# IN THE TRENCHES

Selected Speeches and Writings
of an American Jewish Activist
Volume 2: 2000-2001

## DAVID A. HARRIS

Executive Director,
The American Jewish Committee

KTAV Publishing House, Inc.

Distributed by
Ktav Publishing house, Inc.
900 Jefferson Street
P.O. Box 6249
Hoboken, NJ 07030
201-963-9524 FAX 201-963-0102
Email: info@ktav.com

ISBN 0-88125-779-6

*To my mother, Nelly Harris,*
*who has made it all possible,*

*and*

*To my wife, Jou Jou, and our three*
*sons, Danny, Michael, and Josh,*
*who have made it all so worthwhile.*

# CONTENTS

# 3. TESTIMONY

# 4. MEDIA ACTIVITY

# 5. AJC INSTITUTIONAL

# FOREWORD

The Chinese curse about living in interesting times might well apply to the last two years, when so many of our optimistic suppositions about the future have been shattered—about the prospects for peace emanating from the Oslo Accords, about the withering of anti-Semitism as a worldwide force, and about the invulnerability of America to terrorist attack.

Through these difficult days, David Harris has been on the scene as reporter and interpreter of events. Whether on sabbatical in Europe, involved with the United Nations in Geneva, in Israel sharing his viewpoints on national security with Israeli leaders, or in New York at the helm of the professional operation of the American Jewish Committee, David has been deeply and personally engaged in the struggle for Jewish continuity and strength.

It is clear from the letters, speeches, and articles in this volume, spanning the period 2000–2001, that David combines the diplomacy of a statesman and the ability to communicate with all kinds of people with the probing analysis of a scholar. His observations are both prescient and engaging; his voice, compelling but never strident. When he sounds a wake-up call, there is ample reason to rise and move into action.

The American Jewish Committee is indeed fortunate to have David Harris as its steward at this "interesting" time in history, and I am fortunate to have in him a trusted and knowledgeable friend and colleague in organizational leadership. May his insights guide us to a more secure, perhaps less "interesting" time in the journey of the Jewish people.

Harold Tanner
President, American Jewish Committee
Spring 2002

# IN THE TRENCHES

## Volume 2

# INTRODUCTION

This is the second volume of *In the Trenches*. The first covered a twenty-year span, 1979-1999, while this volume deals only with a two-year period, 2000-2001.

What happened the second time around?

A friend suggested that, whatever the differences in talent—and, truth teller that he is, he couldn't help but point out a few of the differences—perhaps I had taken a cue from Balzac, Dickens, and Dostoyevsky. These great writers were paid by the word. Had I renegotiated my contract with the American Jewish Committee in the same spirit, he asked. An intriguing idea, I responded, but regrettably not in the cards.

Another friend suggested that the kind words I had received about the first volume had gone to my head and mistakenly led me to believe that the world couldn't wait eighteen more years for the appearance of a second volume.

He cited the example of a controversial senior UN official who announced her retirement, only to reverse herself after she claimed to have been moved by the outpouring of complimentary words in honor of her pending departure. Of course, some of the most effusive comments came from precisely those who couldn't wait to see her go. Imagine their shock, then, when they heard the announcement that she was staying on at least one additional year.

I hope I won't experience the same reaction to the publication of this book.

Actually, there are three reasons why this book comes out after only two years.

First, thanks to the generosity of the American Jewish Committee, I was able to take a year-long sabbatical, together with my family, starting in August 2000. We moved to Geneva, Switzerland. The time away gave me the opportunity I had long sought to write, as well as to teach, read, and study.

Second, within weeks of our arrival in Geneva, the latest wave of Palestinian violence against Israel was launched. It was profoundly disturbing to observe from the vantage point of Europe and the Geneva-based United Nations institutions the unfolding of subsequent events, including the resurfacing of anti-Semitism sometimes only thinly masked as anti-Israelism. I couldn't in good conscience remain silent about what I was witnessing.

Moreover, there were larger political and social trends afoot in Europe that I wanted to describe. Among these are the ongoing efforts to achieve greater political and economic integration within the European Union, the ebb and flow of the complex trans-Atlantic relationship, the changing impact of Holocaust consciousness on contemporary Europe, and the emerging challenge of multiculturalism—and especially the rapidly growing Muslim communities—on virtually every West European nation.

And third, the simple fact is that I enjoy writing. That wasn't always the case—just ask my college professors—but the more I write, the more I find myself becoming addicted to it.

Reflecting the changing world situation and my own experiences, this volume of essays, in contrast to the previous volume that focused quite heavily on the USSR, Soviet Jewry, and East-West relations, deals largely with Europe, the Middle East, American Jewish-Israeli ties, and international terrorism.

I am grateful on a daily basis to the American Jewish Committee for the privilege of working for an extraordinary—and entirely unique—institution. Truth be told, I'm convinced that I have the world's best job. AJC blends so seamlessly the universal and the particular in its mission; brings unparalleled sophistication, skill, and reach to everything it does; is that all-too-rare oasis of civility, decency, and integrity; and draws from the ranks of American Jewry's finest volunteers and professionals. What more could I ask for?

Some of those individuals have helped make this book possible.

First of all, I could never have taken my sabbatical without the support of three people.

Bruce Ramer, AJC's president at the time I first asked for a year off, not only agreed to my request but did it so graciously—entirely characteristic for him—that I shall never forget his kindness and friendship.

Harold Tanner, who succeeded Bruce Ramer as AJC's president in May 2001, was equally supportive of my sabbatical, even though it overlapped with his first months in office. And it was he who, without a moment's hesitation, agreed to the publication of this volume. How lucky I am to have the privilege of collaborating with people of Harold's caliber and sensitivity in this extraordinary enterprise we call the American Jewish Committee!

Shula Bahat, AJC's associate executive director, was there to step in for me as acting director. Given her profound commitment to the agency's welfare, I could head off to Europe totally secure in the knowledge that the American Jewish Committee was in the best of hands.

Moreover, I can never say enough good things about the chief librarian of AJC's Blaustein Library, Cyma Horowitz, and her longtime associate, Michelle Anish. They have helped me in countless ways with my never-ending informational requests, big and small, conventional and off-the-wall. It is no wonder that Professor Leonard Dinnerstein of the University of Arizona referred to this jewel of a library as "the best small collection of American Jewish history extant."

Yehudit Barsky, the director of AJC's Division on Middle East and International Terrorism, could not have been more helpful in sharing her vast knowledge for several pieces in this book that touch on the subject of terrorism.

Most of the letters that form the first part of the book, together with several of the speeches, were written while on sabbatical in Geneva.

The dedicated staff of the AJC-affiliated UN Watch, my home away from home in Geneva, helped me in three invaluable ways—as sounding boards, researchers, and demanding critics. They were Michael Colson, UN Watch's executive director; Andrew Srulevitch, Michael's worthy successor; Hannah Gaywood, the office manager and my guide and navigator throughout the year; Josephine Barry and Ian Disend, two talented year-long interns; and Paola Goldstein, a part-time office assistant, who was always encouraging of my work and eager to help.

Some authors are lucky to have one good editor. I've been blessed with three—Bob Rosenbaum, Larry Grossman, and Roselyn Bell. I thank them for many things, including making me look better on paper than I deserve.

Linda Krieg, AJC's graphic artist, sets impossibly high standards for herself and never fails to meet them. Not for the first time, I'm the lucky beneficiary.

Some of the pieces in this book have been published in newspapers and magazines. Ken Bandler, AJC's public relations director, is relentless in seeking to place my articles and op-eds, and I am grateful for his efforts.

Also included in the book are several radio commentaries. The idea for these commentaries originated with Haina Just, who acted as a media consultant to AJC and was a wellspring of creative suggestions.

I am very lucky to be working in an office with two wonderful associates.

Rebecca Neuwirth, who carries the title senior assistant to the executive director, has always been there to help research an issue, organize a presentation, or offer insightful comments about a draft. Her intelligence, dedication, and kindness will carry her very far in life.

Alina Viera, my administrative assistant, is simply the best. In her unassuming and unflappable way, she kept this entire writing project on track and moving briskly. No task was too big or complicated for her. As they say in her native Polish, *dziękuję bardzo*.

This is my second publishing experience with KTAV. I am indebted to Bernie Scharfstein, KTAV's publisher, who has once again made the entire process both smooth and enjoyable.

And last but by no means least, I want to thank my family.

My wife, Jou Jou, is my best friend and my toughest critic. Her passion for all things Jewish, and especially her unwavering love of Israel, have been a constant source of inspiration and motivation.

And our three sons are not only the great joy of my life but also a reason I do the work I do. Banal as it may sound, I desperately want to leave them a better—and more secure and tolerant—world than I found growing up at the height of the Cold War and in the long shadow cast by the Second World War and the Holocaust.

Given the state of things as I write this introduction, however, with the haunting memory of September 11 ever-present, more deadly terror attacks against Western targets anticipated from Islamic radicals, Israel besieged by daily Palestinian suicide bombings, *Newsweek* chillingly asking on its cover how will Israel survive, and Jews around the world jittery about the revival of anti-Semitism, I cannot help but wonder what kind of world our children will inherit.

At difficult moments like these, I look to the two parts of my being that make me whole—my American and Jewish identities—and I find strength and guidance in both traditions, as I hope Danny, Mishy, and Josh will.

Robert Frost, the four-time Pulitzer Prize-winning poet, once wrote:

*Take human nature altogether since time began ...*
*And it must be a little more in favor of man,*
*Say a fraction of one percent at the very least ...*
*Our hold on the planet wouldn't have so increased.*

And Rav Avraham Kook, the much-esteemed and open-minded first chief rabbi of Palestine, reminded us of what we must always aspire to:

*The truly righteous complain not of wickedness, but multiply justice; complain not of a denial of faith, but multiply faith; complain not of ignorance, but multiply wisdom.*

New York, April 2002

# 1. LETTERS

## Letter from a Sanctuary
## March 10, 2000

As we consider those forces in the world today that have the capacity either to foster increased harmony or to spawn violent conflict, the role of religion may be at the top of the list.

Absent the defining global political fault lines of the past century—the battle against Nazism and fascism, the Cold War, and the struggle for decolonization—or anything quite resembling them, it is very likely that religion will be an ascendant force in the new century. In fact, as I write this letter, the newspapers are filled with reports of local or regional conflicts either based on religion or invoking religion as a mask for deeper issues—in Nigeria, Sudan, Algeria, Iran, Indonesia, South Asia, Chechnya, Northern Ireland, and the former Yugoslavia, to name just a few.

Religion can be an extraordinarily potent force for good. Each of the world's major religions provides a moral compass for its adherents, the boundaries between permissible and impermissible behavior, a guidebook and road map for traversing the years of our lives, help for making sense of the daunting challenges of both the here and now and the hereafter, and a sense of community and belonging in an otherwise cruel and unforgiving world.

On the other hand, the historical record shows all too vividly that religion can be turned into a force of evil. Its meaning and intent can be manipulated, corrupted, and perverted. Religious charlatans have often invoked their own narrow, self-serving interpretations of religion to justify violence and carnage. "Received truths," "the word of God," and "I had a calling" can become temptingly convenient pretexts for religious chauvinism, triumphalism, and exclusivity.

Individuals and societies can go either way. As the Jewish sage Maimonides wrote in the twelfth century:

> Every human being has merits and faults. The righteous person has more merits than faults, the wicked one more faults than merits. The average person is (more or less) evenly balanced between the two. A community, too, is judged in this manner; if the merits of its citizens outweigh their faults, it is called righteous; if their faults outweigh their merits, it is called wicked.

In this increasingly crowded world of ours, where the spread of nuclear and other nonconventional weapons raises the stakes further in conflict scenarios, it becomes still more important that the forces of religious tolerance, ecumenism, and open-mindedness prevail.

After all, for many, religion represents the highest calling in us. All the world's major religions embrace, in one form or another, the Golden Rule. Simplistic as it may sound, if only everyone could be persuaded to absorb and practice this basic ethical concept—the very same one Rabbi Hillel identified as the essence of the Torah when asked to summarize its teaching while standing on one foot—how would the world look today? Or what if everyone were to accept the revolutionary Judaic notion that—*whatever* our skin color, our faith, our language, our national origin—we are all created in the divine image of God and therefore members of the same human (not just Jewish, but human) family?

While not for a moment minimizing the contributions and importance of each of the great religions, this point underscores the need for religious leaders to emphasize what unites us rather than what divides us. In the final analysis, adherents of the major religions around the world have a stake in protecting religious freedom and practice for everyone, if for no other reason (though, to state the obvious, there are many far more compelling reasons) than the self-serving fact that they themselves could face limitations or repression. After all, every major religious group that is the majority population in one country is a minority somewhere else.

A prescription might go something like this: My religious rights begin where yours end and end where the next person's begin. Again, it sounds naive and therefore far-fetched, but is there another way to avoid the potential fault lines of religion and the danger of violence unleashed in the name of religion? Can we sustain hope if the theology of the Southern Baptists, for example, demands the denial of the Jewish faith to affirm the "validity" of its own? Or if the theology of many born-again Christians declares that only they, and no one else, are to be admitted to heaven, while all others are destined for a far less appealing fate? Or if the doctrine of Hezbollah (literally, "the Party of God") asserts that they—and they alone—have a direct line to God, and, as a consequence, whatever they do, by definition, is sanctioned, if not ordered, by Him?

We Jews, whatever our internal tensions and divisions, had long thought that we were somehow immune from our people engaging in violence waged in the name of religion. In many respects we were indeed different, and not only because we were so often the targets of religiously inspired violence. But we certainly had our comeuppance in recent years with the tragic murder of twenty-nine Muslim worshipers by Baruch Goldstein in Hebron and, of course, the assassination of Prime Minister Yitzhak Rabin by Yigal Amir. The worlds of both Goldstein and Amir were defined by religion, and both believed they were acting in its name. And the ongoing struggle within Israel to define the relationship between religion and state is another sobering reminder of the wide range of religious voices and agendas battling for supremacy within the Jewish world.

In fact, the outcome of the challenges we face will be determined to a large degree by the balance of forces *within* each of the world's great religions. Who will be in the ascendancy—the moderates or the extremists, the humble or the hubristic? The internal tensions never disappear, of course; they may ebb and flow, but they are always there. Thus, the challenge we face is a permanent one. But we know such challenges. We are taught in *Pirkei Avot*, the Ethics of Our Fathers: "Our task is not to complete the work, but neither are we free to desist from it."

One of the hallmarks of AJC's efforts, especially over the past fifty years, has been fostering a climate of greater interreligious understanding, harmony, and cooperation. In this undertaking, we have had many wonderful partners of other faiths. Together we have achieved a veritable revolution in relations between Jews and, in particular, the Catholic Church and many of the Protestant churches, as well as a very promising dialogue with the Eastern Orthodox churches. Against the backdrop of the largely hostile Christian attitudes toward Jews over the centuries, the significance of the dramatic turnaround that began in earnest in the 1960s with the convening of Vatican Council II, and has since deepened and spread to the other Christian faith groups, especially here in the United States, cannot be overstated.

But our work in the field of Christian-Jewish relations is far from over. And our need to build links with other religions, especially Islam, only grows as they become more significant actors on the world scene and also as the number of their adherents in the United States increases. Moveover, our challenge to forge larger interreligious coalitions—local, national, and international—that reflect the quest for broad-based mutual respect, harmony, human dignity, and, ultimately, peace is always before us.

The American Jewish Committee is energetically and ambitiously at work on all these fronts. Here are four examples of our efforts:

(1) With a generous grant from Harriet and Robert Heilbrunn of New York, we have established the Harriet and Robert Heilbrunn Institute for International Interreligious Understanding, whose principal purpose is to foster greater understanding between Muslims and Jews. One of the institute's first projects is the publication of two scholarly books—*Children of Abraham: An Introduction to Islam for Jews* and *Children of Abraham: An Introduction to Judaism for Muslims*. The books will appear in both English and Arabic, and they will also be available through our Web site. The U.S. State Department has already expressed strong interest in this project.

(2) AJC and Saint Leo University, a highly regarded Catholic college near Tampa, Florida, have jointly established a permanent Center for Catholic-Jewish Relations. Just a few weeks ago, the center hosted

a major national conference on the eve of Pope John Paul II's visit to Israel examining the past twenty-five years of Catholic-Jewish relations.

(3) Six years ago, AJC launched a program to enhance contact and understanding between Catholic and Jewish high school students. Known as the Catholic/Jewish Educational Enrichment Program, the program today operates successfully in five cities—Chicago, Los Angeles, New York, Philadelphia, and San Francisco—with the active cooperation of the local archdioceses and help from a major multiyear grant from Steven Spielberg's Righteous Persons Foundation. Recently, CNN aired a three-minute segment highlighting this initiative.

(4) When tragedy befell Kosovo's Albanian Muslim population last spring due to Serb aggression and, a few months later, Turkey was hit with a powerful earthquake, AJC, thanks to a tidal wave of donations, was able to respond quickly, creatively, and generously. We wanted to demonstrate in deeds, not only in words, our concern for our fellow human beings, who in these two cases happened to be Muslims. Altogether we raised and disbursed over $2 million in relief assistance, a portion of it, incidentally, through Catholic Relief Services. In the very same spirit, when dozens of African-American churches in the South became victims of arson, we joined forces with the National Council of Churches and the National Conference of Catholic Bishops to raise several million dollars to support rebuilding efforts. We at AJC adopted the Gay's Hill Baptist Church in Millen, Georgia, and became personally involved in its reconstruction.

Testimony to our contribution in the field of interreligious relations has come from many distinguished personalities over the years, but no comment has meant more to us than that of our cherished friend John Cardinal O'Connor of New York, who, as we write, is in rapidly declining health. Speaking at our annual Lehman Dinner, the cardinal said: "No organization in this city, in this country, in this world, has done more to advance Christian-Jewish relations than the American Jewish Committee."

## Letter from an Insomniac[*]
### January 2, 2001

In recent months, like many friends of Israel, I've had my share of sleepless nights. With only a few brief moments of either hope or respite, the news has been unremittingly disturbing and depressing. Israel is once again under siege. Every corner of Israel, every Israeli, is a potential target. There is no distinction between soldier and civilian, between adult and youth, between dove and hawk, between believer and atheist, or between those living within and those living beyond the Green Line. It may not be all-out war as we saw in 1967 or 1973, but it is a calculated Palestinian strategy to obtain through violence what they have heretofore failed to achieve by negotiation.

Some Israelis and their friends abroad react to this volatile situation by beating their breasts and asking yet again what more Israel might do to meet the demands of the Palestinians. Others, at the opposite end of the political spectrum, conclude that not only is the pursuit of peace a dangerous dream but, even more, a risk to the very existence of the state.

### Decisions on War and Peace

As I see it, Israel has no clear option, no obvious way to turn, and its predicament is further exacerbated by its complex and polarized domestic situation. In saying this, I do not wish to second-guess the Israeli government and people. I have always taken the view that it is for them, first and foremost, to make the fateful decisions about war and peace and the steps that can lead in either direction. And the sheer survival of Israel over fifty-two years, not to mention its remarkable growth and development, adequately attests to its uncanny ability to overcome the odds, confound the skeptics, and disprove the doomsayers. Even as I openly worry about the future, then, I am inspired and reassured by Israelis' determination to go on, to fight when necessary, to negotiate for peace whenever possible.

---

[*] A version of this piece was placed in the *Congressional Record* by Congressman Tom Lantos on January 31, 2001.

Today we are confronted with a situation that few, especially in the West, might have predicted. A dovish Israeli government—prepared to cross its own red lines, especially regarding the future status of Jerusalem, in the pursuit of an historic peace agreement with the Palestinians—is faced with violence in the streets, calls for jihad, and terrorist attacks in the heart of the country, while the Arab world lines up foursquare behind the Palestinians and seeks to isolate Israel by depicting it as the trigger-happy aggressor, the Nazi reincarnation.

Thus, instead of grasping Israel's outstretched hand and seeking to resolve outstanding issues, however challenging, at the bargaining table, the Palestinians perceived instead a weakened Israel. If proof was needed, it came for them in the unilateral decision to withdraw from southern Lebanon after Israeli mothers led a campaign to bring their sons home before more were killed at the hands of Hezbollah; in Prime Minister Barak's determination to make peace before the end of the Clinton presidency, which was, in the final analysis, an artificial deadline; and in Israel's perceived vulnerability to the sting of international censure, given Barak's efforts to undo the global public relations impact of the Netanyahu years.

In effect, Arafat, though the weaker party by far, has skillfully leveraged his position, emerging stronger than might have been imagined. He has, for example, already managed to prove once again that violence does pay—the current deal being brokered by the White House and given tentative approval by Barak appears to go beyond the package on the table at Camp David in July. If so, why should Arafat, from his point of view, stop here?

### Violence and Negotiations

Eager to see his long-sought Palestinian state emerge from the "honor and blood" of the martyred, ever mindful of the most radical elements among the Palestinians, and determined not to demand less than Anwar Sadat, King Hussein, or Hafez el-Assad in insisting on Israeli compliance with all his territorial demands, Arafat continues his complex juggling act of encouraging violence and talking peace at one and the same time.

At the very least, we can expect from Arafat more of the same brinkmanship through the last days of the Clinton administration. Knowing how eager the American leader is to leave the political scene with substantial progress to show in the Middle East, given his extraordinary investment of time, energy, and the prestige of the presidency, and aware of how committed the Israeli leader has been to making this possible on Clinton's watch, Arafat will squeeze the moment for all it's worth, and then some, in an effort to improve still further his bargaining position.

Not quite, some observers will note. Arafat doesn't hold all the cards. After all, there's an Israeli election around the corner and, without a peace deal, the conventional wisdom is that Barak will fall and Arafat will then have to face his old nemesis, Ariel Sharon, who will make the Palestinian leader's life a lot more difficult. Maybe, but then again, maybe not.

We in the West make a living out of failing to understand the Middle East. We're so busy superimposing our own deeply ingrained ways of thinking on the region—based in large measure on our rationalism, pragmatism, willingness to compromise, and tendency to mirror-image ("Surely they're like us and want the very same things in life as we do")—that we too often end up surprised and puzzled when things don't go as we might expect.

We don't speak Arabic; we have little contact with Arab culture; we have minimal understanding of the nature of Islam and its pervasive role in the life of the Arab world; we spend too little time reading the writings of Judith Miller, Bernard Lewis, Fouad Ajami, and other knowledgeable observers of the region; and we embrace too quickly as representative those selected Arab voices that sound reassuring to us.

Yet none of this stops us from thinking we know enough about the region to offer confident views on diplomacy and strategy. Indeed, the U.S. government, with its far greater resources and expertise, has stumbled more than once, with fatal consequences, trying to make its way across the Middle East minefields.

Isn't it just possible that the prospect of a Prime Minister Sharon not only doesn't frighten Arafat but actually appeals to him? Taking a page from Leon Trotsky—the worse it gets, the better it becomes—Arafat may, in fact, perceive advantages in such an outcome: With Sharon demonized in the international news media and sharply criticized in world capitals, Israel could face new international pressures, including renewed calls for UN intervention and increased sympathy for a unilateral declaration of independence.

### Tests for Barak and Sharon

And this brings us back to Israel's domestic predicament. Barak, the pollsters say, needs a peace deal before February 6 if he is to have a chance at winning the election. Without it, he is saddled with negative images—accusations of political ineptness, willingness to yield to the demands of religious parties despite his calls to marginalize them, and inexperience and imprudence in dealing with the Palestinians. Thus, no matter what he says between now and February 6, no matter how tough his language may be at times, the prevailing assumption is that he needs Arafat to bail him out and both men know it.

On the other hand, Sharon is a known quantity who is a deeply polarizing figure in Israel. He is seen as representing a return to the Shamir years of a "fortress Israel" in eternal conflict with the enemies of the Jewish people. That may not sit well, not for long, with many Israelis living in a prospering first-world country that longs for regional stability and even a chilly peace with its neighbors, so that it can finally one day turn to the future and away from the endless cycles of violence of the past.

After all, if the Israeli left was revealed to be the victim of its own illusions about creating a new Middle East, the Israeli right has been the victim of its own illusions about the possibility of maintaining an indefinite status quo of occupation. If Barak is found wanting by the Israeli electorate in his ability to provide answers and solutions, then it's equally possible that Sharon, if elected prime minister, will face the same prospect.

Of course, whoever is elected, Barak or Sharon, could face the very same unruly and fractionated Knesset, which further clouds the outlook for stable governance. This is precisely what Benjamin Netanyahu is counting on. Although polls showed him leading both Barak and Sharon, he chose not to run this time around unless the

Knesset dissolved itself and also stood for new elections. It was a statesmanlike position, praised by many, including some who do not normally count themselves among Netanyahu's most fervent admirers; it was also a position calculated to elevate his standing in the expectation that whoever is elected in February will not be able to lead for long before yet another round of voting, including parliamentary elections, is needed. At that time, Netanyahu would almost surely step into the political fray.

### Overriding Political and Strategic Factors

In the meantime, as Israeli politics seeks to sort itself out against the backdrop of the deep and seemingly irreconcilable fissures in Israeli society, certain things seem clear and best not forgotten.

First, many of the claims of the Israeli right, especially since the signing of the Oslo Accords in 1993, have proved accurate, though they were largely ignored by those on the left who reflexively dismissed anything said by spokesmen on the right. For example, incitement to hatred among Palestinians has continued unabated and with devastating consequences. Moreover, the accumulation of weapons and the buildup of the Palestinian police and militia, in direct contravention of the Oslo Accords, have created a deadly adversary for Israel. And the wink and nod to Palestinian extremists—many arrested with great fanfare only to be released as soon as no one was paying attention—has undermined the chances for a peaceful settlement with Israel.

Second, many of the claims of the Israeli left have also proved strikingly accurate, despite attempts by those on the right to dismiss them. Palestinians would not docilely remain under Israeli occupation forever. Neither could Israel expect occupation to continue without some corrosive effects on its democratic values, nor could it absorb the Palestinians in the territories without undoing the Jewish character of the state. And sooner or later, Jewish settlers in remote outposts in Gaza, for example, would become flashpoints for violence between Israelis and Palestinians.

Third, as a consequence, no one school of thought has a monopoly of wisdom on what is best for Israel. Ideologues, whether of the left or right, become prisoners of their own preset and imbedded views, and, as a result, tend to adjust the facts to their doctrinal thinking rather than the other way around.

Fourth, regardless of what happens in the short run respecting Israeli-Palestinian issues, the sad reality is that Israel will continue to face severe challenges in the region, requiring a powerful military, eternal vigilance, and close coordination with the United States.

Iran and Iraq pose dangerous, and growing, threats, particularly in the area of nonconventional weapons. Islamic extremist groups operating in the region will not soon go away. Syria possesses missiles and chemical warheads. Disturbingly, Egypt has embarked on a broad modernization program of its conventional forces and is known to be engaged in research on some nonconventional weapon systems as well. An emerging Palestinian state will alter the political and security landscape for Jordan, with unknown consequences, not to mention for Israel.

And, of course, the larger problems of the need for a true reformation in the Arab world, of the glaring absence of democracy and the rule of law, of governmental lack of accountability to its citizens, of endemic corruption and nepotism, of high birthrates and insufficient jobs, of economic stagnation and fear of opening to the world, of the Islamists' influence on society, all continue to plague this vast and important region of the world.

A few pertinent statistics illustrate the dimensions of the problems faced by the Arab world. Fouad Ajami of Johns Hopkins University has pointed out, for example, that Finland, with a population of 5 million, exports more manufactured goods than the entire Arab world combined, with its twenty-two countries and its population well over 200 million. Israel has a higher per capita GNP than its five contiguous neighbors—Lebanon, Syria, Jordan, the Palestinian Authority, and Egypt—combined, and more Internet users by far than all five put together. And impoverished Gaza has a higher birthrate by a multiple of nine than prosperous Bologna, Italy.

Fifth, we should be under little illusion about such notions as a "demilitarized Palestinian state" or "an end to the conflict." A Palestinian state is coming, one way or another. It will happen, and

Israel no doubt will do its utmost to establish harmonious ties, but it must also recognize, as a recent CIA report looking ahead to the year 2015 predicted, that "chilly" relations are likely to prevail at best and constant surveillance and monitoring will be required.

That Palestinian state will certainly not be demilitarized, I believe, regardless of agreements signed, which could well pose a threat to both Israel and Jordan. And there will remain those Palestinians who will seek to continue the struggle with Israel, either because they see Israel proper as their real home, or because they see the Zionists as "infidels" and "modern-day Crusaders" who have no right to be there, or both.

Sixth, we need to take very seriously anti-Semitism emanating from the Arab world. Not only is it pernicious and contrary to the promotion of peaceful relations in the region, but it also fuels anti-Semitic attacks against Jews and Jewish targets throughout the world, as we have tragically seen in recent months.

And finally, we need to remind ourselves of the importance of our own role in making a difference on Israel's behalf. Both in our public education and advocacy efforts in the United States, in which we stress the mutual benefits of close U.S.-Israel ties as well as America's vital national interest in Israel's security, and in our diplomatic, exchange, and public affairs programs around the world, the American Jewish Committee is making a unique contribution to Israel's well-being and its quest for peace. The daunting challenges that lie ahead for Israel will doubtless only heighten the importance of that work.

## Letter from Europe
### January 10, 2001

These last several months of living in Europe, together with my family, have been special in so many respects. Each and every day has brought new encounters and discoveries, even as the cloud of daily tragedy in the Middle East casts its shadow over all of us.

Rather than run the risk of overwhelming you with the many and varied impressions gathered during five months of living in Geneva, rubbing shoulders with diplomats here from many countries, teaching a graduate seminar at the Johns Hopkins University campus in Bologna, and meeting with Jewish community leaders from many European countries, let me try to organize my thoughts and approach issues from four angles.

First, I must say—and I don't mean to rub it in—that the quality of daily life in Geneva is simply unparalleled. I say that as a lifelong and proud New Yorker. Sure, there are many who say that Geneva is boring, boring, boring, but we've found it anything but. It's a beautiful, well-organized, and well-located city, with a remarkable degree of civility and some wonderfully innovative urban elements that New York and other American cities could learn from.

But Geneva also reflects the complicated and schizophrenic nature of Switzerland, a country not easily described. Let me illustrate.

Every morning I go for a jog in a picture-perfect park that's about 100 feet away from our apartment building. It's an ideal park. Hundreds of children play in it every day, yet not a single one cries. Hundreds of parents and housekeepers watch over those children, yet not a single one shouts. Dogs, a very common feature in Switzerland, don't bark, much less defecate. And litter is simply unknown to the park.

But, as I recently learned, under this very same park, 100 feet from our apartment building, is a fully equipped, nuclear-proof shelter for 6,000 residents of our neighborhood. It has everything from nursery schools to medical facilities, and is checked periodically as part of the Swiss civil defense program. No doubt, Switzerland has the most elaborate such civil defense structure anywhere in the world. Near the picturesque city of Lucerne, for example, the tunnel of Sonnenberg was completed in 1976. It has seven bombproof floors underground, room to lodge 20,000 people, and a hospital with two operating rooms and 328 beds.

In fact, this civil defense program is part of a still more elaborate defense plan for Switzerland. Though it is not well known, Switzerland has been among the most militarized countries in Europe. All males must do military service, then serve in the reserves for several decades, and always maintain a weapon at home. Some of the scenic mountains for which Switzerland is justifiably famous have been carved out to provide secure space for planes, tanks, and artillery. Every bridge and tunnel built around the perimeter of Switzerland includes provision for destruction in the case of enemy attack, notwithstanding the fact that no one can remember the last time foreign military forces attempted to enter the country.

Indeed, so great has been the paranoia about possible attack and occupation that a secret government unit, known as P26, was established in the 1960s. Among its very first acts was to purchase land in Ireland, with funds provided by major Swiss banks, in case it became necessary to establish a Swiss government-in-exile. And in 1989, it was revealed that the government had been collecting secret files on citizens, organizations, and foreigners—in all, some 900,000 files. Ruth Dreifuss, the politician who recently became Switzerland's first Jewish president, commented at the time: "Switzerland was the country in Europe that most strongly experienced the Cold War. This was our version of McCarthyism, but fortunately with less damaging consequences."

Yes, Switzerland is a captivating and vexing country at one and the same time. This schizophrenia is also amply reflected in its wartime history and its belated effort to grapple with the meaning and place of that history in its national consciousness.

Second, speaking of history, for us Americans, there is often a kind of romanticization that overtakes us when we travel in Europe.

We visit the palaces, the crumbling fortresses, the chateaus, the walled cities, and the castles, and we succumb to their charm.

But for a Jew living in Europe, history is not so easily romanticized. It is ever present, it is inescapable, and, more often than not, it is a sobering, at times chilling, reminder of the realities of the Jewish past.

History means going to my local branch of UBS, the leading Swiss bank, and recalling that in 1997 a Swiss bank guard named Christoph Meili was fired for trying to stop the bank from destroying records that might have shed light on dormant accounts from the wartime period. He and his family eventually had to flee the country because of death threats, and were given permanent resident status in the United States.

History means going on one of our shopping expeditions to Chambery, a charming town in the Savoy region, and seeing the plaque outside a building in the center indicating that a young man living there had been deported to Mauthausen, never to return.

History means traveling to Bologna, where I teach, and being reminded of Edgardo Mortara, the six-year-old Jewish boy who, in 1858, was secretly baptized by his housekeeper, seized by the Vatican, at the time ruled by Pope Pius IX, and raised as a Catholic, despite the family's protests. Incidentally, Pope Pius IX was just canonized, together with Pope John XXIII, by the current pope.

History means visiting Joschka Fischer, the foreign minister of Germany, in the new quarters of the Foreign Ministry in Berlin, a building that once served as the Reichbank headquarters and, more recently, as the headquarters for the Central Committee of the East German Communist Party.

History means visiting the Olympic Museum in Lausanne, a striking building on the lakefront. One searches there in vain for any reference to the eleven Israeli athletes murdered at the 1972 Munich Summer Games, before coming outside to see the glittering lights of Evian across the lake, a breathtaking sight were it not for the fact that Evian evokes the memory not just of bottled water and thermal baths, but of a failed international conference, in 1938, to assist Jewish refugees when they still might have been saved.

History means crossing the border with France nearly every day, as we are but two and a half miles from the frontier, a border where no one seems to care about our passports, much less visas. Each and every time I cross from France back to Switzerland, I am reminded that sixty years ago it was a sealed border. People risked, and too often lost, their lives as they sought to puncture holes and make their way from occupation to freedom.

To be fair to the historical record, Switzerland accepted 30,000 Jewish refugees during the war, more than the United States. But too many others never made it because of the *refoulement,* the pushing away of refugees.

In this regard, history means the story of Aimee Stitelmann, a sixteen-year-old Swiss citizen, who tried to help Jewish children enter the

Geneva area from France. Twice during the war Swiss authorities arrested her. The second time, she was tried in July 1945, two months after the war's end, for having broken Swiss law by seeking to bring in unauthorized individuals—i.e., Jews fleeing the Nazis—and sentenced to two weeks in prison.

Yes, history here truly is lived each and every day.

I have to tell the truth. Sometimes I cannot help but envy other travelers. I suspect that when they see road signs for Lyons, they think first of art museums and two-star restaurants, not of Vichy and Klaus Barbie; and when they travel to lovely Venice, they are not immediately seized with the thought that the concept of the "ghetto" originated there, but rather might first debate whether the gondola ride is worth the exorbitant cost.

Third, for a friend of Israel, this has been quite a challenging period, to say the least.

Once again, I am reminded how unique is the relationship between the United States and Israel, and how equally special is the American Jewish community.

All the European countries today have bilateral ties with Israel. They range from the special links between Germany and Israel to the more problematic ties between France and Israel. And all the European countries have Jewish communities, ranging from the French, by far the largest, to infinitesimally small populations in such countries as Finland and Portugal. All are vitally important to the well-being of Israel and the Jewish people, but none can match the unique significance of the American role in Israel's quest for peace and security or the part played by American Jewry in advancing that role.

This reminds me yet again of the special responsibility—and remarkable opportunity—that has been placed on our shoulders.

Moreover, in recent times, all of us have experienced the shattering of illusions. Today it's the left whose illusions have largely been shattered, yesterday it was the right.

It was the illusion of those on the right to believe that Israel could have a flourishing democracy and widespread settlement activity, and at the same time rule over 2-3 million disgruntled Palestinians, even if occupation came about as a result of acts of war by Egypt and Syria in the spring of 1967.

Now it's the left's turn. Wishful thinking about peace had replaced hard-nosed assessment of certain developments among the Palestinians. Education for hate, encouragement of violence, misuse of the Palestinian police, accumulation of weapons, release of hard-core terrorists, calls to jihad—these weren't simply propagandistic points made by Israelis on the right, but genuine concerns with a basis in fact.

We all ought to experience a bit of humility. There is no clear path for Israel today. There are no neat and clean choices. There are very real risks whichever way Israel eventually turns. There are no experts with foolproof understanding of the region and prophetic certainty. Israel will continue to lurch from its quest for peace to its need to protect its citizens and back again, seldom being able to keep both objectives in perfect harmony, at least until the situation clarifies itself—perhaps tomorrow, perhaps in a decade, perhaps still longer—and Israelis understand whether a durable peace is truly attainable.

I only wish the European media would grasp these complexities, but that may be a pipe dream. With few exceptions, journalists have been rough on Israel, repeatedly portraying it as the aggressor in the most unflattering possible way. If you feel the American media have too often lacked balance, I daresay it's far worse here.

And though I can't prove it, I have a sense, from a number of conversations in France, Italy, and Switzerland, that there are some in Europe who take a special pleasure in criticizing Israel today. This could be a reaction to the last few years of Jewish criticism of European behavior during the war with respect to refugees, individual and communal property, dormant bank accounts, insurance policies, and art. Here's a way to get back at the Jews, some contend, but in a way that cannot be characterized as anti-Semitic. And, in the same vein, here's a way to show that the Jews really aren't so different from the rest of us. Look, give them a powerful military and they behave no better than other people, despite Jewish talk of morality, ethics, and concern for the oppressed and powerless.

And fourth, as an American living in Europe, it is striking to see what is taking place on this continent today. We Americans need to understand better the developments. Some very exciting and dynamic things are at hand.

The European Union's ongoing effort to define itself, to deepen the reach of its regional institutions, and to expand to include as many as thirteen new members, all have truly profound implications. As the recent summit in Nice suggested, it's not an easy process—far from it—but it's moving ahead. European themselves, as well as Americans, Israelis, and others, must all ask themselves what does this mean for them, and the answers may not always be obvious or internally consistent.

For one thing, it's striking to see borders disappearing. At many points between France and Germany, for example, or France and Italy, there simply are no border crossings.

And of course, widespread prosperity in Europe continues to be very apparent, without some of the glaring disparities between rich and poor that characterize American society, I might add.

Yet at the same time, there are obvious concerns within Europe. Let me just mention three.

One is talked about, but often obliquely or behind the scenes. There is a growing awareness of a resurgent Germany. It's not the case that Germany has behaved irresponsibly or is pushing around other countries; rather, it's simply the realization that Germany is becoming more future-oriented and, ever so slowly, feeling less constrained by the burden of the past. As the largest country in the EU, in terms of both population and economy, its weight is considerable. And as the EU moves eastward, Germany's influence is likely to grow further. In other words, the center of gravity of the EU is moving steadily away from Paris and toward Berlin.

Another is the question of immigration and the related matters of integration and acculturation. Pick up any newspaper in countries like Germany and Italy and there is likely to be at least one article on the subject daily. In effect, many European countries are in a bind. According to studies done by the European Union, the EU will need literally millions of immigrants over the next several decades in order to compensate for its declining and, in some cases, negative birthrates. Yet Europeans, to put it kindly, are, at best, ambivalent about immigration.

By and large, European countries don't see themselves as do New World societies like Australia, Canada, and the United States. We are societies that are constantly redefining ourselves. We are works in progress—we have been and will continue to be. That's not the way European societies have evolved, or at least not the way the popular imagination believes they have developed.

But today, legally and illegally, by air, by sea, and by land, from the east and the south, migrants are seeking to make their way to the thriving countries of Europe. And they are not taking no for an answer. They keep coming, finding the porous points and entering, looking for jobs and new starts.

On the one hand, as in the United States, they often do the jobs that no one else wants to do. On the other hand, talk about Albanian or Russian organized crime is heard throughout Europe. Trafficking in women from Eastern Europe is a major concern, and street crime is often associated in the public mind with this inflow of migrants. Thus, there are very mixed feelings about this migration—a recognition that some of it is necessary, but that it comes with a price and a degree of uncertainty.

And this brings me to my final point. What will happen in the case of that uncertainty? Europe's past challenge was how it dealt with its Jews; its future challenge is largely to be defined, I believe, by how it deals with its growing Muslim populations. In Sweden today, more than 200,000 Muslims live in a society of 9 million; in Switzerland, there are an estimated 250,000 Muslims among 7 million residents; in France, 4-5 million Muslims live in a country of 60 million; and in Germany, mosques are rising everywhere. In Frankfurt alone, there are twenty-seven mosques today, with more being built.

How will Europe face these challenges? Will it turn against the newcomers and fuel populist movements, some of which have already sprung up in such countries as Belgium, Denmark, Holland, and Italy, not to mention the most successful of all, the Freedom Party in Austria, which is a junior partner in the governing coalition? What will be the impact of the newcomers on European societies? Will they seek to change fundamentally the societies in which they live, and, if so, how?

And what will an expanded Europe, with a changing face, mean for Jews and the State of Israel? What will an increasingly strong and confident Europe mean for relations with the United States, which is sometimes seen these days as an adversary as much as a friend and partner?

All are tough questions with no obvious answers. But what is certain is that what happens on the European continent has significance for us all. The American Jewish Committee, with our long-standing interest in and widespread contacts with Europe, will have to pay still more attention in the coming years to developments at work here.

## Letter from Jerusalem
## February 16, 2001

Election day, February 6, seemed to generate more attention outside Israel than inside. Perhaps it was the certainty of a Sharon victory, as the polls had consistently shown him leading Barak in the weeks leading up to the election. The only question was the margin of victory. Or perhaps it was widespread despondency about the choice of candidates, neither of whom sparked much enthusiasm or optimism about the future. Or perhaps it was the overarching realization that peace was clearly not around the corner but rather the likelihood of continued terrorism and street battles, if not a larger conflict.

Nonetheless, the electoral results were striking and reveal that voters were largely uneasy about questions of national security and personal safety. In effect, to borrow a line from the film *Network*, voters were saying: "We're mad as hell and we're not going to take it anymore." Under the circumstances, they were not prepared to renew Barak's mandate, believing that he had shown political clumsiness and naïveté, alternating between tough talk directed at the Palestinian Authority and a willingness to continue negotiations with the Palestinians at almost any price.

Sharon was the beneficiary of this dramatic loss of confidence in Barak, even though in the past he has been seen as a polarizing figure in Israeli domestic politics. Voters hope, by dint of his tough image, that he can persuade the Palestinians to end the violence or, alternatively, at least make them pay a higher price should the violence continue.

Interestingly, many voters stayed home, most notably Israeli Arabs but others as well. As my most informed Israeli source—my longtime taxi driver—told me, he and his family could not bring themselves to vote. Eighteen months ago, they voted for Barak, believing he combined an unsurpassed military record with statesmanship. Today they felt too disillusioned by his "zigzag" leadership to give him a second chance. (More evidence of Barak's inconsistent nature came after he resigned from politics in the wake of his electoral defeat only to return ten days later and enter talks with Sharon on a unity government and cabinet post.) Yet the prospect of Sharon was no more appealing. He had no new political ideas, they believed, and would only further isolate Israel internationally.

But the biggest question of all among Israelis focused less on the election, and the subsequent discussions about the possible creation of a national unity government, and more on future relations with the Palestinians.

In essence, a decisive majority of Israelis have concluded that there is no peace partner with whom to conduct further talks. That view may well change; public opinion, whether in Israel or the United States, can be very fickle. But, for the time being, this is the prevailing opinion and it has cast a pall over the nation. After all, it means the prospect of continued struggle, with all its implications, rather than the chance even for a chilly peace.

In a recent *Dilbert* comic strip, the main character announces: "The secret to happiness is self-delusion."

For those many Israelis who had allowed themselves to believe since the signing of the Oslo Accords in 1993 that an historic corner had been turned and some form of accommodation with the Palestinians was in the making, it turns out their optimism may have been a form of self-delusion.

They didn't quite grasp the force of the so-called "right of return" issue for the Palestinians or the Palestinian agenda in Jerusalem, not to mention the depth of hatred toward Israel or the preparations for the use of armed violence to help achieve their goals. They understood that Arafat was not the most trustworthy negotiating partner, but still were caught by surprise by the vehemence of his rhetoric—for example, calling Israel "fascist" during his appearance at the World Economic Forum in Davos in January or, more recently, referring to the deliberate killing of eight Israelis in a Tel Aviv suburb as nothing more than a "bus accident."

For the moment, the Israeli peace camp is in shambles. What's left of it is on the defensive, although it is only a matter of time before its adherents begin to rally around an anti-Sharon platform, even in the face of a national unity government, and try to rebuild their strength. They will argue forcefully that there is simply no alternative to the quest for peace and Sharon cannot be trusted to pursue it.

And while the Israeli right is for now in the ascendancy, my guess is that it won't last forever. Sharon has publicly stated that he will not negotiate with the Palestinians as long as violence continues. The Palestinians, despite the horrendous economic situation in which they find themselves, are unlikely to stop the violence, both because they do not want to reward Sharon and because they sense Israeli vulnerability.

If the violence then continues, Sharon will either have to renege on his pledge and proceed with talks or else stand firm. Either way, he will find himself facing enormously difficult, indeed unpalatable, policy options, and risk losing some domestic support.* Moreover, he will seek to rule over what could be a rather unruly governing coalition, encompassing diametrically opposing political views, from hawkish to dovish.

Time, the Palestinians believe today, is on their side.

Israel is growing soft, as evidenced, the Palestinians say, by the unilateral withdrawal from southern Lebanon because today's Israel cannot "stomach" casualties. Iran, and especially Iraq, are expressing loud support and banging the war drums; Palestinians have one of the highest birthrates in the world; Israeli Arabs are beginning to raise their voices and flex their muscles; and Sharon, despised by the Western media and many European leaders, is unlikely to win many friends for

*A third possibility is to consider unilateral disengagement, a much discussed option in Israel today. This would not be without potential risk, among them that the Palestinians could perceive the move as an Israel in retreat, that there would be no internationally recognized peace accord, and that the territorial withdrawal would not satisfy Palestinian demands, so the struggle would continue.

Fig. 1.1.

## Ariel Sharon, victoire annoncée d'un homme de guerre

Front-page cartoon entitled: "Ariel Sharon, the victory speech of a warrior." Sharon is depicted in the right panel. One of the perpetrators of the Ramallah lynching of two Israeli soldiers is depicted in the left panel.
Source: *Le Temps* (Switzerland), February 6, 2001

Israel.* Therefore, the tide is turning in the Palestinians' favor, or so they contend.

But their analysis must also take into account other factors. Israel remains the strongest military power in the region, not to mention a first-world economic force. The United States, the world's leading superpower, remains Israel's closest ally. Sharon has proved time and again that he doesn't bend or break very easily. A national unity government in Israel will mean greater internal cohesion, at least for a while. Independent reports suggest that the Palestinian areas are close to anarchy and that living conditions are steadily declining. And sever-

---

* To illustrate media reaction in Europe, on February 6 *Le Temps*, a leading French-language newspaper in Switzerland, carried two prominent cartoons side by side on its front page. One showed a Palestinian with blood on his raised hands participating in the lynching of the two Israeli soldiers in Ramallah; the other showed Sharon campaigning next to an Israeli flag with his raised hands covered with blood. (See fig. 1.1.)

al key Arab countries have shown little desire until now to be drawn into a wider regional conflict by Palestinian provocations.

In other words, we can expect a very difficult, and probably inconclusive, period ahead for Israel.

And over the long term, the tensions and fault lines in the Jewish state will not disappear. To the contrary, they are only likely to grow. The nation's political and social circuitry is overcharged.

In the year 2000, according to one outgoing cabinet minister, 30 percent of all births within the 1967 Green Line were to Israeli Arab families, while 24 percent were to *haredi* (ultrareligious) Jewish families. This trend is likely to continue in the years ahead. It is even more pronounced in Jerusalem.

An Israeli official has revealed that more than half of all *olim* (new immigrants) in the past year are not Jewish according to halakhah (Jewish law), adding to already sizable numbers of newcomers from the Former Soviet Union who are not Jewish. Despite increased numbers enrolled in conversion classes, the conclusion is inescapable.

In an effort to decrease the number of Palestinian workers in Israel, more Poles, Romanians, Chinese, Thais, and other foreign workers have been encouraged to come. Today their numbers are considerable, more than 200,000. It is possible that many will stay, as was the case in Western Europe, and build families, further affecting the population balance.

Israeli Arabs, approximately 18 percent of the population and, as noted, growing in number, are becoming increasingly vocal in demanding equal rights and an equal share of the national budget. Moreover, many do not hide their larger political agenda, which is to transform Israel from a Jewish state into a "democratic state of all its citizens." At what point might Israeli Arabs demand some form of political autonomy, and with what results?

Needless to say, the religious-secular divide in Israel shows no sign of easing, which creates a largely intractable problem between two (actually more) very different notions of Jewish identity and statehood.

And the list of pressing domestic challenges goes on and includes striking gaps between rich and poor,* the future of settlements in Gaza

---

* A recent authoritative study in Israel revealed one of the highest rates of poverty among Western industrialized countries.

and parts of the West Bank, lingering ethnic resentments among Sephardic Jews toward the Ashkenazim, scarce water resources in an area where more than 9 million now live between the Mediterranean Sea and the Jordan River, and a badly flawed electoral system.

Externally, the situation is also complicated, in both the short and longer term.

The new Bush administration is still getting its feet wet and defining its international policy. Some signs have been encouraging, others less so. It is only a matter of time before the administration will be seriously tested in the Middle East, whether by Saddam Hussein, Osama bin Laden, or Yasir Arafat, or all three, and then we shall have a better sense of its worldview and policy orientation. Given the U.S. and British air strikes against Iraq last week, the first such test by Saddam Hussein and his allies might not be far off, with an assumption that other challenges will follow.

Iran, despite its continued domination by religious extremists, is gradually re-entering the community of nations; so, too, Iraq, with France, China, and Russia paving the way. Even Qaddafi's Libya is rapidly shedding its rogue image and attracting commercial attention from Western countries, reportedly including the United States.

At the same time, the Middle East is headed toward a new generation of weapons. Iran and Iraq, in particular, are determined to acquire weapons of mass destruction and the means to deliver them. Syria has short-range missiles and chemical warheads. Egypt, a country with which Israel has had a valuable peace accord for over two decades, has embarked on a significant military modernization program, which has raised eyebrows in Israeli defense circles. And terrorist groups in the region undoubtedly will also seek to put their hands on new weaponry. In other words, an already volatile strategic environment is likely to grow only more so for Israel, absent dramatic and, in the near term, unlikely developments on the peace front.

The Europeans will not give Sharon a long honeymoon, even if Shimon Peres, who is highly regarded in European capitals, becomes the new foreign minister. While the European Union has little direct impact on the course of events in the Middle East, it is not without influence in the region or at the United Nations, where we can expect to see a stepped-up attempt to vilify and isolate Israel.

And the threat of terrorism, as we have witnessed these past five months, cannot be ignored or minimized. The targets have been Jews and Jewish institutions. France, home to the largest Jewish community in Europe, has experienced the bulk of incidents. Israeli and Jewish facilities are very conscious of the menace.

Visits to these facilities provide a sobering reminder of the dangers: Jewish schools hidden behind concrete perimeter walls, synagogues protected by police officers with submachine guns, embassies that resemble prisons, and prominent Israeli and Jewish officials unable to travel anywhere without a retinue of security personnel.

In sum, the agenda is substantial, but then again, what's new? At any given moment in the history of the Jewish people or the life of Israel, logical analysis would always have said that the odds were against us. Yet somehow, through a combination of faith, resolve, and wits, we have always defied the odds, not simply surviving but in recent years flourishing.

The State of Israel has managed in its fifty-three-year history to develop into a remarkably strong and prosperous nation, despite wars, terrorism, economic boycotts, the absence of natural resources, and attempts at diplomatic isolation. Israelis have shown time and again their determination to meet the challenges of building and defending their state.

And the Jewish people in the Diaspora have understood and embraced the need to support Israel. That support has been indispensable in the past; it remains so now.

The American Jewish Committee has been there throughout. I daresay that there is no other organization in the world today outside Israel's borders that has taken upon itself such a far-reaching program to assist Israel in the political and diplomatic worlds—regular meetings with top government leaders on five continents, daily efforts at the United Nations, missions to Israel for influential Americans, ongoing discussions with other religious and ethnic communities, and considerable media activity, including frequent advertisements, op-eds, and letters to the editor in leading newspapers around the world.

It is abundantly clear that the going won't get any easier in the months ahead, but then again when in Jewish history has it ever been easy?

The seventeenth-century French author La Rochefoucauld once said: "Few things are impossible in themselves; it is not so much the means we lack as perseverance to make them succeed."

In general, he may be right, but there can be no doubt that Israel and the Jewish people, including, of course, AJC, continue to have the perseverance to succeed, and we shall.

## Letter from Geneva
## March 12, 2001

After seven months here, I think I can safely say that living in Geneva is one thing, working another.

To begin with, if, as some say, New York is a better place to visit than to live, then Geneva is the reverse, a better place to live than to visit.

Sure, from a sight-seeing perspective, there's the beautiful double-barreled mountain backdrop—the Jura Mountains to the north, the Alps to the south. Then there's the magnificent crystalline lake, which is technically called Lac Léman but the Genevois—the name for the locals—are quite content to hear foreigners refer to it as Lake Geneva.

And there are a handful of attractive museums, a charming Vieille Ville (Old City) which has Roman antecedents and links to the likes of John Calvin, Jean-Jacques Rousseau, Henri Dunant, and Camillo Benso, count of Cavour, and, of course, the imposing UN and International Red Cross facilities. But, when all is said and done, vacationing in London, Paris, Amsterdam, or Europe's hottest city these days, Prague, offers the visitor quite a bit more.

On the other hand, what a wonderful place to live.

It is an attractive, gentle, and efficient urban environment, well placed in the heart of Europe. People are unfailingly polite, children have lots of room to roam, buses run frequently and on time, drivers have yet to discover their horns, joggers and cyclists have unlimited options, the baguette is an art form, and culture is cherished.

There's the added bonus of an impressive, if small by American standards, Jewish community, with a well-developed network of synagogues, youth groups, and organizations.

The Jews hail from many parts of the world, including North Africa, the Middle East, Eastern Europe, and Alsace. A newcomer quickly feels a warm welcome and the peculiarly familiar notion that, no matter how small, the community nonetheless has deeply imbedded fault lines. The Liberal synagogue is snubbed by the other houses of worship, while, in the Sephardic shul, the Syrian and Lebanese Jews, reportedly troubled by the perceived domination of the Moroccans, are determined to build a second synagogue just a few meters away.

If I have one complaint about the quality of life here, it's the ubiquitous smoking, including among teenagers. As an American increasingly insulated from smoking by stringent rules in U.S. public places, the virtual absence of limits on smoking here, a country otherwise deeply concerned about health and environmental issues, comes as a bit of a shock.

Working, though, is another matter. Don't get me wrong. It's a fine place, I'm sure, for those employed by banks, jewelry stores, watchmakers, and the increasing number of multinationals, like Procter & Gamble, setting up shop here. But it's not quite as congenial for friends of Israel, like UN Watch, to conduct their business. In fact, to be honest, it can be downright lonely, frustrating, and depressing.

But that only makes it all the more important to have an organization like UN Watch operating here. The late Morris Abram, AJC's distinguished president from 1964 to 1968 and the U.S. ambassador to the UN here from 1989 to 1993, was right to perceive the need for such a watchdog agency and on the mark in wishing it to become a member of the AJC family. While the agenda of UN Watch touches on a number of issues, at its heart it concerns itself with Israel.

After four years as America's top diplomat here, Abram came to understand that Geneva—because of its vast collection of UN agencies (e.g., the World Health Organization, International Labor Organization, United Nations High Commissioner for Refugees, Commission on Human Rights, and Office of the High Commissioner for Human Rights), the concentration of diplomats from 190 countries, and the presence of literally hundreds of nongovernmental organizations (e.g., the International Committee of the Red Cross, World Council of Churches, International Commission of Jurists, World

Alliance of YMCAs, etc.), many headquartered here—needed much more sustained attention from the Jewish community than it had received until that point.

It must be said that prior to the outbreak of violence in Israel and the territories in September, there were actually a few glimmers of light in the international system regarding Israel's pariah status.

For one thing, last May the Western European and Others Group (WEOG) in New York, urged on by U.S. ambassador Richard Holbrooke, voted to extend Israel temporary and limited membership, ending Israel's anomalous status as the only UN member state ineligible for participation in one of the five regional blocs that play such an important role in the world body.

That story is by now well known. Less known, however, is the intense debate in Israel over whether to accept this limited offer, or to stand firm on the principle of simultaneous inclusion in the WEOG group in all UN cities, including Geneva. In the end, Ambassador Holbrooke prevailed on Foreign Minister David Levy to accept half a loaf, arguing forcefully that once Israel had its foot in the door the rest would come more easily. On the other hand, he said, to insist on everything up front would result in a flat refusal by the Europeans.

Today, nearly one year later, Israel has made little headway here in Geneva on the issue of WEOG membership, and has therefore been compelled to alter its strategy to pursue it on an agency-by-agency basis—beginning with arguably the least political, the World Intellectual Property Organization—rather than across the board. The volatile situation in the Middle East, European diplomats privately acknowledge, has slowed the process once again.

The same can be said for the issue of the Magen David Adom, Israel's humanitarian society.

The International Red Cross and Red Crescent movement does not recognize its emblem, the Red Shield of David. To make a long story short, under the leadership of Dr. Jakob Kellenberger, the president of the International Committee of the Red Cross, a laudable effort was made last year to solve the emblem issue and ensure Israel's full equality in the movement. A diplomatic consultation, attended by UN Watch, was held in September to discuss the adoption of a Third

Additional Protocol to the Geneva Conventions, which dealt with the emblem issue, and plans were under way to organize the elaborate approval process later in the fall.

Despite the objections of some Arab countries, most nations understood the belated need to address Israel's problem in the context of a movement that describes itself as nonpolitical and universal. But then came the September events and the process was immediately put on hold, where it remains to this day.

On March 19, just a week from now, the annual session of the UN Commission on Human Rights will take place and a number of reliable diplomatic sources have predicted an especially rough and highly politicized gathering when it comes to Israel. The only "good" news, if you will, is that while the commission can censure and seek to ostracize, unlike the Security Council it has no power to impose sanctions.

Normally, the commission meets once a year, always in Geneva, for six weeks. But, with my luck, this will be my second session, as the commission met in special session in October for the sole purpose of considering the situation in the Middle East and adopting an especially virulent anti-Israel resolution that, among other things, accused Israel of crimes against humanity.

If I could, I would invite American Jewish leaders to observe these proceedings in order to better appreciate their often Orwellian quality, such as when the Iraqi ambassador denounces the "Zionist entity" (Israel is never mentioned by name in Baghdad) as a Nazi state.

Once again, the deck is stacked against Israel. Among the fifty-three member countries this year, which incidentally are selected by the five regional blocs, are such human rights stalwarts as Algeria, Cuba, Libya, Saudi Arabia, and Syria. Moreover, this year's commission agenda, as usual, is constructed in a very peculiar way.

Item 8 is entitled "Question of the violation of human rights in the occupied Arab territories, including Palestine." The next item, Item 9, is entitled "Question of the violation of human rights and fundamental freedoms in any part of the world." In other words, as far as the commission is concerned, the world is divided in two—the occupied Arab territories on the one hand and literally everything else (Afghanistan, Chechnya, Congo, Iraq, Sierra Leone, Sudan, etc.) on the other.

As if this weren't enough, we are also expecting later this month an indication from the Swiss government, as the depository nation, regarding the Arab request to reconvene the high contracting parties (i.e., the signatories) to the Fourth Geneva Convention, which last met, if only briefly, on July 15, 1999, to discuss Israel's alleged violation of the convention's provisions. The parties are currently being polled and, according to our information, only a handful have expressed opposition; the EU has not yet responded, and its views will, as always, carry considerable weight.

Bear in mind that since the convention went into force in 1949—as a response to the horrors of the Second World War, I might add—this is the *only* time that the signatories ever gathered to discuss an alleged violation of the convention anywhere in the world.

And there's still more.

Intensive planning is under way here in Geneva, under the auspices of the Office of the High Commissioner for Human Rights, for the World Conference Against Racism, scheduled to take place in Durban, South Africa, from August 31 to September 7, 2001. Indications from several Arab and other Muslim countries are that they regard this as another important diplomatic venue to assail Israel. Indeed, in one of the four regional preparatory meetings leading up to the World Conference, held in Tehran two weeks ago, the Asian bloc endorsed language accusing Israel of "racism," "genocide," and "crimes against humanity."

Sadly, I could go on listing other challenges we face, including a renewed effort by the Arab bloc to use many of the specialized agencies headquartered here—from the International Labor Organization to the World Health Organization—to attack and condemn Israel.

Or I could note the fact that when I testified, on behalf of AJC, at the special session of the Commission on Human Rights in October, I was one of just three nongovernmental representatives to defend Israel, while spokesmen for fifty-seven—yes, fifty-seven—groups joined in the chorus of scathing criticism of the Barak regime, according to the Israeli ambassador, who kept a running count.

In the same vein, I could also point out that the World Council of Churches and the World Alliance of YMCAs have gone on the attack, dropping any pretense of balance in openly supporting the Palestinians against the "brutal armed attacks of the Israeli army," to quote from the December 2000 issue of *YMCA World*, the quarterly magazine of the alliance.

But let me mention only one more issue, the one that probably troubled Morris Abram more than any other and that should disturb us all.

In too many cases, nations that should know better, not to mention institutions and individuals, have kept silent or equivocated in the face of this onslaught, which in the end not only affects Israel but also the integrity and credibility of the UN itself.

Rather than stand firm against such bullying tactics and intellectual dishonesty, these nations either blithely go along or seek to appease the instigators. The reasons vary from diplomatic and commercial interests to energy concerns, from fear of igniting terrorism against themselves to the time-honored practice of trading votes—i.e., "I'll vote for you on your important issues if you vote for me on mine." Whatever the reasons, the facts, sadly, speak for themselves.

The towering exception is the United States. It is unafraid to speak out, to lobby, and, if necessary, to stand alone in its vote. At times, it is joined by a handful of others, notably Australia, Canada, and a few Central American and East European states, and, less frequently, by the EU.

By and large, the EU prefers to negotiate with the Arab bloc on Middle East issues and search for common ground, but every once in a while that's simply not possible, as was the case last October. In fact, the Arabs remain furious with the EU for its negative vote at the time. A recent EU-Arab bloc meeting here was described as "stormy" by one insider, who said an Arab delegate accused the Europeans of countenancing "war crimes" by Israel.

In sum, it's been quite an eye-opening experience, but I'm grateful to have witnessed it with my own eyes, if only to understand better the magnitude of the challenges we face.

And when it all seems just the slightest bit overwhelming, those snow-covered peaks beckon and the incomparable baked goods of our local *pâtisserie* tempt, serving as a welcome diversion and as fortification for the next day.

## Letter from Another World
## April 12, 2001

When I was in college in the late 1960s, one of my favorite movies was *King of Hearts.*

Released in 1966 and starring Alan Bates, it told the story of Private Charles Plumpick, who, toward the end of World War I, was ordered to enter the French town of Marville and locate and defuse a bomb reportedly planted by the departing German army. Plumpick, however, was spotted by some Germans and sought refuge, ultimately ending up in the local insane asylum.

For some reason, the inmates were convinced that he was the "King of Hearts" and treated him accordingly. Knowing that there was a bomb somewhere in the vicinity set to go off, Plumpick tried to lead the inmates away, but they resisted, choosing instead to frolic in the otherwise abandoned town and savor their new freedom.

To fast-forward, at the end of the movie the inmates, having witnessed firsthand the tragedy of war, return of their own volition to the insane asylum and want no further contact with the "normal" world. In the very last scene, Plumpick seeks to join them.

Thoughts of the movie kept coming to mind over the past few weeks as I witnessed the United Nations Commission on Human Rights in action. What's normal and what's abnormal? Have truth and fairness been turned on their heads? Is the world going nuts, or am I?

Given the foretaste we had at the special session of the commission in October, when Israel was accused of committing "a war crime and a crime against humanity," it was abundantly clear that this gathering of the fifty-three member nations would be rough as well. But the truth of the matter is that, no matter how many times one witnesses the exercise, it still comes as a shock to the system.

Opportunities to assail Israel abound, for example under Item 5 of the agenda ("The right of peoples to self-determination and its application to peoples under colonial or alien domination or foreign occupation"), Item 6 ("Racism, racial discrimination, xenophobia, and all forms of discrimination"), Item 8 ("Question of the violation of human rights in the occupied Arab territories, including Palestine"), and Item 13 ("Rights of the child").

Not only does the construction of the agenda create endless possibilities to take the floor and attack Israel, but, more importantly still, the political makeup of the UN, of which the commission is a mere reflection, almost inevitably ensures that Israel will find itself with few supporters.

Start with the twenty-two-member Arab League. To be sure, the group is far from monolithic. There are radical, centrist, and moderate factions. Even so, as the friendly ambassador of one moderate country confided to me after I questioned his diatribe against Israel: "I had no choice. The pressure on me from other Arab countries was intense and unrelenting. Had I acted differently, there would have been negative consequences."

Nabil Ramlawi, the Palestinian permanent observer at the UN in Geneva, often sets the Arab tone in the commission and elsewhere. Ramlawi has always been among the shrillest of Palestinian voices. It was Ramlawi, for example, who declared at the fifty-third session of the commission, held in March 1997, that Israeli doctors had deliberately infected 300 Palestinian children with HIV. The Israeli ambassador described this at the time as "a modern-day form of the blood libel—anti-Semitism at the state level."

Usually, though, in the Arab group Egypt plays the key role. Egyptian diplomats posted abroad tend to be particularly well trained and skillful, whether in Washington or Geneva, and they are determined, whenever and wherever possible, to assert Egypt's primacy in the Arab world.

Assessing the Egyptian role here at the UN regarding Israel can be difficult. In truth, the Egyptians almost inevitably tend to be both part of the problem and part of the solution, and that's exactly the way they like to play it. They want to make Israel's life as difficult as possible, and they often succeed; and then they want to be, and be seen to be, the address for last-minute diplomatic compromise and exit strategies.

As if the Arab bloc didn't create enough headaches for Israel, consider the fifty-seven-member Organization of the Islamic Conference (OIC). Here, again, groupthink works quite effectively. Malaysia, as the current chair of the OIC, speaks on behalf of the entire group, and then, just to make sure the point is clear, many individual members, such as Iran and Pakistan, also request the microphone to lambaste the Jewish state.

And if the OIC didn't create enough headaches for Israel, a third and still larger entity is the 113-member Nonaligned Movement (NAM). Solidarity is also a powerful motivating force in this group of African, Asian, and Latin American nations, especially since the Arab League and OIC member nations are also core constituents of NAM. Thus, when Colombia, currently a member of the Security Council, was facing conflicting pressures from NAM on the one hand and the United States on the other regarding a recent Israel-related vote, it went with NAM, despite the close ties with Washington and the substantial U.S. aid package.

In the spirit of the holiday season, *dayenu*, this would have been enough, but there's still more, I'm afraid.

As I wrote in my last letter, perhaps most disturbing of all is the posture of the Europeans. Four things, in particular, strike me.

First, the pursuit of consensus within the European Union and among its associated countries allows individual nations to duck responsibility for actions taken in the name of the group.

Second, many of these very same countries have only recently gone through a process of historical self-examination, a kind of moral reckoning, regarding their actions and inactions during the Holocaust. Yet, with the notable exception of Germany, it is painfully clear that no country today sees any real linkage between the wartime period and its contemporary approach toward Israel.

Third, the United States and Europe, which should be natural partners and allies, with increasing frequency tend to take different approaches to policy issues, including here in Geneva. This is not a healthy development, to say the least.

And fourth, Europe, though comprised of democracies that share basic values with Israel, has often determined that other interests take precedence, certainly in this forum. Elsewhere, I've referred to the commercial and economic interests, the fear of terrorism, and the desire to reach a modus vivendi with an Arab world at Europe's doorstep. But it doesn't end there.

A sympathetic ambassador told me of a Scandinavian colleague who was chairing a UN meeting a few years ago and, in that capacity, blocked an Arab parliamentary move. Within days, the diplomat was visited by an Arab delegation with a very clear message: "You will never again be elected to a post within the UN, as we control the majority; therefore your career here is as good as over." The fact that the story was still circulating a few years later is sobering proof of the mathematical (and political) realities that shape the way the world body works. The European nations, influential though they may be within the UN, are very far from commanding a majority; they need allies to build that majority on any given issue.

To be fair, it's not that Europe has become Israel's adversary; it's far more complicated and nuanced than that.

When the Arab bloc refused to compromise on their tough resolution at the special session in October, the Europeans voted against it, and at other times they may abstain if they feel the Arab language goes too far. But, on the whole, there seems to be a growing impatience with Israel, an unwillingness to give it the benefit of the doubt, a desire to counterbalance American support for Israel with a tilt toward the Palestinians, and an openness to international involvement in the conflict despite Israeli objections.

Lastly, there's one more factor that affects the picture here. The American Jewish Committee has enjoyed consultative status at the United Nations for the past four years. But every time there is a debate on Israel, it is abundantly clear that we are part of an infinitesimally small minority of nongovernmental organizations (NGOs) willing to stand up for balance and fairness where Israel is concerned.

In the current deliberations of the commission, I had the privilege of testifying on Item 8, which is the crux of the Israel debate. (I also testified on two other agenda items.) (See Testimony, pages 257–64.) Of twenty-nine NGOs that spoke, twenty-five vilified Israel, two were tough on Israel but at least mentioned, if only in passing, Palestinian violations of human rights, and exactly two, including AJC of course, sought to provide an understanding of Israel's extraordinary dilemmas.

(In this context, it is worth noting that, according to an April 7 article in *Tribune de Genève*, a number of NGOs from the developing world operating in Geneva are government-funded and government-controlled.)

To say the least, it's very difficult to sit through the speeches of government and NGO spokesmen and hear Israel accused of "deliberately starving" the Palestinian population, of "racial supremacy," of "crimes of war," of "crimes against humanity," of "eliminating a whole people," of "genocide," of "racism," of intentionally "murdering children," of "barbaric massacres," and of "massive violations of human rights." Or to hear references to "usurping Zionist gangs," "occupied territories," when the speaker has in mind Israel's 1948 borders, or, for that matter, to suggestions that it's time to bring back the "Zionism is racism" resolution.

I brought my aunt, a native of Poland who left Europe a step ahead of the Nazis, and my wife, a refugee from the Arab world, to attend one of the sessions. My aunt felt physically sick after an hour and asked to leave, and couldn't manage to sleep that night. My wife was so enraged by the self-righteous comments of the Libyan ambassador—who, incidentally, was elected a vice chairman of this year's Commission on Human Rights—that I was afraid she might verbally assault the envoy.

The sense of shock and loneliness, though, isn't limited to the halls of the UN in Geneva.

When I was about to enter the seventh grade, my family moved to Munich. It was there that I first encountered the challenge of being a Jew.

In the U.S. Army school I attended, there were few Jews and, as I painfully learned, lots of nasty stereotypes about us. Moreover, it wasn't easy standing out as the only student in the class who didn't sing the Christmas songs.

And to this day I still remember my father jumping out of bed late one night, while we were living in a hotel during our first weeks in Munich. I only learned the next morning that it was because he heard a group of beer drinkers in the café below singing Nazi-era songs, and he went down to confront them physically, alone as it turned out.

Maybe because these were the first experiences of their kind for me, or maybe because I was so young and impressionable, or maybe because the setting was Germany and I knew enough at that age to realize that Germany was not just another country, these episodes have stayed with me.

And now, in a way, I see history repeating itself.

Two of our three children are with us. They've had a terrific experience in Europe, but not without incidents. They have confronted "gas-chamber jokes" in the locker room, school bake sales for Palestinian children, the numerical isolation of being among only a handful of Jews in the school, and claims that the Holocaust is a "Jewish lie."

And most recently, our youngest son found himself at school face-to-face with an older Arab student, the son of an ambassador here, I might add. The young man asked my son what religion he was. "Jewish," Josh replied. "I don't like Jews," came the reply. "I'm going to ask you a second time, and I want a different answer." To his credit, but with trepidation, Josh held his ground and repeated that he was Jewish. The older boy then knocked something over and told Josh to pick it up, at which point Josh ran away. At such moments, it's nice to have an older brother, and Michael was there for Josh. But, given the student makeup of the school, both our sons were adamantly opposed to our pursuing the issue with officials.

(They've also learned that their maternal grandmother, who lives in Rome, recently received an anonymous phone call from a man identifying himself as "Adolf Hitler," and they've heard that the eight Israelis killed by a Palestinian bus driver were standing at precisely the stop in Azor that their aunt, my wife's sister, uses daily.)

We American Jews sometimes fail to understand the dangers lurking out there, or the consequences of isolation and vulnerability. We are so blessed to live in a land that has embraced us, that welcomes our full participation, and whose politicians often court us, that we may not always understand the challenges faced by fellow Jews who live not in lands of oppression, like Iran, but in lands of freedom.

Being part of a 6-million-strong Jewish community, in a country that defines itself as unabashedly pluralist, is rather different from being part of a statistically insignificant, if historically important, Jewish community of 30,000 amid 58 million Italians or 14,000 among 40 million Spaniards. The sense of place, degree of self-confidence, access to power, and ability to shape events are all of another order of magnitude for American Jews.

With each passing day here, no matter how much I genuinely relish the travel, the languages and cultures, and the daily joys of life, I realize more and more the unique strengths of the United States, the American Jewish community, and the American Jewish Committee. I thought I knew all this quite well before leaving New York last summer, but the perspective of distance—and new experiences—has given me an entirely new level of understanding and appreciation.

## Letter from Bologna
## May 20, 2001

I had it all planned.

I was going to finish teaching my year-long course at Johns Hopkins University's School of Advanced International Studies (SAIS) in Bologna this month and devote an entire letter—one in the series I've been writing during my sabbatical year—to an extraordinary encounter with a group of outstanding, intellectually curious students against the backdrop of one of Italy's less visited urban treasures.

I was going to talk about the class, entitled Seminar on Post-Holocaust Political and Ethical Issues, and our grappling with such challenging questions as the nature of evil and altruism; the role of memory and mythology in national consciousness and identity; and political, legal, religious, and educational strategies for dealing with hatred and its consequences.

I was going to describe some of the students, all but a few pursuing master's degrees in international relations, who hailed from a score of countries in North America and Europe; whose exposure to the topics under discussion ranged from essentially nil to one German woman who has devoted much of her life to building ties with the Jewish people in Israel and worldwide; and who, judging from alumni of SAIS, are likely to be counted among tomorrow's top diplomats, nongovernmental organization leaders, and multinational corporation titans.

I was going to profile one particular Turkish student, Ceren Ozer, who, as a result of the seminar, will be interning at the AJC Berlin office this summer, helping us better understand the large Turkish community in Germany, with the goal of establishing links between the community and AJC, very much in the tradition of our intergroup activity in the United States.

I was going to recount in detail some of the fascinating classroom discussions and debates on the effectiveness of tolerance-building school curricula; the value today of pursuing suspected Nazi war criminals; the impact of the Holocaust on Israeli domestic and foreign policy; and appropriate responses to extremism, whether in the case of the German government's attempt to ban a political party (NDP) or the European Union's effort to punish Austria after a governing coalition was formed with Jörg Haider's Freedom Party as the junior partner.

I was going to put in a big plug for the city where all this was taking place—Bologna, the capital of Emilia-Romagna, with its well-preserved medieval city center, an estimated twenty-five miles of arcaded sidewalks, a rich academic tradition, a proud antifascist wartime record, and a legendary reputation as home to the best cuisine in Italy.

I was going to discuss the laudable effort to document the complex history of the Jews in Bologna and the surrounding cities and towns (e.g., Ferrara, Modena, and Parma), including the opening by local authorities of the Jewish Museum of Bologna—located on Via Valdonica, once part of the ghetto imposed on the Jews in 1556—and guided tours of the city, sponsored by the museum, on such topics as Jews in ancient, medieval, and contemporary Bologna.

And I was going to end with some thoughts on Italy, a country that just held closely watched national elections to establish the fifty-ninth government in fifty-six years; that remains utterly captivating, if at times frustrating; that is facing its share of domestic political, economic, and social challenges, not least illegal immigration; and that for me has had very special meaning ever since I first met my future wife in Rome in 1975, while involved in the movement of Soviet Jews in transit there and awaiting permanent resettlement in Western countries.

That's what I was planning to do in this letter, but, like most welllaid plans, this one, too, went awry. To be precise, some other things came up.

First, the other day my wife and I went to Annemasse, a French town just over the border, which has a delightful twice-weekly, open-air food market overflowing with fresh fruits and vegetables, home-made breads, jams, and honeys, and the best brie this side of Zabar's.

A short while earlier, I had spoken with my cousin Sacha in Paris. Like several of my other French relatives of her generation, Sacha was a member of the French Jewish Resistance during the war, whose principal task was to smuggle Jewish children from the Savoy region into Switzerland. When I mentioned to her that we sometimes shop in Annemasse, she told me that this is where the Gestapo had first imprisoned her sister, Mila, after being caught, in 1944, trying to take Jews across the border. She even remembered the name of the prison.

This trip to Annemasse, therefore, took on a whole other meaning. We went to the tourism office and asked if anyone had heard of a wartime prison in the area called Pax. Yes, we were told, there was such a prison, which before the war had been the Hôtel du Pax and which today was again a hotel with the same name; it was located no more than 200 yards from where we were standing.

In fact, we learned much more. In September 1943, German troops replaced the occupying Italian forces in Annemasse and requisitioned the hotel and a three-story apartment building across the street, also still standing, as the headquarters for the Gestapo and a prison and torture chamber. Between September 15, 1943, and August 18, 1944, the date of Annemasse's liberation, an estimated 1,500 members of the French Resistance and local Jews, including the elderly and children, were held there, many only temporarily en route to the Nazi camps via Drancy and other French transit centers.

Mila, the cousin I never knew, was eventually sent from Annemasse to Lyons and from there to Ravensbruck, from which she never returned.

This is another potent reminder just how difficult, indeed virtually impossible, it is to take a step in any direction on this continent without coming face-to-face with the full force of Jewish history.

Or, for that matter, discovering yet again how small the Jewish world really is. When David Vannier, a French student in my seminar, mentioned after our final session that his grandmother had been part of the Jewish Resistance, I asked him to check if she by chance remembered the name Mila Racine. He contacted her in Paris and immediately responded by E-mail: His grandmother had been a good friend of Mila's and also knew the rest of the family.

Second, while in Bologna I finished reading James Carroll's *Constantine's Sword*. Carroll, an ex-priest, is a highly regarded author and journalist.

Published earlier this year and reviewed favorably in the *New York Times*, the book is an extraordinary account of the church's relationship, over the span of 2,000 years, with Jews and Judaism. Be warned, though. It does not make for easy reading. The material can be difficult, at least for those readers without firm grounding in Christian, especially Catholic, theology and history.

But that's not the only reason it's a hard read. The story it tells, with few exceptions, is an exceptionally painful one.

Even those who may know something about the subject, I suspect, will learn a great deal more, as well as experience a range of emotions, from following the author as he seeks to answer such central questions as "What is the relationship of ancient Christian hatred of Jews to the twentieth century's murderous hatred that produced the death camps?" and, referring to the seven-meter papal cross placed at the entrance to Auschwitz, "If Auschwitz must stand for Jews as the abyss in which meaning itself died, what happens when Auschwitz becomes the sanctuary of someone else's recovered piety?"

To be fair to the record, Carroll's book has come in for heavy criticism from some in the Catholic hierarchy, who have accused him of faulty scholarship or, in a few cases, of being a self-hating Catholic. I am not in a position to judge all the charges, but for me the cumulative effect of over 600 pages of painstakingly documented history was both powerful and persuasive.

And reading the book while in Italy gave it special meaning, especially as I walked through the Bologna ghetto, the second ghetto in the Papal States after the papal bull segregating Jews was issued by Paul IV in 1555.

It also prompted me to recall my visits to the Rome ghetto, now— what else?—a trendy residential area, which stood until 1870, and to the church adjoining the ghetto, still there, which Jews in the ghetto were required to attend. If I remember correctly, the church is called San Gregorio alla Divina Pietà.

As the guides explain, on entering Jews had their ears checked because some inserted balls of wax so as not to hear the fiery sermons aimed at conversion, and those working in the church carried long poles to waken Jews seeking to sleep through the homilies.

But Carroll's book didn't simply depress, not at all. It also served as yet another important reminder of the compelling need for ongoing, in-depth, constructive, and soul-searching interreligious dialogue between Christians and Jews, precisely what the American Jewish Committee has been vigorously pursuing for the past half century.

There is much to show for our pioneering effort—unquestionably, far more progress has been achieved in the past fifty years than the previous 1,950 years combined—but more remains to be done, and Carroll helps us understand the unfinished agenda.

And third, each day brings still more bleak news from the Middle East. Two Jewish youngsters brutally killed in the West Bank, five Israelis killed in a suicide bombing in a Netanya shopping mall, and Syrian president Assad's raw anti-Semitic words in the presence of Pope John Paul II (and the failure of the Vatican to condemn explicitly those words) are just a few of the examples of the escalating violence accompanied by ever shriller rhetoric and growing pessimism about what the future holds.

For now, both sides stand firm—Israel making clear not only that it will not succumb to Palestinian violence but also that it is prepared to step up its military response, the Palestinians contending that popular anger and resentment against Israeli occupation, settlements, and use of force neither can nor will be contained.

What happens next? Truthfully, it's anyone's guess.

Will the United States, which has largely stayed on the sidelines since President Bush took office in January, ratchet up its diplomatic efforts to halt the violence and get the parties talking about short-term measures to improve the situation on the ground?

With the European Union, spurred in particular by France and Belgium (the EU's next president), growing increasingly irritated by Israeli behavior, especially regarding the settlements question, will it seek a more active political role, especially if the United States does not? Would the EU try to leverage its association (and other) agreements with Israel, an idea that has been in the air, or, far less likely, use its substantial aid package to the Palestinians, as diplomatic weapons?

Will pressure increase in the UN Security Council to fulfill the long-standing Palestinian desire to create an international protection force, an initiative strongly opposed by Jerusalem? In such a case, would the United States continue to hold firm in opposition by exercising its veto power?

Will Arafat be more successful in drawing the Arab world into the conflict by seeking to isolate Israel still further in the region, reintroducing the Arab economic boycott (we heard rumblings of this during a recent visit to Germany), stepping up vilification of Israel in the international community by pressing for the reconvening of the high contracting parties to the Fourth Geneva Convention and reawakening the "Zionism is racism" canard, or convincing the oil-producing states to flex their muscles?

Will the Israeli domestic consensus, which has strongly supported the national unity government, hold over the coming weeks and months? Or will opposition to the government grow from those who believe its present course is misguided, creating a more politically divided nation?

What is abundantly evident sitting here in Europe is that there is a huge gap in how the current conflict is seen.

For many of us, the sequence of events is quite clear.

The Barak government, with American support, offered the most far-reaching concessions to the Palestinians in an historic effort to conclude a durable peace agreement. The deal would have met virtually every reasonable Palestinian demand. Instead of either accepting the deal or remaining at the bargaining table and negotiating for more, Arafat walked away and returned to a more familiar role instigating violence rather than implementing peace. Under such circumstances, Israel had no choice but to respond militarily to defend the nation and to make clear that the Palestinian strategy had no chance of success.

But reading the newspapers, listening to television commentary, and talking with European diplomats, I find that, for a variety of reasons, they choose to see it rather differently.

With only a few exceptions, most notably in Germany, they don't care to remember the Barak offer or the Palestinian rejection. Nor do they seem to focus on the political and psychological significance of the Palestinian call for the "right of return," or appear especially bothered by President Assad's anti-Semitic remarks or denigration of the Holocaust in the Arab world. Nor do they truly understand the fear and frustration that has gripped Israel these past eight months, as it faces repeated terrorist attacks and finds itself with no peace partner. Nor, with a postwar generation in positions of power and influence in Europe, do they fully comprehend the lingering sense of vulnerability that many Jews continue to feel even with a strong and resolute Israel.

Instead, they tend to see a militarily imbalanced situation, with Israel using advanced weaponry against what they regard as a beleaguered and impoverished population with few arms at its disposal. They view Israel as an occupying power that must leave all the lands taken in 1967, pure and simple, if the conflict is to end, and they want this conflict, at Europe's doorstep, over and done with. They do not take as a serious threat those Arabs who make no distinction between the 1948 and 1967 borders. They may or may not have high regard for Arafat, but consider him the only game in town. And they most certainly do not like Ariel Sharon, who was initially given a little, but only a little, breathing space, principally because Peres came on board as foreign minister, nor do they have much sympathy for Israel's settlements or those who live in them, even when they fall victim to Palestinian violence.

In sum, we, friends of Israel, have quite a full plate and, as the American poet Robert Frost wrote, "miles to go before we sleep."

Believe me, I would much rather be talking about "full plates" in Bologna, with its suggestion of heaping portions of tortellini and other sumptuous regional specialties.

But, in thinking about the current challenges, it is important to bear in mind that this is not the first moment, nor surely the last, when we have faced a daunting agenda and mountains to climb. Yet we have never flinched or failed to rise to the challenge since the rebirth of the Jewish state in 1948. This time surely will be no exception. Just as Israel remains determined, so shall we in the Diaspora.

## Letter from Madrid
## June 11, 2001

Truth be told, I don't need much prompting to go to Madrid. In my book, together with Paris and Prague, it's among Europe's most beautiful and seductive cities. But the prospect of attending the Second General Assembly of European Jewry, organized by the European Council of Jewish Communities (ECJC) and bringing together 700 delegates from thirty-nine countries, made this particular trip to Madrid all the more enticing.

I had participated in the First General Assembly in Nice two years earlier, another "rough" assignment. Whoever chooses these locations deserves a medal, not that there's much time for sight-seeing. Years in Jewish communal life have taught me that we sometimes suffer from a masochistic streak; we select wonderful sites to hold conferences and then too often lock ourselves in windowless meeting rooms from morning till night discussing our communal ills.

Actually, in this case the Madrid organizers included a plenary session at the Sinagoga de Santa María Blanca in Toledo, a synagogue that was taken over as a church in the fifteenth century and has remained a Catholic house of worship ever since. I had a predictably schizophrenic reaction to the venue.

On the one hand, there was a sense of joy that, more than 500 years later, committed Jews in large numbers entered this building to discuss the *future* of Jewish life in Europe and were greeted warmly by a leading Spanish Catholic prelate.

On the other hand, the inescapable sense of historical loss was ever present. Here was a once-magnificent synagogue taken away from the Jewish community centuries ago, in the center of a city that once housed a significant Jewish community and today counts not a single Jew.

Toledo was not unique, of course.

From the Golden Age of Jews in Spain—one of the most remarkable periods in the entire sweep of Jewish history, which included such illustrious individuals as Yehuda HaLevi, Maimonides, Solomon Ibn Gabirol, and Nachmanides—to the fifteenth-century era of the

Inquisition, forced conversions, expulsion, and autos-da-fé, the slide was rapid and the results devastating.

Not until the twentieth century did Jewish life slowly reemerge, culminating with the visit of King Juan Carlos to the Madrid Synagogue on March 31, 1992, 500 years to the day from the edict of the Catholic kings expelling all the Jews from Spanish territory. Moreover, Spain was the last Western European nation, in 1986, to establish diplomatic ties with Israel, although, happily, the bilateral relationship has grown rapidly over the past fifteen years.

These two European Jewish gatherings—first in Nice, then in Madrid—suggest history in the making. Something exciting is happening to European Jewry, and the ECJC is in the vanguard. There's a new spirit and it is palpable.

For one thing, the fall of the Iron Curtain has created previously unimaginable opportunities for the reawakening of Jewish life in Central and Eastern Europe. Jewish communities, big and small, have reemerged, and there is a desire, actually a hunger, for links with other Jewish communities.

For another, the bug of European integration has bitten the Jews of Europe. As fifteen European countries move toward closer political and economic integration, and thirteen other aspirants seek to align policy with the European Union, Jewish communities recognize not only the opportunity but also the necessity to establish the groundwork for pan-European cooperation.

And for a third, European Jewry, long considered the stepchild in a world Jewish community dominated by Israel and American Jewry, now appears determined to flex its muscles and insist on a place at the table with its numerically larger counterparts.

The going, though, will be anything but easy. For all the obvious enthusiasm displayed at Madrid, the delegates themselves acknowledged the long road ahead.

In some European countries, Jewish population numbers, according to the *American Jewish Year Book 2000*, are barely noticeable—for example, 1,100 in Finland, 1,000 in Ireland, 1,200 in Norway, and 300 in Portugal—even as these communities admirably seek to sustain a strong commitment to Jewish life. In fact, of all the European countries, ironically the only one to experience any significant Jewish population growth in recent years is Germany, largely due to the steady influx of immigrants from the Former Soviet Union.

Moreover, resources remain scarce. The tradition of philanthropy, which has characterized American Jewry, is not yet equaled in Europe—far from it. The levels of communal development vary widely within Europe. Long and proud histories distinguish each community. English is becoming the continent's lingua franca, but linguistic barriers remain. Approaches to Jewish pluralism differ from country to country and also, at times, from city to city. Competition among Jewish organizations—a phenomenon not entirely unknown to American Jews—exists in Europe. And the historical and psychological barriers to establishing a strong, effective European Jewish community are not insignificant.

Let me dwell on this last issue for a moment. It's always dangerous to make sweeping assertions, but there are some profound differences between the basic European and American models.

Israelis and American Jews often ask, for instance, why their European colleagues aren't more politically active on behalf of Jewish concerns. To the extent that this is true, one must consider that there is not the same tradition of lobbying by interest groups in Europe as there is in the United States.

And that's not all. When my wife moved with me to New York in 1979, she helped me understand a profound perceptual divide.

Having lived all her life first in North Africa, then in Europe, she was instinctively used to separating her private and public identities. At home, she was profoundly Jewish, but elsewhere, she had learned, Jews didn't make too many waves.

There was always unease, even in a fully democratic country, about drawing too much attention to the Jews. There were the heavy weight and long shadow of history, the unhealed scars, the residual trauma—not easily shed—from centuries of Christian-dominated Europe, from the isolation, scapegoating, and persecution, culminating in the Shoah, that too many European Jewish communities experienced. As a consequence, there was a lingering uncertainty about whether Jews could consider themselves equal *participants* in society, even if they had become full citizens and lived in the country for generations or longer.

To some, especially in Israel and the United States, this was outdated Jewish thinking, but nonetheless it was, and to a degree remains, a feature, albeit diminishing, of the Jewish psyche in parts of Europe, especially in those countries where Jews constitute a minuscule percentage of the population.

In others, most notably France, home to the revolutionary doctrines embodied in the Declaration of the Rights of Man (1789) and the French National Assembly's Law Relating to Jews (1791), the Jewish community, numbering 600-700,000, has maintained a high profile. The community enjoys good access to the government and media, and Jews are remarkably prominent in the nation's intellectual life. Even so, influence is circumscribed by a number of factors, including, again, a limited tradition of lobbying by interest groups and a sizable Arab population that outnumbers Jews approximately seven to one.

At first, my wife was shocked to see the American Jewish model. She was uneasy watching as American Jews loudly and proudly asserted their identity in public, petitioned the government, placed advocacy ads in newspapers, and took on one policy battle after another.

But it wasn't long before she came to admire this behavior—even if she sometimes wondered whether the public identity of American Jews outweighed the private—and to understand that it stemmed from a different societal conception than she had previously known.

American Jews in this era are not regarded, nor do they see themselves, as guests, but rather as equals with other Americans. Accordingly, they don't hesitate to jump into the fray when they feel their interests are at stake. Nor do they fear that such activity might jeopardize their place in society or alienate the majority population.

To the contrary, the genius—and I use the word advisedly—of American Jewish political advocacy has been to seek a broader base of support for core concerns by making the case, often successfully, to other Americans that these concerns—whether standing with a fellow democracy, Israel, or defending the human rights of Jews in danger—reflect the highest American ideals and values.

I was reminded of the differences last fall when a Jewish activist in Geneva planned a pro-Israel rally opposite the UN headquarters, a week after anti-Israel demonstrators had gathered at the same spot to call for jihad and chant "*Mort aux juifs*," "Death to the Jews."

We were chatting a few days before the demonstration, and she asked me for program suggestions. In typical American Jewish fashion, I proposed inviting non-Jewish groups and elected officials to join the rally; after all, that's what the American Jewish Committee would instinctively do in similar circumstances. She said it was a fine idea, but then asked where I expected to find them.

With the exception of Germany, and even there things are slowly changing, it is becoming ever harder to find coalition partners in Europe when it comes to Israel. And without such partners, it can feel painfully lonely.

Which brings me back to the phenomenon of growing European Jewish identity and cooperation. One obvious way to overcome this numerical disadvantage is to develop links across borders, all the more so when those borders are in any case beginning to melt away. It is far more impressive to speak of 2-3 million European Jews who feel strongly on an issue rather than just a single national community.

To illustrate, when the Swedish parliament, on June 1, passed legislation that would interfere with the Jewish community's right to perform circumcisions on newborn Jewish males, the community's president sought the support of all the thirty-nine countries represented in Madrid so that she could speak with a louder voice in Stockholm, and indeed she was able to carry back with her a declaration adopted unanimously (and also supported by several international Jewish agencies).

And when Israel experienced the devastating terrorist attack outside a Tel Aviv nightclub, in which twenty-one youngsters were killed and 120 others wounded, the Madrid delegates adopted a strongly worded resolution targeted as much at Europe as at the world.

It is worth quoting the three references dealing with Europe, both for their content and for the signal they send that a cohesive pan-European Jewish community is forming and is determined to become a factor in the life of Europe as a whole:

"We, the 700 delegates representing thirty-nine countries ... urge the governments of Europe to speak out forcefully against the escalating campaign of Palestinian terror and violence ... further urge the governments of Europe, who are the principal financial supporters of the Palestinian Authority, to state clearly that such actions violate European moral values and undermine the search for a just and lasting peace in the Middle East ... request the European media to adopt a balanced approach to coverage of the Middle East, and to avoid simplistic, one-sided portrayals that present Israel as the aggressor and the Palestinians as innocent victims."

Among delegates, there was a recognition that, despite the pro-Israel stance of some politicians, many European governments had shown little understanding, much less sympathy, for Israel's difficult position in the face of Palestinian rejection and terror during the past nine months in particular. Thus, a far greater effort would be needed to advocate on Israel's behalf. If not spearheaded by Jewish leaders, then by whom? At the same time, they were fully aware that they faced a steep uphill climb.

(In a related aside underscoring Israel's isolation in the international community, the Israeli ambassador to the United Nations in Geneva, speaking at a Jewish function last night, noted that, with the exception of the Americans, not a single diplomat or UN official approached him to offer condolences after last week's suicide bombing outside the Tel Aviv nightclub.)

The same concern was expressed by many delegates in Madrid about media treatment of Israel and the need to grapple with it more effectively than in the past, though this, too, everyone admits, is no easy assignment. While in Spain, for example, I was shown a number of cartoons in mainstream periodicals that illustrate all too well the problem.

One cartoon, which appeared in *El Periodico* (October 6, 2000), shows a young Palestinian male crucified on a Star of David (fig. 1.2).

Another, in *El Pais* (May 23, 2001), depicts Prime Minister Sharon and a small figure flying in his direction with the caption: "Clio, the muse of history, placing the mustache of Hitler on Sharon" (fig. 1.3).

Fig. 1.2.

Source: *El Periodico de Catalunya* (Spain), October 6, 2000

Fig. 1.3.

Cartoon depicting Prime Minister Sharon and a small figure flying in his direction with the caption: "Clio, the muse of history, placing the mustache of Hitler on Sharon."
Source: *El Pais* (Spain), May 23, 2001

Fig. 1.4.

An Orthodox Jew carries an Israeli flag in his right hand with a rifle hanging
from his shoulder. He is reading from a Bible held in his left hand: "We are
the chosen people for the manufacture of weapons."
Source: *El Pais* (Spain), May 24, 2001

Fig. 1.5.

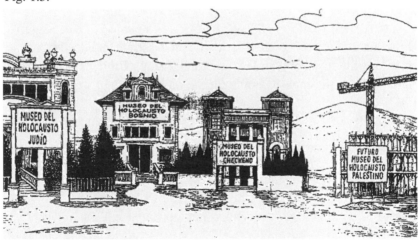

From left to right, building signs read: "Museum of the Jewish Holocaust,"
"Museum of the Bosnian Holocaust," and "Museum of the Chechen
Holocaust." Building on the far right is under construction. The sign reads:
"Future Museum of the Palestinian Holocaust."
Source: *La Vanguardia* (Spain), May 25, 2001

Fig. 1.6.

Cartoon picturing Prime Minister Sharon with a yarmulke saying: "From bad can come good. At least, Hitler taught me to invade a country and exterminate every living vermin." Notice the swastika inside the star of David on his chest. Source: *Cambio 16* (Spain), June 4, 2001

A third, also in *El Pais* (May 24, 2001), is a picture of a caricatured Orthodox Jew carrying an Israeli flag in his right hand with a rifle hanging from his shoulder. He is reading from a Bible held in his left hand: "We are the chosen people for the manufacture of weapons" (fig. 1.4).

A fourth, in *La Vanguardia* (May 25, 2001), presents three buildings, each with a sign in front of it—"Museum of the Jewish Holocaust," "Museum of the Bosnian Holocaust," "Museum of the Chechen Holocaust"—and a fourth building, under construction, with the sign "Future Museum of the Palestinian Holocaust" (fig. 1.5).

And the fifth and most recent, which appeared in *Cambio 16* (June 4, 2001) just a few days after the Tel Aviv discotheque bombing, is of Sharon with a hook nose, wearing a kippah, and with a swastika inside a Star of David emblazoned on his shirt, and his comment: "From bad can come good. At least, Hitler taught me to invade a country and exterminate every living vermin" (fig. 1.6).

There's much more such outrageous material, and not just from Spain, of course; it's not limited to cartoons either, but also, as I have suggested in previous letters, includes radio and television reporting, newspaper headlines, photographs and captions, content and placement of articles, and editorials across Europe. (See Appendix.)

But rather than end on this depressing note, let me finish on the more hopeful note with which I began.

Something exciting and important is happening among Europe's Jewish communities fifty-five years after the war's end. It didn't start yesterday, and it won't take full form overnight; there will doubtless be many obstacles along the way. Still, there's a growing determination to create something larger than the sum of its parts, and, in doing so, to establish European Jewry as a truly vibrant force in the social, cultural, and political life of the new Europe.

Is it a realistic goal? The skeptics say no way, the national differences and rivalries are too entrenched and, in any case, "there's not enough there there."

But the effort deserves the full support and assistance of Israel and American Jewry, because the potential dividends of success, even partial success, would serve the interests of both European and world Jewry, and that's something well worth pursuing.

And this is precisely why, as one practical step to assist the European effort, the American Jewish Committee and the European Council of Jewish Communities announced an association agreement in Madrid, following on the heels of the formal links we have developed with the Bulgarian, Czech, and Slovak Jewish communities and the offices we have established in Berlin, Geneva, and Warsaw.

Just as AJC, after the war, opened a Paris office to help in the Herculean task of rebuilding Jewish life on the continent after the devastation wrought by the Shoah, today we seek to participate in the writing of a promising new chapter in the history of European Jewry, which has come an impressively long way in the past half century.

## Letter from Parc Bertrand
## June 22, 2001

Wow, was I naive! When I first fantasized about a sabbatical year in Switzerland, I had visions of hiking alone in the Alps and, in that pristine setting, thinking about some of the "big questions" concerning the Jewish condition. Without the daily distractions and inspired by the magnificent scenery, I thought, I could see the larger picture.

It didn't quite work out that way.

Actually, things were going reasonably well the first six weeks of our year abroad, and I felt pretty confident that I could balance the various pieces of my life—family, professional, and personal—allowing me time to read, study, and, yes, think. But then Arafat launched his premeditated campaign of violence in September, and things haven't been the same since.

Knowing that there are just a few weeks left before we return to New York, and recognizing that Arafat is not going to change his stripes anytime soon, if ever, I figured that my morning jogs would have to replace the unrealized Alpine walks as my contemplative time. In fact, I can't complain. Our neighborhood park, Parc Bertrand, is quite special—a well-tended sea of green shared harmoniously by users of all ages. As a matter of fact, it has an inspiring view of the surrounding mountains, all of which, incidentally, are located in France, to the consternation of the Geneva tourist board.

But the answers may not necessarily be found in the Alps anyway. A cartoon in the *New Yorker* made the point. It showed a bearded guru up in the mountains sitting cross-legged with a hiker facing him in the same position. The guru says to the hiker, "If I knew the meaning of life, would I be sitting in a cave in my underpants?"

In other words, the park may be as good a place as any to look for answers to life's big questions.

\* \* \*

It's said that in politics where you stand depends on where you sit. That normally refers to whether a given politician or party is in power or in the opposition.

In this instance, it has to do with the fact that I've been sitting in Europe for nearly a year, visiting various countries on the continent and following closely the media here. That may give me a case of "localitis," a disease not unknown to diplomats stationed abroad who often see the world through the prism of their particular assignment. (Lawyers, I believe, use the term "clientitis.") Suddenly, the Duchy of Grand Fenwick becomes the center of the universe and needs to be the single greatest foreign policy priority for the diplomat's home country simply because he (or she) happens to be located there. I'll try to steer clear of the syndrome.

That said, and benefiting from my time in Parc Bertrand, please indulge me as I reflect on some of the pressing challenges we are currently facing.

Israel's safety and well-being are at the top of my list.

Those who were Pollyannaish about a pending peace deal have surely had a rude awakening in the last nine months.

Many Israelis have sadly concluded that in some respects the current situation eerily suggests a return to 1947-48, when the very existence of a Jewish state was in question. As Ze'ev Schiff, the respected *Ha'aretz* journalist, wrote on June 11: "... Arafat is doing everything possible to turn back the clock and to bring both the Palestinians and the Israelis to the initial stages of the 1948 War of Independence."

That's a sobering realization and enormously difficult to fathom, even as we all pray that the prospects for an accord, which both Israelis and Palestinians desperately need, have not entirely vanished. To drive the point home, one Israeli diplomat told me, "If I thought that peace was an impossibility for the next twenty or forty years, could I find the strength to go on?"

It may be out of place for a comfortable Diaspora Jew to proclaim confidently that Israelis will somehow find the strength and determination, as they always have, to carry on, defend their country, and make clear, lest there be any doubt among Israel's adversaries, that the country's will cannot be broken.

But if I say it, it is principally to remind us Diaspora Jews that Israelis have been shouldering an impossibly heavy physical and psychological burden. They do so with enormous courage and stoicism, but no one should underestimate the toll. They cannot be expected to carry on alone, even if they will always bear the brunt of it.

It is Israelis, after all, who face years of military service, decades of reserve duty, daily fear of terrorism, international vilification, and the constant anxiety that the next phone call or television or radio report will bring feared news.

I try to put myself in the shoes of my wife's sister and brother-in-law in Israel.

Deeply committed Zionists, they quietly go about their lives—he as an engineer dealing with the nation's dwindling water supply, she as a social worker. They have two children, the older of whom, Omer, was called to the army last fall. Omer failed the medical test because he was overweight.

For many in my Vietnam-era generation, this would have been cause for jubilation, but for Omer it was an unmitigated disaster. He spent the next several months single-mindedly exercising and dieting. In March he entered the Israel Defense Forces, where he promptly sought admission to one of the elite fighting units. No sooner was basic training completed than he was assigned to a combat zone.

Omer's story is repeated every day in Israel. No doubt he'd prefer to be in front of his computer or traveling abroad, but he, like other young Israeli men and women, recognized his responsibility and answered the call to serve his country. Even at the risk of sounding excessively saccharine, for me the Omers of the world inspire confidence in Israel's future.

Yet, at the very same time, given the volume of intrafamily telephone traffic, I have some idea of what his parents are enduring. Proud though they are of his military service, they are also living a daily nightmare—at any given moment wondering where he is, what he is doing, and whether he is in harm's way. And this will go on for at least three years.

In the meantime, our son Michael was selected to play on the Swiss national soccer team at the World Maccabiah Games, the quadrennial Jewish Olympics, this summer. (No, we haven't defected; eligibility is based on residence, not citizenship.) Concern about security and fear of terrorism prompted several national teams, led by the United States, to call for the games' postponement, although in the end the Americans reversed themselves and agreed to attend.

For now the games will take place, but the understandable apprehension among parents and players has not disappeared. How could it? Still, there is a laudable determination to demonstrate support for Israel and to make clear that the terrorists will not prevail. That very same thinking prompted the American Jewish Committee to announce a solidarity mission to Israel for July 22-24, which I hope will be oversubscribed.

After all, it is we, the Jews of the Diaspora, who represent Israel's only permanent ally. And if we don't fulfill our responsibility, including political support and travel, then we have left Israel—this miraculous Jewish state that was created after 1,900 years of yearning—to fend entirely for itself.

Yet, with all the truly remarkable advocacy efforts of the organized American Jewish community on behalf of Israel, I remain dumbfounded at the number of Jews—and not just the young generation but many of my contemporaries as well—who have little interest in Israel and even less sense of the historical moment. Israel is simply not a significant factor in their lives.

Speaking to some of these individuals, I'm reminded of the Jewish mother who wanted to teach her reluctant son new vocabulary words. "Bubeleh," she said, "what's the difference between 'ignorance' and 'indifference'?" He shrugged his shoulders and muttered: "Mom, I don't know and I don't care."

There is no one-size-fits-all explanation for this attitude toward Israel, and I'm not sure that adequate research has been done on the underlying causes of the detachment, though theories abound. Thanks to AJC surveys, we know the numbers on basic attitudes of American Jews toward Israel, including subgroup data, but we don't have a sufficient qualitative appreciation of what's behind the numbers, and we need it.

To add to the mix, Israel faces not only potent and well-known external threats, but daunting internal challenges as well, many of which simply will not wait for the regional situation to resolve itself. Indeed, the domestic social circuitry is so overheated that it's hard to imagine any country confronted with so many issues, on so many fronts, at the same time.

A rapidly increasing ultra-Orthodox population, a seemingly unbridgeable religious-secular divide, a restive and growing Israeli Arab community, and large numbers of new arrivals from the Former Soviet Union who are not Jewish, or only remotely so—not to mention several hundred thousand foreign workers—all raise fundamental questions about the future character of a Jewish state that has never been adequately defined in the first place.

At best, these questions have been dealt with episodically; at worst, they suffer from neglect. But each of these issues demands attention. The popular Israeli phrase *yih'yeh beseder*, "it'll be okay," can't be the beginning and end of the discussion, any more than a resigned defeatism that says there are no workable solutions, so why even bother.

To illustrate the complexity of these issues, take the case of Israeli Arabs. Of late, there has been discussion about their second-class status. Israel has devoted insufficient resources to these communities, and there can be no justification for this policy. Still, the discussion can't end here. Some difficult—and uncomfortable—questions must also be asked.

Are current events in Macedonia of possible relevance? Perhaps. In this case, an Albanian minority, variously estimated at 25-30 percent of the population, alleging discrimination in all spheres of life and emboldened by Albanian nationalism in neighboring Albania and Kosovo, has challenged the Macedonian regime. Under certain unfolding circumstances, could the same happen in Israel among Israeli Arabs? Already we see some Arab members of the Knesset making astoundingly anti-Israel statements.

Some would argue that Israeli Arabs, for all their grievances, realize full well the benefits of Israeli democracy and economic prosperity and would not wish to risk losing access to these advantages, but recent history has again reminded us of the power of ethnic and religious identity.

Or there could be another possible scenario. Given the fact that 30 percent of all births today within the pre-1967 borders are to Israeli

Arab families, at what point might some leaders, asserting that the community is denied full equality in a society defined as a *Jewish* state, demand some form of political autonomy? And what would be the implications of such a development for Israeli sovereignty and national identity?

Moreover, the Palestinian campaign launched in September has unleashed a new wave of anti-Jewish attacks at the United Nations, in Europe, and elsewhere. With few exceptions, I might add, the international response has been less than heartening. Consider:

- As the *Washington Post* reported on June 19, "The Zionism and racism debate is back, this time in the preparations for the United Nations World Conference Against Racism to be held at the end of August in ... Durban." The allusion, of course, is to the infamous UN General Assembly Resolution 3379, adopted by the world body in 1975, and finally repealed sixteen years later.

- In the negotiations over the final document for the Durban conference, there has been a vigorous effort, led by the Arab world, to remove any reference to the Holocaust and instead to speak of "holocausts."

- In Egypt, which signed a peace treaty with Israel over two decades ago, a government newspaper, *Al-Akhbar*, has once again defended Hitler. According to the Middle East Media Research Institute, the paper recently published an article that stated: "Even if we cross off one zero from the 6 million and are left with a tenth of the number, it would still seem exaggerated and would have to be investigated.... No one can ask why Hitler punished the Jews.... The Zionists were a fifth column in Germany, and they betrayed the country that hosted them in order to realize their aspirations. They had to be exposed...."

- Earlier this month, an Orthodox rabbi from Israel was killed on the street in Zurich. No motive has yet been established, but this is at least the third violent attack in recent years on an Orthodox Jew in Zurich, and the Jewish community is apprehensive.

- In a leading French daily, *Le Figaro* (June 7), the president of the International League Against Racism and Anti-Semitism (LICRA) wrote: "Arson attacks and Molotov cocktails thrown at synagogues, attacks with rocks against Jewish schools, racist writings on Jewish-owned businesses, anti-Semitic insults.... Where and when are we? In Berlin in the 1930s? No. In fact, in Bondy, Trappes, Lille, Toulouse, Strasbourg, Bagnolet, Noisy-le-Sec, Meudon-la-Forêt, Paris ... in France." Indeed, France's National Consultative Commission on Human Rights reported to Prime Minister Jospin that in 2000 there was "a stunning fivefold increase in anti-Semitic violence."

- Syrian president Bashar Assad, who libeled the Jewish people in the presence of Pope John Paul II, and who said to Spanish prime minister Aznar that "Israel's racism has surpassed the Nazis," is soon to visit Paris and Berlin. Will he repeat his utterances? If so, will his French and German hosts also respond with silence? By the way, this is the same Assad who was described by Patrick Seale, a leading British specialist on Syria, as having "absorbed Western values" during his years studying and working in the United Kingdom (*Ha'aretz*, June 8, 2000).

What I also find very troubling, especially here in Europe, is that the impact of the Holocaust—which should have sensitized governments and individuals to the slippery slope of anti-Semitism—doesn't always seem to register. In some ways, it's as if the Holocaust, which continues to receive a good deal of attention in public discourse, is viewed as a discrete event in history, unrelated either to the contemporary condition of Jews or, for that matter, to the self-identity (and sense of vulnerability) of Israel.

This issue would require a separate letter, but suffice it to say that, if I am correct, it may be due to some combination of the following factors: (a) the advent of a new century and the symbolic "turning of an historical page"; (b) the rise to political leadership of a postwar generation, leaving only Pope John Paul II, Polish foreign minister Bartoszewski, and a handful of other leading personalities with any firsthand recollections of World War II; (c) the sense that Israeli "aggressive behavior" reveals that when Jews have power they act no better than anyone else, including the Europeans historically; and (d) the belief that the negotiations on financial settlements of the past few years have effectively "closed the books" and allowed the European nations to feel that debts have been settled.

As the challenges facing the Jewish people once again mount, we are slowly declining in number, except in Israel and, for the moment, in Germany (at the expense of Jewish communities in the Former Soviet Union). The reasons are clear and needn't be repeated here.

Decisions about family, faith, and children are so sensitive, so personal, that it is illusory to believe that any of us can have much impact on the larger trend or even, in many cases, on those closest to us. Unless we adopt the policy of French president de Gaulle or Romanian dictator Ceausescu to encourage births by providing substantial subsidies (and medals)—and I'm not sure how successful they were—we may have no choice but to make the best of a discouraging situation, while hoping for a reversal and ensuring family-friendly policies throughout the Jewish community.

What are the implications of a drop in Jewish population figures? For one thing, it has a demoralizing psychological impact on the Jewish people globally. For another, in small communities it may mark the end of Jewish life, as we have already witnessed in some European cities and also, if for very different reasons, in several southern U.S. towns. Third, it could erode the perception, vital to Jewish interests, of power and strength.

This last point is especially, though obviously not solely, relevant to the United States. The role of American Jewry as an effective political force and advocate—on issues ranging from the U.S.-Israel relationship, to the dangers posed by rogue states and terrorist groups, to the protection of Jews in danger—is absolutely vital, indeed irreplaceable in today's world.

But even as we worry about our numbers, we also have to be concerned about the nagging fissures in our midst—along denominational, national, ethnic, and other lines—that too often sap our strength and divert our time and resources.

The Talmud teaches us that conflict among Jews led to the destruction of the Second Temple in 70 C.E. Have we learned anything since, or are we destined to keep repeating our self-defeating behavior?

When a motion to recognize formally Geneva's long-standing Liberal Jewish congregation (in American terms, "Conservative lite") was introduced a few months ago—motivated by a desire to unite all the Jews here in the struggle on Israel's behalf—it was defeated. And in Europe, Geneva is far from unique in this regard. Such an attitude makes me wonder how much we've actually learned.

Here we are, a tiny Jewish people, some 13-14 million in a world of 6 billion, meaning that roughly one of every 450 people on this planet is Jewish. In a few years the ratio will be one in 500. Today we have challenges and threats galore. In response, we need an intensified spirit of commitment and cooperation, and a reaffirmation of our common destiny.

I hope I'm not asking for the impossible, but, as they say in Italian, *A mali estremi, estremi rimedi*–"Extreme ills require extreme remedies."

## Letter from Paris
## July 14, 2001

The story goes that UNESCO, the United Nations specialized agency headquartered in Paris, announced "the year of the elephant" and invited countries to sponsor research on the huge animal.

At year's end, UNESCO published the titles of the various research projects. From France came "101 Ways to Make Love to an Elephant," from Denmark "1001 Recipes for Using Elephant Meat in Open-Faced Sandwiches," from Italy "Can Elephants Be Trained to Sing Verdi Arias?" and from Israel—what else?—"Elephants and the Jewish Question."

This story came to mind recently as my wife and I were sitting with some Geneva-based Jewish friends at a lakeside restaurant. The setting couldn't have been more picture-perfect and the company more agreeable, yet for the first hour or two we found ourselves talking obsessively about the respective difficulties we had encountered as friends of Israel during the past year in Europe.

At this point, I'm inclined to invoke for the reader a National Car Rental slogan I saw on one of their trucks in Paris, which in English translates as: "We're not here to complicate your life." Bear with me; our dinner conversation may have begun on a down note but it ended on a happy one.

Concerned about their professional positions in the UN system, our friends would not wish to be identified, but they described a work atmosphere in Geneva that ranged from chilly to openly hostile. They spoke of instances when anti-Israel bureaucrats tried to target those few officials seen as "too eager" to hire Jews (not just Israelis, which would have been bad enough, but Jews generally).

We, in turn, described, among other episodes, the most recent incident at our children's school.

On June 1, the school organized an International Day. A high school girl from Israel chose to wear an Israeli flag as part of her dress that day. It wasn't long before she found herself face-to-face with a student from an Arab country. He told her to remove the Israeli flag. She refused. He brandished a knife and reportedly said: "I feel like killing someone today." She ran away, only to be surrounded by a group of Arab students a short while later.

She was still wearing the flag, and this time one of the older students ordered a younger student to throw a cup of soda on the girl. She began crying and ran away. She saw two school administrators and told them what happened. Their astonishing response: "This is a matter between countries. It does not involve us."

To date, despite the efforts of several students and parents, as well as the intervention of a respected Swiss antidefamation organization, CICAD, the school has taken no action, choosing the path of denial instead. Over the course of the past few weeks, we learned that more or less similar events had occurred at several other private schools in Switzerland.

So here we were, with delicious fresh fish from Lac Léman on our plates and a magnificent sunset filling our view, and yet the four of us were managing to depress one another all the same. But then one of our friends turned to us and said: "Let's change the subject. What's been your happiest discovery this year?" Without a moment's hesitation, my wife and I both blurted out in more or less identical words: "France. We have fallen in love with France." And our friends immediately responded by saying that they, too, had developed a passion for what the French sometimes call the Hexagon, referring to the six-sided shape of France.

In my case, this requires full disclosure.

I grew up in a predominantly French-speaking home. Until my parents both learned fluent English, their only common language was French, though in both cases it was not their native language. In fact, every person in my family older than I spoke French and had lived in France until the war or, in some cases, during and after the war as well.

My parents were not uncritical of France. Despite their love of the language and memories of happy moments, they harbored some negative feelings. My mother recalled how, as a refugee child from the Soviet Union, she was made to feel unwelcome in her Paris school, and later how French anti-Semitism affected the lives of Jews, especially after Nazi troops occupied the country in June 1940.

The authorities, with malice aforethought, sent my father, who had volunteered for the French army's division for foreigners, to the very different Foreign Legion in Algeria, where, as a Jew, he received a less-than-welcome reception. Later, when France fell, he was arrested by the Vichy regime and put in Kenadsa, a concentration camp in western Algeria. He spent three difficult years there before managing to escape.

Moreover, I could never forget that France was the country that had had intimate ties with Israel from the very creation of the state until the 1960s, only to do an about-face on the eve of the Six-Day War, when it imposed an arms embargo on the region. For practical purposes, the embargo damaged only Israel, a major purchaser of French weapons, including fighter planes. This was followed by President de Gaulle's notorious comment after the war, which was ostensibly directed at Israel but which some Jews assumed was more widely aimed: "An elite people, proud and domineering."

France, once Israel's most valued ally, redefined its national interest in the mid-1960s and concluded that, in this post-Algerian war era, there was much more to be gained politically, strategically, and commercially from close links with the Arab world than with Israel. Franco-Israeli cooperation suffered a major blow, as France over the years vigorously pursued Saddam Hussein's Iraq, pushed the European Common Market to take a more critical line on Israel, and made back-room deals with the PLO.

And as an American who had traveled to France often since my teen years, I was acutely conscious of the strain of anti-Americanism that seemed to pervade France and that often translated as well into what Americans perceived as a barely concealed arrogance in personal contacts.

Today, I can't, in all honesty, report a totally revamped country, especially when it comes to Israel, but some things have undeniably changed for the better.

It took decades and several presidents, but, to his everlasting credit, President Chirac, shortly after assuming office in 1995, accepted France's responsibility for the crimes of the Vichy regime when he said: "Yes, the criminal folly of the occupier was assisted by French people, by the French state."

Two years later, the Roman Catholic bishops of France issued a Declaration of Repentance in Drancy, the notorious wartime detention and transit camp, which declared in part: "In the face of the magnitude of the tragedy and the unprecedented nature of the crime, too many of the church's pastors, through their silence, committed an offense against the church itself and its mission. Today we confess that this silence was a mistake…. We beg God's forgiveness and ask the Jewish people to hear our words of repentance."

Most recently, in a letter to the American Jewish Committee dated June 28, 2001, the French foreign minister, Hubert Védrine, referring to the outrageous attempt by some nations to avoid speaking of the Holocaust and instead talk of "holocausts" at the upcoming World Conference Against Racism in Durban, reaffirmed the European Union position that "the Holocaust is a unique tragedy in history and this term must be reserved exclusively for this tragedy of European history."

On the other hand, French policy toward the Middle East, I'm sorry to say, hasn't experienced a turnaround, as witnessed by last month's red-carpet reception in Paris for Syrian president Bashar Assad, the eagerness to engage Iran, pro-Palestinian sympathy, and the frequent second-guessing when it comes to Israel. ("What Gaul!" friends of Israel might well say.)

At the same time, France regards itself as a major diplomatic player; after all, it holds a permanent seat on the UN Security Council, is a key factor in European Union decision-making, and has long-standing interests in the Middle East. Accordingly, being sidelined on Arab-Israeli peace process issues while Washington enjoys the confidence of the major parties cannot be a happy state of affairs.

This may have been on Chirac's mind when Israeli prime minister Sharon visited Paris on July 5. Sharon didn't get quite the same warm reception he received at his first stop in Berlin, but he could not have missed hearing President Chirac declare: "France is an ally of Israel."

What exactly the word "ally" means in Chirac's mind remains to be seen. Was the French leader simply angling for the image of greater evenhandedness, the assumed entry card required for a more active role in Arab-Israeli diplomacy?

Sharon, who doubtless recognized that Israel's interests were not served by publicly emphasizing the political divide between the two countries, replied by speaking of "the friendship" between the two countries.

Nor has France suddenly become an uncritical admirer of the United States. A headline in the current issue of the prestigious *Le Monde Diplomatique* said it all: "The dreams of empire of the American presidency."

French politicians and intellectuals, with few exceptions, have their laundry list of concerns about America and are seldom shy about articulating them.

The French anxieties are quite well known: concerns about America's "disproportionate" power, the tendency toward American "unilateralism," a "cowboy" instinct in foreign policy, competition for influence in Francophone Africa and elsewhere, accusations of industrial spying using the Echelon satellite system, the persistence of the death penalty, perceived indifference to the danger of global warming, cultural "imperialism," etc.

That said, the truth of the matter is that France and the United States really do have far more in common than that which divides them. Yes, Airbus and Boeing are in a bitter struggle for supremacy in the world market for planes—and this should not be glossed over—but the common history and shared values of these two nations do form a very strong bond, whatever the current differences may be.

And I am convinced that the French have improved in their attitude toward Americans generally. As one letter-writer to the *International Herald Tribune* recently stated: "As an American living in Paris, I remember the bad old days, but things have changed for the better. Subject to rare exceptions, the French, even in Paris, are as friendly to Americans as anyone would want."

Our family has spent time this year traveling throughout France and can only report pleasant encounters. Imagine, the French—the very same people who not only didn't speak English but showed disdain for the language—now speak it, so much so that it's been hard at times for us to practice our French.

Okay, maybe I'm going soft; after all, France is a magnificently alluring country. Indeed, it is the number-one tourist destination in Europe, if not the world.

Paris is for me the ultimate urban expression, especially bearing in mind that its uninspiring physical location meant that the city's magic was entirely created by the genius of its people, save those responsible for the atrocious 685-foot skyscraper in Montparnasse that stands as a permanent defacement of the city skyline.

In reality, it's easy to understand the words of Montaigne, the sixteenth-century essayist, who wrote: "I love Paris dearly, including its warts and stains."

The rest of the country, including such cities as Lyons and Strasbourg, the Alps, the Côte d'Azur, Provence, Lake Annecy, the Atlantic coast, and the farmland, is equally breathtaking. Throw in the vitality of French intellectual and cultural life, the enviable sense of style and elegance, the celebration of great cuisine, and the sheer beauty of the French language—or the language of Molière, as it is often called—and it creates quite a heady mixture.

Not that the country doesn't have problems; it has its share.

To begin with, France has had an awkward governing structure since 1995, the "cohabitation" of right-of-center President Chirac and the left-of-center government led by Prime Minister Lionel Jospin. The two men are expected to vie for the presidency in the next elections, scheduled for 2002, and current polls suggest it will be a very close contest.

Further, it has been slowly losing power within the European Union to a more assertive Germany, which is coming out from under the shadow of its past. And as EU enlargement proceeds, the center of gravity will almost inevitably shift further away from Paris.

Domestically, there are the ever-present financial scandals, including accusations of the misuse of secret funds by Chirac, stepped-up investigations of torture during the Algerian war of independence, and revelations of Jospin's previously hidden Trotskyist past.

Beyond the immediate issues, France faces the ongoing challenge of integrating the millions of North Africans, Algerians in particular, who arrived decades ago and are in danger of becoming a permanent underclass.

While there are many individual success stories, especially in the fields of entertainment and sports (sound familiar?), entire suburbs have become breeding grounds for unemployment, Islamic fundamentalism, crime, and social alienation. French authorities are now grappling with a set of responses, from debates over affirmative action in elite institutions of higher education to policing methods.

To their collective dismay, the French, who tend to portray America as a crime-ridden and violent nation, learned from a just-published study that in the year 2000 the per-capita crime rate in France exceeded that of the United States, though the murder rate was three times higher in the States.

In the midst of this vibrant and complicated country live 600-700,000 Jews, who form the largest Jewish community in the Diaspora after the United States. During the course of this sabbatical year, I've spent time with the community in Paris, most recently when CRIF, the national umbrella organization, organized an impressive demonstration at the memorial site of the Jewish martyrs at the Vélodrome d'Hiver.

The occasion was the official visit to France of Syrian president Assad, and the protest was focused on Assad's anti-Semitism. As one of the flyers announcing the demonstration declared: "We cannot accept that the country of the Rights of Man receives with honor a head of state who expressed violently anti-Jewish statements in the presence of the pope."

By framing the gathering in this way, rather than as an anti-Syrian political rally, CRIF was able to attract the participation of several leading human rights organizations and representatives of most of the major political parties, as well as the support of the Catholic and Protestant hierarchies. The crowd was variously estimated at 6-8,000, and media coverage was quite extensive.

Subsequently, the mayor of Paris and several local politicians expressed publicly their opposition to Assad's anti-Semitism. In doing so, they were obviously unmoved by the major ad campaign on Assad's behalf sponsored by the "Syrian community in France." For example, one full-page ad in the national daily *Le Figaro*, which appeared on June 26 and showed a large photo of Assad and Chirac smiling and shaking hands, declared: "The dialogue is above all one between men.... Because France shares the values of tolerance with Syria where, for the past fourteen centuries, exponents of various philosophical and religious beliefs have lived."

The French Jewish community, given a major boost in the 1950s and 1960s by the influx of Jews from North Africa, is proud, active, and undaunted, despite the frightening spate of attacks directed at Jews since the surge in Middle East violence last year.

(There had been previous devastating attacks as well, including those against the Copernic synagogue in 1980 and Goldenberg's Restaurant two years later, both in Paris. Memorably, the French prime minister at the time of the Copernic tragedy, Raymond Barre, said in the heat of the moment: "They [the terrorists] wanted to strike at the Jews and hit innocent French," referring to the fact that two of the four victims were non-Jewish passersby.)

And French Jewry has built a thriving communal life in Paris, as well as in other cities such as Lyons, Marseilles, Nice, Strasbourg, and Toulouse.

More generally, Jews have played an extraordinarily important role in virtually every aspect of the life of France. As but one illustration, two Jews, Léon Blum and Pierre Mendes-France, served as the country's prime minister in the last century, in Blum's case on three separate occasions.

Truly, the "City of Lights," like New York, Los Angeles, London, Montreal, Toronto, and a handful of other world-class cities, is a place where the Jewish presence is strongly felt, adding to its magnetic appeal.

Now if only we could return to the glory days of Franco-Israeli friendship....

Happy Bastille Day!

## Letter from 38,000 Feet
## August 1, 2001

In *Lady Windermere's Fan*, Oscar Wilde penned the memorable words that my wife likes to quote: "In this world there are only two tragedies. One is not getting what one wants, and the other is getting it."

True enough perhaps, but not in the case of a much-anticipated sabbatical year just ended.

We're actually on our way home now, one year to the day after leaving New York. I've been on Swissair Flight 104 many times, but this trip is special, filled with a seemingly endless stream of feelings, images, and thoughts prompted by a remarkable experience abroad with my family.

The idea for the year began in 1998, although in a way it started long before.

When I was about to enter the seventh grade, my father was asked by CBS, his employer, whether he'd move to Munich to help implement a cooperative agreement with a German network. It wasn't an easy decision. My father hadn't been back to Germany since 1933, the year he left for the "safety" of Vienna after Hitler became chancellor.

CBS suggested he give it a try for a few weeks before deciding whether the family would follow. He reluctantly agreed. Forty years later, I can still vividly remember the day the call came from my father telling my mother and me to start packing.

We traveled on the majestic SS *America*. It was a thrilling adventure for an eleven-year-old. Most memorable of all was waking up on the sixth morning, looking through the porthole, and seeing a magical sight. We were in the harbor of Cobh, Ireland, anchored a few hundred yards offshore, surrounded by verdant hills dotted with picturesque houses.

It was my very first glimpse of Europe and I was smitten. In the ensuing months, I became completely enamored with the landscape and the rhythm and quality of daily life in the various countries we visited.

I loved the quaint street trams and sometimes rode them back and forth all day. I stood outside the bakeries, soaking in the tantalizing aroma of fresh breads while eyeing the meticulously arranged pastries. I was fascinated by the idea that a few hours in the car could take us across borders to new lands with different languages, architecture, and cuisines. And I was struck by the ever-present sense of history, recent and remote, even if I was far too young to grasp its full meaning.

After we returned to New York, I knew that I wanted to go back to Europe when I grew older. Some wishes do come true. In my twenties, I spent more than five years there, studying and working. And as parents, my wife and I took our three sons abroad several times, which only whetted my appetite to give them something more substantial, the same kind of living and school experience I had had as a child.

The chance came when my tenth anniversary as AJC's executive director approached. It more or less coincided with a certain midlife birthday that puts an unmistakable end to any lingering—and self-deceptive—claims of youth, making the prospect all the more timely.

I broached the idea of a sabbatical year with Bruce Ramer, AJC's president. Despite the disruption my absence might cause, to his ever-lasting credit and, after consulting with his fellow officers, he gave me the green light. Shula Bahat was ready to step in as acting executive director, which meant I could leave secure in the knowledge that the organization would be well managed.

Our family thought about where to go. In theory, everything was possible—in Europe and, for that matter, beyond. My initial instinct was to find a country unreachable by E-mail. I could only identify three.

The first was Syria. Enough said.

The second was North Korea. No E-mail, but then no food or anything else either.

The third was Afghanistan. Maybe we should reconsider Syria.

In truth, we first thought about Israel. Much as I love the country, though, I visualized myself working from morning till night and unable to hide long enough in such a small and intimate place to catch my breath, much less enjoy a respite. Remember the joke about Cohen, the Soviet spy, sent to Israel?

Then came England. I fantasized about returning to Oxford, buying a bicycle, attending occasional seminars, prowling through the libraries, and, in an act of defiance against that milestone birthday, maybe even picking up rowing again. This time, though, my wife put the kibosh on the idea, arguing that our children should be exposed to another language while abroad. Surely, Oxford English counted as a foreign, if not totally exotic, language for our children, I argued, but she was unpersuaded.

Then came Italy, and it took us the better part of a nanosecond to agree. After all, who doesn't love the country? Italy it was, then. As luck would have it, I was offered a visiting professorship in Bologna that would allow me to indulge a work addiction I feared I couldn't entirely shake, yet give us the time we craved for travel and other pursuits.

But then life took an unexpected turn, and Bologna became Geneva. Still, we couldn't complain. No, Switzerland may not be Italy, and Geneva has never been confused with Bologna, but, for the record, there are street trams in Geneva (there are none in Bologna), the French influence makes the *boulangeries* and *pâtisseries* here worth a visit, and if the key to choice of residence is "location, location, location," then it doesn't get much better than Geneva's placement in the heart of Europe.

What most struck me about this year is how much Europe has changed since I first set eyes on it four decades ago, though it has lost none of its allure and charm, far from it.

True, some things aren't very different.

For many Italian drivers, a red light is still an opinion, not an order. In some French homes and hotels, we were faced with those infamous bathtubs that double as showers, with no curtains and a handheld shower just eighteen inches off the ground. In England, there remain otherwise nice houses with separate hot- and cold-water faucets that can make washing perilous business. In Germany, the beer starts flow-ing in some cafés before I've had my first glass of orange juice. And in Spain, there continues what is, for me, a totally inexplicable fascination with the bull, whether it's in the streets of Pamplona or the arena of Seville.

Moreover, many Europeans still have a complex attitude toward America and Americans involving some combination of admiration, envy, and disdain. Intrinsic to this mindset is the notion that America as a nation is capable of brilliant achievements—from medical discoveries to computer advances to moon shots—but that individual Americans are often intellectually challenged.

Thus, in Switzerland I heard the following story: What do you call someone who speaks three languages? Trilingual. What about someone who speaks two languages? Bilingual. And what about a person who only speaks one language? An American.

In the Netherlands it was a variation on the same general theme: An American is standing at a street corner waiting for the light to turn green. He hears a distinct clicking sound and turns to a Dutchman standing next to him and asks what this means. "That's to alert blind people that the light has changed," the Dutchman proudly explains. "That's strange," replies the stunned American. "In the United States we don't let blind people drive."

So, too, in England: An American is flying to London. As the plane descends toward Heathrow Airport, he looks out the window and sees an impressive building. "What's that?" he asks the Englishman in the adjoining seat. "That's Windsor Castle, the home of the royal family," the Englishman responds. "But why would anyone want to build a home so close to an airport?" inquires the puzzled American.

Incidentally, this genre of joke extends to Israel. An American visits a flourishing kibbutz in the middle of the Negev Desert. "Gee, the kibbutz founders were lucky to find an area so green and fertile to build on," the American comments to his host.

On a more serious note, as I mentioned, there have been truly profound changes in Europe.

Most obviously, this continent is no longer bifurcated by the Iron Curtain that Winston Churchill first referred to in his historic 1946 speech at Westminster College in Fulton, Missouri.

As a child of the Cold War, I can still picture going to school one morning in the fall of 1962 convinced we'd all be dead before the day was out because the Soviet-American face-off over Cuba would trigger a nuclear war. Later, I experienced communist tyranny firsthand.

Even a decade after the dramatic collapse of the Soviet empire, I'm still awestruck by the extraordinary events that have brought to an end Europe's physical and political division. I'm especially mindful of the singular American role—not always appreciated or even remembered these days—in bringing about this previously unimaginable outcome, another reminder of America's immense contribution to Europe's post-war freedom, security, and development.

I pinch myself each time I walk through Berlin's Brandenburg Gate or pass what was once Checkpoint Charlie. I still marvel seeing the cars in Vienna with Slovak, Czech, and Hungarian license plates—mind you, cars that actually work, unlike the old Soviet and East German models—touring the city sights or heading for points farther west. I frequently catch myself staring at the departure monitors in Ben-Gurion Airport and smiling as I count the many daily flights to Central and East European cities that had previously had few links with the West, much less with Israel. And I still do a double take when I see the Estonian, Latvian, and Lithuanian flags.

As the walls between East and West have come tumbling down, the last barriers among the member states of the European Union have all but disappeared. Once a traveler is inside the EU, customs formalities range from limited to nonexistent, which has only one downside—it's next to impossible to request a souvenir stamp for a passport.

The visionaries of European integration, particularly Monnet, Schuman, De Gasperi, and Adenauer, began in the 1950s by linking six countries—France, West Germany, Italy, Belgium, Luxembourg, and the Netherlands—around the issues of coal and steel.

But, in point of fact, they were embarking on a much more ambitious effort. They were planting the seeds for the most far-reaching peace project in modern history. It was Monnet, columnist Flora Lewis reminded us, who believed that "the only way the lessons of history stay learned is when they are embodied in institutions."

These great men understood the desperate need to overcome the legacy of decades, if not centuries, of devastating wars that had torn Europe apart and wreaked such unparalleled havoc. Moreover, they grasped the essential point that France and Germany had to be at the center of any new regional mechanisms.

Today, even with the difficulties that plague the European Union—the Irish vote against enlargement, the Danish rejection of the common currency, Franco-German differences over a future governing structure, and polls showing that many Europeans feel detached from Brussels—it remains an extraordinary success story. (A Eurobarometer survey released in July revealed that only 54 percent of Europeans have any trust in the European Commission, the EU executive body, the *International Herald Tribune* reported.)

The EU now counts fifteen member countries, with thirteen others, including Turkey, seeking entry. A vast zone of democracy and prosperity has been established. The once poorer countries—Greece, Ireland, Portugal, and Spain—have developed rapidly. Aspiring member states on the fast track—Cyprus, the Czech Republic, Estonia, Hungary, Poland, and Slovenia—understand full well the norms and values, not to mention the reams of rules and regulations, they must embrace if they are to be admitted.

Add NATO to the mix. The enlargement in 1999 to include the Czech Republic, Hungary, and Poland was another important step not only in unifying Europe but also in solidifying its democratic structure. Those *New York Times* editorial writers who railed against enlargement in one essay after another were proved wrong.

In 2002, NATO is expected to invite additional countries to join. Without wishing to minimize the problems associated with expansion, the benefits of such growth far outweigh the potential risks. Yes, as Henry Kissinger has written, there's always a danger that this security alliance will turn into "multilateral mush," but that need not be. Importantly, countries seeking entry have been taking historic steps to enhance their chances. That helps explain, for example, the Hungarian-Romanian accord. Both countries knew that, as one price of admission, they needed to solve their long-standing differences, and they did.

In the same spirit, the Serbian prime minister recently acknowledged that the decision to hand over Milosevic to the Hague tribunal was prompted both by the need for Western aid and the recognition that this step was necessary to link his land closer to Europe and the West.

With all the remarkable strides achieved in Europe, much remains to be done.

For one thing, there are still unresolved conflicts. Progress toward a peaceful settlement of the long-simmering dispute in Northern Ireland has suffered a recent blow. Terrorism by Basque separatists continues to plague Spain. The division of Cyprus since 1974 has been a sticking point in Greek-Turkish relations. And, not least, multiple challenges bedevil the Balkans.

For another, as I've written on previous occasions, the demographic issues facing Europe pose profound social, political, economic, and cultural challenges. While EU countries like Germany debate new immigration policies (the *Frankfurter Allgemeine Zeitung* recently reported that, given current population trends, "by 2030, it is estimated that Germany will have just as many pensioners as it has workers"), illegal migrants keep trying to enter in search of new lives.

Every day in the press there are articles about intercepted migrants who were found clinging to train undercarriages, crammed in unseaworthy vessels, posing as tourists, or hidden in sealed trucks.

The majority of current and potential migrants, both legal and clandestine, are neither European nor Christian. Instead, they come from Asia, the Middle East, and North Africa. Europe will need to come to terms with the prospect of continuing, perhaps accelerating, ethnic and religious changes.

To understand just how difficult this can be, it's worth seeing a wonderful movie called *Pane e Cioccolato* ("Bread and Chocolate"), starring Nino Manfredi. Released in 1973, it tells of the difficulties faced by a poor immigrant working as a waiter in Switzerland—and he was an Italian! More recently, a British film entitled *East Is East* recounted the societal and family hurdles faced by a Pakistani migrant, his British wife, and their seven children in an English working-class town.

As we know, rapid social change can create a political backlash (and, as we witnessed recently in northwest England, violent clashes).

This helps explain the rise of Jörg Haider and the Freedom Party in Austria. In the last national elections, campaigning on blatantly xenophobic themes, the party garnered 27 percent of the vote and, troublingly, is now the junior member in the governing coalition. Fortunately, Umberto Bossi and his extremist Northern League Party in Italy didn't do nearly as well in the recent Italian elections, yet still managed to enter the governing coalition, landing Bossi a cabinet seat.

Another striking change in Europe is the widespread use of English. When I first lived in Italy in 1975, I used a dry cleaner across the street from my apartment. Not only did the owner not speak a word of English, but each time I brought him clothes—and I'm not making this up—he would mark my name as "x" because, as an Italian, he couldn't fathom the notion that a surname might begin with the letter H, much less end with a consonant. He simply assumed, I suppose, that I was pulling his leg.

That dry cleaner was very much in the spirit of Primo Levi's memorable character, Cesare, in Levi's second book, *La Tregua* ("The Truce"), who firmly believed that the Russians and Germans he met immediately after the war "pretended not to understand Italian" because of "malice or extreme and scandalous ignorance…."

I can't say if that dry cleaner speaks English today, but just about everyone else in Europe seems to.

I was sitting in a Geneva park when an adorable girl, maybe five years old, smiled at me and said a few words in French. I thought to myself: Here's a rare chance to speak French. However, the moment I began to reply she interrupted me and said in perfect English, "Oh, I can see it's easier for you to speak English, unless you want to speak Chinese, which I can also speak!"

I could go on, but the flight is almost at an end. Suffice it to say, then, that this has been a terrific year.

True, in some ways it was much more than we bargained for. As I've written before, the troubling events in the Middle East and their ripple effects consumed us day in and day out, dominated my work at UN Watch, affected the lives of our children at school, brought us still closer to Europe's Jews, made us even more aware of the challenges faced by friends of Israel in Europe, and powerfully reminded us yet again of the unique position of the United States and the American Jewish community—and within it, the American Jewish Committee—in defending Jewish interests.

But I wouldn't have traded this year for anything, not least because of its significant and, I hope, enduring impact on our kids.

In French, there's a wonderful expression—*l'esprit de l'escalier,* which literally means "the spirit of the staircase." It refers to that moment, after leaving a meeting and heading downstairs, when an afterthought hits us, something we wish we had said or done during the meeting.

As our plane approaches JFK, that afterthought still hasn't come regarding the year just ended. Instead, there's only gratitude for the extraordinary opportunity my family and I were given, indelible memories, and a sense of anticipation about the year ahead—once we get past the unpacking, that is.

## Letter from East 47th Street
## September 6, 2001

On September 23, where do you plan to be? Enjoying a relaxing Sunday at home? Doing the *Times* crossword puzzle? Watching the Giants play the Kansas City Chiefs? Escorting your children to their soccer game? Or taking advantage of the last warm days at the beach?

As they say in New York, "fuhgedaboudid."

A major solidarity rally with Israel is planned for that day, at 47th Street and Second Avenue. Jewish organizations across the ideological and denominational spectrum, spearheaded by United Jewish Communities (UJC), are sponsoring the event. Your participation is urgently requested.

Israel faces a real crisis. Its people are struggling valiantly to defend the country against daily threats, while never abandoning the hope for peace.

During this difficult period, as Israelis have buried the victims of terrorist attacks throughout the country, they have often wondered whether they are alone in their struggle. Tourism has come to a screeching halt, foreign media treatment has too often been slanted, and, as we have witnessed most recently in Durban, many of the world's nations are ready, at the drop of a hat, to bash Israel.

Tough as all this is, the Israelis can deal with these developments, as they have in the past. But the looming questions repeated again and again in Israel to any visitor are: Where are our fellow Jews? Do they understand our difficult situation? Are they raising their voices in support?

The September 23 rally gives us all the chance to answer those questions resoundingly.

The world will be watching on September 23—quite literally, in fact.

Not only will the rally be covered by U.S. and international media, but many government leaders will be in New York at the time for the opening of the fifty-sixth session of the UN General Assembly.

We have an extraordinary opportunity, by our presence, to send a powerful message to world capitals—and not least to the people of Israel—that we stand with Israel, never more so than in its hour of need.

Fast-forward and imagine for a moment the electrifying effect of masses of participants filling the East Side streets, joined by leading politicians, clergymen, and entertainers, voicing their solidarity with Israel.

In my case, it's easy to visualize. All I have to do is think back fourteen years to Freedom Sunday for Soviet Jewry, the last megademonstration organized by American Jewry. I had the privilege of serving as national coordinator for the event, the largest rally in American Jewish history.

Held in Washington on the eve of Soviet president Gorbachev's first visit to the White House, it was an unforgettable event—for those who participated, for Kremlin leaders who couldn't fail to see the extraordinary breadth and depth of support for the rights of Jews in the USSR, and, not least, for beleaguered Soviet Jews, who felt strengthened in their resolve to carry on the struggle by this outpouring on their behalf.

We usually don't get to choose the important moments in life. The moments come, linger briefly, and compel us to make choices. Those choices, in turn, reveal a great deal about ourselves, and they also tell our children and grandchildren a great deal about us.

The September 23 rally is one of those important moments. Be there, even if it means changing your plans for the day. You'll feel good about the decision, you'll have a memorable day, and together we'll send a loud and clear message to the world about exactly where we stand.

Letter from New York<br>September 15, 2001

As I write this letter in the wake of the calamitous events of the past week, rescue workers in lower Manhattan continue to sift through the rubble, while families of the nearly 5,000 unaccounted persons who worked in the World Trade Center search frantically for any sign of their missing relatives.

Fear of the possibility of other terrorist attacks persists, the Federal Bureau of Investigation is engaged in a massive hunt for the terrorists still at large and those who may have assisted them, and President Bush and his senior advisers are considering the range of military options.

The president has begun to prepare the American people, as he indicated in a radio address to the nation earlier today, for the fact that American-led action will constitute a "comprehensive assault on terrorism," to include organizations and those countries that harbor and support the terrorists. He said that our nation's response would be "sweeping, sustained and effective," and asked the nation for "patience, resolve, and strength."

The United States is currently engaged in a full-court diplomatic press to line up international support for a coalition of forces to attack terrorism at its sources, and has made clear that those who are not with us in this struggle will be considered against us. Significantly, the nineteen NATO members, for the first time since the collective security alliance was established in 1949, have invoked Article 5, which stipulates that an attack from abroad against any NATO member constitutes an attack on all.

The Congress, with only one dissenting voice, has lined up square-ly behind the president, giving the White House authority to use mili-tary force against the perpetrators of these horrific terrorist attacks, authorizing the call-up of up to 50,000 military reservists, and allocat-ing $40 billion to help rebuild the damaged sites and provide a down payment on the massive expenditures required to mount an appropriate military campaign.

While all this activity is going on at the national and international levels, daily life in New York, needless to say, has been affected.

Given that 50,000 people worked in the two towers and another 150,000 passed through the buildings every day, not to mention those employed in the immediate vicinity, the sheer number of people direct-ly touched was huge. It meant that just about everyone in the New York area knew someone who worked in or visited the towers or the nearby buildings.

From the moment American Airlines Flight 11 flew into the north tower, followed eighteen minutes later by United Airlines Flight 175 striking the south tower, sirens began wailing in the streets of New York, as fire engines, police cars, and other emergency vehicles raced to the southern tip of Manhattan Island.

Billowing smoke from New York's two tallest buildings was clearly visible from our vantage point three miles from "Ground Zero." Within an hour, Third Avenue was clogged with pedestrians making their way north—in some cases fleeing on foot from the stricken area, often cov-ered in dust and ash, in other cases evacuating office buildings in the midtown area. People were trying to get away from the center and reach their homes and families, but for many it proved impossible, at least in the short run. Trains stopped running, bridges and tunnels were shut down, and buses were few and far between. And for those from other cities or countries who were in New York at the time, getting home proved a lot tougher. In fact, five days later, some are still strand-ed here, unable to find seats on reduced flight schedules.

Strikingly, there was no panic. People looked grim, stunned, wan, but instinctively seemed to understand that everyone was in this togeth-er and behaved accordingly. A city celebrated for its diversity—a diver-sity that was reflected in all its richness among those who worked at the World Trade Center—was dramatically reminded on September 11 of the ties that bind.

There were appeals for blood donations. The response was overwhelming. People lined up outside donation centers to the point where the centers could not keep up with the supply. It reflected a remarkable outpouring of community spirit, fulfilling words from a poem written on another ominous date in history, September 1, 1939—the Nazi invasion of Poland: "May I, in the darkness and dust, show an affirming flame."

New Yorkers wanted to help. Our city had been attacked and, for the moment at least, the only way we could fight back was to unite and to volunteer whatever skills we had to offer. As with the pool of those eager to donate blood, the supply of volunteers exceeded the demand, and the city eventually announced that no additional help, by volunteers at least, was required.

A reporter asked one New Yorker if she planned to leave the city after the attacks. The woman looked horrified and said the thought had never occurred to her. Still, no one could know if more attacks were planned. As a matter of fact, in the days after September 11, there have been a number of threats and alarms, resulting in the temporary evacuation of area airports, Grand Central Station, midtown office buildings, and at least one school, but slowly the tempo of life is picking up and some sense of normalcy is returning, even if nerves are more than a bit frayed.

America has been desperately in need of heroes, of role models for our nation and especially our youth. For years, the country has made do with often deeply flawed personalities from the worlds of politics, entertainment, and professional sports. Today, out of unspeakable tragedy have emerged the true dimensions of heroism—unsung individuals who exhibited staggering courage.

Several passengers on hijacked United Airlines Flight 93, traveling from Newark to San Francisco—who realized they were headed for certain death in a hijacked plane that had become, in effect, a lethal missile bearing down on the nation's capital—attacked the terrorists and forced the plane to crash near Pittsburgh, thereby averting an even worse disaster. What can one say about such remarkable people, whose lives were extinguished in the crash?

And here in New York, the firefighters, police, medical personnel, and emergency rescue workers have been working around the clock in an effort to save as many people as possible. In the process, many have made the ultimate sacrifice. The image of firefighters rushing into the World Trade Center towers as people were fleeing the burning and crumbling buildings has been etched in the nation's consciousness.

As Fire Chief William Feehan said in an interview on National Public Radio shortly before he gave his life on September 11, "A firefighter has to be ready at any moment to go into harm's way and be ready to help in any way. The culture of the Fire Department is very special. It's to go to the aid of those in peril. It's not about money. It's about much more." Chief Feehan had been a firefighter for over forty years. He died at the age of seventy-one and was buried yesterday.

Even as I write these words, the reality hasn't fully sunk in.

America was attacked in a breathtakingly bold and well-coordinated attack that revealed our nation's striking vulnerability and represented a colossal failure of our intelligence and security capacities.

More than 5,000 people are presumed dead, and countless other lives are shattered. The World Trade Center, the symbol of America's soaring economic power, is gone, and the Pentagon, the emblem of America's military might, lies badly damaged.

The world's unquestioned superpower was left gasping for air. What the Axis nations in World War II and the Soviet bloc during the Cold War couldn't even contemplate, a shadowy enemy had accomplished. America was caught totally unprepared, dealt a body blow, and left badly shaken.

It's always tempting to second-guess. Hindsight, after all, affords perfect vision. Even so, who could have foreseen such an act of war? At the same time, the truth is that terrorism against American targets by the forces of radical Islam didn't start yesterday. Time and again, these forces have made clear their hatred of the United States and everything it represents. They detest American, indeed Western, secularism, modernity, culture, and power. They cannot fathom the notion that "infidel" troops are stationed on "holy" Islamic soil in Saudi Arabia. They hold the United States responsible for "aggression" against Iraq, a Muslim country. And they long for the restoration of Islamic unity and glory.

Just as Hitler spelled out in *Mein Kampf,* in 1924, the diabolical program he intended to pursue, so did Osama bin Laden offer his worldview for all to see. According to Professor Bernard Lewis of Princeton University, the text of bin Laden's views was published in London in 1998. Entitled a "Declaration of the World Islamic Front against the Jews and the Crusaders," the document includes the following passage:

> By God's leave, we call on every Muslim who believes in God and hopes for reward to obey God's command to kill the Americans and plunder their possessions wherever he finds them and whenever he can. Likewise, we call on the Muslim *ulema* [authorities on theology and Islamic law] and leaders and youth and soldiers to launch attacks against the armies of the American devils and against those who are allied with them from among the helpers of Satan.

As a nation, the United States has dealt with the threat of radical Islamic terror episodically, not consistently, approaching it less as a war than as a matter of law enforcement. We had our share of successes in tracking down wanted terrorists and managed to curtail the activities of Libya's Qaddafi, but the total effort has been less than the sum of its parts.

Can anyone argue that the United States reacted with sufficient resolve to the bombing of the Marine barracks in Beirut in 1983? Or to the destruction of the American embassies in Nairobi and Dar es Salaam in 1998? Hundreds of people were killed in Lebanon and East Africa in those attacks, yet the inadequate American response sent a clear message that Washington wasn't prepared for what would necessarily be a dirty war. And these were far from the only terrorist attacks against American targets by various Middle Eastern groups united by a desire to inflict the maximum possible damage on American interests.

Throughout the years, there were those persistent voices—including that of the American Jewish Committee—urging the United States and the rest of the Western world to recognize the true nature of the peril, to connect the dots and draw the appropriate conclusions, and to meet the challenge head on in such a way as to leave no doubt about our will. Otherwise, the toll would only mount.

But our intelligence agencies had come to rely increasingly on electronic collection rather than human sources—though no one should underestimate the difficulty of penetrating groups like bin Laden's loosely organized worldwide network—and the FBI was faced with various political and legal hurdles in its ability to monitor effectively Arab and Islamic activity. And, as a nation with global interests and a vast agenda, our nation had to juggle its counterterrorism objectives with other, at times conflicting, diplomatic, political, and commercial concerns.

In addition, the United States received uneven support abroad. Our European allies at times claimed that Washington—ever in need of an enemy, some Eurocynics asserted—was exaggerating the threat of radical Islam. But then again, it was France and Italy, and perhaps other European nations, who made a deal with the devil in the 1970s, when they secretly reached agreement with the PLO to keep terrorism off their soil in exchange for tacit support of some kind—so what could one expect? And European nations, dependent on export markets and imported energy, have been especially eager to court such countries as Libya, Sudan, and especially Iran, despite credible evidence that these countries have been supporting international terrorism.

But that was then and this is now. The more pressing issue is what happens next.

The United States has set down the markers. This will be a war against terrorism, not simply the firing of a few missiles at terrorist training camps in Afghanistan or a one-shot strike at a suspected chemical weapons factory in Sudan.

As Francis Quarles, the seventeenth-century English poet, wrote: "Beware of him that is slow to anger; for when it is long in coming, it is the stronger when it comes, and the longer kept. Abused patience turns to fury."

He could have been describing the United States today. The fury is there. So is the government's determination.

As American leaders plan our nation's response, some questions come to mind:

Will the national consensus, so strong today in the United States, remain intact, or will it begin to splinter as time passes?

Do Americans have the stomach for what could be a protracted and complex conflict? The last two major military actions in which we were involved—the NATO bombing of Serbia and the Gulf War—were far more straightforward in their objectives, our enemies were clearly defined, and relatively few American fatalities resulted.

What will be the objectives of such a war? What exactly constitutes victory? The Bush administration speaks of a war against international terrorism, including the nations that offer refuge and support to terrorist groups. Apart from Afghanistan, Iran, Iraq, Libya, Sudan, and Syria are all on the State Department's list of countries involved with terrorism. Does that make them all potential targets?

Who will comprise the coalition? It's clear that the democratic nations will participate, and the administration is eager to enlist Arab and Muslim countries as well, both to refute any impression of a civilizational conflict between the West and Islam and, as a practical matter, to have access to staging areas close to the intended targets.

But will the administration be asked to pay a price for their inclusion? In the case of the Gulf War, for example, Egypt received a huge and largely unnoticed dividend—cancellation of billions of dollars in debt owed the United States, and that wasn't all. This time, might it be the promise of new weapons deliveries to such countries as Egypt? Or a willingness to try to move the Israeli-Palestinian peace process faster than Jerusalem feels it is safely prepared to go? Or perhaps an unspoken understanding to define the aims of the war more narrowly than the U.S. administration might otherwise wish in deference to the insistence of, say, Egypt or Saudi Arabia?

What will Washington do about Syria? The American position, as noted above, is clear—either a country is with us or it's against us. If Syria "agrees" to end its involvement in terrorism, would it be eligible to join the coalition, bearing in mind that it was part of the U.S.-led group during the Gulf War, for which it was handsomely rewarded, even if its contribution to the effort was essentially nonexistent?

Can a common understanding of what, in fact, constitutes terrorism be reached, or will differences be glossed over for the sake of appearances?

For example, would Syria be asked not only to end its long-standing hospitality for radical Islamic groups seeking Israel's destruction but also to halt all support for Hezbollah in Lebanon—a country whose independence Syria does not even formally recognize—including the transshipment of weapons originating in Iran and destined for the terrorist group?

How will the administration handle Chairman Arafat's offer to participate in the coalition? And conversely, how will it deal with Prime Minister Sharon's insistence that the Palestinian Authority should not only be excluded from the coalition but, as a terrorist infrastructure, ought to be among the targets of the entire exercise?

Speaking of Israel, Sharon has said that the coalition should comprise "democratic countries," but, by definition, that would exclude any Arab country. The Bush team will not heed that request because it needs an Arab and Islamic cover, which brings us to the question of whether there is a place in the coalition for Israel.

As is well known, during the Gulf War the earlier Bush administration excluded Israel from its coalition. Israel was told to keep its head down and place its trust in the United States. It absorbed thirty-nine Iraqi-launched Scud missiles, but exercised remarkable restraint under the leadership of Prime Minister Shamir.

Would Sharon insist on a place in the coalition this time around, all the more so given Israel's unrivaled experience in coping with Middle Eastern terrorism? Or would Israel again agree to lie low—perhaps limiting itself to unpublicized assistance—based on Sharon's oft-stated confidence in President Bush's commitment to Israel and recognition that Jerusalem stands to gain greatly from a successful outcome to the military campaign? Would Israel show the same restraint if, for any reason, it was attacked in a region where missiles have become almost commonplace?

How about the Europeans? Will they see eye-to-eye with Washington on the objectives of a potentially wide-ranging war against terrorism that could target not only Afghanistan but also, say, Iraq? How would they react if asked, as an initial step, to reconsider their growing commercial ties with Iran, arguably the leading bankroller of international terrorism in the world today? Will the facade of unbreakable unity begin to fray at the edges down the road, with the British likeliest to stand shoulder-to-shoulder with the United States till the very end, the Germans growing nervous if antiwar demonstrations should start taking place in the streets of major cities (as occurred during the Gulf War), and the French becoming uneasy about pursuing anything more than a narrowly defined military mission for fear of hurting other national interests?

The Europe that I saw up close over the past year could find itself divided if the conflict endures and there is no clear consensus on military objectives.

On the one hand, most governments feel an abiding loyalty to the United States right now, which, after all, came to Europe's rescue in two world wars, helped rebuild a ravaged continent, and extended its protective umbrella during the Cold War, and is now asking for full support against what is, in truth, a common enemy.

On the other hand, in many European quarters there is a growing repugnance to war as an instrument of state policy, a belief in dialogue, peaceful conflict resolution, and international tribunals as alternatives, and little sympathy for America's recent approach to world affairs, which has been described by some Europeans as insufficiently sensitive to the views of allies.

The Europeans would do well to heed a front-page column in the influential left-of-center Italian daily *La Repubblica* (September 13):

> It is in tragedies that individuals and peoples rediscover the deep roots of their real identity. The terrorist attack against America is one of those historical moments that require us to undertake this assignment.... An absolute rejection [of Western values] which today strikes the Americans but involves both sides of the Atlantic Ocean. Because in the final analysis, even if in ordinary times we emphasize the reciprocal differences [between the United States and Europe], we are linked together in a world of its own. The West, to be precise. One family. The decision of our alliance to consider the attack on America as an attack on us all, according to Article 5 of the NATO Charter ... leaves no space for ambiguity or waltzing around. If someone tried to, they would immediately and irremediably lose any claim to membership in the Western community.

How about the objectives themselves? Afghanistan clearly would be the immediate target. But it is a rugged, inhospitable country, as Soviet forces discovered at great cost over a span of ten years. And bombing the country couldn't bring it back to the Stone Age because that's precisely where it is today.

Will Pakistan sever, once and for all, its vital support for the Taliban and permit the country to become a staging ground for a vast military operation against its neighbor without internal repercussions? Osama bin Laden, observers note, is practically a folk hero in Pakistan. As elsewhere in the Muslim world, "Osama" has become one of the most popular names for newborn males in honor of the Saudi exile. Given the country's inherent instability, could we witness internal turmoil in Pakistan as a result of the courageous green light from General Musharraf to U.S.-led forces?

In some respects, Pakistan encapsulates within its borders all the longer-term challenges of impoverished, corrupt, aggrieved Islamic states, which have high birthrates, a shaky economy, weak institutions of civil society, and, in this particular case, possession of the nuclear bomb.

And is it possible to duck a large, foreboding question? Can the battlefield be transferred to the region without enduring more terrorist attacks on the United States or American personnel and property spread around the world?

The support base for radical Islam in the United States extends well beyond the hundred or so terrorists identified by the FBI since September 11. And this does not even begin to address the universe of latent sympathy for Osama bin Laden and his ilk that exists in other Western countries, much less the actual network of operatives, sleepers, and supporters scattered around the world.

This threat will challenge domestic law enforcement as never before, and could be further complicated by an inherent tension between national security and civil liberties concerns that is likely to resurface after the initial wave of revulsion passes.

It also means, I earnestly hope, a careful reexamination by government and other sectors of American society of those U.S.-based Muslim organizations that have inexplicably been conferred legitimacy and accorded high-level access while serving as mouthpieces for radical Islam and apologists for the use of terror.

Further, it suggests the need for far more careful scrutiny by law enforcement officials of fund-raising efforts in this country to channel money to Middle Eastern terrorist groups, often under the guise of assistance for "widows and orphans."

And it requires the media to emerge from what appears to be a self-imposed censorship, hitherto failing to tackle these and related topics, despite repeated urging, for fear that they will be labeled anti-Arab or anti-Muslim. The *Wall Street Journal* editorial page has been a notable exception, as has the reporting of Judith Miller of the *New York Times*.

Speaking of the press, what about the latest Palestinian attempt to muzzle the foreign media?

After reports of the destruction wrought by the terrorists in New York, Washington, and Pennsylvania, Palestinians began assembling in the streets to celebrate. In Nablus alone, as many as 4,000 people gathered. The attempts by Western film crews to record these events met with intimidation, just as occurred when Western media attempted to film the gruesome lynching of the two Israeli soldiers in Ramallah. Fortunately, in the latter case a private Italian television crew was able to smuggle out footage, which was subsequently broadcast around the world. This time, though, the Associated Press has been unwilling to air its footage from Nablus because of fear for the life of its correspondent.

None of this, of course, has stopped the leading Palestinian spokeswoman from denying that joyous demonstrations ever took place and trying to shift the focus of discussion to Israel, in repeated television interviews with uncritical, at times sycophantic, reporters.

Such a Palestinian voice, no matter how glib, is unlikely to serve as a credible source on the subject of terrorism for the vast majority of Americans. In any case, I believe, Americans are too smart to buy the line that the nightmarish events of the past week should somehow be blamed on Israel or America's ties with Jerusalem. They understand that Osama bin Laden and his followers target the United States because of what we stand for, pure and simple. These religious fanatics seek America's disappearance from the face of the earth; nothing less will satisfy them.

Moreover, I trust that Americans understand that bin Laden is not at all interested in a peace deal between Israel and the Palestinians, to the extent that he even thinks about the issue. He would not be content unless Israel were completely destroyed and Muslims *in his image* were in control of the land.

That said, it doesn't help our efforts in the United States at this time to see some of the comments made by Israelis, either of the "we told you so" variety, which comes across as self-serving, or the "America ought to push Israel to the peace table right now," which suggests a connection between the terrorist attacks and Israeli-Palestinian issues. These Israelis should heed the advice of Plutarch: "Silence at the proper season is wisdom, and better than any speech."

As I write this letter, every once in a while the radio punctuates its round-the-clock broadcasting with the names of more victims from the World Trade Center and Pentagon. It's so horrendously painful to imagine that just a few days ago these people were spending time with their families, thinking of the future, perhaps wondering who to vote for in the New York mayoralty primaries, or speculating whether Michael Jordan might actually resume playing pro basketball. Instead, as their bodies are identified, funeral plans are made, the lives of their loved ones are shattered, and a weeping nation expresses its condolences.

This great country will regain its footing. Of that I am absolutely certain. Notwithstanding all the daunting challenges before it, I have every confidence that the American people will exercise the "patience, resolve, and strength" that President Bush asked for and that our nation will successfully meet the test before it.

It might be worth remembering the words of an exceptional statesman, Winston Churchill, whose nation also faced and met the ultimate test: "An optimist sees an opportunity in every calamity; a pessimist sees a calamity in every opportunity."

Optimism has always been a defining feature of this extraordinary country. Despite the tragic events of this past week, it will continue to be so.

And as for my beloved New York, who said it best? Maybe it was none other than Frank Sinatra in that legendary song of his—"I'm going to make a brand new start of it in old New York.... It's up to you, New York, New York."

This has been a difficult twelve months. It began with Arafat's repudiation of the peace process and a new wave of Palestinian-instigated violence, followed by repeated deadly terrorist attacks against Israelis and persistent efforts to isolate Israel in the international community, culminating with the Durban fiasco. And it ended with a deadly war brought to American soil.

We should never forget that, no matter how daunting the challenges, our tradition teaches us to believe in the possibility of a better tomorrow.

*L'shana tova.* May 5762 be a better year for all of us.


## Letter from East 56th Street[*]
## October 1, 2001

As we begin the year 5762, most of us surely are gasping for breath from the year just ended. It's been a rough twelve months, with little respite in sight.

It started last Rosh Hashanah with the eruption of Palestinian-instigated violence. This could have been a year that built on the historic peace offer presented by Prime Minister Barak, with the active support of President Clinton. Instead, we were compelled to ask whether the whole Oslo process had been a fraud, a diplomatic sleight of hand by Chairman Arafat to weaken Israel and move the Palestinians that much closer to their real goal, one that many believed was no longer part of their vocabulary—the destruction of Israel through stages.

However painful, it is ultimately unavoidable to ask the difficult questions prompted by the experience of the past year: Is there, in fact, a Palestinian partner for peace? Is there any reason left to believe that Arafat is either capable of or willing to settle the conflict peacefully on terms that could conceivably be acceptable to any Israeli government? Did Israel so hopelessly delude itself about the entire venture as to help arm an adversary, in the belief that the weapons it transferred were intended for domestic law enforcement in the emerging Palestinian state?

---

[*] This letter draws on speeches I made at the American Jewish Committee's New York Chapter Town Hall meeting, at New York University, and to a visiting delegation of senior German (and other NATO) military officers during the week of September 24.

Did the reintroduction of the so-called "right of return" issue at Camp David signal the death knell of the peace process? Do the continuing incitement of and education for hate, not to speak of the glorification of suicide bombers, mean that the Palestinian objective is nothing less than unrelenting struggle till the very end? How else are we to interpret the opening of a new Palestinian exhibit last week at the largest university in the West Bank, in Nablus, that pays tribute to suicide bombers, an exhibit that includes, as the *New York Daily News* reported on September 24, a replica of the August 9 Sbarro pizzeria bombing in Jerusalem "complete with fake body parts and pizza slices strewn all over," accompanied by a tape recording that announces: "O Believer! There is a Jew hiding behind me. Come and kill him."

Does the persistent effort to deny a Jewish religious and historical link to any part of the land, including Jerusalem, reflect a deeply embedded Palestinian view that the Jews are nothing more than interlopers, no different than medieval Crusaders or other "foreign occupiers" over the centuries, who must be expelled in one way or another?

What about the world's reaction to events unfolding in the region over the course of the year? Could we find much solace in seeing how many countries—with the United States standing out once again as a laudable exception, joined, on occasion, by a handful of other principled nations—blithely ignored the facts on the ground and, for the sake of expediency, accepted the Palestinian interpretation of events?

And what conclusions could we draw from the way the United Nations and other international organizations treated Israel entirely differently than any other of the 189 member states?

A few examples:

- The UN Commission on Human Rights, for the third year in a row, adopted a resolution on the defamation of religion, which, in its "list" of the world's religions that are unfairly portrayed, mentions only Islam by name. Needless to say, there is not a peep about the defamation of Judaism in the Arab and Islamic press, much less the destruction of Jewish holy sites in Palestinian hands, including Joseph's Tomb, over the past year.
- While Israel has no chance even to serve on the fifty-three-nation Commission on Human Rights, Libya was elected a vice-chairman of this year's session.

- Syria is about to be elected to a two-year term on the powerful UN Security Council, a body Israel has never served on since joining the UN in 1949.
- Among the UN's many special rapporteurs examining specific country situations, only the rapporteur for Israel and the Occupied Territories has no time limit, whereas all the others must have their mandate renewed periodically.
- The signatories to the Fourth Geneva Convention are preparing to convene for the second time in order to discuss Israel. These countries have never, not once, met to consider any other country situation since the convention was first adopted in 1949.
- The International Red Cross movement continues to violate its own core principles of universality, neutrality, and impartiality by excluding the Magen David Adom, Israel's humanitarian society, from full participation in the global movement.

To be sure, as painful as all of these developments are, in the end they are only irritants. The UN body with teeth is the Security Council, where the United States, as one of five permanent members, has veto power. There the Palestinians and their supporters have been consistently unable to muster the support required to achieve their overriding goal—the internationalization of the conflict.

In the fall of 2000, we also witnessed an unprecedented spate of anti-Semitic attacks around the world in democratic countries, especially in France. Jews once again experienced a profound sense of vulnerability, and Jewish institutions required increased protection. Yet, despite the number and viciousness of many of the scores of documented attacks in France, not a single person today, I am told, sits in a French prison for any of the crimes committed.

By the spring of 2001, our attention was increasingly drawn to the World Conference Against Racism, to begin at the end of August in Durban. While the final outcome of the official governmental conference was not as bad as originally feared, it provides small comfort. The months of negotiation preceding the gathering were troubling in the extreme, and those Jewish delegates who attended the conference will not soon forget the harrowing experience.

How galling it was that a forum aimed at combating hatred was turned into a vehicle for its promotion. How tragic it was for those countries and NGOs that truly sought a discussion on the ills of racism and the best ways to grapple with it to see this international gathering hijacked by Arab nations and their supporters. How outrageous it was that everything was put on the table by the anti-Israel crowd—the Holocaust, anti-Semitism, Zionism, you name it; nothing was off-limits. How disturbing it was that, despite an understanding long in advance that no country-specific situation would be discussed, Israel was once again the exception. How dismaying it was that many countries, and even more nongovernmental organizations, went along with this charade. And how shocking it was that Durban became the venue for an "orgy of anti-Semitism," as one participant described it, where Jewish delegates were harassed and threatened to the point that many required police protection, while the infamous *Protocols of the Elders of Zion* was being distributed together with publications equating Zionism with Nazism.

Within days of the Durban debacle, we were faced with the calamitous attack on America, about which I wrote in a letter dated September 15. Since then, the focus of attention has broadened from the human drama of the tragedies themselves, the thousands of lives lost, the heroic rescue efforts, and the nation's anguished mourning, to a closer look at the enemy, an examination of the military and geopolitical challenges faced by the United States in pursuing the investigation, the creation of an international coalition, and the coordination of a multifaceted response.

In considering the current situation, we need the intellectual wizardry of a chess grandmaster, who is able to visualize a board on which every move can trigger six, eight, ten countermoves, and who, at the very same time, must be thinking several moves ahead.

In fact, it's even more complex, since the board, in this case, is not two-dimensional, but multidimensional. Imagine one axis lined with dozens of countries, while other axes deal with the diplomatic, political, strategic, military, intelligence, religious, and other dimensions of this unfolding drama, and add to this geometric structure the element of time—i.e., what may obtain today in a given situation may or may not be different in a week, a month, a year.

No one can predict with any degree of certainty what will happen. To be sure, there are more and less well-educated guesses, but no one has a monopoly of wisdom when it comes to the period ahead.

That applies to our government as well. I say this as someone who strongly supports our government, but for whom such support can never be allowed to translate into blind faith.

Previous administrations, both Republican and Democratic, have on occasion made serious policy errors when navigating the shoals of the Middle East generally and responding to international terrorism in particular. If I cite a few examples, it is to remind us that in the conduct of international relations, the precision of science is tempered by the vagaries of human nature. This is especially true in a region of the world where the cultural divide with the West is especially pronounced.

It was, for example, President Jimmy Carter who, in December 1977, declared: "Because of the greatness of the shah, Iran is an island of stability in the Middle East." Less than thirteen months later, the shah left Iran never to return, paving the way for the Islamic fundamentalists to gain power, which resulted in incalculable damage to American interests in the region.

In the 1980s, we armed the mujahideen, the Afghans and their supporters from the Arab and Islamic worlds who came to fight a jihad against the Soviet occupiers of the land. They were more than a match for the better-armed Soviets, killed tens of thousands of Soviet troops, and eventually forced the Kremlin to withdraw its army in humiliating defeat.

But in a perfect illustration of the Law of Unintended Consequences, many of the mujahideen, including Osama bin Laden, flush with victory and confident that God was on their side, next turned their wrath—and their American training—on nations supporting the United States, and then on America itself.

Throughout the years, we chose to ignore—or so, at least, it seemed—the link between Saudi Arabia and the spread of Wahhabism, a fundamentalist form of Islam, in the Muslim world, which, in turn, fueled more religiously driven extremism.

And we misread Saddam Hussein in the months leading up to his occupation of Kuwait in August 1990, failing to grasp his aggressive designs on his tiny, oil-rich neighbor, indeed, perhaps even inadvertently encouraging him by the ill-chosen words of the American ambassador in Baghdad at the time. Subsequently, after an impressive military campaign, spearheaded by Washington, that ousted Iraqi troops from Kuwait, the coalition forces declared victory. There was one small detail, though: Saddam Hussein remained in power, his elite troops free to commit wanton massacres against Iraqi Shiites and Kurds, and his appetite for weapons of mass destruction undiminished, if temporarily disrupted by the UN inspection teams (which haven't been able to visit the country for nearly three years).

In the same vein, we have, at times, erred in our approach to international terrorism.

Yes, it's easy to second-guess, to look back on history with perfect clarity of vision, but in these particular instances the American Jewish Committee was right on the money. Just as we tried to sound the alarm about Saddam Hussein in 1990, as the earlier Bush administration was opposing congressional sanctions against Iraq and a group of senators was being charmed by the Iraqi leader, so, for many years, have we been urging a more consistent, persistent, and resilient policy to deal with the worldwide phenomenon of terrorism.

Without doubt, our nation had its share of successes in the war against terrorism—important investigations and courtroom verdicts, and any number of terrorist actions foiled through early detection.

Too often, though, our nation struggled with terrorism as if the struggle were a legal issue and not a war. Admirable though this approach may have been in adhering to the rule of law and high-minded principle, it meant we had at least one hand tied behind our back, hampering our effort to fight what is, in essence, a dirty, shadowy war with enemies who flout the law and scoff at principle.

Can anyone truly say that our nation's response to previous terrorist strikes against American targets was adequate?

President Reagan pulled U.S. troops out of Lebanon after 241 Americans were killed in a suicide bombing of the U.S. Marine headquarters in Beirut in 1983, sending a message that we didn't have the will to take on the murderers.

The missile strikes ordered by President Clinton against targets in Afghanistan and Sudan, in the wake of the 1998 bombings of the American embassies in Kenya and Tanzania that killed at least 220 people, were totally ineffective, and if there were other, below-the-radar actions, they obviously didn't produce the desired results.

I could go on.

The United States has experienced damage to its own intelligence capabilities, both domestic and international, particularly in the realm of human intelligence gathering. We created a number of budgetary, political, and legal hurdles that inevitably took their toll.

Remember the 1993 attack on the World Trade Center? Later, it was revealed that the FBI had piles of tapes of intercepted recordings, all in Arabic, which sat in storage rooms for weeks, perhaps months, because the bureau didn't have enough Arabic-language translators— and the funds necessary to hire them. Perhaps some of the information would have been relevant to the attack.

Further, in AJC's many conversations with law-enforcement officials, it has become abundantly clear that, because of political and diplomatic concerns, from time to time they have had to tread very lightly.

This was true overseas, where we had to be acutely sensitive to Egypt, for example, in the investigation of the 1999 crash, off Nantucket, of the EgyptAir flight that resulted in 217 fatalities (Egypt unconvincingly insists the crash was due to mechanical failure, while American technical experts believe the plane was brought down by a suicidal act of the copilot), or to Saudi Arabia, in a frustrating effort to identify the perpetrators of the 1995 and 1996 bombings of American military installations there that killed twenty-six people.

It has also been true here at home. While law-enforcement agencies long suspected the presence in the United States of groups sympathetic to radical Islamic movements, the impression we got was that these agencies were often held on a tight leash. The administration was skittish about pursuing at least some of the suspect groups for fear of being labeled anti-Arab or anti-Muslim, an accusation the groups were quick to level.

Regrettably, the Clinton administration went a step further by conferring legitimacy on several Arab-American and Muslim organizations operating in the United States that have defended radical Islamic ideologies. Despite warnings, the White House and State Department opened their doors to representatives of these groups.

The Bush administration has continued the practice. Last week, for example, the president met with a delegation of Arab and Muslim American leaders who represented some of the more notorious groups, including the American Muslim Council, the Muslim Public Affairs Council, and the Council on American-Islamic Relations (CAIR).

It was a spokesman for CAIR, for instance, who, just last month, defended a *fatwa* issued against Khalid Durán, the Muslim author of a book on Islam in the AJC-sponsored *Children of Abraham* series. Durán and his family have been in hiding ever since the Jordanian fundamentalist cleric announced the *fatwa*.

And it was the leader of the Muslim Public Affairs Council, present at the White House meeting, who declared on radio station KCRW on September 11:

> If we're going to look at suspects [for the four plane hijackings and the carnage that ensued], we should look to the groups that benefit the most from these kinds of incidents. And I think we should put the State of Israel on the suspects list, because I think this diverts attention from what is happening in the Palestinian territories....

Why this seemingly shortsighted, if not self-defeating, practice? There appear to be two principal reasons: First, the Arab and Muslim communities, whatever their actual numbers—there are widely varying estimates—are seen as a factor in American life, not least on Election Day. Second, genuinely moderate spokesmen for these communities have been marginalized, blocked by the more extreme voices that dominate communal life.

All this said, the United States has been light-years ahead of European countries in trying to cope with the global challenge posed by Islamic extremist terrorism.

While Washington was trying to isolate the regime of Saddam Hussein, one of the principal addresses of international terrorism, it could count on the unstinting support of London. But Paris was another matter.

While Washington was trying to isolate the mullahs in Tehran, arguably the biggest backers and bankrollers of international terrorism in the world since the 1979 overthrow of the shah and the 444-day captivity of fifty-two American hostages (1979-81), many of the European Union nations were falling all over each other to penetrate the Iranian market, especially its oil and gas sectors.

While Washington put Syria on the annual list of states sponsoring terrorism, the French government rolled out the red carpet for Syrian president Assad in July 2001, and he was also received in Germany, albeit with less fanfare, and Spain.

While moderate Arab states like Tunisia were practically begging Whitehall to curb the political activity and fund-raising of groups seeking to topple the Tunisian regime, the British turned a deaf ear to the requests, citing the values of an open society. (The United States, it must be said, has been similarly accused by some moderate Arab regimes, which fear that America has been naive and gullible in offering extremist exiles the protections of a democratic country.)

And even a brief look at the history of Middle East terrorism on European soil suggests that too many countries sought to appease or negotiate quietly with violent groups—and the countries that offered the terrorists sanctuary and support—rather than to confront them head-on.

But that was then and this is now. As Marlin Fitzwater, the spokesman in the first Bush White House, said in 1990 regarding a national security matter: "This strategy represents our policy for all time. Until it's changed."

September 11 marked a turning point. Whatever happened before—and, yes, it is very relevant to the discussion—a moment of truth has now arrived. War has been declared on the United States.

The Bush administration has handled the national response with remarkable skill and has enjoyed record public support. It resisted the understandable impulse to unleash the military immediately, recognizing instead that the best decisions are made not in the heat of the moment but with the benefit of careful deliberation. The added benefit is that such deliberation keeps the enemy off guard, uncertain where, when, or how the response will come, but under no doubt that there will be a certain reply.

(The public may not be the first to know about military action, either, because of the shadowy nature of any pursuit of Osama bin Laden and his associates.)

The tactic of deliberation has permitted the government to consider carefully the eventual scope of a war against terrorism. Clearly, that's not an easy issue, both because of the internal debate in the administration and because Washington seeks to build the widest possible international coalition.

On the one hand, the broader the coalition, the narrower the consensus among the members on possible targets, military or otherwise, is likely to be.

On the other hand, some members of the coalition believe the terrorist threats they face have been given short shrift over the years. For example, when an American Jewish Committee delegation met with Russian foreign minister Ivanov for a ninety-minute meeting on September 21, he emphasized that the Chechen threat was cut from the same cloth as Al Qaeda, Osama bin Laden's "holding company," as this terrorist network has been described. He suggested in no uncertain terms that Washington ought to rethink its hitherto sympathetic approach to the Chechens.

The careful planning has also allowed the Bush team to put in place a multipronged strategy, with both military and nonmilitary dimensions, that suggests a far-reaching assault, at least on the Al Qaeda network worldwide. Savvy diplomacy has won the endorsement and cooperation of NATO, the European Union, the UN Security Council, and key countries around the world, including those closest to Afghanistan. And the president and his advisers have gone to great lengths to ensure Arab and Muslim participation in order to avoid any hint of the civilizational conflict that Harvard professor Samuel Huntington foresaw in his important book, *The Clash of Civilizations*.

(Italian Prime Minister Berlusconi introduced the civilizational element last week by declaring that the West is superior to the Islamic world because freedom is not part of the "patrimony of Islamic civilization." Notwithstanding the withering criticism he received from many quarters, he reaffirmed the view the next day. No doubt the timing, if not the substance, of the Italian leader's comments was not appreciated by Washington.)

Looking ahead, there are several issues that particularly concern me as an American Jew.

First, will Israel somehow be linked in the public's mind with the events of September 11? It shouldn't be, unless the connection is to prompt greater sympathy and understanding for the wave of suicide terror attacks Israel has endured and Israel's need to respond forcefully.

After all, this was an attack on America, not because of any link to Israel, but rather because of who we are and what we stand for. As President Bush said in his eloquent address on September 20:

> Americans are asking, "Why do they hate us?" They hate what they see right here in this chamber, a democratically elected government. Their leaders are self-appointed. They hate our freedoms—our freedom of religion, our freedom of speech, our freedom to vote and assemble and disagree with each other. They want to overthrow existing governments in many Muslim countries, such as Egypt, Saudi Arabia, and Jordan. They want to drive Israel out of the Middle East. They want to drive Christians and Jews out of vast regions of Asia and Africa.

Former Israeli prime minister Benjamin Netanyahu made an important related point during his testimony before the Government Reform Committee of the U.S. House of Representatives on September 20:

> The soldiers of militant Islam do not hate the West because of Israel; they hate Israel because of the West—because they see it as an island of Western democratic values in a Muslim-Arab sea of despotism.

Even so, we need to be aware that Israel-bashers are trying to link Israel to the events of September 11 in two ways.

For one thing, rumors are being spread that the Mossad was behind the terrorist attack. Absurd as the idea may be, these rumors persist and have made it into the press from Greece to Pakistan. Among the accusers has been none other than the father of Mohammed al-Atta, one of the hijackers on the American Airlines Flight 11 that crashed into the north tower of the World Trade Center. Al-Atta, senior, met with a *New York Times* reporter after the attack and gave entirely new meaning to the definition of chutzpah:

> Someone like Israel's intelligence agency had the capacity to organize such an attack, the father said. But his son, an urban planner, did not. "I do not believe my son did it; I am sure he is alive," he said. "He was afraid of flying."

For another, some are suggesting that American support for Israel, or Israel's alleged unwillingness to negotiate with the Palestinians, is at the root of the problem. The argument is demonstrably false, but it is being peddled by those who wish to do Israel harm.

Second, what will be the impact on Israel and the U.S.-Israel relationship of the American effort to build a worldwide coalition against terror?

In the long run, it should further strengthen ties between two democratic states that have the shared experience of facing suicide bombers bent on mass destruction. (Bear in mind, for example, that the June bombing of the Tel Aviv discotheque resulted in twenty-one fatalities. Given that the United States is close to fifty times more populous than Israel, that would translate into over 1,000 deaths in American terms. Indeed, since the signing of the 1993 Oslo Accords, more than 400 Israelis have been killed in terror attacks, the equivalent, in American population figures, of approximately 20,000.)

Moreover, the success of the American-led coalition becomes Israel's success as well. Any weakening of the Islamic terror network also benefits Israel, as does any dent in state sponsorship of the terrorists.

In the short run, though, it is less clear where Israel will stand. Washington is putting intense pressure on both Israelis and Palestinians to resume talks, any talks, and get the conflict out of sight of the cameras of Al-Jazeera, the Qatar-based television station that broadcasts throughout the Arab world. But the Palestinians aren't necessarily cooperating, and Israel must continue to defend itself against waves of violence that may be calculated to put additional pressure on Jerusalem at this delicate moment.

Third, what will be the price demanded by Arab and Islamic countries for their entry into the U.S.-led coalition? And what will be the price demanded by the United States for the admission of Arab and Islamic countries into the coalition?

These questions have particular relevance for such countries as Syria. Here's a nation that, by any reasonable standard, ought to be a target of a war on terrorism, but could end up, as it did during the Gulf War, on the American side. And what about Hamas and Hezbollah, both of which were noticeably absent from the terrorist list issued by the White House last month (though they were part of President Clinton's executive order on terrorist groups signed in 1995)? How, if at all, will this be addressed by the coalition? It's not yet clear.

Fourth, what exactly constitutes the scope of the war on terrorism? If it doesn't target state sponsors, then what long-term impact will the current effort have? After all, terrorist groups will continue to organize and operate as long as they have the protection of sovereign states that harbor, finance, and, in some cases, train and equip them.

Fifth, recalling the Gulf War experience, is it conceivable that Saddam Hussein or, say, Hezbollah might try to attack Israel as a diversionary measure to divide the coalition? If so, how would Prime Minister Sharon react? How would Washington handle the situation?

And sixth, here at home, is it just possible that the Arab and Muslim communities will emerge from the current crisis with enhanced political strength? Counterintuitive as it may seem, it could happen, and the Jewish community will have to assess the long-term impact of such a possibility.

The wave of sympathy for those Arab- and Muslim-Americans (not to mention Sikhs) who have reportedly been harassed after the events of September 11 speaks volumes about the great reservoirs of kindness and compassion that characterize America's pluralistic society. In this spirit, American Jews, including prominently the American Jewish Committee, have always stood foursquare against any form of bigotry and defamation and in favor of extending the hand of friendship to America's increasingly diverse racial, religious, and ethnic communities.

But every once in a while there's more going on than meets the eye.

Take, for example, a feel-good *New York Times* article (September 21) entitled "Abhorring Terror at an Ohio Mosque." It recounted the story of Imam Fawaz Damra, the spiritual leader of the Islamic Center of Cleveland, who "prayed" for a man who, in a fit of anger after September 11, rammed his car into the center. Sounds inspiring: the cleric is represented as a man of peace and forgiveness. But had the *Times* dug deeper, it would have discovered something else, as the *Tampa Tribune* did a year ago (October 9, 2000).

The Florida newspaper published an article describing an Immigration and Naturalization Service tape showing Sami Al-Arian, head of the active arm of the Islamic Jihad, with the same Imam Damra at a rally. "[Al-Arian] walked behind Damra as the introduction began … no visible reaction is displayed when Damra mentions a direct relationship between his organization and the Islamic Jihad," the newspaper reported.

Damra's new public posture of solidarity with terror victims prompted AJC's Cleveland office to reintroduce that city's news media to the imam's record of support for terrorism—a record that included, as the *Plain Dealer* reported on September 27, his calling for "directing all the rifles at the first and last enemy of the Islamic nation and that is the sons of monkeys and pigs, the Jews."

Or consider a speech given by a Chicago rabbi in the wake of reports of hate crimes. Apart from making an unfortunate comparison to Kristallnacht, the rabbi spoke about his willingness to help form a human chain around the Bridgeview (Illinois) Mosque to protect it from anyone who might seek to damage it. This speaks volumes about his admirable sensitivity. Unfortunately, he may not have known what the FBI, the *New York Times*, the American Jewish Committee, and others long knew—the Bridgeview Mosque, as reported by Judith Miller in the *Times* on September 21, is a center for Hamas activity in the United States.

As they say, "The road to hell is paved with good intentions."

I suspect that by now some readers of this letter may be suffering from an acute case of depression. After all, this has been a very difficult period in our lives. But I want to end on an upbeat note—not because of any sense of guilt, much less manufactured optimism, and not because I underestimate the difficulties ahead, but rather because I believe it may actually be warranted.

When told that a man who had been unhappy in his marriage remarried shortly after his wife died, Samuel Johnson, the eighteenth-century English writer, remarked famously that "it was the triumph of hope over experience."

In my case, it is the triumph of hope *because* of experience.

Despite a wrenching year militarily, economically, and, not least, psychologically, Israel remains strong, unbent, and determined to defend itself, as it has since its founding in 1948, and, at the very same time, unwilling to abandon the hope for an eventual peace accord.

Despite all the challenges connected to the Middle East, anti-Semitism, and Durban, the Jewish people throughout the world—from France to South Africa, from the United States to Russia—continue to stand tall, proud, and committed.

And despite an unprecedented attack on America, this nation's beacon of freedom shines as brightly as ever, and the resolve to hunt down and destroy our enemy should leave no one in doubt.

## Letter from an Ex-HIAS Employee
## November 15, 2001

In 1973, I was moonlighting in New York as a teacher of English as a foreign language. Increasing numbers of Soviet Jews began showing up in our school. I was immediately drawn to them for reasons of family, language, culture, and solidarity. During coffee breaks, they would speak to me of their migration to the United States, via Vienna and Rome, and laud the assistance rendered by the Hebrew Immigrant Aid Society (HIAS) en route.

The next year, I had the unusual opportunity to live and teach in the Soviet Union on a government-to-government exchange program. Until being expelled by Soviet officials for political activities, I was deeply involved in the lives of many Soviet Jews, especially refusenik families.

Shaken by the sudden departure but determined to continue my involvement in the historic awakening of Soviet Jews, I remembered what my students in New York had told me and took a train to Rome. Without an appointment or even the name of anyone, I simply showed up at the HIAS office on Viale Regina Margherita and said I was a Russian-speaking American Jew who had been profoundly moved by my three-month experience in the USSR and was hoping to work with Soviet Jewish migrants. Shortly thereafter, I was hired by Irving Haber of the Geneva office and spent two and a half years working with HIAS, first in Rome, then in Vienna.

They were difficult years, but they were also exhilarating and inspiring. All of us in the HIAS frontline offices felt we were involved in an historic mission, an aboveground railroad to move Jews who had previously been thought lost to world Jewry to new homes and new lives in freedom and safety. The workload was enormous, the security concerns were ever-present, and the daily challenges of dealing with an extraordinarily diverse and complex refugee population were sometimes overwhelming.

I kept a diary. Here's one excerpt from my time in Vienna:

August 29, 1978. There were dozens of Soviet Jews filling the corridor and only three of us at HIAS to deal with them. Each of the refugees wanted priority in the handling of his or her case; each person insisted there was a sick parent or child involved. Every time one of the three of us would go out into the corridor we would be surrounded by the refugees. *"Molodoy paren, budtye lubyezny, pomogite nam"* ("Young man, be so kind and help us.") *"U menya k vam malenkaya prosba"* ("I have a small favor to ask you.") *"Kak ya mogu popast v San Francisco?"* ("How can I make my way to San Francisco?") And so on. It never ended, yet at the same time here were people in literally the first or second day of their new lives in the West, entirely unprepared, totally disoriented, still dazed from the departure experience, subject to endless rumors circulating among the new arrivals, and hell-bent on protecting their families.

I wanted to experience at least part of the journey with the refugees, so I took an eighteen-hour train ride from Vienna's Sudbahnhof with a group of eighty-three Soviet Jews one December day. The destination was Rome, the next transit point on their journey to new lives, or, more accurately, Orte, a stop before Rome that presented fewer security challenges for the Italian police than the bustling Rome station. I remember the refugees' wide-eyed curiosity about everything, mixed with understandable fatigue and anxiety. The attachment to luggage was especially striking. People didn't let their belongings out of their sight. Other than family, it was all they had; it represented the remnant of the life just ended and the meager start of the life just begun.

And I recall the meticulous planning of the entire process. HIAS was there every step of the way. Believe me, it wasn't easy. There was the coordination with the Austrian and Italian governments, the security dimension, the transportation arrangements, the special medical and other needs of the refugee population, and the temporary housing on arrival. What a massive organizational undertaking, and all done in a precomputer era!

Moreover, there was a very particular psychological dimension to the work. All the migrants had been raised in a communist society and few had ever before visited the West. Only a handful had any real sense of Jewish identity or knowledge, though almost everyone had endured discrimination in one form or another because they were Jews. And all had experienced hardship in applying to emigrate, going through the labyrinthine bureaucratic maze and facing countless humiliations along the way.

This meant that many of the refugees were initially apprehensive, even suspicious of a voluntary Jewish organization. Sure, they were grateful to have a ready guide and a safety net, but the nature of a voluntary Jewish agency was so alien that it took a while to register. After all, to survive in the Soviet Union, citizens had to navigate the idiosyncrasies of a hostile system far beyond the comprehension of residents of Western countries. To do so meant developing a certain instinct, cover story, and protective shell.

Grappling with this unfamiliar psychology was a permanent challenge for the HIAS staff. At times, it tested our patience, but on reflection it was unavoidable. Two contrasting cultures—Western and Soviet—came into close contact with one another, and the natural bridge, our common Jewish identity, was tenuous at best, since few Soviet Jews had ever been given the chance to explore the meaning of that identity, at least in a positive sense.

For me, that made our efforts all the more important. The sooner we got people out of the USSR and resettled in Western countries, the greater the chances for rebuilding their Jewish connection, especially in the case of the children.

I must acknowledge the HIAS role in laying the foundation for building that connection. For example, when I saw how little Soviet Jews knew of their heritage, I proposed to conduct evening seminars in Ostia, the seaside town where the bulk of the refugees lived. HIAS supported the effort. And when I wanted to go a step further and write a bilingual book on Judaism, Jewish history, and Israel specially designed for Soviet Jews, HIAS once again came through.

Daily inspiration for our challenging work, of course, came from the refugees themselves, some of whom had extraordinarily powerful stories to tell. So, too, from my HIAS colleagues in Rome and Vienna. They worked hard, unimaginably hard, and endured unrelenting pressure from a steady stream of people in need. They performed magnificently, with grace, efficiency, humor, and respect for the refugees. They were unsung heroes—people like Evi Eller, Suzy Hazan, Cathy Bottone, Ida Pompucci, Marita Dresner, Walter Hitchman, Marilla Haggiag, Sylvia Zimmaro, Gert Miller, Hedva Hassan, Dahlia Boukhobza, and Vera Morse—who made a substantial difference in the lives of fellow Jews.

They processed, counseled, and guided thousands upon thousands of refugees through the first critical steps of a new life in the West and facilitated their onward migration to permanent new homes. *Yad b'yad*, hand in hand, we worked; *regel b'regel*, together we walked.

This encounter with HIAS also left two other enduring imprints on me. First, it persuaded me to pursue a career in Jewish communal work. Frankly, when I first arrived in Rome, I thought I might do the work for a couple of years and then, with that out of my system, go on and pursue a career in the State Department or the UN. Instead, the HIAS experience convinced me that there could be no higher calling than a lifetime spent in the Jewish community. And since joining the American Jewish Committee in 1979, I've learned what should have been obvious all along: There certainly is no shortage of compelling and vitally important diplomatic and political challenges facing the Jewish people.

Second, it led to my marriage. Yes, that's right, to my marriage. Thanks to Hedva Hassan, my wonderful and utterly charming colleague in the HIAS office in Rome, I met my future wife, Giulietta, Hedva's cousin, in 1975. I'll save the reader the details, but trust me, it wouldn't have happened without HIAS.

Since leaving HIAS over twenty years ago, I've never had a proper chance to express my appreciation to the organization for those memorable years in Rome and Vienna, for launching me on my professional career, and for being the *shadkhan*, the matchmaker, that made possible my marriage and family life. Allow me to voice that gratitude now.

*Mazel tov*, HIAS, on the celebration of your 120<sup>th</sup> anniversary as a lifeline for Jews in need everywhere.

# 2. SPEECHES

## Tribute to
## Greek Foreign Minister George Papandreou
## AJC 94th Annual Meeting
## Washington, D.C.
## May 3, 2000

There are many people here this afternoon for whom this is a very special event. I am one of them, having worked in the vineyards of Greek-Jewish relations for some two decades, beginning at a time when, as the foreign minister said, relations between Greece and Israel were not all that they could have been. Therefore, it has been especially gratifying to see the remarkable revolution that has taken place in Greek-Israeli relations, as described so eloquently today by Foreign Minister Papandreou.

Throughout these years, there was always a common denominator of shared values between Greeks and Jews that we never lost sight of. And there were many who helped to build what is today a warm and close link, not only between Greece and the State of Israel, but between Greece and the Jewish people worldwide, including centrally this organization.

One of those who worked so hard toward our shared goal is our esteemed friend, a leader of the Greek community of the United States and of all Hellenes abroad—Andy Athens.

Although Foreign Minister Papandreou acknowledged her, I think it is only appropriate that we in the Jewish community also recognize the pathbreaking work that was done by Fotini Konstantopoulou in creating the magnificent archive of documents on the history of Greek Jewry, which are today available in book form in English and which have also been provided to the Holocaust Memorial Museum.

The Greek ambassador to the United States is not simply the envoy of his country; he also embodies the country to all of us who don't have the pleasure of spending as much time as we might wish in Greece. Ambassador Alexandre Philon has been an able representative of Greece to the United States and a valued friend of the Jewish community and the American Jewish Committee. We are delighted that you are here, Ambassador.

Sometimes there are "sung" heroes in life; more often there are unsung heroes. One unsung hero of the remarkable change in the Greek-Israeli and Greek-Jewish relationship is a senior official in the Ministry of Defense in Athens. He has been a close colleague for many years, and I'm delighted he is with us today—Andreas Mitzis.

The Greek Jewish community is well represented here—its leaders are with us for our entire meeting, as they have been for previous annual meetings. They are our dear friends. I would like them to please stand up and be recognized.

Greek Jews are the heirs and trustees of a remarkably long and rich history that goes back in two directions: one to the Roman Empire and the other to the Spanish Inquisition. Both paths brought them to Greece at different periods of history and led to the establishment of vibrant communities in such places as Salonika, Ioania, Athens, Larissa, Rhodes, and Crete.

But then the war came, and so much of Jewish life was destroyed. Eighty-six percent of the Jewish community was murdered. So was an entire civilization.

But those with us today were determined to rebuild in their native land, the land they loved. And they have done so. We applaud them for their valiant efforts to reinvigorate the community and to generate optimism about the future.

Still, they are a deeply scarred and traumatized community. There is not a single Jewish family in Greece today that was not directly affected by the Shoah. And so, for them the notion of "friends" is not something they take lightly. They cherish their friends, as we do at the American Jewish Committee. They remember their friends, as we do. And Minister Papandreou, there is simply no better friend of the Greek Jewish community, of Israel, and of the United States than you.

The American Jewish Committee, in recognition of this historic occasion, would like to present you with a special gift. We do so for being a man of peace and vision, for being an architect of the relationship between Greece and the State of Israel, for being a stalwart friend of the Jewish community of Greece, and for being a champion of that revolutionary concept called democracy—born perhaps when another Papandreou was around, but long before even your distinguished grandfather. It is, of course, a Greek word and the ultimate Greek contribution to civilization.

For being a champion of all that it represents, including the liberation of the human spirit and unswerving respect for human dignity, it is a distinct honor, as well as a personal pleasure, to present you with this token of our profound esteem and appreciation.

The plaque contains a quoation from the seventeenth-century philosopher Baruch Spinoza that reads: "The true aim of government is liberty." The words beneath are: "Presented with appreciation and respect to His Excellency George Papandreou, Foreign Minister of Greece, for his steadfast support of the Greek Jewish community and his relentless pursuit of democratic values and ideals. The American Jewish Committee, May 3, 2000."


We Remember
AJC 94th Annual Dinner
Washington, D.C.
May 4, 2000


Secretary of State Albright, (Swedish) Prime Minister Persson, (German) President Rau, (Israeli) Ambassador Ivry, your excellencies, members and friends of the American Jewish Committee:

This Tuesday we marked Holocaust Remembrance Day. To commemorate the date, we placed a statement I wrote in the *New York Times*. Let me read it to you.

In the Jewish tradition, we are commanded to remember (*zakhor*) and not to forget (*lo tishkach*). Today is Yom HaShoah, the Day of Holocaust Remembrance. On this solemn occasion, 55 years after the end of World War II:

We remember the six million Jewish martyrs, including 1.5 million children, who were exterminated in the Holocaust.

We remember not only their tragic deaths, but also their vibrant lives—as shopkeepers and craftsmen, scientists and authors, teachers and students, parents and children, husbands and wives.

We remember the richly hued Jewish civilizations that were destroyed—from Salonika, Greece, to Vilnius, Lithuania.

We remember the slippery slope that began with the rantings of an obscure Austrian-born anti-Semite named Adolf Hitler and led, in the course of less than 15 years, to his absolute control over Germany.

We remember the fertile soil of European anti-Semitism—cultivated over centuries by cultural, political, and religious voices—that created an all-too-receptive climate for the Nazi objective of eliminating the Jewish people.

We remember Denmark, as well as Albania, Bulgaria, and Finland, for their extraordinary efforts to protect their own Jewish communities.

We remember the courage of thousands of Righteous Persons who risked their own lives that others might live.

We remember the millions of non-Jews—Poles and Russians, Roma and the disabled, political opponents and homosexuals—murdered under the relentless Nazi onslaught.

We remember the valiant soldiers of the Allied nations who, at such great human cost, vanquished the Third Reich.

We remember the survivors of the death camps, who endured such unimaginable suffering and who have inspired us all with their indomitable courage, spirit, and will to live.

We remember the absence of an Israel in those wartime years, an Israel which, had it existed, would have provided a haven when so shamefully few countries were willing to accept Jewish refugees.

We shall never forget those who perished.

We shall never forget those who saved even a single life. As it is written in the Talmud: "He who saves one life has saved the world."

We shall never forget the importance of speaking out against intolerance, whenever and wherever it occurs.

We shall never forget the inextricable link among democracy, the rule of law, and protection of human rights.

We shall never forget the age-old prophetic vision of a world of justice, harmony, and peace.

And we shall never forget that each of us, in ways large and small, can help bring us closer to the realization of that prophetic vision.

Ladies and gentlemen, I often ask myself whether humankind has really learned anything lasting from the darkness that descended on the world in 1933 and resulted in such unparalleled suffering, whether the words "never again" have any real hold on our collective conscience or are more often than not invoked ritualistically or mechanically on appropriate occasions.

In truth, many who aspire to the greatness of which humankind is capable have learned—or at least should have learned—important lessons, though the daily headlines remind us that ending the scourges of dehumanization and demonization based on race, religion, or ethnicity, and the murderous rampages and genocide that can too easily follow, is a permanent uphill battle.

We have learned—or at least should have learned—the importance of institutionalizing and commemorating memory, of educating our youth about the tragedy of the Holocaust and its contemporary meaning. We are especially grateful to our distinguished guest this evening, the prime minister of Sweden, for taking a lead in the field of Holocaust education and remembrance—for without memory, what are we?

We have learned—or at least should have learned—the need to confront the past squarely and openly, and not to seek shelter in the company of myths, denials, or half-truths. Germany's president, Johannes Rau, has confronted the past unblinkingly, and his nation today stands taller as a result.

We have learned—or at least should have learned—the meaning of the sovereign State of Israel to the Jewish people both as the realization of our national yearning and as a refuge for the dispossessed.

We have learned—or at least should have learned—the importance of supporting regional and global institutions to extend and protect human rights and human dignity. One such institution, the Council of

Europe, has recently adopted a powerful statement on anti-Semitism. I am pleased that the admired secretary-general of the council, Walter Schwimmer, could be here with us this evening.

We have learned—or at least should have learned—the importance of building a vibrant nongovernmental sector that serves as a prod to sometimes reluctant governments when it comes to human rights violations and threats to human dignity.

We have learned—or at least should have learned—the importance of extending the principles of the Nuremberg trials that crimes against humanity ought to be punished by the international community.

We have learned—or at least should have learned—the importance of collective international action to stop genocide when diplomacy alone fails, and here I wish to pay particular tribute to Secretary of State Albright for acting as a national and international conscience in response to ethnic cleansing and genocide.

And we have learned—or at least should have learned—that the individual does matter. Could there possibly be better examples of our potential capacity to make a difference than those who, in times of nightmarish adversity, put at risk their careers, their lives, even their families' lives, to help victims of tyranny and injustice?

It is such truly rare and remarkable people whom we honor this evening: diplomats featured in an inspiring exhibit entitled "Visas for Life" that the American Jewish Committee is hosting at the Capital Hilton Hotel and that was conceived by Eric Saul, who is with us tonight. These diplomats went well beyond the call of duty—in some notable cases defying official orders—and, as a result, rescued tens, indeed hundreds, thousands of Jews.

We shall always remember the lifesaving efforts of Carl Lutz, Switzerland's consul in Budapest; Dr. Feng Shan Ho, the consul general of China in Vienna; Hiram Bingham, American vice consul in Marseilles; Paul Komor, Hungary's honorary consul in Shanghai; George Mandel-Mantello, El Salvador's honorary first secretary in Geneva; Dr. Aristides de Sousa Mendes, Portugal's consul general in Bordeaux; Don Angel Sanz-Briz, the Spanish ambassador in Budapest; Chiune Sugihara, the Japanese consul in Kovno, Lithuania; and Selahattin Ülkümen, the only surviving diplomat in this group, who was the Turkish consul general on the island of Rhodes.

These diplomats are represented here this evening by members of their families, many of whom traveled long distances, and I would like to ask them to stand and be recognized.

During the holiest period of the Jewish calendar that begins with Rosh Hashanah, the Jewish New Year, we read the following passage in our prayer book:

> And yet even in the inferno, even there
> were those we call the *Hasidei Umot Ha'olam*,
> the righteous of the nations.
> Some gave their lives to keep Jews from harm.
> Who can measure such courage?
> When so many were afraid to act,
> They bore witness to the greatness
> Men and women can reach.
> Look and take heart.
> If ever such days return,
> Remember them and find courage.
> Consider what can be done, what must be done
> Not to banish from our souls the image of God.

May the courage and compassion, the humanity and humility, of these righteous diplomats forever be a blessing and an inspiration to us all. And may we be worthy of the examples they set.

### Eulogy for Jan Karski
### Washington, D.C.
### July 18, 2000

Only a few, so few listened to their cries of pain, their pleas for help when darkness descended over the earth.

Said one Polish Jew:

> A coat of snow shines and twinkles in the light of the matchless, golden Polish fall. That snow is nothing other than the down feathers of Jewish bedding left along with all our goods—chests, trunks, suitcases

full of clothing, pots, pans, plates—by the 300,000 Jews deported eastward. Abandoned goods covered by that "snow" of the period of the German mass murder of Jews.

The ghastly silence is cut by revolver shots, the rattle of machine guns, the clamor of doors broken in and the shattering of furniture, the hoarse cries *"Alle juden raus"* ("All Jews out"), the macabre march of Jewish victims sentenced to death, under the watch of SS officers. Complete emptiness. This is the picture of the Warsaw ghetto in September 1942.

Said another Polish Jew:

I have no words with which to picture the life of the ghetto during those days. All of us looked upon ourselves as living corpses, as ghosts who no longer belonged to this world. Our every thought and every word was about death. Death seemed to be the only way to escape from the indescribable hell in which we lived.

But even amid the vast industrialized killing fields, there were a few, so few, rays of sunshine. One of them, perhaps the brightest ray of sunshine of all, was the man we pay final tribute to today, Jan Karski.

It is asked: If a tree falls in the forest and no one hears it, does it make a sound? Similarly, one can ask: If humanity cries out in anguish and no one listens, does the pain go unfelt?

Jan Karski listened. Yes, he listened. Jan Karski—son of Poland, son of the Catholic Church, and son of the human family—devoted his life, indeed risked his life again and again, so that these cries of woe of Polish Jews during the World War II would not go unheard. This courier of courage of the Polish underground took to the world community—to presidents and prime ministers, to foreign ministers and supreme court justices, to famous writers and Jewish leaders—his eyewitness accounts of the systematic extermination of the Jews by the Nazis. Many found his stories of gruesome atrocities in the ghettos and camps hard, even impossible, to believe, but Jan Karski told them and retold them to anyone who would listen.

Here is a part of the story he told:

A Jewish leader said he wanted to organize a visit to the Warsaw Ghetto for me so I could offer testimony about what I saw. And I saw terrible things. I saw naked old men lying dead on the street. I saw a woman walking with her baby at her breast which was no breast—it was just a piece of skin. Some Hitler Youth entered the ghetto, and everyone ran. A shot shattered the window in the apartment where I was. A woman who was there put her hand on my arm and said: "You came here to see what is happening to us. Now go, go."

The Jewish leaders also organized a more dangerous expedition for me to what I now think was a transit camp. A civilian told me to follow him and not to say anything. We entered a gate, and the guard obviously knew him. The Germans were shooting into the air and pushing people onto a train. There was shouting, chaos, confusion. The cattle cars were filling up with Jews. A soldier tore a child from a mother's arms and threw the child, just like a sack, over the heads of the people into the wagon. It was horrible. I'd never seen anything like this. I must have had a sudden nervous breakdown, and I don't know what I did then. I only know that my guide was shouting "Follow me!" and he was angry. He got me out.<sup>*</sup>

Jan Karski modestly referred to himself as a "human tape recorder," replaying the messages he was asked to deliver. In actuality, he was a trumpet: a man who heralded the harsh tones of human indifference and cruelty so loudly that no one could deny hearing them, while at the same time personifying the softest melodies that make up the indomitable spirit and inherent goodness that mankind can still possess.

Many years after the war's end, Karski was asked if his mission to inform the world and seek help for the beleaguered Jews had had any results. He replied: "As to the Jewish part of my mission, it was an obvious failure. Six million Jews died and no one offered them effective help. Not any nation, not any government, not any church. The help they did receive, heroic help, was provided only by individuals."

Jan Karski was most certainly one such individual. As Martin Peretz wrote in the *New Republic* in 1993, while in Poland for the fiftieth

* *Newsweek*, March 8, 1999.

anniversary of the Warsaw ghetto uprising: "When Polish president Lech Walesa spoke and mentioned that Karski was in our midst, the crowd's sudden hush indicated that the people knew they were in the presence of one of those obsessives whose obsessions make him both brave and good."

It is precisely for these obsessions—this remarkable courage; this lifelong commitment to combating evil—first Nazism, later communism; this friendship to the Jewish people that was so manifest in our darkest days and continued to his last breath in the relentless determination to fight anti-Semitism, to promote understanding between his fellow Poles and Jews, and to stand with Israel, of which he became an honorary citizen in 1994, a day he described as the most meaningful of his life; and to bear witness again and again and again—that we shall always remember Jan Karski. Still more, we shall teach our children and our children's children about this moral giant, about this most righteous of the Righteous Among the Nations.

There was a famous nineteenth-century Polish poet, Juliusz Slowacki, who wrote *Mój Testament*. Let me read just one couplet from this beautiful poem:

*Zylem z Wami, cierpialem, I plakalem z Wami,*
*Nigdy kto szlachetny, nie byl mi obojetny.*

I lived with you, I cried with you, and I suffered with you,
I was never indifferent to any human being.

These words could have been written for Jan Karski. Indeed, these words could have been written by Jan Karski.

May Jan Karski find eternal peace in his final resting place.

May we cherish his memory as near to our hearts as he cradled the souls of the millions of Jews he never knew but tried to rescue.

And may we, those fortunate enough to have known him, always be inspired by the example of his life to be rays of sunshine, no matter how few or many we may be, to hear and heed the cries of anguish from our fellow human beings, and to have the physical and moral courage to act on our beliefs.

In Guy de Maupassant's famous novel *Une Vie*, the very last line of the book, spoken by Rosalie the maid to Madame Jeanne, her boss, is as follows: "*La vie, voyez-vouz, ça n'est jamais si bon ni si mauvais qu'on croit.*" "Life, you see, is never as good or as bad as one thinks."

I don't know what Jan Karski would have said about that formulation, but I do know that some lives, just a precious few, are lived better than any of us could ever believe or imagine. His was one such life, and we are its lucky beneficiaries.


## The United Nations, the Middle East, and American Jewry
### American Jewish Committee/UN Watch
### Human Relations Award Dinner
### New York
### October 18, 2000


When I was eleven years old, my family moved from New York to live in Europe. There I discovered what soon became my favorite newspaper in the world, the *International Herald Tribune*. To me it was the *New York Times* in miniature but with cartoons and the humor columns of Art Buchwald.

Now I am back in Europe enjoying a sabbatical year, and the first thing I did on moving was to get a subscription to the *International Herald Tribune*. And what the *New York Times* doesn't have today is Dave Barry, who has in a way succeeded and perhaps even surpassed Art Buchwald.

Some of you in this room are very partisan, I know, in one direction or another. Indeed, it's a good time in the electoral season to be partisan, but, as I'm on the job, I'm officially nonpartisan. So permit me to share with you just a couple of paragraphs from a recent Dave Barry column on the current presidential race:

"I hope you don't get the impression that the whole campaign has been about trivial matters. In fact, Al and George have spent weeks arguing about a crucial issue that will determine the fate of the entire world for centuries to come, the format of the presidential debates. The Gore camp struck first, boldly proposing a series of 140 seven-hour debates, each one including a segment where the candidates will have to identify tree species by looking at bark samples. The Bush campaign countered with a proposal for one twenty-minute debate with each candidate being allowed to phone a friend and ask the audience, and the question categories being Famous Movie Dogs and Name that Golf Club. The two sides are hammering out a compromise format which I am sure will attract a nationwide television audience consisting of whoever is operating the camera.

"Al and George, though, are not your only choices. I am still running," says Dave Barry, "and here is my platform. *Taxes*. I favor a tax cut for the middle class, defined as anyone who owns at least five remote controls. This cut will be offset by a 100-percent tax on all money won by contestants on 'reality based' television shows. *Social Security*. I say we scrap the current system and replace it with a system wherein you add your name to the bottom of a list, and then you send some money to the person at the top of the list, and then you.... Oh, wait, that is our current system. *Cell phone conversations in restaurants*. I favor on-the-spot confiscation of the phone, as well as the hand holding it." And finally, the fourth pillar of Dave Barry's presidential platform, *drugs for seniors*. Says the humor columnist, "Go ahead, seniors. But don't be playing your stereo at all hours."

There's my contribution to this election season, thanks to Dave Barry.

On a more serious note, let me pick up on some of the themes that were mentioned by Ambassador Holbrooke in his characteristically eloquent remarks earlier this evening.

The United Nations, as we know, was established at an historic conference in San Francisco in 1945. It was a world body that offered great promise. No one was more committed to its development, I believe, than the Jewish community. Indeed, the American Jewish Committee played a singular role in helping to ensure the inclusion of human rights protections in the United Nations Charter.

The United Nations was established by the Allies as a response to the catastrophe that had befallen the world in the years just prior. Surely, we Jews had a stake in its success. And since that time the UN has had many successes. Take the field of peacekeeping, something we sometimes overlook. There are today at least fourteen major UN peacekeeping operations around the world, including on the Golan Heights as well as in Croatia, Kosovo, Lebanon, Cyprus, Sierra Leone, Congo, and West Timor, though the UN record is far from perfect, as the massive tragedies in Bosnia and Rwanda tellingly remind us.

The work of the UN specialized agencies goes on, sometimes unheralded, but always important—the United Nations High Commissioner for Refugees, the World Health Organization, the Food and Agriculture Organization, the World Intellectual Property Organization, the World Trade Organization, the World Bank, the International Monetary Fund, the World Meteorological Organization, to name but a few.

Indeed, the United Nations has a vast and compelling agenda. It may not be a panacea for all the world's problems, but its role nonetheless is indispensable. Consider that as we sit here this evening in New York, 1.2 billion people on our planet are subsisting on less than one dollar per day. Consider that 1 billion people have no regular access to potable water. Consider that 100 million children permanently live on the streets. Consider that there are 39 million externally or internally displaced persons as a result of conflict. Consider that there are 133 million women in the world who suffer from female genital mutilation and their numbers increase at the rate of about 2 million a year. Consider that local and regional conflicts in different parts of the world continue to flare up, triggered by tribal, racial, religious, ethnic or other differences. And consider that the gap between the wealthiest and the poorest nations of this world continues to widen.

These are tasks where United Nations leadership is needed. That work merits our understanding; it deserves our country's support. It is important, therefore, as Ambassador Holbrooke has said many times, that the United States no longer hold the dubious distinction of being Debtor Number One at the UN. It is shameful, and, frankly, it runs against our national interest. This is not simply a feel-good exercise of giving money to do good, though that might be sufficient reason for some. It is also what serves our country's highest needs. America's influence is diminished by our debtor status. With Ambassador Holbrooke's leadership, some progress on the debt has been made in the U.S. Congress, but more work needs to be done, and we have a role to play.

When Morris Abram finished his four years as America's ambassador to the UN in Geneva—the culmination of a distinguished public career that included the presidency of the American Jewish Committee, a key role in the landmark one man-one vote Supreme Court decision, the presidency of Brandeis University, and many other achievements—he understood that what was missing from the universe of nonprofit organizations was an agency that would keep a close eye on the world body, praising it when it did its work well, critiquing it when it failed to meet its own high standards as set forth in its charter.

In 1993, Morris Abram established United Nations Watch. Among the things that had rankled him most during his years of service was the stark realization that the UN was too often still on automatic pilot when it came to treatment of Israel and sometimes, less well known, in its broader approach to the Jewish people. And he believed that this worrisome situation was being largely neglected by world Jewry at our own peril. That's why Morris created UN Watch, with the invaluable help of Edgar Bronfman, and chaired it for seven years. In his declining years, though, he felt it important to establish a permanent home for this institution. He strongly believed that the right home was his other home, the American Jewish Committee. And so we agreed to take on the sponsorship of UN Watch, which is headquartered in Geneva and has an outstanding international board and a staff team ably led by a young Canadian attorney, Michael Colson.

Secretary-General Kofi Annan, speaking to the American Jewish Committee and UN Watch last December, paid tribute to Morris and acknowledged the difficulties faced by Israel. He said: "The exclusion of Israel from the system of regional groupings, the intense focus given to some actions taken in Israel while other situations sometimes fail to elicit similar outrage, these and other circumstances have given regrettably the impression of bias and one-sidedness." This is precisely why we decided that taking on UN Watch was important. And in doing so, we wanted to further augment the agency's already top-drawer leadership.

We approached Connie Milstein earlier this year and asked if she would join the board of UN Watch. To her great credit and to our immense benefit, she immediately said yes. As you heard earlier from

Ambassador Holbrooke and Congressman Gephardt, Connie understands full well both the potential and the pitfalls of the United Nations.

And while I am speaking about the leadership of UN Watch, permit me to introduce a very special public citizen.

As assistant secretary of state for international organizations, this individual led the ultimately successful effort to repeal Resolution 3379. Remember that odious resolution known in shorthand as "Zionism is racism," a resolution first adopted at one of the lowest points in the history of the General Assembly, in 1975, and repealed sixteen years later? You can literally count the number of UN resolutions that have been repealed on the fingers of one hand. That individual, who today serves on the board of UN Watch, is Ambassador John Bolton.

We have a weighty agenda before us and Ambassador Holbrooke set out a good chunk of it. While the United Nations Charter says that the equal rights of all member states, large and small, shall be upheld and protected, that principle most assuredly does not apply to the State of Israel.

You have already heard from Ambassador Holbrooke about the issue of Israel's exclusion from one of the five UN regional groupings. I won't repeat it. What about the annual agenda of the Commission on Human Rights, an agenda that is rather peculiarly constructed? You see, it has two parts to it. One part deals with "Israel and the Occupied Territories" and the other refers to general country situations—in other words, to the rest of the world. No, I am not joking. Under the second part, you will find human rights crisis zones, at least some of them, perhaps Rwanda, Burundi, Kosovo, Afghanistan, Chechnya, and so on. All are lumped together, while Israel stands as a separate and permanent agenda item. That's the way the world has been mischievously and disingenuously divided up, and too many nations that should know better mindlessly go along with this absurd bifurcation.

Speaking of the Commission on Human Rights, as some of you may know, it is holding a special session this week called for by the Arab bloc, with the support of the Islamic movement and many nonaligned countries. It's quite a sight. You have to see it to believe it. I was there all day yesterday and had the opportunity, representing AJC, to address the fifty-three member countries present. Before me, the Israeli ambassador, Ya'akov Levy, spoke about the current situation in the region. Let me excerpt briefly from his forceful statement:

I cannot think of a worse time for this special session to take place in Geneva. At this point what is needed is a supreme diplomatic effort to take us beyond the current violence and bloodshed, to stabilize the situation. The UN secretary-general has been working ceaselessly with us, with the Palestinians and other parties. So, too, the president of the United States and the leaders of Israel, Egypt, Jordan, and major European nations. Any effort that could conceivably inflame the situation is counterproductive. This gathering, the speeches we have heard, and presumably the speeches we have yet to hear, could be counterproductive at best, distracting us from our major efforts. That is why Israel was opposed to the session from day one, and why we are still opposed to it.

In my testimony, I said:

The present special session of the Commission on Human Rights underlines the tragic consequences that result when the road of violence is chosen over the road of dialogue. This Commission on Human Rights has the obligation to confront the complex—and I wish to underscore the word "complex"—realities of the present situation. A one-sided discussion that ignores inconvenient truths to the contrary will not help. And a one-sided, politically charged outcome can have grievous results on the ground and therefore must be avoided at all costs.

Some of you may know the story about Henry Kissinger's first visit to Israel, when Golda Meir was prime minister. After a day of intensive discussions, he said to the Israeli leader: "Golda, I've always had a desire to visit the Western Wall. Would you take me?" "Really, Henry, I didn't know. I'd be delighted," she replied.

They went, and he watched as people at the wall took pieces of paper, wrote things, and stuffed the notes in the wall's cracks. "Golda, what are they doing?" "They are expressing to God their hopes and wishes." Kissinger took a piece of paper and wrote, "May there be peace in the Middle East for years to come." He showed it to Golda. "To God?" "To God!" said Golda. He shoved it in the crack. He took a second piece and wrote, "May there be economic prosperity for all the peoples in the Middle East." "To God, Golda?" "To God, Henry." And into the wall it went. On the third piece he wrote, "May Israel soon withdraw from the eastern half of Jerusalem, as well as the Golan Heights and the West Bank." "To God?" "No," said Golda. "That one is to the wall."

Sadly, Ambassador Levy, U.S. ambassador Nancy Rubin, and I were talking to the wall in Geneva. Let me give you a taste of the rhetoric we were subjected to yesterday by delegation after delegation from the Arab and Islamic worlds.

Here is one particularly outrageous example: "Mr. Chairman, never before in the history of mankind, be it in primitive societies or civilized ones under a fascist regime, have we ever seen civilian children who protest for the rights of their people confronted with a heavily armed army. The Zionist occupation army is using all kinds of weapons to exterminate children. As a result, thousands of Palestinian civilians have been injured or killed, and as for the Palestinian youth, Assam, he was savagely killed. He was captured by Zionist troops who used his eyes as an ashtray in which they extinguished their cigarettes. Then they broke his bones and crushed his skull. Mr. Chairman, those who have always been claiming to be the victims of Nazism are committing today the same Nazi crimes." This statement was made by the Iraqi ambassador.

We face other challenges as well. There is the anomalous status of the Magen David Adom, the Israeli equivalent of the Red Cross, which does not have full standing in the world movement because its symbol—the Star of David—is not recognized as a legitimate emblem. One hundred twenty-five years ago, the Ottoman Empire was permitted to use the red crescent of Islam because the Turks refused to use the cross. At the time, the Swiss tried in vain to explain that the red cross had no religious connotation, but was simply the inversion of the symbol on the Swiss flag.

But once the red cross became infused with religious meaning, and it did the moment the red crescent of Islam was added, how could Israel be expected to use either a cross or a crescent? Yet that is precisely what its choice has been until now, or else remain excluded from full participation in the movement.

In recent months, we witnessed remarkable progress toward solving the emblem issue. In fact, we were on the verge of a breakthrough by the end of this month when events in the Middle East exploded; now the timetable has been set back. Still, I am convinced that within the Red Cross movement there are many who share our commitment to solving this issue, including, importantly, the president of the ICRC, Jacob Kellenberger. They recognize that the exclusion of Israel undermines the core principles of universality, impartiality, and neutrality that define the humanitarian movement.

We at UN Watch and AJC know that it is not enough to vent frustration or anger, nor is it sufficient to rail against hypocrisy or selective morality. To achieve results in the international community much more is needed: a firm grasp of the issues; an understanding of personalities, structures, modalities, and national interests; an awareness of the mechanisms for getting things done; the respect and the ear of decision-makers; and the determination to stick with it, recognizing that in complex institutions like the International Committee of the Red Cross or the United Nations things seldom happen overnight, especially without the support of the "automatic majority."

That explains, I believe, the significance of the marriage between UN Watch and the American Jewish Committee.

I cannot close without a few thoughts on the situation in Middle East in the wake of the tumultuous events of the last three weeks.

First, at the risk of stating the obvious, I pray that the opening created at Sharm-al-Sheikh, and it is very narrow and fragile, will bring the parties back to the negotiating table, because in the final analysis that is the only path toward peace. In this connection, I would like to express our appreciation to President Clinton for the time and effort he has devoted to the search for peace, and also to Secretary-General Kofi Annan, who has distinguished himself as a sensitive and principled leader of the United Nations.

Second, if any additional proof were needed of the importance of the U.S.-Israel relationship, these last three weeks were Exhibit A. Israel once again found itself largely isolated in an international community that suddenly became blind and deaf when it came to Israel's side of the story. But as long as Washington and Jerusalem stand shoulder to shoulder, not only is Israel's security substantially enhanced, but the chances for peace in the region are extended. Conversely, any perceived diminution in the relationship between Washington and Jerusalem could only have disastrous consequences for the peace process. In the Arab world, any gap between the United States and Israel would be seen as an opportunity not for peace but rather, I fear, for exacerbating the conflict.

Third, friends of Israel in the United States are an indispensable factor in maintaining our country's support for that bilateral relationship. We must never, ever, become complacent about the tie or simply leave it to others to tend. If not us, who?

Fourth, everyone who follows events in the Middle East should be humbled by the last few weeks. None of us, it seems, knows the region as well as we might have thought. Fouad Ajami, the distinguished Johns Hopkins University professor, made this point in the *New York Times* yesterday. Our country is reminded again and again of how complex, inflamed, and unpredictable this region can be.

Let me read for you what a respected journalist, writing just days before the outbreak of the current round of violence, had to say:

> It is common wisdom that if the peace process with the Palestinians fails to come to fruition, all hell will break loose, that there will be panic, pandemonium and terror. Though usually the pessimist, I beg to differ. I think this peace deal is done, that fruition is relative, and that even if the sides do not sign a final status agreement, they have essentially already made their peace. Life is now in the details. The peace process has also placed 6 million insatiable Israeli consumers on Palestine's doorstep. To ensure they keep coming to Palestinian markets, Israelis need to be made to feel secure. It is in the Palestinian interest to do so. The above coupled with the passage of time, the hope created by even stalled negotiations, the withdrawal of troops from Lebanon, creates a

new normalcy. Whatever, *this is the healthiest situation I have sensed here in the region in a long time* [emphasis added]. And one can only hope that it prevails.

This piece was written by Hirsh Goodman, the founding editor of the *Jerusalem Report*. I repeat his words not to embarrass him—he is usually among the most astute observers of the region. But he got it 180 degrees wrong, perhaps because, like so many of us, he allowed himself to yield to his own logical way of thinking and assume, if only for a moment, a similar outlook on the other side.

Fifth, beyond the daily headlines, let us be absolutely clear what else is going on. There is a systematic and pernicious attempt underway to strip away the Jewish narrative, to question the connection between the Jews and this land that is at the heart of our history. Now we are told, for example, that the Western Wall was nothing more than the last point of departure for Mohammed to leave earth and never had any connection whatsoever to the Jews. We are told that Jesus was not a Jew but a Palestinian. And on it goes.

Some in the Arab world are also chipping away at the Shoah to undermine the notion that the Holocaust revealed the desperate need for a Jewish sovereign state—by branding Jews as Nazis, as the Iraqi ambassador did; by questioning whether 6 million were killed, as the mufti in Jerusalem did in the presence of the pope earlier this year; and by assaults on Holocaust history in the Syrian government newspaper.

All these efforts are aimed at calling into question the very foundation of Israel's raison d'être.

Sixth, as we saw previously with the "Zionism is racism" resolution, and as we also witnessed with the selection process at Entebbe in 1976—where German and Palestinian terrorists, working together, separated the Jews and the non-Jews just as the Nazis had done—the line between anti-Israelism and anti-Semitism is once again being blurred. There have been over ninety attacks on Jewish religious and cultural institutions in France alone in the last couple of weeks. There have been attacks elsewhere in Europe, most recently in Britain, and the United States is now experiencing its first incidents as well.

This ugly situation has reached my family. Our eighteen-year-old son, who is with us in Geneva, was sitting in the locker room after a soccer game the other day when other children, not knowing that he was a Jew, began making "jokes" about gas chambers and the Jews. And my fourteen-year-old son, who is also with us in Geneva, was so shocked by what he had read about in France that, knowing of my work, he insists that we shutter our windows at night regardless of the weather outside.

Finally, this is yet another reminder that we need strong institutions like AJC and UN Watch because, in the final analysis, we are represented far more effectively when we come together in organizations that skillfully represent our interests at the highest levels in this country and around the world.

Let us leave this wonderful evening renewed in our determination to work together, to succeed together.

## The Balance of Israel's National Security and Strength: The American Jewish Factor
### First Herzliya Conference
### Israel
### December 20, 2000

Permit me to step back from the temptation to look through an American Jewish lens at the issues of the moment, including the peace process, the forthcoming Israeli elections, and the upcoming Bush administration, and instead to consider the larger role played by American Jewry on the U.S. political scene. This is a unique audience comprised of Israel's leading political, foreign policy, military, and strategic thinkers, and I simply cannot pass up the opportunity to discuss with you an issue that too often receives insufficient attention here.

Before doing so, however, let me express my admiration to the organizers of this pioneering and timely conference, and particularly to Dr.

Uzi Arad and his colleagues at the Interdisciplinary Center. The American Jewish Committee is proud to be a partner and sponsoring institution.

And let me add my pleasure at sharing this podium with Zalman Shoval, Israel's distinguished ambassador in Washington for two tours of duty and a cherished friend, and Rob Satloff, one of America's foremost experts on the Middle East and a voice of clarity and reason often heard, but never often enough, in the media.

In mathematical logic, we are taught on the first day that if $a = b$ and $b = c$, then $a = c$.

Using that same logic, if American Jewry has an indispensable role to play in shaping American foreign policy regarding Israel, and if American foreign policy toward Israel has an indispensable role to play in advancing Israel's quest for security, peace, and normalization in the community of nations, then American Jewry clearly has an indispensable role to play in advancing Israel's quest for security, peace, and normalization in the community of nations.

This is my starting point today; it was the same twenty years ago when I first became involved in political advocacy on behalf of the Jewish community in the United States; and as I look ahead, I see no countervailing factors on the horizon that would diminish, much less reverse, this logic.

At times, some in Israel's political echelons have questioned the premise. They have argued that American Jewry, however well intentioned, is amateurish, only partly informed, and undisciplined at best, intrusive at worst, and therefore should remain on the sidelines, while Israel and the United States, two mature sovereign states, shape their bilateral bonds through the personal links established between leaders in Jerusalem and Washington and through the pursuit of congruent national interests.

I would not, I dare not, for a moment question the importance of both factors—that is, the role of close personal ties forged at times, though certainly not as a given, between Israeli and American leaders, and the defining of overlapping national interests. History has time and again demonstrated the overriding significance of both factors in the conduct of Israeli-American relations.

Still, more than one Israeli leader in recent memory—and not just from the right side of the political spectrum—has stumbled badly in discovering that the force of personality alone may not always carry the U.S.-Israel relationship, and indeed that, depending on who occupies the White House and what else is happening in the world at any given moment, Israel's efforts to assert congruent national interests may or may not find a receptive ear in the White House, State Department, or Pentagon.

At the same time, while there may occasionally be truth to some of the unflattering descriptions of American Jewry heard in various Israeli quarters, surely they do not tell the full story. Even worse, by the way, is the striking ignorance about organized American Jewry and its role in political advocacy among many Israelis who should, frankly, know better.

To cut to the chase, I would argue strenuously that without the American Jewish factor, America's Middle East orientation might not look as it does, even to the point that America's national interests in the region would be framed rather differently.

Not only have American Jews maintained an effective presence in the American political arena for decades, but also have managed to extend the reach and hold of Israel on American society more broadly. Bear in mind that when you meet pro-Israel American policy-makers, the likelihood is that they have had significant contact with, and input from, American Jews, whether as individuals or as representatives of Jewish institutions.

Is it far-fetched to believe that, absent the dynamic American Jewish factor, U.S. foreign policy might begin to resemble the rather "evenhanded" approach of many European nations, who tend to define their national interests more narrowly, focusing on the importance of maintaining stability in the Middle East at all costs because of a plethora of concerns—from energy supplies to energy costs, from export markets to historical ties, from fear of terrorism on European soil or against European targets in the region to anxiety about growing and at times restive Arab and Muslim populations within their own borders—and, as a consequence, too often throwing principle and justice to the wind?

Should we not, somewhere in the deep, dark recesses of our minds, always recall the example of France's volte-face. Here was a democratic nation, closely tied to Israel until 1967 and vital to its well-being, that reassessed its national interests—first under President de Gaulle, later under President Pompidou—and, as a consequence, downgraded its bilateral ties with Israel while vastly expanding its links with the Arab world. And France is not the only example of such a turnaround regarding Israel, though it may be the most dramatic.

Not that the United States doesn't share many of the same strategic, diplomatic, and commercial concerns as its European partners; to a very large degree, it does.

But Washington has also usually been able to see the larger picture as well, and not simply because of the benefit of geographic distance.

A number of factors, of course, have had significant influence on the place of Israel in the American consciousness, including:

- sympathy for the Jewish people after the Holocaust revealed the tragic effects of powerlessness and statelessness;
- American admiration for Israel's steep uphill battle to establish and defend a state against numerically superior foes;
- recognition, especially during the Cold War, of Israel's steadfastness and reliability as an American ally;
- common value systems, as Abba Eban has pointed out, built on an immigrant culture, a democratic tradition, and a pioneering spirit;
- a deep link to the Holy Land as the cradle of Judeo-Christian civilization;
- a lack of affinity with the Arab world, whose cultural and intellectual reach, as opposed to its oil, have had relatively little impact on American society to date;
- and, in a related vein, until recently the absence of a well-organized and politically savvy Arab-American lobby able to pursue its agenda effectively at the highest reaches of the American power structure.

Each of these factors, however potentially compelling at first glance, cannot be sustained over the long haul simply through the force of inertia, nor can it be safely assumed that they can forever be immune from challenge or change. That should be abundantly evident.

The one constant in this mix has been the American Jewish community's determination to build support for Israel across a broad spectrum of American life by summoning those arguments that make the most compelling sense at any given moment in time and tailored to the recipient groups.

By the way, this role has been played by American Jews since well before the establishment of Israel.

As but one illustration, it was the efforts of American Jewry that led, in 1944, to the adoption by both the Republican and Democratic platforms of statements endorsing the founding of a "Jewish Commonwealth" in mandatory Palestine, not to mention, if one seeks examples of the place of the individual in international relations, the role played by Eddie Jacobson in encouraging his close friend President Harry Truman to extend U.S. recognition to the embryonic Jewish state.

It follows that any diminution in the effectiveness of the American Jewish community could have harmful consequences for Israel. I must add here my belief that even if, as we earnestly hope, comprehensive peace is one day achieved in the region, its long-term success will in no small measure depend on a continuing Arab perception of airtight U.S.-Israeli bilateral relations, hence an ongoing role for American Jewry.

What are some of the potential areas of concern? Let me divide them into the internal and external.

On the internal front, and at the core of the discussion, is whether there is any reason to be concerned about the long-term commitment of American Jews and their organizational structure to sustained advocacy on behalf of Israel.

I would argue that there is at least some reason for concern, perhaps not immediately but certainly over time.

First, our numbers in the aggregate and as a proportion of the American population are not growing.

Counting Jews anywhere, including the United States, is no easy task, but let's take the 1990 National Jewish Population Survey as our baseline, as we await the results of the delayed 2000 Survey.

**Table 2.1**
**Jewish Percentage of**
**the U.S. Population**

| Year | % |
|------|-----|
| 1900 | 1.2 |
| 1925 | 3.5 |
| 1950 | 3.3 |
| 1975 | 2.4 |
| 2000 | 2.2 |

Source: *To Count a People:*
*American Jewish Population*
*Data*

The omnibus survey revealed the following numbers:

| | |
|---|---:|
| Jews by religion | 5,485,000 |
|     born Jews whose religion is Judaism. | 4,200,000 |
|     converts to Judaism | 185,000 |
|     born Jewish with no religion | 1,100,000 |
| Born or raised Jewish and converted out | 210,000 |
| Adults with Jewish parents who practice another current religion | 415,000 |
| Children under 18 being raised in another religion | 700,000 |
| Total of all categories | 6,810,000 |

As a proportion of the American population, whereas Jews constituted 3.5 percent of the American population in 1925 and 3.3 percent
in 1950, today we are barely 2.2 percent (see table 2.1). And with a rising American population that could reach 600 million by the year
2100, according to current immigration and birthrates, and with at best
stagnant Jewish population numbers, this percentage will only continue to decline.

Second, the intermarriage rate hovers near the 50-percent mark,
compared with less than 10 percent in the 1950s. Study after study conducted by the American Jewish Committee reveals that in intermarried

**Table 2.2**
**Intermarriage Among Jews,**
**Per 100 Marriages**

| Year | Rate |
|------|------|
| 1957 | 7 |
| 1972 | 32 |
| 1990 | 52 |

Sources: Census study 1957;
National Jewish Population
Studies, 1972, 1990

families where no conversion or, at the very least, sustained outreach takes place—i.e., the vast majority—ties to Israel tend to be much weaker (see tables 2.2 and 2.3).

And third, American Jewish success on behalf of Israel could never, in any case, be explained by sheer numbers alone. The breathtakingly active involvement of Jews in virtually every aspect of an increasingly open America, including the marketplace of ideas and public opinion and the political system, helps us understand the success. (The nomination to the Democratic presidential ticket this year of a practicing Jew, Senator Joseph Lieberman, amply illustrates the degree of America's openness today, a stark contrast to the situation prevailing just a few decades ago.) Throughout, a critical mass of Jews, devoted to helping Israel, has succeeded in making support for Israel not only a Jewish but a fundamental American issue as well.

Whether 3.5 percent or 2.2 percent of the population, the main question before us is whether the intensity of feeling for Israel on the part of future generations of American Jews will be maintained, as it has for generations of American Jews since 1948. If not, then we shall inevitably face a growing problem.

Current thinking suggests that younger American Jews are not driven by the same degree of passion for Israel as their parents and grandparents. Born long after the Holocaust and the struggle for Israel's establishment, born or raised after the defining wars of 1967 and 1973, born increasingly to families that have lived in America for two or

**Table 2.3**
**American Jews' Feelings Toward Israel,**
**By Religion of Spouse (in percents)**

| Feeling | Spouse Jewish | Spouse not Jewish |
|---|---|---|
| Close | 79 | 56 |
| Distant | 20 | 45 |

Source: AJC National Survey, 1999

three generations and more often than not have "distant relatives," if that, in Israel, the magnetic pull of Israel may not be nearly as intense or reflexive.

No, as some of my Jewish graduate students at Johns Hopkins University told me the other evening when we got together for dinner, we care about Israel and we know it's a part of our makeup as Jews, but even so we're not sure how significant a role it plays and, frankly, we're confused about imagery. Reflecting generational differences, they said, our parents and grandparents worry endlessly about the very existence of the state, while we see media images of a powerful army portrayed as an occupier and aggressor. And it is, of course, the Jewish state, they note, but are all Jews equally welcome, or are there elements of religious monopoly and sectarian domination that clash with entrenched American Jewish notions of pluralism and tolerance?

In brief, neither Israel nor the American Jewish establishment can simply assume that the high levels of energy and activity on the part of American Jewry regarding Israel are simply a given and will continue unabated for years to come; it could be a fatal miscalculation. Therefore, current initiatives such as Birthright Israel must be supported and sustained, while other equally creative and ambitious ideas are developed to awaken an interest and to sustain involvement in Israel among younger American Jews. This is our joint responsibility; we must share the load.

At the same time, the sky is not falling, certainly not in the near term at least. From year to year, we at the American Jewish Committee

**Table 2.4**
**American Jews' Relationship to Israel**
**(in percents)**

| Year | Very close | Fairly close | Distant |
|------|------------|--------------|---------|
| 1993 | 27 | 48 | 24 |
| 1994 | 25 | 41 | 32 |
| 1995 | 26 | 43 | 30 |
| 1996 | 25 | 45 | 29 |
| 1997 | 23 | 46 | 31 |
| 1998 | 25 | 44 | 31 |
| 1999 | 25 | 49 | 26 |
| 2000 | 28 | 46 | 25 |

Source: AJC National Surveys, 1993-2000

expect to see a drop in feelings of closeness and kinship toward Israel simply because of the inexorable passage of time and the toll it can take on consciousness and identity, yet strikingly it is not revealed in our annual surveys of American Jewish attitudes.

In 1993, we asked the following question of a representative sampling of American Jews: "How close do you feel to Israel?"

Twenty-seven percent of the respondents said "very close" and 48 percent said "fairly close"; 24 percent said "fairly" or "very distant."

This year we asked the same question. The results? Twenty-eight percent said "very close" and 46 percent said "fairly close." Twenty-five percent said "fairly" or "very distant" (see table 2.4).

In the 1993 survey, we posed the statement "Caring about Israel is a very important part of my being a Jew," and asked people to respond.

Seventy-nine percent agreed that "caring about Israel is a very important part of my being a Jew"; 19 percent disagreed.

In the 2000 survey, 80 percent agreed that "caring about Israel is a very important part of my being a Jew," and 18 percent disagreed (see table 2.5).

**Table 2.5**
**American Jews Who Say**
**That Caring About Israel Is**
**an Important Part of**
**Being a Jew**

| Year | % |
|------|------|
| 1993 | 79 |
| 1994 | 76 |
| 1995 | 78 |
| 1996 | 76 |
| 1997 | NA |
| 1998 | 74 |
| 1999 | 76 |
| 2000 | 80 |

Source: AJC National Surveys,
1993-2000

And when asked in 1994, the first year we posed this particular question, "Looking ahead three to five years, do you see Jews in Israel and the United States becoming closer, drifting apart, or neither?" 33 percent said "becoming closer," 8 percent replied "drifting apart," and 56 percent said "neither."

Six years later, the numbers had changed only marginally—32 percent said "becoming closer," 12 percent said "drifting apart," and 50 percent said "neither" (see table 2.6).

Again, in the short term, the basic indices of connection to Israel, caring about Israel, and, though I haven't presented the quantitative data, activity on behalf of Israel have not changed dramatically.

Yet discouraging demographic trends among American Jews (except in the Orthodox community, which today comprises approximately 8 percent of American Jewry), a weakening of identity among some segments of the community, question marks about the attitudes of youth, and increasing debate within communal organizations about the allocation of time, energy, and resources between the very real

**Table 2.6**
**American Jews' Expectations of Future**
**Relations with Israelis (in percents)**

| Year | Becoming closer | Drifting apart | Remaining same |
|---|---|---|---|
| 1994 | 33 | 8 | 56 |
| 1995 | 29 | 11 | 56 |
| 1996 | 34 | 12 | 51 |
| 1997 | 31 | 13 | 54 |

Source: AJC National Surveys, 1994-1997

needs of Israel and American Jewry must give pause for thought and concern (see table 2.7).

Externally, the situation affecting American Jewry's political role vis-à-vis Israel is not static either; no such situation can be.

While identification with Israel in America remains quite high, especially in the Congress but also in public opinion, when measured against support for the Palestinians or the Arab world, the Jewish community will continue to have its work cut out for it.

We do remain a notable factor in American elections, though who would have foreseen that a few thousand elderly Jews living in Palm Beach County, Florida, and having understandable difficulty reading a complicated ballot, might have given the election to George W. Bush by inadvertently voting for Pat Buchanan? If that's not real political power....

Still, I wouldn't count on the situation necessarily providing a permanent source of political leverage.

Remember, in the final analysis, Jews constitute a slowly declining percentage of the American population and its registered voters.

This is true even if Jews are as much as 50 percent more likely than the general American public to vote on election day—Jews presumably having taken to heart the old Chicago political slogan, "vote early, vote often" (Jews constitute 3-4 percent of voters nationally on election day, depending on overall turnout); even if Jews remain active in both polit-

**Table 2.7**
**American Jews' Feelings Toward Israel, By**
**Denomination (in percents)**

| Feeling | Ortho-dox | Conser-vative | Reform | "Just Jewish" |
|---------|-----------|---------------|--------|----------------|
| Close   | 93        | 83            | 69     | 61             |
| Distant | 7         | 17            | 31     | 39             |

Source: AJC National Survey, 1999

ical parties (especially the Democratic Party); and even if Jews constitute a potential swing vote in a handful of key states, such as Florida, New Jersey, and New York, and, to a lesser degree, in California, Illinois, and Pennsylvania (see table 2.8).

Let me add here that for years I have been urging, as a matter of practical politics, that Jews be active and visible in both political parties.

Neither the Democratic nor the Republican Party should ever assume Jewish voting behavior—the Democrats, for example, taking the Jewish vote for granted and the Republicans writing it off as largely unobtainable. That would be a dangerous position to be in. In truth, while the popular perception is that Jews tend to vote overwhelmingly Democratic, there is some surprising elasticity in the Jewish vote (see table 2.9). Forty percent of Jewish voters, for instance, voted for Ronald Reagan in the 1980 presidential contest, and on the state and local levels the numbers have at times been still higher.

(In the 2000 election, the Jewish vote went 79-19 percent for Vice President Gore, but in the closely watched New York Senate race between Democrat Hillary Clinton and Republican Rick Lazio, the first lady won the Jewish vote, according to a *New York Times* exit survey, by a narrow 53-45 percent margin.)

There are a number of external factors requiring our constant monitoring and attention, and they are well known to this audience, so I will mention only a few of the most important in passing.

**Table 2.8**
**Percent of Population Jewish in States with the**
**Most Electoral College Votes**[*]

| State | Electoral votes | Estimated % Jewish of state population |
|---|---|---|
| California | 54 | 3.0 |
| New York | 33 | 9.1 |
| Texas | 32 | 0.6 |
| Florida | 25 | 4.3 |
| Pennsylvania | 23 | 2.3 |
| Illinois | 22 | 2.3 |
| Ohio | 21 | 1.3 |
| Michigan | 18 | 1.1 |
| New Jersey | 15 | 5.8 |
| North Carolina | 14 | 0.3 |

Source: *American Jewish Year Book, 1999*
*270 electoral college votes are needed to win a presidential election. These ten states have 257.

First, there is the traditional American lack of interest in foreign affairs and an instinctive reluctance—not always, but often enough—to become entangled in conflict situations far from our shores.

Closely connected are the perennial unpopularity of foreign aid programs generally, an exaggerated sense of their cost to the American taxpayer as a percentage of the overall American budget, and the prominent share of the small foreign aid budget earmarked for Israel.

Moreover, the election of new members to the U.S. Congress always raises concerns about whether they will sustain the important role of Congress on behalf of Israel or succumb to a more parochial, domestically focused agenda. Or, alternatively, reflecting the changing demographics in America, especially the rapidly rising Latino and Asian communities, lawmakers might one day insist on more aid being committed to other areas of the world, possibly at the expense of Israel (and its neighbors). Among other things this will test the coalitional

**Table 2.9**
**American Jewish Voting Patterns in Presidential Elections (in percents)**

| Year | Democrat | Republican | Third party |
|------|----------|------------|-------------|
| 1932 | 82 | 18 | 0 |
| 1936 | 85 | 15 | 0 |
| 1940 | 90 | 10 | 0 |
| 1944 | 90 | 10 | 0 |
| 1948 | 75 | 15 | 10 |
| 1952 | 64 | 36 | 0 |
| 1956 | 60 | 40 | 0 |
| 1960 | 82 | 18 | 0 |
| 1964 | 90 | 10 | 0 |
| 1968 | 81 | 17 | 2 |
| 1972 | 65 | 35 | 0 |
| 1976 | 71 | 27 | 2 |
| 1980 | 45 | 39 | 14 |
| 1984 | 69 | 31 | 0 |
| 1988 | 73 | 27 | 0 |
| 1992 | 78 | 12 | 10 |
| 1996 | 78 | 16 | 3 |
| 2000 | 79 | 19 | 2 |

Sources: *Public Opinion Quarterly*, 1997; *New York Times*, Nov. 9, 2000

strengths of organized American Jewry, which has always made a priority of building cooperative ties with other ethnic and religious communities.

Also in the same vein, friends of Israel need to counter the possible impression that the Middle East is a sand trap, sapping American prestige and resources, and exposing American targets overseas to terrorism and the wrath of the Arab street, with possibly little payoff, and therefore warranting less, not more, American attention and direct involvement. After all, more than one U.S. administration has been hurt trying to navigate the dangerous shoals of the Middle East.

America's Achilles' heel is its dangerous and still growing dependence on imported oil, which requires the constant juggling of a multiplicity of sometimes conflicting interests in the Middle East. Can't the many talented Israeli scientists and engineers give the world the technological breakthrough needed to begin to move us away, once and for all, from the gas-dependent engine to reliable battery-operated or hydrogen-operated cars?

But there is one external threat that I would like to dwell on because it represents a direct challenge to the American Jewish community's role on behalf of Israel and has heretofore been given insufficient attention. I am speaking of the emerging Arab and Muslim lobbies in the United States.

This challenge began in earnest in the late 1980s, during the Palestinian intifada. At that time, Arab-American organizations orchestrated anti-Israel demonstrations throughout the United States to coincide with activities taking place in the West Bank and Gaza. During that period as well, Arab-American organizations began to cooperate with Muslim-American organizations.

Until that point, Muslim organizations had largely rejected any relationship with groups that promoted a secular rather than an Islamist Palestinian state. This coalescence of interests was a precursor to the coalitions of Arab- and Muslim-American organizations that are actively participating in the American political process today.

Interestingly, in the 1970s and early 1980s, Arab-Americans debated among themselves if their political involvement on the American scene could make a difference for the Arab world. A major part of this debate focused on the perceived power of American Jews and whether Arabs in America could ever break what they called the "stranglehold" that American Jews had over the U.S. government. In contrast to the majority of Arab-American organizations that firmly believed that "Jewish power" in America was an invincible force, a few leaders took the opposite viewpoint.

Throughout the last fifteen years, these leaders, principal among them Jim Zogby of the Arab-American Institute, have relentlessly pursued the goal of building the Arab-American community into a viable political force approaching the influence and standing of the Jewish community.

Zogby's first political shot in the battle over U.S. Middle East policy was the 1988 Democratic primary season and convention. He and his colleagues translated the energy of the pro-intifada street demonstrations into a viable mainstream political force of grassroots activists who became delegates at that year's Democratic National Convention in Atlanta, blindsiding a largely unprepared and somewhat complacent American Jewish community.

In every subsequent election, the Arab American Institute, together with the American Arab Anti-Discrimination Committee, has pursued national voter registration drives and political campaigning on behalf of both the Democratic and Republican Parties for the purpose of "empowering" Arab-Americans.

Zogby realized a long-standing goal by becoming the first Arab-American leader to host a U.S. president. "I understand that I am the first sitting U.S. president to address an Arab-American conference," said President Clinton as he spoke to the National Leadership Conference of the Arab-American Institute on May 7, 1998.

The convention was held jointly with the Palestinian American Congress, and was viewed as a "coming of age" by the Arab-American community. A photograph circulated by the Arab-American Institute at that time depicted Zogby with President Clinton, a tested friend of Israel, standing under a banner that bore the theme of the conference— "50 Years of Occupation." To this day, I might add, no one in the White House can explain how President Clinton allowed himself to be put in such an awkward visual (and political) position.

Next came the rise of Muslim-American organizations, many with a rather extremist agenda. Our natural counterparts and even potential interreligious partners—moderate Muslim leaders—sadly have been few and far between, bullied and intimidated by the extremists. Both major political parties, in their eagerness to attract a potentially numerous bloc of Arab- and Muslim-American supporters, have largely, and regrettably, chosen to ignore warnings about the company they may keep by associating with many of these groups.

The Muslim organizations are aggressively promoting themselves as a rising force on the American scene and an alternative political voice to that of the Jewish community. In interviews with the media, for example, representatives of the American Muslim Council have put the Muslim-American population at "over 6 million," and the press has too often unquestioningly repeated the number as if it were fact.

Professional demographers have disputed the figure, however, and the researcher who performed a survey for the American Muslim Council later admitted that he was pressured by the group to arrive at the figure of 6 million, implying that the actual figure was, in fact, a good deal lower.* But 6 million has a special resonance, of course; it would mean that Muslims outnumber Jews in the United States and it would buttress calls for a redefinition of America's heritage as "Judeo-Christian-Muslim," a stated goal of some Muslim leaders. (Note: In 2001, AJC commissioned a study of Muslim population figures in the United States by the highly regarded demographer Tom Smith of the University of Chicago that concluded that the actual number of Muslims in America lies between 1.9 and 2.8 million. A contemporaneous research study by a team of scholars at the City University of New York estimated the number at 1.8 million.)

The first serious efforts at political outreach to the American Arab and Muslim communities occurred in the early 1990s, when President Bush initiated the custom of sending 'Id Al-Fitr greetings to the leaders of religious and community organizations. These communities have also garnered legitimacy from the Clinton administration's determined efforts, especially in the White House, State Department, and Justice Department, to identify interlocutors, raising eyebrows along the way by some of the choices they have made.

Further, over the past several years a new generation of Muslim-American activists has formed a coalition, American Muslims for Jerusalem (AMJ), focusing on the issue of Jerusalem as their central concern and often parroting the views of Hamas and Islamic Jihad.

The AMJ's first major campaign was an anti-Israel boycott of the Disney Company's international exhibit commemorating the millenni-

---

* "Gap in Census Leaves Need for Religious Data," *Los Angeles Times*, April 17, 2000.

um. The AMJ demanded that an Israeli exhibit on Jerusalem be altered to reflect Muslim sensibilities on the issue. The group strenuously objected to the exhibit's portrayal of Jerusalem as the capital of Israel.

American Arab and Muslim groups have also attacked other companies to flex their muscle and prove that they are a force to be reckoned with. Recent targets of attack have included Ben & Jerry's ice cream, which was criticized in October 1998 for an advertisement depicting Golan Heights water as an ingredient. The ad was dropped. In July 1999, Sprint Communications was attacked similarly for using the Dome of the Rock in an advertisement for cheap phone rates to Israel—the point being that its status as part of Israel was still under international discussion. And Burger King was targeted for opening up a franchise in Ma'aleh Adumim.

Not only have American Arab and Muslim groups sought to use their numerical and economic weight as a force in American politics and society, which in itself is not unique, but they have also been quick to level charges of racism—i.e., anti-Arab or anti-Muslim sentiments—as another tactic of choice. This effort at intimidation, to call it by its real name, has been used to good effect, especially when dealing with law-enforcement officials, publishing executives, and representatives of the media.

The latest manifestation of a coalescence of interests between Arab- and Muslim-American groups is the response to the so-called Al-Aksa Intifada.

In a sophisticated and strikingly well-funded public relations campaign, and hoping to take maximum advantage of the beating Israel has taken in media coverage since September 28, they have made an effort to portray the Palestinian struggle as nothing less than akin to the American Revolution, claiming that perpetrators of Palestinian violence "died in the pursuit of liberty and independence." Another series of newspaper ads conjures up the imagery of Tiananmen Square, with an Israeli tank facing a lone Palestinian youngster standing in its way.

Make no mistake about it. These groups are determined to establish themselves as political and social counterweights to the American Jewish community and its political objectives in the Middle East.

Their aim over time—and this promises to be an extended political struggle for the hearts and minds of fellow Americans—is to take Arab interests more fully into account in the formulation of American foreign policy and to reposition the image of the Arab world in the American mind. In this overall effort, the aim, inter alia, is to reduce American foreign aid to Israel, deemphasize Israel's strategic importance for the United States, redefine American notions of terrorism, and end sanctions against Iraq.

In recent American elections, Arab and Muslim groups have demonstrated that they are indeed coming of age. They have pursued strategies common to other immigrant groups and perhaps most effectively used by American Jewish groups.

Still, in comparison to the Jewish community, Zogby's Arab-American Leadership Political Action Committee raised a comparatively small sum for candidates who demonstrated sympathy on issues of concern to the Arab-American community—"more than $125,000" in the 1998 primary and general elections. Nevertheless, Zogby's strenuous effort to portray the Arab-American and Muslim-American communities as an emerging political force during the extremely close 2000 election—and particularly as a "swing vote" in the key state of Michigan, with its estimated 400,000 registered Arab-American voters—was rather successful. In essence, Arab-American leaders—not uniquely, it must be said—tried to play it both ways in order to position themselves as helping the eventual presidential winner, be it Bush or Gore.

And, yes, the presidential candidates paid attention this year.

On October 5, Governor Bush held a closed meeting with Arab-American leaders in Michigan, most of whom went on to endorse him. Vice President Gore met with Arab-American leaders a week later in Michigan.

Bush publicly indicated his support for the Secret Evidence Repeal Act in one of the national debates with Gore; Gore followed suit in the next, indicating that at least this agenda item for Arab-American groups had made it onto the candidates' agendas. Many American Jewish organizations, including the American Jewish Committee, have opposed the bill, arguing that it puts immigrant rights over national and international security concerns.

In the bigger picture, Arab-American and Muslim groups have certainly managed to gain political and electoral legitimacy, even if several of their favored candidates for Congress were defeated this year. Yet who can begrudge them their involvement in the political arena? After all, the U.S. Constitution invites citizens to "petition the government," and that is precisely what they are doing, just as we do; we just always have to do it better.

These communities have become a focus of serious attention, with candidates coming to their meetings for the first time, and with the media seeking their communal views. That being said, they have yet to muster sufficient numbers of voters and opinion-makers to compete with the American Jewish voice, but their numbers are growing, principally through immigration, and so is their political savvy and self-confidence. We dare not underestimate them or delude ourselves about their Middle East objectives, even as they may also pursue a domestic agenda reflecting concerns about integration into American society, where, potentially, at least, there might at times be overlapping interests with the Jewish community.

I close, therefore, where I began.

America is crucial to Israel's well-being, to its quest for peace and security. Of course, there are other global power centers that are and must be of enormous interest to Israel—the European Union, most notably, and Germany, in particular, Turkey, China, India, Japan and South Korea, and Russia—but the U.S. role in the life of Israel remains both unique and indispensable, of an entirely different character than any other.

American Jewry is crucial to America's continued special relationship with Israel. In essence, as some commentators have dubbed it, we have a "strategic triangle." It is incumbent on Israeli and American Jewish leaders to do everything possible to maintain the ties that bind us together and to be alert to the very real internal and external factors that could negatively affect our joint interests. We can ill afford to do less.

## Jews and Germany: Remembering the Past,
## Planning for the Future
### University of the Bundeswehr, Hamburg
### Fuehrungsakademie of the Bundeswehr, Hamburg
### University of the Bundeswehr, Munich*
## January 29, 2001

As they say in the United States, "Before I begin speaking, I'd like to say a few words."

I am honored to have this opportunity to speak to the faculty and student body of such a renowned institution.

Moreover, I am grateful to Defense Minister Rudolf Scharping, who has lent his invaluable support to the fruitful cooperation between the German armed forces and the American Jewish Committee.

And I am especially pleased that Colonel Jochen Burgemeister, my friend and partner over the past seven years—who has contributed so significantly to the growing dialogue between the Bundeswehr and the Jewish people—is here with us today.

Also, allow me to introduce two of my German-speaking colleagues from the American Jewish Committee—Deidre Berger, the director of our Berlin office, and Rebecca Neuwirth, my special assistant in New York—who are deeply involved in our extensive German-Jewish programming.

There is much I would like to discuss with you today. Accordingly, time is not my friend. Thus, I hope you will forgive me if I avoid the traditional habit of many American speakers, myself included usually, to begin with a joke or two. Actually, truth be told, you probably should be thankful that I've spared you my sense of humor.

I had occasion to read the speech of Defense Minister Scharping, a cherished friend of Israel and the Jewish people, which he gave at Tel Aviv University last month during an official visit. It was an important and timely presentation, whose theme was "European Security in the Twenty-first Century—Perspectives and Requirements." But what most struck me about it was not what was in the speech but what was not.

* In English: University of the German Armed Forces, Hamburg; Command and Staff College of the German Armed Forces, Hamburg; University of the German Armed Forces, Munich.

There was only one reference to the past, when the minister said: "The Israeli people knows that it can, for historical and moral reasons, count on our support for the protection of its security." Otherwise, the themes revolved around the quest to ensure security and stability in Europe and the related search for peace in the Middle East.

Now one might note that this was not a speech given at Yad Vashem, the Israeli national memorial to the Holocaust, or here in Germany on January 27, Holocaust Remembrance Day and the anniversary of the liberation of Auschwitz, so why should there be more references to the past?

In fact, though, it was not so long ago that any speech by a top German political official, whatever the ostensible topic, if delivered in Israel or before a Jewish audience in the Diaspora, would necessarily have included references to the past.

But the contact, at the leadership levels in particular, between Germany and the Jewish world, especially Israel, has been so extensive, so frequent, that the language of these encounters is slowly but perceptibly changing.

Indeed, light-years have been traveled since the first secret meeting between the esteemed German chancellor Konrad Adenauer and an Israeli delegation, at the Hotel Crillon in Paris on May 6, 1951. The topic was indemnification, or, as you called it in German, *Wiedergutmachungsabkommen*, between the Federal Republic and Israel.

It is worth noting that, although an historic agreement was, in fact, signed, in Luxembourg, by Chancellor Adenauer and Israeli foreign minister Moshe Sharett on September 10, 1952, the principle of such indemnification—as Avi Primor, Israel's former ambassador to Germany, recalls in his book, *The Triangle of Passions*—was supported by only 11 percent of the West German people, according to polls taken at the time. Meanwhile, in Israel, the debate over accepting German funds was so bitter that it led to mass demonstrations and violence.

Yes, relations between Germany and the Jewish world have come a very long way over the past fifty years, especially between Germany and Israel. There have been more than a few complications along the way, some undoubtedly known to this audience, but the overall direction has been extraordinarily positive.

I would only mention for now two notable dates along this historical path—1960, when Chancellor Adenauer and Israeli prime minister David Ben-Gurion met, in New York, for the very first time; and 1965, when formal diplomatic ties were established.

In point of fact, the exigencies of statecraft required Israel rather early on to make painful but necessary decisions regarding links with Germany that Jews elsewhere in the world were not compelled to do.

Jews in the Diaspora could choose to ignore Germany if they wished, boycott its products if they so desired, and avoid travel there. Israel, on the other hand, faced with the Herculean challenge of building a state while defending its borders against those who sought its destruction, could ill afford to reject out of hand the possibility of relations with West Germany, however painful that idea might have understandably been for many Israelis.

Today, by contrast, Israelis regard Germany as a close ally, indispensable to Israel's well-being in a wide variety of fields on both the bilateral and multilateral fronts.

The special relationship forged between Berlin and Jerusalem, to which Minister Scharping made reference, has been a matter of great consequence to Israel and of benefit to both countries. We trust that this special relationship will continue to grow and develop in the years ahead, even as the process of integration of European foreign and security policy advances.

Diaspora Jewish groups, with one notable exception, were a few steps behind Israel in their views, but they have been catching up. There is a growing willingness to recognize the vast strides made by Germany in facing its past, building a democratic society based on the rule of law, serving as an anchor of NATO, seeking to create a European Germany rather than a German Europe, and reaching out to the Jewish world and Israel.

From the start, the one exception was the American Jewish Committee. Not only did it not lag behind, but, to the contrary, it took the lead in its understanding of Germany's dynamic postwar history.

Grasping the enormity of the Shoah, the American Jewish Committee began to follow the wise counsel of Confucius, who said in another era, "Better to light a candle than to curse the dark."

Germany would not suddenly disappear, the American Jewish Committee reasoned; it would always be there in the heart of Europe and, sooner or later, it would reemerge from the shambles and the occupation.

The only question was whether this postwar Germany would evolve in a positive or negative direction. History had taught us that we could ill afford to sit on the sidelines and simply wait for the question to resolve itself; we had to seek a role, however modest, in ensuring that light prevailed over darkness.

Yet, even as the comfort of light has, over time, replaced the terror of darkness, the past remains with us. The wounds have not fully healed, nor are they likely to anytime soon. The ghosts and shadows and cries of anguish continue to torment us. The questions, ultimately unanswerable perhaps, nevertheless persist.

Another Chinese philosopher, Tao Te Ching, once wrote, "The more you know, the less you understand."

The perfected industrialization of genocide still awakens us from our deepest sleep, fifty-six years after the machinery was silenced.

We Jews remain a scarred and traumatized people. Centuries of the teaching of contempt for Jews, persecution, exile, forced conversions, and pogroms had surely taken their devastating toll, but—at the very least, we thought—had created an acute sixth sense, a built-in radar, that could help Jews anticipate the onset of danger.

But nothing, nothing at all, could have prepared us for the systematic extermination of 6 million Jews, one-third of the Jewish people.

Nothing could have prepared us for the murder of 1.5 million children.

Nothing could have prepared us for what Winston Churchill, in August 1941, denounced as "a crime without a name."

Nothing could have prepared us for the terrifying sense of abandonment, as too many nations, institutions, and individuals callously turned their backs on the fate of European Jewry.

And nothing could have prepared us for the destruction of a civilization that had been part of the European landscape for two millennia.

Even long after the war's end, therefore, we learn not one, but two alphabets. We learn the alphabet that gives us the building blocks for creating language in all its beauty and richness. We also learn the alphabet we dare not forget, which sixty years ago created a new language of unprecedented evil.

In this second alphabet, the letter *a* stands for Auschwitz-Birkenau; the letter *b* for Babi Yar, the killing field on the outskirts of Kiev; the letter *c* for crematorium; the letter *d* for deportation; the letter *e* for *Einsatzgruppen*, the notorious Nazi killing units; the letter *f* for the Final Solution; the letter *g* for gas chamber; the letter *h* for Hitler, the personification of evil.

The letter *i* stands for I. G. Farben, the industrial employer of slave labor; the letter *j* for Jasenovac, the concentration camp in Croatia; the letter *k* for Kristallnacht, the night of the broken glass; the letter *l* for the Lodz ghetto in Poland; the letter *m* for Mauthausen, the concentration camp in Austria; the letter *n* for the 1935 Nuremberg Laws; the letter *o* for Oranienburg, the concentration camp in Germany; the letter *p* for Ponary, the site of mass extermination in Lithuania; the letter *q* for Quisling, the notorious Norwegian traitor.

The letter *r* stands for Ravensbruck, the concentration camp in Germany; the letter *s* for the *Sonderkommando*, the deadly special commandos; the letter *t* for Treblinka, the extermination camp in Poland; the letter *u* for the fascist Ustashe in Croatia; the letter *v* for the collaborationist Vichy government in France; the letter *w* for the Wannsee Conference, where Reinhard Heydrich first outlined the plan for the Final Solution in January 1942; the letter *x* for Xanthia, the town in Thrace that had not one Jew left after the war; the letter *y* for the yellow star Jews were forced to wear; and the letter *z* for Zyklon B, the insecticide turned lethal killing agent in the gas chambers.

Besides us Jews, who else today continues to struggle so intensely with this language and its meaning? Who else agonizes so much over the history of the Third Reich, sees the films, reads the accounts and memoirs, seeks out the survivors, visits the fields of ashes, the museums, and memorials, and attempts to connect this information to the contemporary world?

The answer, I believe, is that, more than anywhere else, the struggle persists right here in Germany. This remains the case, even as we leave behind the twentieth century, and even as a new generation of German political leaders, largely born after the war, assumes the mantle of national responsibility.

Not among all Germans, to be sure, but among many. Yes, there are those who feel the time has long since come to close the history books, or who find false comfort in the writings of those relativists who seek to challenge the singularity of the Nazi crimes.

But I have met an impressive number of Germans—in schools and universities, in churches and clubs, in the government and the military—for whom the intellectual and emotional struggle goes on, for whom it is not yet possible to turn the page and put the past fully behind them.

For them and for us, the result is to bring us closer together. We might come at the issues from very different starting points, but, in fact, we are drawn nearer to one another than might seem obvious.

There is, then, much that we can, that we should, do together.

Let me suggest that our common agenda today, as Germans and Jews, comprises at least four parts: (a) preserving memory, (b) building a world respectful of democracy and human rights, (c) serving as an early warning system against extremism and xenophobia, and (d) standing firm against those in the international system who flout the rule of law and threaten the precepts of peaceful coexistence and peaceful conflict resolution.

Why preserve memory? The answer is really very simple, or is it? It is to ensure that those who were consumed in the flames of the Shoah did not die in vain. It is about them, but also, truthfully, it is about us.

It is to remind us all, as Dr. Jonathan Sacks, the chief rabbi of Great Britain, said in London last week, of what happens "when we deny the humanity of those who are not like us."

It is "for the sake of our children," said Nobel laureate Elie Wiesel at the ceremony marking the fiftieth anniversary of the liberation of Auschwitz-Birkenau in 1995. "We must remember Birkenau, so that it does not become their future."

Unless we are somehow able to understand how an otherwise educated nation could fall under the spell of an obscure, Austrian-born madman and go to war against the world, leaving tens of millions of people dead, countries laid to waste, and countless shattered lives among those who survived, how can we realistically hope to prevent it from happening again?

Unless we are somehow able to understand how a demented, anti-human ideology could take root in a nation's soil and lead so many to participate so energetically in the implementation of genocidal policies without parallel in human history, what world will await our children and grandchildren?

Yes, memory is about the victims, and memory is also about us.

And this brings me to our second joint responsibility, building a world respectful of democracy and human rights.

In this endlessly complex world in which we live, some things are abundantly clear from even a brief glance at history and offer the ray of hope we so desperately need.

Among them is the simple, irrefutable fact that democratic nations do not as a matter of habit declare war on other democratic nations; they resolve their differences peacefully.

Thus, to yield to wishful thinking for just a moment, if the world's nations all suddenly embraced the essential tenets of democracy, the likelihood of international conflict would rapidly diminish, if not disappear, and the chances of respect for human rights would dramatically increase.

Democratic governments feel, or at least are supposed to feel, a sense of accountability to all their citizens, whether because of a system of checks and balances among the various branches of government, or because of regular elections that can reward or punish politicians, or because of an independent press that doesn't simply parrot the government line, or, especially, because of an inherent belief in the dignity of their citizens.

Democratic governments don't deliberately starve their populations as an instrument of state terror, as the Soviet Union did in Ukraine, with devastating consequences, in the 1930s. Or as North Korea has done more recently.

They don't use poison gas against their own citizens, as was the case in Iraq just over a decade ago.

They don't assassinate dissidents, or imprison journalists who expose the failings of the state or Jews simply because they are Jews, as Iran does today.

They don't totally subjugate women, denying them education, employment, and even health care, as we have witnessed in Afghanistan under Taliban rule.

They don't limit access to the Internet out of fear of the impact of unauthorized sources of information, as Syria does right now.

And they don't seek murderously to suppress minority religions, as has taken place in the Sudan against Christians and animists for too many years now.

By nature, democracies may be imperfect, but, as Winston Churchill said in the House of Commons in 1947, "Democracy is the worst form of government, except all those other forms that have been tried from time to time."

Democracies are a permanent work in progress and—yes, let's admit it—many remain deeply flawed.

Some democracies have been associated with slavery, colonialism, racism, anti-Semitism, costly military misadventures, and abuse of political power and legal authority.

But the strength of a democratic system lies in its ideological under-pinning, namely, that government is meant to reflect the will of the people and therefore is beholden to the people, not the other way around. When things go off track, sooner or later corrective mecha-nisms go to work, and the system tends to emerge healthier and a step closer to realizing its own enduring ideals. I have seen this process at work in the United States, as in other democratic countries.

Democracy has formed the cornerstone of the Federal Republic since 1949. Democracy is the common denominator of the fifteen members of the European Union. The thirteen candidate members waiting more or less patiently for entry into the European club know full well that the price of admission includes an unquestionably democratic system of governance. Greece, Portugal, and Spain made the successful transition just a few decades ago; others, I trust, will follow suit.

This spread of democracy in Europe—and, despite the occasional setbacks, the breathtaking regional cooperation that has been fostered—allows us to believe that the bloody wars of the past will not be repeated, at least not on the territory of the European Union. Given the scope and magnitude of conflict that has taken place over the centuries on European soil, that is no small feat.

National rivalries are now played out on the football field, not the battlefield. This is something worth celebrating, regardless of the outcome of the match, though I suspect you might not entirely agree that it's almost beside the point who wins and who loses.

Thus, I profoundly believe that the world's democratic nations, including the European countries, the United States, and Israel, have a unique tie that binds them together, and which must never be underestimated. Our governments are answerable to the people, not the reverse. It is the rights of the individual, not the exaltation of the state, that forms the foundation of our societies.

Europe and the United States may increasingly face trade wars; disputes over global warming, genetically modified foods, or the death penalty; tensions over the respective roles of NATO and the new European defense initiative, or the plans to build an American missile defense shield; and differences from time to time over unilateralism versus multilateralism.

I don't for a moment minimize these challenges—far from it—especially as a new administration takes office in Washington, raising concerns in some European capitals about its outlook, priorities, and policies.

I wish I could confidently predict the manner in which the Bush administration will pursue relations with our European allies, but it is simply too soon. In any case, forecasting is a rough business, even for the most experienced among us. A recent headline on the front page of the *International Herald Tribune* said it all: "The Unpredictable [U.S.] Economy: Experts Missed Last 9 Recessions."

No matter how serious, these potentially divisive issues must never be allowed to overshadow the common values and ideals that link us as nations, as peoples, and as societies. No one in Europe understands this better than the Federal Republic of Germany.

Therefore, we look to Berlin to continue emphasizing the vital significance of the transatlantic partnership, countering any sign of what one veteran American journalist fears may be an emerging "Euro-isolationism."

In this regard, I was delighted to read Chancellor Schroeder's words in the *Frankfurter Allgemeine Zeitung* the other day. He wrote: "The peace and welfare of the world's people depend on consolidation and development of the transatlantic alliance.... Germany and America can and will undertake the great tasks of the twenty-first century."

You can be assured that on the other side of the Atlantic, the voice of the American Jewish Committee will continue to be heard, as it has been consistently, in support of strengthening the transatlantic partnership, maintaining an active and enlightened American role in world affairs more generally, and, not least, supporting those international conventions and treaty bodies that enhance respect for and compliance with the universal protection of human rights.

Democracy is a strategic necessity, not a tactical option. It represents the best chance we have to transform the conduct of interstate relations and human behavior, the best opportunity to ensure that you—whether one day serving as officers of the Bundeswehr, NATO, a European Rapid Reaction Force, or peacekeeping operations—will always be underemployed, not overemployed. Please note that I did not say unemployed, just underemployed.

Our third common agenda item is to serve as an early warning system. This is an essential element of what militaries do to guard against armed threats to the security of a nation.

The early warning system that I am talking about is somewhat different, though not entirely. I have in mind the image of the miner's canary, who can sense danger and serves as an alarm bell in those risky underground settings.

By virtue of our historical experiences and rather acute understanding of human nature, Jews and Germans today can serve as a miner's canary when threats to a spirit of tolerance and mutual respect occur, when extremist political parties seek to infiltrate the political mainstream, and when the prospect of ethnic cleansing or genocide looms.

In essence, these tasks require of us some of the same basic elements as the military employs—carefully monitoring developments on the ground, interpreting data, planning for a variety of contingencies, and, when necessary, responding quickly and effectively.

We know from the past that menacing words and threats cannot be ignored. Hitler quite revealingly laid out his plans when he wrote *Mein Kampf* while in the Landsberg fortress, but how many took him and the book seriously?

We know that demagogues may test the waters to see how far they think they can go, just as Hitler first moved into Sudetenland and then paused, and just as he gradually imposed restrictions on Germany's Jews over the span of years. We know—don't we?—that denial or appeasement in response to such probes doesn't work; to the contrary, they are only likely to encourage further brazen steps.

More recently, we saw Saddam Hussein confidently conclude that the world would look the other way while he seized Kuwait, and Slobodan Milosevic similarly assume that his international critics did not really have the stomach to translate words of condemnation into a tough-minded plan of action against his murderous regime.

In the face of evil all of us have to choose among three basic courses of action—support, opposition, or silence.

No one should be fooled. In the final analysis, there is no such thing as moral neutrality in the face of evil. Individuals must choose; so, too, must political leaders, religious groups, and local, national, and international institutions.

Accordingly, we must demand of ourselves no less than we demand of others. And we must demand of others no less than of ourselves.

Over the past decade, Germany has faced its share of domestic social challenges, largely, though not solely, created by the magnitude of the task of unification and the slowly changing face of Germany to a more multicultural society. One result has been the disturbing rise in hate crimes, including murders, assaults, and cemetery desecrations, by the extreme right. In the year 2000, there was a reported 40 percent increase in such crimes over the previous year. This is a matter of profound concern.

As you know, Chancellor Schroeder undertook an unprecedented tour of eastern Germany last summer. At each of his forty stops, he spoke of a three-pronged response to the rise in neo-Nazi violence. He called on his fellow Germans to exercise "civil courage" in confronting neo-Nazis and the larger problem of xenophobia.

The chancellor's appeal reminded me of the words of the late Robert Kennedy, when he spoke in Cape Town, in 1966, to the National Union of South African Students. He said: "Each time a man stands up for an ideal, or acts to improve the lot of others, or strikes out against injustice, he sends forth a tiny ripple of hope, and crossing each other from a million different centers of energy and daring, those ripples build a current that can sweep down the mightiest walls of oppression and resistance."

I heartily applaud the chancellor's initiative; it is both timely and necessary. At the same time, I was struck by the results of a poll conducted in Germany, in October 2000, which revealed that 78 percent of the respondents believe that public officials and politicians are still not doing enough to combat the extreme right.

Exactly my point. The government urges citizens to practice "civil courage" against the extreme right, and the citizens call on the government to increase its efforts. Both are right, and both need to hold the other accountable for their actions.

No one should be let off the hook. No one should be permitted to argue that it is someone else's problem alone. And no one should too confidently minimize the significance of these violent acts, whose target is both their intended victims and the fabric of German democratic society.

Needless to say, such a discussion about the role of the individual and the role of government is not limited to Germany.

I would only add that, with Germany and the other fourteen European Union countries in need of millions of immigrants over the next decades to fill gaps in their workforces and compensate for aging populations and low birthrates, not to speak of a rapidly growing Jewish community right here in Germany, the challenges you will face from various quarters to a spirit of tolerance and openness will not quickly disappear.[*]

[*] A recent study, sponsored by the Center for Strategic and International Studies in Washington, D.C., indicates that, according to current domestic demographic trends, Germany's population could be reduced by up to 17.5 million by 2050.

Continued vigilance will surely be required, including in the Bundeswehr, to guard against stepped-up activities by extremist elements to recruit new members and to target the newcomers.

As I said, the test of our conscience most assuredly does not stop in Germany.

To give you only one example, just this past Sunday in London my family and I heard a group of five Arab men in a city park publicly calling for the killing of Jews, claiming the Holocaust was a Jewish lie to evoke the world's sympathy, and laughing as one told the following story: "What is the difference between a pizza and a Jew? Both must go into the ovens, but at least the pizza doesn't scream."

This episode comes in the wake of numerous recent attacks on Jews and Jewish institutions in Europe, believed to be linked both to the Middle East and to extreme right-wing groups in Europe. (Interestingly, in the 1970s, at the height of terrorism in Europe, the links were most frequently between Middle Eastern groups and the extreme left.)

On a different but related note, let me share with you a revealing and instructive story that took place thirty-seven years ago.

In the early morning hours of March 13, 1964, in a middle-class area of New York City, a twenty-eight-year-old woman parked her car and began walking the thirty meters to her home. Her name was Kitty Genovese. The time was 3:20 A.M.

She was grabbed and stabbed. She screamed. Lights went on in a nearby ten-floor apartment building, and someone yelled out, "Leave that girl alone." The attacker walked away, but then came back and stabbed her again. Again, she cried out for help. Again, the lights came on in the building and the attacker walked away. But then he came back for the third time, at 3:35 A.M., and this time he killed her.

It was not until 3:50 A.M., thirty minutes after her first plea for help, that the police received their first phone call. Within two minutes they were on the scene, but, of course, it was too late.

The only person to call the police, after waiting thirty minutes, indicated that he had thought a lot about whether to call and, he added, had first phoned a friend to get advice on what to do.

Moreover, it was later learned that thirty-seven other people, residents of the nearby building, had been witnesses to the attacks, but not a single one called. Each predictably had a self-justifying excuse—"I wasn't sure if it was a family dispute," "I was certain someone else would call," "I didn't want to get involved with the police," etc.

Just as too many Germans in cities like Rostock remained silent when violent attacks first occurred against foreigners in the early 1990s, so did the residents of Kitty Genovese's neighborhood in Queens, New York, fail to act when a neighbor was assaulted. Whatever the differences in circumstances may have been, the tragic results of indifference to cries for help all too poignantly speak for themselves.

And conversely, just as hundreds of thousands of Germans have participated in demonstrations to protest the acts of violence and to stand against xenophobia, so have we had similarly inspiring examples in the United States.

In December 1993, a Jewish family was celebrating the holiday of Hanukkah in the town of Billings, Montana. Billings has a tiny Jewish community.

A menorah was placed in the bedroom window of Isaac, the five-year-old son of Brian and Tammie Schnitzer. Someone came along and threw a cinder block into the window. Fortunately, Isaac was not in the room at the time or he might have been seriously injured or even killed.

Led by the police chief and the editor of the local newspaper, the town reacted quickly. Thousands of paper menorahs were printed and distributed, and they began appearing in the windows of just about every home in Billings, sending a message to the attacker, or attackers, that if Jews were the target, then everyone in the town had just become Jewish.

The strategy worked. Indeed, it has been cited again and again as a model of community response to acts of hatred. I repeat that the initiative came from a public-private partnership—the police and the newspaper.

Yes, there is much that we have learned, or at least should have learned, about the nature of hate and about how to respond to it, as individuals and as nations. Let us always be sure that our voices are heard and our presence felt.

That is precisely why, in 1999, when Slobodan Milosevic began driving Kosovar Muslims out of their homes, we at the American Jewish Committee felt it important to send a powerful message to a region where hatreds never seem to be buried.

We raised $1.3 million from our members to help the refugees. Before disbursing the money, however, we decided to visit several refugee camps in Macedonia and a field hospital run by the Israel Defense Forces to assess the situation on the ground.

We were deeply touched by what we saw.

The Israeli field hospital was superbly run. Today there are a number of Kosovar Muslim children with Israeli names, in gratitude to the doctors and nurses who helped bring them into this world.

Of the four refugee camps we visited, one in particular especially impressed us. It was, you will be interested to know, a Bundeswehr operation. There was a special effort made to provide a measure of dignity to the refugees by serving hot meals and building wooden floors for the tents; these amenities existed nowhere else. It may not sound like a lot, but, believe me, it was. And we were also moved by the medical assistance being provided by Die Johanniter, the German humanitarian organization.

When we returned to the States, we approached our friends in Germany and proposed a joint humanitarian operation to assist the refugees. The response was immediate and enthusiastic.

The result was a pioneering effort, jointly sponsored by the American Jewish Committee and Die Johanniter, with cargo planes provided by the Bundeswehr, to bring relief supplies to thousands of refugees.

Our goals were three, and I believe we accomplished all of them.

First, to assist people in need, in this case Muslims who were victims of intolerance, and thereby underscore the sacred notion of one human family.

Second, to send a message to the peoples of the Balkans that history could move forward, using our German-Jewish project as a concrete example.

And third, to give shape and form to our belief that Germans and Jews were at a stage in our relationship where we could act together in such times of humanitarian crisis.

And this brings me to the fourth and final part of what I believe to be our common agenda.

There remain, as you know, real dangers to the international system that we must stay alert to, that challenge you and us both.

Let me mention briefly those most pertinent to my discussion today, leaving aside such greatly consequential matters as demographic trends; ecological threats, including global warming, water resources, deforestation, and desertification; growing gaps between rich and poor nations; the spread of infectious diseases; and the continued potential for internal and interstate conflicts, especially in sub-Saharan Africa and Asia.

I am especially worried about several developments.

First, although lately out of vogue in American diplomatic parlance, the term "rogue states" continues to apply to certain countries. I especially have in mind such nations as Iraq, Iran, and Afghanistan.

Of special concern is the determination of Iran and Iraq to acquire nonconventional weapons and the means to deliver these weapons, at short and medium range for now, with some measure of precision.

For a while, many in the West thought that Iran had turned a corner, that the arrival of President Mohammad Khatami on the scene had shifted the ratio of domestic power in the direction of the so-called moderates.

It is now abundantly clear that, much as we all hoped for an improvement in the internal situation, it has not yet occurred. To the contrary, the fundamentalists still hold the reins of real power. They are determined to wage their struggle against perceived enemies both within the country and beyond, including, of course, Israel or the "Zionist entity," as they call it, and the West more generally, although sometimes their policy in this regard is subtly cloaked.

And for a while, many in the West thought that the UN inspections regime in Iraq could prevent Saddam Hussein from resuming his long-standing quest for weapons of mass destruction. Those inspections, however, have not taken place for two years now, the international sanctions regime is fast eroding, biological and chemical weapons production is assumed to be under way, and it is only a matter of time before Saddam Hussein once again stirs trouble.

In Afghanistan, the Taliban do not have the resources to acquire major weapon systems, but they have managed to create a terrorist haven—providing sanctuary for known terrorists, training facilities, and theological centers that transform Islam into a religion of violence locked in permanent battle with the West.

These and a handful of other nations, coupled with terrorist groups operating in the region and supported by networks in Europe and North America, do pose a real menace to the international system. There is no escaping it, no wishing it away.

And the collapse of the Soviet Union, while an unquestionably welcome development, has also made it easier, especially for terrorist groups, to acquire weapons and know-how, either on the open market or with the help of organized crime. Moreover, dramatic advances in information technology, encryption, and communications are assisting these groups as well.

In this regard, a recent study by the Central Intelligence Agency, entitled *Global Trends 2015*, reached the following pertinent conclusions:

> Export control regimes and sanctions will be less effective because of the diffusion of technology, porous borders, defense industry consolidations, and reliance upon foreign markets to maintain profitability. Arms and weapons technology transfers will be more difficult to control.... Prospects will grow that more sophisticated weaponry, including weapons of mass destruction—indigenously produced or externally acquired—will get into the hands of state and nonstate belligerents....

There are several conclusions I would draw.

First, as I said earlier, denial or appeasement as government strategy will not work.

Second, cooperation and coordination, not competition, among allies is vital in the face of such threats.

Third, moderate, forward-looking countries in the region need to be supported.

Fourth, in this respect I would add a special word about Turkey. The EU's decision in Helsinki to open the way for negotiations with Ankara was a historic step. I am under absolutely no illusion about the difficult talks ahead, but the signal it sent was unmistakable and of incalculable diplomatic and strategic importance.

And fifth, the challenges faced by Israel in this volatile region need to be clearly understood. No one, I believe, should ever question Israel's yearning for a secure and lasting peace, nor the bold risks it has taken in an effort to achieve that peace. But the margin for error in Israel's decision-making is virtually nil, given the precarious geography and the complex regional climate.

And events of the past several months underscore once again the extraordinarily difficult dilemmas faced by Israel in its search for peace. An Israeli government prepared to go to unprecedented lengths to achieve a negotiated settlement with the Palestinians is faced instead with armed violence, erratic behavior, and unrealistic negotiating demands.

The Israeli statesman Abba Eban once said of the Palestinians, "They never miss an opportunity to miss an opportunity."

Is this to be another missed opportunity? If so, it would be a tragedy for all the peoples in the region, both Arabs and Israelis.

Together, then, we must continue to do what we can to help ensure Israel's security in the context of a Middle East where peace one day replaces war, where prosperity replaces poverty, and where harmony replaces hatred. It will most certainly not be easy, but the objective is worth the struggle and the alternative is simply too frightening to contemplate.

In sum, we, Germans and Jews, have a full plate and a daunting agenda. The stakes could not be higher. But I am persuaded that our efforts, both individually and collectively, can make a profound positive difference on the direction of this new century.

And to quote a line from the movie *Apollo 13*, the NASA controller in Houston, when faced with the news of the ill-fated moonshot, declared, "We dare not fail."

No, we dare not fail.

<br>

### The Middle East: Hope versus Fear
### Diplomatic Academy
### Vienna, Austria
### April 24, 2001

I am grateful to the Diplomatic Academy and, in particular, to Ambassador Sucharipa, whom I first met in New York when he was serving as Austria's permanent representative to the United Nations, for extending me an invitation to speak here today. It is an honor to appear at such a renowned and admired institution.

Also, I must confess that I was pleased to be invited because I have very personal memories of Vienna, where I lived with my wife in the late 1970s while working here. Our office was just across the street, in fact, on Brahmsplatz, and we were assisting some of the hundreds of thousands of Jews from the Soviet Union whose first point of arrival in the West was this city.

For those leaving a land of oppression, Austria was their initial glimpse and taste of freedom. The refugees were thankful to this country for opening its doors and welcoming them, and those of us helping this massive human flow were equally appreciative.

My work with Jewish refugees was an outgrowth of a belief that my generation—the first generation born after the Holocaust—had a special obligation, as well as an unprecedented opportunity, to contribute to the security, well-being, and, if you will, normalization of the Jewish people.

Moreover, there was an important lesson for me in this work. Here I was, the son of a Jew who had lived in Vienna until the Anschluss in 1938, working in this city exactly forty years later, with the full cooperation of the Austrian government, to save Jews fleeing persecution. What a dramatic, and welcome, turn of events, suggesting the possibilities of change and progress.

There were other signs of change as well. Soviet Jews, in 1978, were prepared to openly challenge the most powerful totalitarian state on earth in their quest for freedom. What gave those Soviet Jews the courage to do so? What made it so different from 1938?

Soviet Jews never felt alone, though they were obviously isolated. They believed that their efforts could and would capture the imagination of the world and generate support, even with all the risks they faced of harassment, imprisonment, and denial of exit visas.

Why did they believe this, when forty years earlier the plight of Jews in Germany and subsequently other European countries so obviously failed to capture the world's imagination?

Perhaps it was because some nations, institutions, and individuals had absorbed at least a few of the lessons of the Holocaust, including the need to place human rights high on the political agenda, as the

United States so admirably did in its bilateral dealings with the Soviet Union.

Perhaps it was the realization that human rights protections had become part of the international vocabulary. The postwar global architecture included increasing mechanisms for monitoring and safeguarding fundamental rights, including the right to leave one's country and the right to practice one's religion.

While the international community could not compel the Kremlin to change its laws on emigration, or to permit the study of Judaism, or to end the practice of anti-Semitism, it could challenge Moscow at every step, citing the Universal Declaration of Human Rights, the Helsinki Accords, and other international agreements to which the USSR was a party.

And not just states were in a position to do this. A vast network of nongovernmental organizations emerged after the war, many committed to advancing international human rights protections. They became a constant irritant in the side of the Soviets and an important source of support for Jews still inside the country.

Perhaps it was the recognition that the media were now a force to be reckoned with, an international actor that could not only mobilize public opinion but also, as we have seen on numerous occasions, shape government policy.

And perhaps Jews in the Soviet Union found strength in the fact that in 1978 there was an Israel—a Jewish sovereign state concerned with the fate of as many as 3 million Jews living behind the Iron Curtain, eager to help them both openly and clandestinely, and prepared to extend resettlement and citizenship to those able to reach its shores.

I often ask myself one of those ultimately unanswerable historical questions: If Israel had existed in 1938, how might the course of history have changed for the Jewish people in the ensuing seven years?

I can only guess at the answer, of course, but I have clearly seen what Israel means for Jews since the birth, or rebirth, of the state in 1948.

Permit me to dwell on this for a few minutes, especially because tomorrow evening Israel will celebrate its fifty-third birthday. Moreover, it allows me to put my cards on the table regarding Israel in the context of this discussion.

Incidentally, I hope that many of you in this audience will agree with my sentiments. After all, as the seventeenth-century French intellectual La Rochefoucauld wrote in his legendary *Maximes*: "There are few sensible people, we find, except those who share our opinions."

I believe that the very establishment of the state in 1948 and its record of development over the ensuing fifty-three years are nothing short of extraordinary.

And it was all accomplished not in gentle Scandinavia but in the turbulent Middle East, where Israel's neighbors were determined from day one to destroy it and were prepared to use any means available to them. They tried it all.

There have been full-scale wars and wars of attrition; diplomatic isolation and attempts at international delegitimation; primary, secondary, and even tertiary economic boycotts; terrorism in the skies, in airports (including Vienna's), on trains (including one carrying Soviet Jews across Czechoslovakia to Austria), in an Olympic village, and in crowded marketplaces, packed buses, and even elementary schools.

Israel's enemies hired Nazi-era scientists to build advanced weapons, and they spent vast sums to build modern armies.

They have propagated Holocaust denial, fearing that the reality of the Shoah would otherwise bring world sympathy to the State of Israel.

They have spread the poison of anti-Semitism, often thinly veiled as anti-Zionism, to Arab populations through schoolbooks, Friday sermons at mosques, and government-controlled newspapers.

Yes, they have tried it all, but they have never succeeded in breaking Israel's national will.

No other country, certainly no other democratic country, has been subjected to such a constant challenge to its existence, to its very legitimacy, though the age-old biblical, spiritual, historical, and physical connection between the Jewish people and the Land of Israel is quite unique. Indeed, it is of a totally different character from the basis on which the United States, Australia, Canada, New Zealand, or the bulk of Latin American countries were established, that is, by Europeans, with no legitimate claim whatsoever to these lands, decimating indigenous populations and proclaiming authority.

No other country has faced such overwhelming odds against its survival or experienced the same degree of international vilification by an automatic majority of nations that has reflexively followed the will of the energy-rich and more populous Arab world.

Yet throughout, Israelis have never succumbed to a garrison mentality, never abandoned their yearning for peace or willingness to take significant risks to achieve peace, and never flinched from their determination to build a thriving state.

To be sure, nation-building is an infinitely complex process.

In Israel's case, the nation-building took place against a backdrop of intercommunal tensions with a local Arab population that laid claim to the very same land; as Israel's population literally doubled in the first three years of its existence, putting an unimaginable strain on severely limited resources; as the country was forced to devote a vast portion of its budget to defense despite the compelling socioeconomic needs of its citizens, especially the new arrivals, including many Holocaust survivors and hundreds of thousands of Jewish refugees from Arab countries, forgotten victims of the Arab-Israeli conflict; and as the country coped with the daunting challenges of forging a national identity, common culture, and social consensus in a population that could not have been more geographically, linguistically, socially, and culturally diverse.

I might add to the list of challenges Israel's total lack of natural resources. As Golda Meir, the late prime minister, once said: "Let me tell you the one thing I have against Moses. He took us forty years into the desert in order to bring us to the one place in the Middle East that has no oil."

Moreover, it is one thing to be a people living as a minority in often inhospitable majority cultures, as Jews did in countless countries over the span of more than 1,900 years; it is quite another to exercise sovereignty, as the majority population. Inevitably, there will be clashes between a people's faith and ideals, particularly when they are rooted in a religious expression that places emphasis on ethical values, and the sometimes messy and amoral requirements of statecraft.

Without doubt, the Israeli record is imperfect. What country's is not, though few are as microscopically scrutinized from the outside as Israel's?

Mistakes, big and small, have been made in this young country, in the realm of both foreign and domestic policy. And many tough issues remain unresolved, including the elusive search for a common understanding of what it means to be a Jewish and democratic state; how to bridge the seemingly irreconcilable worldviews of the religious and secular populations of the Jewish majority; what to do about an electoral system that too often creates political paralysis; and how to achieve the integration of the Arab minority in Israel while, at the same time, retaining the state's distinctive Jewish character.

Yet for all the bumps in the road, the strains and tensions in Israeli society, and the unresolved issues that still loom large, Israel remains an astonishingly impressive work in progress.

In just fifty-three years, Israel has built a thriving democracy; a powerful military with a formidable deterrent capacity; an economy whose per-capita GNP exceeds the combined total of its five contiguous neighbors—Lebanon, Syria, Jordan, Egypt, and the Palestinian Authority; a thriving culture utilizing an ancient language rendered modern; and an agricultural sector that has served as an example to developing nations of how to conquer an arid land.

In sum, this is an epochal story of return and renewal, of courage and tenacity, of faith and fulfillment, of the triumph of hope over despair.

But it is also the story, of course, of an unfinished journey to achieving lasting peace, security, and stability in a complex region. The last seven months are a sobering reminder, if reminders are even needed, of the difficulties that still lie ahead.

Let's look at some of those difficulties. At this point, I'm tempted to quote Dante's inscription on the door to Inferno: *Lasciate ogni speranza o voi che entrate,* "Abandon all hope, those of you who enter."

Israel is confronted by three major diplomatic and strategic challenges. The first and most obvious is with the Palestinians, the second is with Syria and Lebanon, and the third is with those dangerous states beyond Israel's immediate borders, notably Iraq and Iran. In addition, of course, Israel faces the transnational threat of terrorism by political and religious extremists.

In the short term, at least, I cannot be optimistic about significant progress on any of these fronts. To the contrary, and I say this with a sense of profound sadness, things are likely to get still worse before there is any possibility of an improvement on the ground.

After all, if the Palestinians could not reach a settlement with Prime Minister Barak in power and willing to offer an historic, and previously unimaginable, compromise, can we really expect a major breakthrough now with a clear majority of the Israeli public unprepared to offer still more concessions?

Can the gap between the two sides for even restarting talks be bridged, with Chairman Arafat insisting on resuming where Barak left off, even though the Palestinian leader rejected the deal, and Prime Minister Sharon asserting that talks will not begin until Palestinian violence ends and further stipulating, with the support of the United Statres, that he is not obligated to pick up the talks where they ended under Barak since Arafat turned down the offer?

And what about the growing belief on both sides that peace may not be achievable?

Recent polls in Israel show the population growing ever more distrustful of Arafat, supportive of a tough military response to Palestinian-instigated violence, and once again fearful that the true Palestinian intention, over time and in stages, is to destroy Israel.

On the Palestinian side, there is, to say the least, fury at the Israeli handling of Palestinian unrest, deep resentment of the Jewish settlements and the actions of some settlers, and suspicion that Sharon's objective is not negotiation but subjugation.

Finally, assuming that Arafat genuinely seeks an accommodation with Israel, has he prepared the Palestinian people for the possibility— and price—of peace? Or has he raised Palestinian expectations—for example, regarding Jerusalem and the so-called right of return—to such a point that serious compromise, a necessity on both sides if a deal is ever to be reached, could trigger an uncontrollable backlash?

Since 1947, the Palestinian approach has essentially been all or nothing, and the result speaks for itself. Maximalism has been shown not to work.

David Ben-Gurion, the leader at the time of Israel's establishment, and Habib Bourguiba, the leader at the time of Tunisia's independence from France, were two political leaders who understood, each in his own way, the necessity for pragmatism in pursuing statehood, the need to accept certain realities in the interests of the greater good for their respective peoples. That sense of pragmatism has been sadly missing from the Palestinian leadership.

A Jordanian commentator, Dr. Fahed Al-Fanek, tellingly made the point in an article in *Al-Rai* (March 2, 2001). "In recent months," he wrote, "Yasir Arafat could have, all at once, saved the Barak government, saved the good reputation of President Clinton, and turned himself from a reckless president into a peacemaking president. In return, he could have had a recognized independent Palestinian state over most of the territory of the West Bank and Gaza Strip, with Jerusalem as its capital…. It is entirely clear that the Palestinian side has made a mistake by missing a rare opportunity that may never return…. In the last century, there has been a sequence of opportunities that the leaders of the Palestinian people rejected in order to avoid being accused of leniency and negligence of Palestinian rights. Nobody has learned the lessons from this sequence of missed opportunities."

Will the Palestinians continue to languish in their fanciful and unattainable dreams, hoping that Saddam Hussein or, for that matter, even the UN will somehow achieve for them what they have not been able to gain for themselves? Or will they finally grasp the opportunity to establish a viable state next to, and at peace with, Israel?

In doing so, I fully understand, they would be forgoing a part of their national narrative, but then so would Israel in any final settlement. An end to the conflict becomes possible only if each side recognizes and accepts that the prize of peace is worth the price of peace, and the price is compromise, painful compromise, for both sides.

Successive Israeli governments, with the support of a clear majority of the Israeli public, have time and time again demonstrated their understanding of this cardinal rule of negotiation, whether in talks with the Egyptians, Jordanians, Syrians, or Palestinians.

It remains to be seen whether the Palestinian leadership and people—and, above all, Arafat—can reach the same understanding. I hope against hope that they will be able to do so and sooner rather than later, with the steady encouragement of the United States, the European Union, other major powers like China, Japan, and Russia, and moderate Arab countries, especially Egypt and Jordan.

But, again, the obstacles are daunting. As Dennis Ross, the former

U.S. peace negotiator, told the Israeli daily *Ma'ariv* in an interview published April 13: "Arafat did not prepare his people for peace and—more important—he did not prepare himself for it. The Palestinian leader has lived in conflict all his life. His fame and stature were built by the struggle, and when the moment came to give up the struggle, he was incapable of doing so."

Regarding Syria, there is periodic talk about secret contacts between Jerusalem and Damascus. Whenever word is leaked, it always seems to come down to the same thing.

Prime Minister Barak offered the late Hafez al-Assad 99 percent of what he was seeking on the Golan Heights. Assad, however, held out for the remaining 1 percent, direct access to the shoreline of the Sea of Galilee, based on his disputed claim as to what border actually constitutes the basis for Israeli-Syrian talks.

When Barak traveled to Camp David for talks with the Syrian foreign minister facilitated by the United States, he visited the exercise room one morning. There he saw a Syrian negotiator running on a treadmill. Barak's comment about the Syrian became a metaphor for the bilateral talks: "He's pointed in the right direction, but he's going nowhere."

Will Bashar al-Assad, one of three sons who recently inherited power in the Arab world from their late fathers, budge on the long-standing and hitherto intransigent Syrian position?

Is he in a strong enough position domestically to do so, even if he wished?

Would Syria allow itself to settle for less than Egypt or Jordan, which held out for every last inch of disputed land from Israel and eventually got it?

Can the United States and Europe help entice Syria toward a settlement with the prospect of closer cooperation with the West?

Does Sharon have either the interest or the mandate to go beyond the previous positions of Israeli leaders in pursuit of a deal?

On Lebanon, nothing will happen bilaterally between Lebanon and Israel unless and until Syria gives its okay. After all, though the fact is largely and inexplicably ignored by the international community, Syria occupies and dominates Lebanon. Indeed, Syria does not even recognize the country's sovereign independence, which explains the absence of a Syrian embassy in Beirut. Further, Lebanon provides Syria with yet another front against Israel, whether through terrorism or in war, and it offers an outlet for up to 1 million Syrians to work and send remittances home.

Last spring, Israel, under Prime Minister Barak, withdrew unilaterally from its security zone in southern Lebanon. UN secretary-general Kofi Annan has confirmed that the withdrawal fulfills the requirements of UN Security Council Resolution 425, though the Lebanese and Syrians insist otherwise and continue to make noise in the UN.

Ominously, today it is the Iranian-backed Hezbollah, and not the Lebanese army, that controls the region. Recent events, such as occurred on April 14 when Hezbollah violated Resolution 425 and fired at an Israeli tank, killing one Israeli soldier and injuring three others, underscore quite dramatically the dangers posed by this terrorist group.

Interestingly, a number of diplomatic observers, including some in Europe, now wonder whether the call on Israel for unilateral withdrawal was right. Several Palestinian leaders of the current uprising cite the withdrawal as proof that what Arab armies could not do— namely, defeat Tzahal, the Israel Defense Forces—was accomplished by Hezbollah and can be replicated in the West Bank and Gaza, thus further fueling the violence there.

The late Yitzhak Rabin believed that Israel urgently needed to make peace with Syria and the Palestinians—if peace was possible—because of the looming threat from the outer perimeter, namely, Iraq and Iran. At best, peace with Israel's neighbors could persuade these regional powers to end their anti-Israel crusade; at the very least, Israel would be able to concentrate its military on the more distant threat without quite as much concern about its contiguous neighbors.

Today, Israel, but surely not Israel alone, faces a resurgent Iraqi threat. The German intelligence agency recently published its estimate that Iraq is three to six years away from producing a nuclear bomb with domestically enriched uranium. And while work proceeds on developing a nuclear bomb, Iraq is also devoting significant resources to biological and chemical weapons, as well as to its missile program, in order to achieve greater distance and precision than was the case with the Scud missiles launched in the 1991 Gulf War.

With no international inspection regime for two years now, and with many of the world's nations openly flouting the sanctions imposed on Iraq, the Iraqi danger cannot be easily disregarded. Or have we all forgotten the devastating eight-year war with Iran, the use of poison gas against Kurdish villages in Iraq, the occupation of Kuwait, and the missiles fired at Israel and Saudi Arabia?

Some were dismissive of the Iraqi threat in 1990, even though Saddam Hussein telegraphed his aggressive designs on Kuwait. Now Saddam Hussein, seeking to assert leadership in the Arab world, calls for war against Israel, which he threatens to destroy "from sea to sea," and once again looks longingly at Kuwait. Just bluster? Perhaps, but can we really afford to ignore or minimize it?

Apropos, there was a recent cartoon in the *New Yorker*, a prominent weekly magazine of culture and politics. It showed a patient after a medical exam asking his doctor: "Give it to me straight, Doc. How long do I have to ignore your advice?"

I pray that Western nations will not ignore the warning signs from Iraq, although watching the behavior of certain countries, I fear we are proving once again how little we sometimes learn from history.

The case of Iran is both similar and different. There is no question about Iran's ambitious programs to develop weapons of mass destruction, which have just been given another major boost, it appears, by Moscow. There is also no question about Iran's active financial and logistical support for international terrorism. And there certainly is no question about Iran's desire to export its brand of Shiite Islam to other countries.

Of course, what makes Iran different is the obvious desire for reform among an important segment of the population, especially youth, and the battle under way between fundamentalist and reformist elements for control. Sadly, the reins of real power continue to rest with the fundamentalists, though some in the West still delude themselves, largely to justify increased commercial ties.

How to contain Iraq at this late hour, and how to strengthen the forces of genuine reform in Iran, which are very much on the defensive, are two of the most significant policy challenges facing the international community today. Both will require courage, creative vision, and, needless to say, at least some degree of multilateral cooperation, if we are to have a chance of success.

Taking a longer-term view, however, I would like to believe that the nations in the region, one by one, sooner or later, will come to recognize, as did Egypt under the late Anwar Sadat, that peaceful development is not simply a political option but a strategic necessity.

And this was the very same Sadat, I might add, who, in 1970, stated: "Don't ask me to make diplomatic relations with [Israel]. Never. Never."* Yes, as I suggested at the outset, progress may not be preordained, but it certainly is possible.

The people of the Middle East deserve and are desperately in need of both peaceful development and progress.

Dr. Patrick Clawson, a Middle East expert, recently addressed this issue in a speech to the Middle East Forum:

> Economically, the Middle East is the odd man out in the world race to globalize. The region grew at only half the rate of other developing countries during the 1990s.... Its share of exports fell from 3.1 percent in 1990 to 1.9 percent in 1998.... The average number of Internet subscribers per 10,000 people in the United States is now 1,940; in the Middle East, it is just 0.6.... According to Freedom House, five of the world's eleven most repressive countries are members of the Arab League.... Arms constituted 14.5 percent of all Middle East imports versus a 1 percent average worldwide.

And Dr. Clawson's argument was reinforced by a journalist, Hazem Saghia, in the Arabic daily *Al-Hayat* two months ago:

> While the modern world is engaged in an unprecedented technological and communications revolution, we [in the Arab world] are busy with questions and concerns that belong to the Cold War era or to the time of the creation of independent [Arab] states in the 1940s or the first encounter between the Arab world and the West in the late nineteenth century.... Rarely does someone talk about the need to achieve invest-

---

* Quoted in Chrisopher Cerf and Victor Navasky, *The Experts Speak* (New York: Villard, 1998), p. 288.

ment, to stop the emigration of youth from the Arab world, about educating youth for the global economy, about freedom, about the status of women, etc.

In sum, the challenges and dangers facing the region are daunting and not likely to disappear anytime soon.

Regrettably, the points made by Clawson and Saghia are not echoed sufficiently in the Arab world, at least not yet, and, frankly, are not high enough on the agenda of Western nations in their bilateral and multilateral dealings with the countries of the region.

Over the years, while pressing for democracy, human rights, and market reform in Eastern Europe, Latin America, Asia, and Africa with some notable success, Western nations have been far more reluctant to do so in the Arab world. Why this inconsistency and double standard?

But Clawson and Saghia raise important issues that need to be confronted, not avoided, for they contain within them the essence of modernity and development, the prospect of regional cooperation and advancement, and an alluring alternative to the increasingly dangerous spirals of conflict and violence.

And, therefore, even as we follow the daily, troubling events on the ground in the Middle East, we should never, not for a moment, lose sight of, or stop working toward, the larger goal of a promising new era for all the nations and peoples of the region.

## Tribute to Denmark's Rescue of Jews
## U.S. House of Representatives
## Washington, D.C.
## May 2, 2001

There are some who contend that too much attention is paid to the men and women who rescued Jews during the Holocaust.

According to this line of thinking, those who saved Jews were few in number, certainly in relation to the overall population, and those who were saved were also few in number. Therefore, historical reality and imagery are distorted by focusing inordinately on this relatively rare phenomenon.

I beg to differ. It is precisely because the efforts to protect Jews were so limited that we need to understand better those who became involved. It is no exaggeration to say that if we can learn from these examples of exceptional moral and physical courage, then we offer a ray of hope for the future of our world.

As Sholem Asch, the Polish-born Yiddish writer, noted: "It is of the highest importance, not only to record and recount, both for ourselves and for the future, the evidence of human degradation, but side by side with it, to set forth evidence of human exaltation and nobility. Let the epic of heroic deeds of love, as opposed by those of hatred—of rescue, as opposed to destruction—bear equal witness to the unborn generations."[*]

This is precisely why the American Jewish Committee supported the groundbreaking research and publications of Pearl and Samuel Oliner into the nature of the altruistic personality during World War II.

The question is whether we human beings are capable of learning. On that single question may hinge nothing less than the future of mankind living on an increasingly crowded planet, practicing hundreds of different faiths, speaking countless languages, professing allegiance to some 200 flags, and exhibiting a wide range of skin colors.

Either we learn a sense of respect and responsibility for one another, or we are doomed to endless cycles of violence and conflict, in which apathy and indifference become the handmaidens of hatred and intolerance.

From an early age, I learned the story of Denmark's rescue of its Jewish population on the eve of the Nazi order to arrest and deport the Jews. It is a story I have taught my children.

It is an extraordinary story, and it is a unique story.

I have spoken with many Danes who participated in the nationwide effort to smuggle the Jews from Denmark to neighboring Sweden

---

[*] Quoted in Samuel P. Oliner, "Rescue of Jews During the Holocaust," in Michael Berenbaum and Abraham J. Peck, eds., *The Holocaust and History* (Bloomington: Indiana University Press, 1998), p. 678.

before they could fall into the clutches of the Nazi occupying forces. What most strikes me in each conversation is the genuine, not feigned, sense that there was nothing exceptional in what happened. The Danes have never called attention to their heroism. In fact, they modestly believe they were simply helping their neighbors who were in grave danger, and who wouldn't help a neighbor? After all, it was fellow Danes who were the target of the Nazi plan.

As Jorgen Jenk, a member of the Danish Resistance in World War II who later became a prominent international businessman, said in response to praise from Jewish organizations: "Of course we appreciate the gratitude, but please understand that these were our friends—the baker on the corner, the postman, the family down the street. We just couldn't let them down."

And that's the key, I believe. It was Danes helping Danes. It was neighbors helping neighbors. It was human beings helping fellow human beings. It was people with a clear sense of right and wrong exercising what Jean Piaget, the child development expert, called their "autonomous" morality.

The Jews weren't seen as the other, the outsider, the alien. No, they were regarded as part and parcel of Danish society, citizens who happened to attend a different house of worship and had a different holiday calendar, neither of which posed a threat nor undermined the sense of well-being of the majority population.

And if a very clear majority, though by no means all, of the Danish people felt this way toward the Jews, this attitude couldn't have developed overnight. It must have evolved over time.

Surely, it was reflected in the way Danish political leaders spoke about the nation and national identity.

Surely, it was reflected in the way Danish religious leaders talked about other faiths and the need to practice, not just preach, ethical behavior.

Surely, it was reflected in the way the Danish school system inculcated civic values in generations of children.

And surely it was reflected in the way families raised their children in a spirit of compassion for all people and a sense of personal responsibility for the society in which they lived.

To seek to understand the valiant Danish rescue, then, is to come to grips with the essence of the individual, the place of family, the role of schools, the meaning of faith, the nature of society, and the definition of leadership.

With this in mind, the American Jewish Committee was proud to have merged earlier this year with Thanks To Scandinavia, the distinguished organization founded in 1963 by the late musician and entertainer Victor Borge and New York attorney Richard Netter. The aim of Thanks To Scandinavia is precisely to keep alive the memory of rescue and protection, to teach the lessons of history, and to honor Scandinavians by providing educational scholarships for future generations.

Finally, to borrow a phrase from Vaclav Havel, the distinguished president of the Czech Republic, we live in a "contaminated moral environment." He was referring to those who lived under communism, but in a way these words are also apt to describe the larger world in which we live.

The Danish experience looms ever present as the archetypal model for strengthening our moral environment and as a constant challenge to the temptations of comfort, complacency, and inaction.

It allows us to believe that William Faulkner was right when he said, on the occasion of receiving the Nobel Prize for literature in 1950: "I decline to accept the end of man. It is easy enough to say that man is immortal simply because he will endure…. I believe that man will not merely endure; he will prevail. He is immortal, not because he alone among creatures has an inexhaustible voice, but because he has a soul, a spirit capable of compassion and sacrifice and endurance."

The actions of those heroic Danes during the war vividly remind us that the human "soul" and "spirit capable of compassion and sacrifice and endurance" were not entirely indifferent to the "silent screams," as Nobel laureate Elie Wiesel phrased it, of those marked for extermination.

And for that glimmer of humanity, that divine spark, we shall be eternally grateful.

## The American Jewish Committee at 95
### AJC 95th Annual Dinner
### Washington, D.C.
### May 3, 2001

President Bush, [Mexican] President Fox, [Israeli] Foreign Minister Peres, [German] Foreign Minister Fischer, Bruce Ramer—AJC's outstanding president these past three years—distinguished guests, ladies and gentlemen:

You join us as we proudly mark the ninety-fifth anniversary of this great organization.

It was the persecution of Jews in czarist Russia that prompted a number of prominent American Jews to attend a meeting in New York in 1906. And out of that meeting was born the American Jewish Committee.

Through ninety-five years of tumultuous global history, the American Jewish Committee has never wavered in its mission to ensure the well-being and security of Jews in a world respectful of democratic values, human rights, and mutual understanding.

We have witnessed the Jewish people's darkest hour during those ninety-five years, the Holocaust, and we have witnessed its finest, the birth of the State of Israel.

Yes, we have witnessed the gamut—the peril and the promise, the darkness and the light.

And as we move ahead along the journey, we have found, as the painter Marc Chagall once said, "Life makes one laugh and cry at the very same time."

On the one hand, there are challenges aplenty.

Israel's quest for a secure and lasting peace sadly remains incomplete. Tonight we reaffirm our steadfast commitment to Israel, never more so than during these difficult times, as well as our dedication to strengthening still further the unique bilateral ties that bind Washington and Jerusalem.

We were painfully reminded once again of the dangers to Jews when this past fall a shocking wave of anti-Semitic threats and assaults was documented in a number of Western countries, most especially France.

Living in Europe this year, my family, including our children, have had the misfortune of experiencing this resurgent hatred personally.

The AJC stands, as we have always stood, in solidarity with fellow Jews wherever they live.

We will not stand idle—how could we?—while nine Jews remain unjustly imprisoned in Iranian jails on trumped-up charges.

Nor can we forget the four Israelis kidnapped by Hezbollah last fall and not heard from since.

We are appalled by those who would distort or even laud the Holocaust—the focus of full-page ads we placed in the *New York Times* and *Washington Post* this week—and, equally, by those who would deny the Jewish people's biblical, historical, and spiritual link to Israel and the city of Jerusalem.

We remain profoundly concerned by the determined efforts of Iran and Iraq—two countries that openly call for Israel's annihilation—to acquire weapons of mass destruction and the means to deliver them.

We vigorously applaud the democratic revolution that has swept through large parts of the world. But too many governments are still maintained by the bullet, not the ballot, and it is precisely those undemocratic regimes that pose the gravest threat to human rights and peace.

And the often daunting task of promoting harmonious relations among the world's many religions, races, and nationalities remains with us, both within countries and across borders.

Yet, on the other hand, we can take heart from the remarkable human progress we've been privileged to witness, and from the age-old Jewish belief that better days lie ahead, if only we dedicate ourselves to their realization.

Was it Yogi Berra who once said, "The future ain't what is used to be"?

In fact, the future holds great promise, and this evening suggests why.

The United States, under the leadership of President Bush, remains a powerful force for democracy and decency, and all I can say is thank goodness for this great country. America has always defined itself as a permanent work in progress, and that work only gets better and better.

Mexico has turned an important corner in its history with the election of President Fox, and its recent political, economic, and social development has been impressive.

Germany has, over the past half century, become a model democratic nation and an indispensable partner for the State of Israel. Foreign Minister Fischer is both a reflection and a leader of today's dynamic Germany.

And Israel has defied all the odds. It has become a metaphor for the triumph of hope over despair. No one understands this better than Shimon Peres, who has played a leading role in Israel's remarkable saga from 1948 until the present day.

Could the American Jewish Committee's founders have ever envisioned an occasion such as this dinner? Probably not in their wildest dreams. But surely they would have been thrilled to see the results of their efforts.

The tree they so wisely planted ninety-five years ago has grown tall and proud and, as with any healthy tree, we, the American Jewish Committee, draw strength and nourishment from its deep roots.

As our tradition teaches us, just as previous generations planted for us, so must we plant for the generations to come. And you can be sure that we will.


## A Brief Strategic Look at Israel and the Jewish People in the International System
## Second Herzliya Conference
## Israel
## December 16, 2001

President Katsav [of Israel], General Gilboa, Professors Uriel Reichman and Ehud Sprinzak, our chairman, Dr. Uzi Arad, and distinguished guests:

The American Jewish Committee is honored once again to cosponsor this important gathering, and I am delighted to be with you this evening, just as I was privileged to participate in last year's inaugural conference.

It's traditional for American speakers to lead off with a joke, seemingly regardless of the subject matter or the circumstances, but you'll be pleased to know that I've decided not to do so.

After all, as the story goes, when you tell a joke to a peasant, he laughs three times—once when you tell the joke, the second time when you explain it, and the third time when he understands it.

But when you tell a joke to a Jew, even before you've had the chance to finish it, he's already interrupting you—first, because he's heard it before and wants you to know it; second, because he thinks you're not telling it well; and third, because *he* decides to tell you the joke, but in a much better version than yours.

So, no jokes for this audience; it's simply too risky.

On a more serious note, to state the painfully obvious, a great deal has transpired since last December's conference, more than any of us could have envisioned. We meet while the United States is leading a war against terrorism and while Israel seeks to defend itself against repeated and heinous acts of terror.

Therefore, our meeting during these three days becomes all the more timely and important.

I begin with a very simple and hopefully self-evident proposition: The Jews of the world need one another, we depend on one another; never more so than during turbulent times such as these. From our unity and solidarity comes strength. Conversely, from our disunity and division comes weakness. To some, this may sound hopelessly naive, born of an idealism still deeply rooted in America's soil; perhaps so, but it remains central to my strategic view of the world.

In saying this, I recognize fully, and always have, the profound imbalance in responsibility and risk shouldered by Israelis and Diaspora Jews.

Still, Jewish communities around the world continue to have an important role to play in advancing Israel's national interests in the international system.

Nowhere is this more evident than in the United States. As I noted here last year, American Jewry is an indispensable factor in the American-Israeli equation. Consequently, it is in our collective interest to ensure the continued resilience and standing of American Jewry.

Conversely, anything that serves to weaken American Jewish strength and resolve will ultimately diminish the U.S.-Israeli bilateral relationship, which in turn could only have catastrophic long-term consequences for Israel's diplomatic, security, and other vital interests.

Other Jewish communities also serve important roles in buttressing support for Israel in their respective countries.

Significantly, this is not necessarily a function of a community's size. After all, there is no Diaspora community in the world today where Jews constitute more than 2 percent—or one in fifty—of the population. And in virtually every case, Jewish numbers, both in actual and proportional terms, are at best static and more often in decline.

A community of no more than a few thousand Jews in, say, Costa Rica or Panama, however, has been able to play an influential role, well beyond its actual size, in enhancing Israel's standing and image. Why?

The simple answer is that members of the community integrated well into the fabric of the country, contributed significantly to all the major sectors from economy to culture, took an active interest in political life, and were unhesitating about placing concern for Israel at the top of their agenda, without—let me stress this as emphatically as I can—taking sides in Israel's internal political debates.

Thus, from a strategic perspective, rather than bemoan our thin numbers, I take as my starting point the remarkable success of Jews in virtually every Diaspora country, and the possibilities this indisputable reality continues to present for reaching the highest level of policy-makers and affecting public opinion.

I continue to believe that advocates for Israel in world capitals have a powerful case to make. It is built on four solid legs.

The first leg is that Israel is a democracy. It is self-evident to us, no doubt, but too often overlooked in places it shouldn't be. That celebration of democratic values must always be made to count for something in the corridors of power of other democracies.

The precious fraternity of democratic nations needs to remain mutually respectful and supportive. And due recognition must be given to the undeniable fact that democratic governments reflect the will of the governed, and if they don't, then there are mechanisms available for peaceful transition.

Israel stands out in this region as a uniquely democratic state, with all the attributes of such a state, and we need to remind the world of this central fact again and again, all the more so after September 11.

We need to state unequivocally: Those who stand with Israel stand for democracy, and those who stand for democracy should stand with Israel. This is not to argue for an Israel-right-or-wrong policy, but it is to call for a clear and unambiguous demarcation between democracies and dictatorships.

The second leg is Israel's unquenchable thirst for peace and a concomitant willingness to make painful—and risky—compromises to achieve that often elusive peace.

This began with acceptance of the United Nations Partition Plan in 1947 and continued through earlier this year, when Prime Minister Barak and President Clinton still hoped to strike an historic peace deal with an ultimately unwilling Chairman Arafat. But just as it takes two to conceive a child, so it takes two to conceive a peace. The world cannot expect Israel either to make peace in a dangerous vacuum or, for that matter, to negotiate peace in earnest with a partner whose very commitment and integrity are seriously in doubt.

The third leg is Israel's legitimate right to defend its citizens against acts of violence and terror, a right that all nations reserve and many exercise.

No nation can be expected to demonstrate infinite self-restraint, least of all in a region where such a posture is interpreted as a sign of weakness, not strength. The United States has certainly learned this lesson in recent months. Why should Israel be expected to behave differently?

The fourth leg is the unique historical connection among a land—Israel; a people—the Jewish people; a faith—Judaism; a language—Hebrew; and a vision—Zionism. As a result of recent events in the Middle East, we have been compelled to return to fundamentals, to remind the world of the basic case for Israel's very legitimacy and right to exist. No other country in the world, fifty-three years after its establishment, finds itself in an even remotely similar situation, yet that cannot deter us from the vital task at hand.

Whatever has been done to date, and it has been a great deal, world Jewry must be mobilized in a sophisticated and systematic manner, as a matter of the highest priority, to build increased support for Israel and understanding of its truly unenviable policy challenges and dilemmas, whichever way it turns. And Israel itself has a much greater role than it has heretofore played in helping mount such a mobilization.

Those Diaspora communities that until now have hesitated to jump into the fray for a variety of psychological, sociological, and historical reasons—more often than not related to their skittish sense of national place and identity—need somehow to overcome these hurdles and be heard clearly in the Middle East debate.

As the nineteenth-century French writer Victor Hugo said, "Nothing is so irresistible as an idea whose time has come."

In this regard, I was pleased to see as but one example the recent intensified efforts of the German Jewish community in taking out full-page ads in leading newspapers to protest the visit to Berlin of Syrian president Assad and in vigorously making the case for Israel in the electronic and print media. This is a welcome development.

Of course, the challenge of defending Israel around the world must not rest solely on the shoulders of world Jewry. It never has, nor should it today.

But we have some serious challenges. Let me briefly mention a few.

First, we have lost many of our traditional nongovernmental coalition partners.

Some have chosen the path of least resistance and retreated to a form of studied neutrality; others have opted to join the chorus of critics of Israel. The reasons could fill a separate speech. Suffice it to say that we need to pay more attention to this arena, including encouraging the creation of new nongovernmental groups supportive of Israel. NGOs are key actors in the international system today, and their voices carry considerable weight in areas ranging from human rights to the environment. Thus, we ignore them at our peril.

I witnessed firsthand the magnitude of our isolation this past year in Geneva when I testified twice at the United Nations in support of Israel and against pernicious resolutions submitted by Arab countries. In both cases, literally dozens of NGOs—some legitimate, others transparently state-sponsored front groups—rose to assail Israel, while friends could literally be counted on the fingers of one hand.

We need to take into account not only the impact of heavy lobbying of NGOs by Arab and other Muslim nations, but also the growing role of anti-Israel Arab and Muslim groups based in the West. These groups have energetically sought to build alliances with labor unions, student groups, antiglobalization forces, and other religious and ethnic communities to further their political objectives pertaining to the Middle East.

This campaign of intense lobbying and coalition-building is clearly evident in the United States, even as many of these groups scramble to reinvent themselves after September 11, revise their Web sites to remove potentially incriminating information, and seek to explain how they could have brazenly claimed a population figure of 6-8 million Muslims in the United States, when two recent authoritative academic studies, one sponsored by the American Jewish Committee and conducted at the University of Chicago, found the actual number to be in the range of 2 million.

Second, some of the moral icons who understood so clearly the trajectory of Jewish history in the twentieth century, and who believed so profoundly, not only in Israel's right to exist but also its absolute need to exist, are no longer with us. Giants like Andrei Sakharov, the Reverend Martin Luther King, Jr., Senator Henry Jackson, Jan Karski, Father Benjamin Nunez, and Indro Montanelli—powerful and respected voices in their own countries and on the world scene—have passed away, and their places are not easily taken.

Third, a new generation of politicians has emerged around the world, whose formative years were the 1960s and 1970s. They were eyewitnesses neither to the Shoah nor to Israel's birth and early struggle for survival. Instead, they came of age when Israel was in possession of the West Bank and Gaza, and when, absent a thorough grasp of history, it could sometimes be difficult to sort out competing claims in a tableau that appeared very simplistically to pit Israel as the occupier and the Palestinians as the occupied.

Fourth, at the risk of stating the obvious, the role of the media has continued to grow as an actor in the international system in the past decade. No serious discussion of national security can take place today without due reference to the emergence of the media as a major factor not only in heavily shaping public opinion, but also in profoundly affecting governments' decision-making.

As a related aside, I cannot help but wonder whether the course of history might have been changed had the *New York Times*, America's most influential newspaper, treated the Holocaust differently. Last month (November 14), Max Frankel, the paper's former executive editor, revealed the following startling facts about the *Times*'s failure to report and condemn Hitler's extermination of the Jews:

> Only six times in nearly six years did the *Times*'s front page mention Jews as Hitler's unique target for total annihilation. Only once was their fate the subject of a lead editorial. Only twice did their rescue inspire passionate cries in the Sunday magazine.

More than five decades later, however, whether we always like it or not, Jews are news.

Thus, I'm pleased that the subject of the media has been added to the agenda this year and will be addressed in detail in the coming days.

As one who has dealt extensively with both electronic and print media in Europe and the United States, I know how rough things can be when it comes to Israel, but I also know that the situation is not hopeless, though it may sometimes appears to be. We simply cannot afford to abandon our efforts to press for balanced coverage of the Middle East; the stakes are too high, and at the end of the day, we must never forget that we are in possession of the ultimate weapon—the facts.

Fifth, the power of the Holocaust to affect understanding of Jewish vulnerability and the consequent need for a strong and viable Jewish state has diminished in recent years.

Again, this is a complicated subject, requiring more careful examination, but what has been striking for me, especially in Europe, is the growing inability to connect the experience of the Shoah with the contemporary history of world Jewry and Israel. Instead, many now see the Holocaust as a discrete event in history—to be remembered and memorialized, yes, but, in a subtle way, to be sequestered.

Thus, the foreign minister of a European country could in one breath speak of his country's many efforts to restitute stolen property and examine its less-than-laudable wartime record, but in the next breath largely dismiss concerns about documented acts of violence against Jews in his country and defend his decision to participate in the reconvening of the high contracting parties to the Fourth Geneva Convention, even if the gathering was a blatantly anti-Israel exercise, and the convention itself was drafted as a direct response to the tragedy of the Second World War.

If the Holocaust has not adequately sensitized this top diplomat either to the slippery slope of anti-Semitism or to the dangers of treating Israel, the Jewish state, by an entirely separate standard than all other nations, then what hope is there?

On the subject of violence against Jews, here, too, we must become more vigilant and supportive of one another. Once again, the interdependence of our fates has been revealed.

The Palestinians trigger violence here, and Jewish targets are attacked with abandon in France.

Bin Laden seeks Israel's destruction as part of his larger demonology and declares war on "Jews and Crusaders."

Barbara Spinelli, writing in the pages of *La Stampa*, one of Italy's most respected newspapers, calls on Jews around the world to beg forgiveness for Israel's "original sin" of disenfranchising the Palestinians, and Jews throughout Italy shudder as a national debate ensues, with several prominent left-of-center politicians supporting Spinelli.

The Arab students' group at New York University, seeking to cast blame on Israel for September 11, circulates to its members a diatribe by David Duke, a notorious extreme right-winger connected with the anti-Semitic Ku Klux Klan.

A prominent imam in New York disappears after September 11 and resurfaces in Egypt, to assert that Jewish doctors are poisoning Muslims in the United States and presumably to join in the unremitting, if little publicized, effort to Islamicize the Arab world's leading country.

Yes, a great deal has happened since last December's conference.

We have new administrations in power in Washington and Jerusalem, and may I add that the Bush administration has been quite remarkable in its steady support for Israel, confounding the skeptics who thought we would likely see a repeat of the sometimes cool and detached first Bush administration with regard to Israel.

We have had a seemingly endless number of brutal terrorist attacks against Israeli civilian targets, and, in response, the recent Israeli decision to break off contact with Arafat and the PA.

We have witnessed the dismaying buildup to the Durban gathering, the inaptly named World Conference Against Racism, and the eruption at the parallel NGO forum of unadulterated anti-Semitism, the likes of which have not been seen for a very long time.

We have had other disturbing manifestations of anti-Semitism, most notably in France, home to the world's third-largest Jewish community.

We have experienced the horrific events of September 11 and the subsequent American decision to wage war on terrorism, beginning, but most certainly not ending, with Osama bin Laden, Al Qaeda, and the Taliban.

We have seen European and other countries crack down on real and potential terrorist networks on their own soil, a step that many countries had been reluctant to take prior to September 11.

We have learned exactly what is being taught in some schools in the Muslim world, and it turns out that the material is overflowing with contempt for our very existence as non-Muslims.

Jewish organizations around the world need to grapple with the manifold implications of recent events from a geostrategic perspective and seek the appropriate role they can play in helping to foster new foreign policy opportunities to:

- build renewed international support for Israel in Europe, Latin America, Africa, and Asia;
- quarantine more effectively terrorist-sponsoring countries;
- bolster moderate nations that have hitherto been targets of radical Islam;
- strengthen long-term international cooperation in the war against terrorism;

- slow down the ominous prospect of proliferation of weapons of mass destruction;
- encourage greater energy independence in oil-importing countries like the United States;
- and expose the hypocrisy of those countries that cunningly seek to play off the West against the Islamists.

This is a moment rife with opportunity, even as we dare not underestimate the perils.

In this spirit, President John Kennedy once remarked: "When written in Chinese, the word 'crisis' is composed of two characters. One represents danger and the other represents opportunity."

Jewish communities can and must play an important part in seizing the moment and helping shape the emerging world order.

In times such as these, it is all the more important to have an active dialogue between Israel and the Diaspora, far more extensive than we currently have.

Putting our heads together, the total becomes far greater than the sum of its parts; working separately, the total becomes far less. To me, the choice is obvious.


A World Changed Forever?
Berlin, Germany
December 4, 2001


On September 11, the United States was attacked in an act of war. More people were killed than on December 7, 1941, the day that Japan bombed Pearl Harbor. Indeed, more people were killed on September 11 than in America's Revolutionary War against Britain.

I applaud President Bush, his administration, and the bipartisan leadership of the U.S. Congress for the steady, steely, and deliberate way they have gone about organizing our nation's response on both the military and nonmilitary levels.

Those who feared that the United States would act precipitately, lashing out in blind rage, were wrong, just as were those who predicted that the United States would meet the same fate in Afghanistan as the British and Soviets before them—though I wouldn't underestimate the challenges ahead for Washington and the international community.

Bending over backward to avoid being lured into the trap of a war on Islam, the United States carefully formulated its response and covered all the bases—NATO, the European Union, the UN Security Council and General Assembly, key allies around the world, including those in the Middle East and Central and South Asia, and, of course, Russia, with which we now have a promising new bilateral relationship.

The United States has pursued the military campaign with remarkable precision. Overwhelming air power, specially trained forces, high-tech weaponry, sophisticated intelligence-gathering capacity, and local forces opposed to the Taliban have come together in a remarkable way to bring about the Taliban's collapse far more quickly than anyone might have predicted.

I also wish to acknowledge those nations that have not hesitated to stand with America in its hour of need. Difficult times like these remind us very clearly who our real friends are and on whom we can count, whether for diplomatic support or military assistance.

In this regard, permit me, on behalf of the American Jewish Committee, to express profound admiration to the German government, and in particular to Chancellor Schroeder, Foreign Minister Fischer, and Defense Minister Scharping. They have been principled and unwavering in leading this country into a new era of international engagement and, in so doing, underscoring the unshakable bonds that link our two nations.

There have also been many moving and deeply appreciated expressions of support from the German public, including pro-American demonstrations, full-page advertisements in American newspapers, and solidarity visits to New York.

For those of us who have attended too many funerals, who have seen a huge gaping hole created in the landscape of our city, who have had to comfort and reassure our children, and who have had to take a crash course in bioterrorism—including learning about the difference between inhalation and skin anthrax—the sense that others stand with us is terribly important, more than I might ever have thought.

At the same time, some in Germany and other European countries have suggested that America somehow brought this calamity upon itself, and there are those who have taken to the streets to protest American-led military action. While I certainly respect their right to do so, such people, I believe, have failed to learn the central lessons of the twentieth century.

There is such a thing in human nature as unadulterated evil. Left unchallenged, that evil can wreak unimaginable death and destruction. In the face of such evil, therefore, the politics of appeasement, the culture of moral equivalency, and the spirit of so-called forgiveness are not only doomed to failure but, even worse, can serve as recipes for self-destruction.

On an uplifting note, let me share with you a touching story about German-American friendship that recently came to my attention.

An American naval officer aboard the USS *Winston Churchill*, a guided-missile destroyer, sent an E-mail to his father. Here is an excerpt:

Dear Dad,

About two hours ago, we were hailed by a German navy destroyer, the *Lutjens*, requesting permission to pass close by our port side.... As she came alongside us, we saw the American flag flying half-mast and her entire crew topside standing at silent, rigid attention in their dress uniforms. They had made a sign that was displayed on her side that read, "We stand by you."

There was not a dry eye on our bridge as they stood alongside for a few minutes and saluted.

The German navy did an incredible thing for this crew, and it has truly been the highest point in the days since the attack.

It's amazing to think that only a half-century ago things were quite different.

Your loving son.

As we speak about September 11 and its aftermath, let's not forget that these horrific events—which caught our nation totally by surprise, shattering the comforting illusion that the blessings of power and geog-

raphy could somehow insulate America from such a daring assault—
didn't come from out of the blue. There is a history, which we dare not
ignore.

We would need to go back quite far in time to understand what this
is all about—difficult, if not impossible, though it may be for those of
us from outside the region who are unfamiliar with the languages and
cultures.

We would need to explore basic precepts of Islam. For example,
Professor Bernard Lewis of Princeton University, a leading scholar of
the Middle East, recently wrote:

> One of the basic tasks bequeathed to Muslims by the Prophet
> [Muhammad] was jihad. This word, which literally means "striving,"
> was interpreted to mean armed struggle for the defense or advancement
> of Muslim power. In principle, the world was divided into two houses:
> the House of Islam, in which a Muslim government ruled and Muslim
> law prevailed, and the House of War, the rest of the world, still inhabit-
> ed and, more important, ruled by infidels. Between the two, there was
> to be a perpetual state of war until the entire world either embraced
> Islam or submitted to the rule of the Muslim state. (*New Yorker*,
> November 19, 2001)

We would need to understand the pride in the Muslim world for its
extraordinary contributions to science, medicine, and culture during
the medieval period, which turned into bitterness and recrimination as
this world began to decline and the Western world started its rapid
ascent.

We would need to grasp the significance of certain important historical events, among them:
- the military victory of Saladin over the Crusaders in the twelfth
  century;
- the expulsion of the Moors from Spain in the fifteenth century;
- the defeat of the Ottomans at Vienna's doorstep in the seven-
  teenth century;
- the founding in the eighteenth century of Wahhabism, the deeply
  conservative Muslim doctrine that today dominates Saudi Arabia
  and that has been actively exported by the Saudis as well;

- the collapse of the Ottoman Empire just after World War I;
- the historic revolution launched by Ataturk to create a modern, Western-oriented state in Turkey beginning shortly thereafter;
- the record of European colonialism in North Africa and the Middle East;
- the creation of the Muslim Brotherhood in Ismaila, Egypt, in 1928, the brainchild of Hassan al-Banna, whose dream, according to Middle East expert Judith Miller, was "to build an Islamic society with neither Western democracy nor a constitution but with *sharia*, the Koran-given law of God";
- the impact of the discovery of oil in Saudi Arabia in the 1930s;
- the ideology of Sayyid Qutb, a firebrand leader of the Muslim Brotherhood in Egypt in the 1960s and, according to Professor Fouad Ajami, a highly regarded scholar of the Middle East, "the true ideological father of modern Islamic militancy";
- and, not least, the Arab humiliation when a determined population of only 650,000 Jews defeated the armies of five Arab states in Israel's 1948 War of Independence, and as Israel continued successfully to defend itself against Arab aggression in the decades thereafter.

But let's fast-forward and pick up the thread of history in 1979, a crucial year in the Middle East that had direct impact on the period that followed.

It was in 1979 that the pro-Western shah of Iran lost his grip on power and was forced to flee, paving the way for the imposition of anti-Western clerical rule that branded America as the "Great Satan."

It was in that same year that Egypt and Israel signed a historic peace treaty. Let's recall that, with the exception of Oman and Sudan, the Arab League subjected Egypt to isolation in the Arab bloc because of that treaty, and that President Sadat was assassinated by Egyptian Islamic Jihad in October 1981.

Less well remembered, it was also in 1979 that religious extremists, drawn from various Arab countries, briefly took over the Great Mosque in Mecca, with the declared aim of "purifying Islam" and "liberating the holy land of Arabia from the royal 'clique of infidels,'" according to Professor Lewis.

And it was in that same year that the Soviet Union brazenly invaded Afghanistan, launching a long and bloody war that drew Arab volunteers alongside the Afghan mujahideen in an ultimately successful jihad against the "infidel" invaders.

Among the results of the war in Afghanistan were two especially important developments.

First, thousands of Arab volunteers received a first-class education in guerrilla warfare, which they were only too eager to apply in other "jihad" situations. And second, the defeat of one of the world's two superpowers emboldened the mujahideen and their Arab allies to believe that God was on their side and that nothing, not even the world's strongest superpower, the United States, could ever stop them.

In 1983, a suicide terrorist attack against the U.S. Marine headquarters in Beirut, widely believed to be the work of Hezbollah, resulted in the deaths of 241 American military personnel. The American response? President Reagan ordered a hasty retreat from Lebanon.

In 1993, two terrorist events of particular importance occurred, one in Somalia, the other in New York.

In Mogadishu, eighteen American soldiers were killed. The attackers were subsequently linked to Osama bin Laden. The American response? President Clinton ordered our troops' evacuation from Somalia.

And in New York, an attempt was made to topple one of the World Trade Center towers. Six people were killed and many more were injured. The perpetrators—and their spiritual gurus—came from the same pool of fanatics driven by Islamic radicalism. The American response? Successful investigative work tracked down the attackers and led to their convictions in the courts, but there was a notable failure to come to grips fully with the broader network that saw American targets at home and abroad as fair game.

According to Milton Bearden, a former top CIA official, writing in the prestigious journal *Foreign Affairs* (November/December 2001), Sudan, then housing bin Laden, offered to expel him in 1995-96. The United States, though, wouldn't take him because officials feared that they couldn't mount a successful legal case. The Saudis, who were also given the chance, wouldn't touch him for fear of creating domestic turmoil. In 1996, then, bin Laden was expelled from Sudan and moved on to safe haven in Afghanistan, which came under Taliban rule the same year.

In 1995 and 1996, there were deadly terrorist attacks against U.S. servicemen in Saudi Arabia, attributed to radical Islamic groups that opposed any U.S. presence in this land, the home of Islam's two holiest sites.

In 1998, there were more suicide attacks linked to bin Laden, this time against the American embassies in Nairobi and Dar es Salaam, resulting in the deaths of 224 Americans and local residents, and injuries to 5,000. The American response? A one-time volley of missiles fired at terrorist training camps in Afghanistan and an attack on a single pharmaceutical factory suspected of producing chemical weapons in Sudan.

That same year, 1998, bin Laden issued his Declaration of the World Islamic Front against the Jews and the Crusaders, calling "on every Muslim ... to kill the Americans and plunder their possessions." At the time, his words weren't taken seriously enough in the West.

In 2000 came the attack on the USS *Cole,* the American naval ship in the port of Aden, which resulted in the deaths of seventeen American sailors. Again, bin Laden was the presumed mastermind.

All these terrorist attacks set the stage for the calamitous events of September 11.

It is typical for some members of what we in America call the punditocracy, or the chattering class, to appear after the fact and confidently explain events and patterns that they missed entirely while these events and patterns were actually taking place.

We at the American Jewish Committee did not foresee the tragedy of September 11, but for years we had been alerting our government— and other Western governments—about the dangers posed by the radical Islamic terrorist network, and the consequent need for greater coordination and consistency in facing the challenge. Anything less, we argued, would inevitably be perceived as weakness and lack of national will.

We had been warning Western governments that Islamic radicals, often expelled from their own lands, were taking advantage of our democratic freedoms to settle, study, raise funds, and plot violent attacks on countries friendly to us, such as Egypt, Israel, Jordan, Tunisia, and Turkey.

And we had stressed that terrorist groups do not operate in a vacuum. To survive, much less train and organize, they need sanctuaries. Those havens were provided by the Taliban, which received vital assistance over the past five years from Saudi Arabia, the United Arab Emirates, and especially Pakistan. Without that aid, it's not clear if the Taliban would have survived. But few nations seemed genuinely eager to press these three countries to end their support for the Taliban before September 11.

It doesn't stop there. According to the U.S. State Department, there are seven countries in the world that sponsor terrorism, five of them in North Africa and the Middle East. They are Libya, Sudan, Syria, Iran, and Iraq, to which I would add Lebanon, because of the state-within-a-state that Hezbollah has created in southern Lebanon; Yemen, which traditionally has harbored terrorist groups, a policy that only now appears to be under review; and Somalia, a chaotic country known to be hospitable to bin Laden and Al Qaeda.

The West, including the nations of the European Union, must do more to make these sponsors of terrorism rethink their policies.

The leading state sponsors, however, have calculated that they can have it both ways. They can take advantage of the all-too-frequent Western need for energy and export markets, the political and economic competition among Western nations, and the Western self-delusion that such engagement, ipso facto, brings reform, all the while continuing their support for terrorism.

Take the case of Syria. Damascus is home to at least ten identifiable terrorist groups. Damascus airport is the intermediary point for weapons flown from Iran and destined for Hezbollah terrorist units in Lebanon. Syrian troops continue to occupy Lebanon and refuse to recognize the country's national sovereignty, which explains the absence of a Syrian embassy in Beirut. And Syria's leader publicly uttered vile anti-Semitic remarks during the visit of the pope earlier this year.

Yet President Assad believes that he can maintain these policies and, simultaneously, be well received in world capitals.

Tragically, he may not be wrong. I was in Paris earlier this year when the red carpet was rolled out for him on a state visit, on the eve of which *Le Figaro* (June 23-24, 2001), one of France's leading newspapers, described him, with a straight face, as the "elected" leader of his country. And in New York a few months later, UN member states overwhelmingly endorsed Syria for a two-year term on the powerful Security Council.

In other words, the threat posed by international terrorism includes but goes well beyond Osama bin Laden and Al Qaeda. We would be utterly naive to think otherwise, to believe that the crushing of the Taliban, and even the hoped-for capture of bin Laden, will allow us to return to a comforting complacency.

Permit me to engage in the Washington political habit of quoting myself.

In June 1999, at a public meeting in New York, here's what I said on the subject of terrorism:

> My nightmare scenario is really made up of four elements. First, I worry about countries like Iran and Iraq, which are hell-bent on acquiring weapons of mass destruction.
>
> The second element is the collapse of the Soviet Union. Don't get me wrong; the collapse is good news.... What is bad, though, is that we now have hundreds of thousands of scientists, engineers, and technicians who are underemployed, if not unemployed.... Some, at least, are going to be vulnerable to tantalizing offers from outside—offers to move abroad, to look the other way while material is being taken, to assist with valuable information.
>
> Third, Russia today, to a large degree, is dominated by organized crime, and organized crime does not live by a code of ethics, at least not ours. The prospect of outsiders seeking to acquire individual talents or material via the organized crime network—or conversely, the network looking for prospective buyers—makes this scenario frighteningly realistic.
>
> And fourth, recall the Sarin attack by followers of the Aum Shinrikyo cult in a Tokyo subway in March 1995. Twelve people were killed and 5,000 were hospitalized. And disaster workers in Japan said that the toll could have been far worse.

What happens when you have determined and single-minded individuals, ad hoc groups, or organized groups, who want to wreak havoc and, in doing so, call attention to their cause? We have seen the results in Tokyo, Nairobi, and Dar es Salaam, at the World Trade Center, and in Oklahoma City.

Who can preclude the possibility that this threat will only get worse with the growing availability of technology and weaponry? If even two of these elements, much less three or four, come together, what kind of challenges will we have to face in the years ahead?

Well, now we certainly have a much better idea of the challenges we must face, so what can we do about them?

(1) As I said earlier, we can never again afford complacency. The threat of terror in all its horrific possibilities will be with us for a very long time to come. It will require constant vigilance, with emphasis on effective intelligence and prevention techniques and sustained multilateral cooperation.

(2) The threat is global. America may be the principal target at the moment, but it is not the only one. Germany understands well the transnational threat posed by terrorism. In two major terrorism trials in this country, the Iranian and Libyan intelligence services have been directly implicated. And, as investigators learn more about the planning for September 11, we see just how many countries were in one way or another extensively used by the plotters, including, of course, Germany. Hamburg's Marienstrasse 54 has now become a well-known address for you and us.

Al Qaeda operatives have established themselves in literally dozens of countries, and Al Qaeda is only one of several groups we need to be concerned about. There are an estimated 5,000 or more "graduates" from fifty countries who have passed through bin Laden's training camps in Afghanistan, and thousands of others have attended different camps. Many Taliban supporters—be they Afghan, Pakistani, or Arab—will try to escape to neighboring countries and then eventually link up once again with the terrorist network.

Ominously, these "holy warriors" have wider support. To cite just one example, *Le Figaro* reported (October 16, 2001) on a Gallup poll in Pakistan that found that "82 percent of the respondents consider bin Laden not a terrorist but a hero of holy war."

(3) Those nations that continue to harbor terrorist groups, often justifying their actions by making false distinctions between "good" and "bad" terrorism, must be made to understand that they will no longer be allowed to get away with such state policy.

It will be especially important to see what comes in future stages of the Bush administration's promised multiphase war on terrorism, especially concerning Iraq, a country very much on the minds of American political and military leaders for understandable reasons.

And speaking of Iraq, doesn't the world owe Israel a long overdue debt of gratitude for having destroyed the Osirak nuclear reactor in 1981? Just imagine for a moment how the strategic calculus would look today—or, for that matter, how it might have looked in 1990 when Iraq occupied Kuwait—had Iraq been able to proceed with nuclear development at the site.

(4) We must make a distinction between Islam, one of the world's great religions, and Islamism, as it has come to be called, which is a form of political fascism masquerading as faith.

Moderate Muslim leaders must be strongly encouraged to stand up and seek to isolate those who would hijack their religion and profane its name with acts of cold-blooded murder. And these leaders must explore without flinching the relationship of Islam to modernity.

As the author Salman Rushdie recently wrote: "The restoration of religion to the sphere of the personal, its depoliticization, is the nettle that all Muslim societies must grasp in order to become modern" (*New York Times*, November 2, 2001).

(5) Those in the Muslim world who teach hatred of non-Muslims must be exposed. Let me cite just a few examples:

The textbook for one of the five religion classes required of all tenth graders in Saudi public high schools tackles the complicated issue of who good Muslims should befriend. After examining a number of scriptures which warn of the dangers of having Christian and Jewish friends, the lesson concludes: "It is compulsory for the Muslims to be loyal to each other and to consider the infidels their enemy." (*New York Times*, October 19, 2001)

Meanwhile, in Pakistan:

In many of the 7,500 *madrassas* [religious schools], with a student body of 750,000 to a million, students learn to recite and obey Islamic law, and to distrust and even hate the U.S. (*New York Times*, October 14, 2001)

And in England, the Al Ansaar bookstore in Birmingham sells videotapes in which "Jews and Americans are referred to as 'monkeys and pigs'" (*New York Times*, October 24, 2001).

(6) Anti-Semitism remains a pressing problem in the Arab world. This was revealed again after September 11, as scurrilous accusations against Israel, the Mossad, and Jews generally began circulating.

Trying to deflect attention from the incontrovertible fact that the nineteen plane hijackers were all Arabs, including fifteen Saudis, and that those behind them were Arab as well, including bin Laden himself, the Arab press tried to pin the blame on the most marketable scapegoat; in this part of the world, that is the Jews.

And in New York, Sheikh Muhammad Gemeaha, leader of the city's most prominent mosque, suddenly disappeared after September 11, only to resurface in Cairo. There he was quoted in an October 4 interview as saying "that Muslim children were being poisoned by Jewish doctors in American hospitals, and that 'Zionists' in command of the nation's air traffic control towers aided the suicide hijackings."

It reached a point where President Bush, in his forceful address to the UN General Assembly on November 10, felt it necessary to denounce these baseless allegations.

For much too long, Arab nations have tried to hide behind the intellectual sophistry that, by definition, they cannot be anti-Semitic since they themselves are a Semitic people. Or else, like the Egyptians, they claim that sickening anti-Semitic diatribes and cartoons in the press are "the price" for a free press, as if the media in most Arab countries were actually free.

Too few Western countries have paid this anti-Semitism adequate attention, instead lamely ascribing it to Arab "passion" and the propensity for "hyperbole," or to a "reaction" to the Arab-Israeli conflict.

The Western attitude may have begun to change at the World Conference Against Racism in Durban, South Africa, in September, when delegates witnessed what one observer described as an "orgy of anti-Semitism" fueled by the Arab world, but only time will tell.

(7) Isn't it long overdue to press those Muslim countries lagging far behind to move forward with democratic change, emancipation of women, respect for minorities, and education for tolerance? The cultural relativists will argue that this is nothing more than a strategy to impose Western values on nations with their own perfectly "valid" norms, but such thinking is in fact condescending in the extreme.

If the experience of the twentieth century has taught us anything, it must be that freedom is indivisible and that human rights are universal.

Are we to ignore the fact that not a single country in the twenty-two-member Arab League has universal suffrage, free and fair elections, and a government that reflects the will of the people?

Or that in Saudi Arabia, according to the U.S. State Department: "The Government prohibits the public practice of non-Muslim religions.... Conversion by a Muslim to another religion is considered apostasy, a crime punishable by death if the accused does not recant.... In a *sharia* court, a woman's testimony does not carry the same weight as that of a man: The testimony of one man equals that of two women."

Or that in Egypt last month twenty-three men were sentenced to jail terms ranging from one to five years for engaging in homosexual activity? Or that Egypt, a country of 60 million people, produces fewer than 400 books a year, because of a suffocating mix of political authoritarianism and religious obscurantism, compared with Israel's 4,000 titles from a nation of 6 million?

Or that in Pakistan Dr. Younus Shaikh, a physiology teacher, was sentenced to death earlier this year on charges of blasphemy? His crime? He had discussed with his class whether the Prophet Muhammad had become a Muslim before the age of forty and whether he or his followers were circumcised.

Or that an Islamic court in Nigeria's Sokoto State last month sentenced a woman convicted of adultery to death by stoning (Agence France-Presse, November 15, 2001)?

How can we in good conscience sit idly by while this part of the world remains frozen in a time warp regarding democracy, human rights, and economic and social development, as if they were of no particular consequence to us? Don't the inhabitants of the Muslim world deserve better from their rulers and from those on the outside who purport to take an interest in the region?

Izzat Majeed, a businessman, wrote a remarkably courageous piece in the *Nation*, a Pakistani daily (November 9), which was cited in a column by Thomas Friedman. Here's an excerpt:

> We Muslims cannot keep blaming the West for all our ills…. Without a reformation in the practice of Islam that makes it move forward and not backward, there is no hope for us Muslims anywhere. We have reduced Islam to the organized hypocrisy of state-sponsored mullahism.

(8) We need to give very careful consideration to the delicate balance between national security and civil liberties in democratic societies. At the risk of stating the obvious, this is not a simple matter.

We cannot give the terrorists the satisfaction of forcing us to compromise on our basic freedoms, yet, at the same time, to adapt Lenin's famous phrase, we must not be the ones to sell the rope that will be used to hang us.

Britain will be a good case study.

To the consternation of several moderate Arab regimes, including those of Egypt and Tunisia, Islamic extremists from these countries have been given wide latitude to operate in Britain because of the nation's proud commitment to an open society. Indeed, several British citizens reportedly responded to the call for volunteers and joined the Taliban in the struggle against the U.S. and British troops. But that should have come as little surprise.

A limited-access British-based Web site urged the "Muslim *ummah* [people] to help our fellow Muslim *ummah* in Afghanistan…. It is a bigger priority for Muslim organizations to help the Taliban at this time than to help any other Muslim cause in the world, whether Chechnya, Kashmir, or Palestine."

The same site advertised "The Ultimate Jihad Challenge." Let me quote from the text:

The ultimate jihad challenge is a two-week course in our 1,000-acre state-of-the-art shooting range in the United States. Due to the firearms law of the United Kingdom, all serious firearms training must be done overseas.... You will be taught the following skills: weapons familiarization, live fire shooting on the move, live fire combat jungle run, live fire sniper, live fire hostage rescue, etc.

And this British-based Web site also offered "Islamic military summer camps in France, Holland, and Italy," as well as "Islamic military training for women."

Will this kind of sanctioned activity continue post-September 11? One encouraging sign is that the British government arrested the individual principally responsible for this Web site, but it took the events of September 11 for such action to be taken.

And finally, where does Israel fit into this complex post-September 11 picture?

There is *no* country in the world that better understands what the American people, and especially the residents of New York, have been going through since September 11 than Israel. Tragically, as we have witnessed again in recent days, Israel has lived with such demented terror for far too long.

Consider this news item from *Corriere della Sera*, the Italian daily (July 5, 2001), which reveals the lengths to which gullible Palestinian youngsters are drawn into the terrorist web:

An aspiring Palestinian kamikaze is seated in front of Israeli policemen who are interrogating him. This time the police managed to prevent the attack. The youngster reveals: "I told the person preparing me for martyrdom that I can only do it on Monday because on Tuesday I have to take a school exam." This report comes from a serious source—Shimon Peres, who was giving an example of the level of craziness in the region.

Israel has considerable experience to share with the United States regarding everything from technical and human intelligence-gathering about radical Islamic groups to the difficult balance between national security imperatives and civil liberties protections, from keeping airplanes safe to refusing to yield to fear.

When attacked by suicide bombers, the United States adopted many of the same strategies as Israel—going to the source, using overwhelming firepower, attacking not only the terrorist groups but those who provide them with sanctuary, and shifting from legal pursuit to open warfare. The only difference is that Israel has been roundly criticized by many countries for pursuing these very strategies.

There was speculation that Israel would be asked to pay a price for the needs of the American-led coalition. After all, to avoid the appearance of the civilizational conflict that Professor Samuel Huntington foresaw in his noted 1993 article in *Foreign Affairs*, Washington had to enlist Arab and Muslim support, yet these very countries made clear their unwillingness to go along if Israel were included in the coalition.

Moreover, Egypt and Saudi Arabia—two countries that have disappointed many Americans by their limited cooperation since September 11—have put considerable pressure on Washington to exact concessions that Jerusalem might not otherwise be prepared to make.

(A recent cartoon showed two Saudis digging a hole in the desert. Upon completing their work, they hide in the hole and put up a sign nearby with the words: "Call us when it's over." And the caption beneath the cartoon reads: "Our Saudi allies dig in for the long fight.")

While the Bush administration has stepped up efforts in recent weeks to get the Israelis and Palestinians back to the peace table and has reaffirmed America's commitment to a two-state solution, it fully understands two key points:

First, the Palestinians spurned a historic chance to achieve peace based on just such a two-state solution when they rejected out-of-hand the Barak-Clinton proposals in Camp David and at Taba. Second, the Palestinians have used terror against Israel to this very day. For an administration waging war on terrorism, this is totally unacceptable, as President Bush made unambiguously clear in response to the latest horrific suicide bombings in Haifa and Jerusalem.

Led by Prime Minister Sharon, Israel is not prepared to succumb to the terrorists' sword of Damocles any more than the United States is, and it rightly insists that the world must make a clear moral distinction between the "arsonists"—the Palestinians—and the "firefighters," the Israelis.

Once the terror ends, if it ends, then the course of action for putting the peace train back on the tracks is well known to all. It is laid out in the Mitchell Plan and the Tenet guidelines. And I have no doubt that trusted friends like German foreign minister Fischer will be there alongside the United States to help nurture any peace process.

But, given Palestinian behavior these past fifteen months, including outright rejection of the Barak-Clinton proposals, the calculated use of violence and incitement, insistence on the so-called "right of return," and the denial of any Jewish historical link to Jerusalem, the peace camp in Israel has all but collapsed—for now, at least—and many Israelis feel they have been transported back to 1947-48, when the very existence and legitimacy of the Jewish state were in question.

When the American Jewish Committee meets with foreign leaders, we sometimes have the sense that they believe they want peace for Israel even more than Israelis want peace for themselves. Let me be clear: No people on earth yearn for peace more than the Israelis, precisely because they have never known a day of real peace since the state was established fifty-three years ago.

Does any serious person believe that Israelis, residing in a democratic and first-world country, are actually content to live with the constant threat of war, frequent acts of terror in population centers, and the immense physical, psychological, and economic burden of defending a tiny country in a volatile region?

Israelis have time and again shown their unquenchable thirst for peace and their concomitant willingness to make painful—and risky—compromises in its pursuit. And I have no doubt that should future talks with the Palestinians reach a point where the majority of Israelis believe the benefit is worth the cost, the spirit of compromise will once again be forthcoming.

As Israeli foreign minister Peres said in an eloquent speech to the UN General Assembly last month:

> Our neighbors—Palestinians and Arabs—know that Israel is committed to contribute whatever she can to renew a real peace process. Not by force, not by imposition, not by unilateral action, but through a negotiated agreement—and an agreed peace.

But durable Israeli-Palestinian peace must be built on a solid foundation, not on shifting sands. It cannot be artificially constructed. It has to evolve, first and foremost, from a strategic decision by both parties that this can be the only path forward, that there can be no other.

Israel has made that strategic decision, but until such time as the Palestinians reach the same conclusion, Israel has no choice but to take those military measures it deems necessary to defend its citizens.

And therefore, to close the circle, if the world needed a reminder of the kind of neighborhood in which Israel is forced to operate and the rules of the game there, then September 11, tragically, provided both in spades.

# 3. TESTIMONY

## Letter to National Commission on Terrorism
## March 2, 2000

Dear Ambassador [Paul] Bremer:

On behalf of the American Jewish Committee, I thank you for the opportunity to submit the following comments regarding the effectiveness of current U.S. laws and policies in response to terrorist threats against America, its citizens, and interests. We are honored to have been given this chance to share our views.

AJC is the nation's premier human relations organization with some 105,000 members and supporters in thirty-two regional chapters across the country. Since 1906, AJC has been dedicated to defending civil rights, religious freedom, and human rights, and promoting respect for American pluralism and democratic principles. In recent years, AJC has paid particular attention to the menace of terrorism fueled by, or linked to, militant Islamic extremism that threatens America and its allies and the core values and institutions of democratic societies around the world.

As an organization, we have consistently advocated a broad, multifaceted response to the global scourge of terrorism, including the enactment of tough and comprehensive federal counterterrorism legislation that, at the same time, respects due-process safeguards. Against this backdrop, AJC has followed with interest the ongoing efforts of the administration and Congress as they consider legislation and other measures regarding encryption, the rights of U.S. citizens to bring civil actions against state sponsors of terrorism, and the government's use of classified evidence in INS deportation proceedings. The following comments reflect our views and concerns regarding these and other important aspects of the American response to terrorism.

### *The Terrorist Threat Today*

Four categories of terrorism confront the United States today:

- Terrorism carried out by organizations that possess an international infrastructure, such as Al Qaeda, headed by Osama bin Ladin, and Hezbollah;
- Domestic terrorist organizations located in the United States that are comprised of American citizens, such as The Order, the Aryan Nations, and certain extremist militia groups;
- Acts of terrorism carried out by individuals motivated by the extremist ideology and propaganda of a terrorist group, but with no formal ties to such groups. One example of such an incident was the August 1999 attack carried out by Buford Furrow against a Jewish day-care center in the Los Angeles area;
- Terrorism carried out via state sponsorship. While state-sponsored terrorism has declined through the 1990s, it has continued to play a role in regard to Middle Eastern terrorist organizations, such as Hamas and Hezbollah, that have received funds and logistical support for their activities from Iran.

### *Recent Trends*

The first factor heightening the threat of terrorism against the United States over the last two decades has been extreme religious fanaticism. Leaders of terrorist groups who employ this type of ideology present a perverted form of religious tenets to justify their attacks. These organizations' abuse of the trappings of religion give them the ability to take advantage of the freedoms provided by Western societies. In contrast to terrorist organizations that have a specifically declared political goal, the potential of these organizations to carry out ever more frequent murderous attacks is much higher.

The second factor is the willingness of terror organizations to pursue ever more deadly means of carrying out attacks. These include the use of powerful improvised explosive devices, as were employed in the suicide attack carried out by Hezbollah against the U.S. embassy in Beirut in 1983 and the truck bombing attacks carried out at the World Trade Center in 1993 and at the Murrah Building in Oklahoma City in 1995. Over the past decade, terrorist organizations such as Al Qaeda have made efforts to acquire weapons of mass destruction. And although the Japanese terrorist organization Aum Shin Ri Kyo does not include the United States among its declared targets, its devastating use of Sarin gas in the Tokyo subway in 1995 has paved the way for other groups to attempt the same elsewhere.

Although there are hundreds of terrorist groups active in the world today, the international organizations that represent the principal threat to Americans at home and abroad are Middle Eastern terrorist groups. Many of these groups have publicly declared their main targets to be Americans and Jews. Noteworthy among them is the International Front to Fight Jews and Crusaders, also known as Al Qaeda.

### Counterterrorism: A Comprehensive Approach

The terrorist acts that the world has witnessed over the last several decades indicate that such politically motivated violence can be carried out by two models of terrorist operatives. The first model is a terrorist organization that recruits individuals who receive training and indoctrination directly provided by that organization. The individual receives orders from the hierarchy of the group and takes action as an operative of the organization. Traditionally, indoctrination and training have taken place through personal contact between ranking members of an organization and the individuals who are recruited to carry out an attack.

Terrorist operatives who are affiliated with an organization benefit from a society created within a society. While smaller organizations may establish training camps to indoctrinate their operatives, other organizations, particularly those that employ religious extremism as a motivating factor, create an entire social service support system for the terrorist operatives, their families, and supporters. This system not only offers support for the terrorist operatives themselves, but also provides the basis for the perpetuation of the movement. In this manner, followers of the movement are indoctrinated in its extremist ideology from a very early age.

To maintain their current capabilities and ensure the continuity of these organizations, funds are raised to support the social service systems of such terrorist movements. Terrorist organizations have taken advantage of the freedom of movement and privacy enjoyed by citizens of the United States and other Western countries to establish ostensibly charitable organizations to raise funds for their activities abroad.

The second model is an individual, or an "independent operator," who generally functions apart from the activities of an organized group. The independent operator, however, is inspired by indoctrination generally identical to that of a terrorist operative trained by a particular organization. In essence, the independent operator exists on the fringes of a terrorist movement. He imposes upon himself his own self-prescribed course of indoctrination and training by accessing materials all too readily available via the Internet or distributed through the mail.

In seeking to counter the activities of these two types of operatives, it is important to recognize that neither operates in a vacuum. The affiliated operative exists within the social support system of a terrorist group, while the independent operative benefits from indoctrination and training materials that are today readily accessible via electronic distribution.

As one means of weakening the infrastructure that produces terrorist operatives, AJC supports the implementation of provisions of the Effective Death Penalty and Anti-Terrorism Act of 1996 that would impede the efforts of Middle Eastern terrorist organizations to raise money on American soil. To date, certain organizations have been investigated for these activities but, regrettably, further concrete action has yet to be taken.

Nearly a decade ago, senior federal law-enforcement officials testified that every significant Middle Eastern terrorist organization has an infrastructure in the United States. There is no reason to believe that the situation is any different today. AJC supports the aggressive investigation of terrorist organizations and their apparatus in the United States, consistent with existing investigative guidelines.

### Legislative Efforts

#### Encryption

This past December, AJC adopted a policy supportive of the administration's collaborative efforts with industry to develop and promote recovery-capable encryption products and other means to crack impenetrable codes. We have urged the administration to continue its consultation with the various interested parties to perfect modes of voluntary key recovery. Likewise, we have called for legislation providing law enforcement, in the absence of plaintext, with lawful technical assistance to use its own facilities for bypassing, disabling, decrypting, or otherwise neutralizing the encryption in question.

As a matter of public safety, law enforcement should be provided with reasonable means to preserve existing investigatory capability, without compromising privacy and due-process safeguards. To this end, we believe funding for research and development must be maintained to address gaps in national security and public safety that may be created by the approaches now being promoted. We urge Congress to provide essential funding in the FY2001 budget for the FBI's Technical Support Center, which serves as the primary technical resource for federal, state, and local law enforcement against cyber-criminals.

## Justice for Victims of Terrorism Act (S. 1796)

In October 1999, Senators Frank Lautenberg (D-NJ) and Connie Mack (R-FL) introduced S. 1796 to assist American victims of terrorism and enforce judgments against state sponsors of terrorism permitted under the 1996 Anti-Terrorism Act.

Several lawsuits have been brought against terrorist-supporting countries pursuant to a provision of the 1996 Anti-Terrorism Act. One of the earliest suits was filed by Steven Flatow against the Iranian government for financially supporting a terrorist group that murdered his daughter, Alisa, in a 1995 bus bombing in Israel; it resulted in a $247.5 million judgment against Iran. Although the administration supported this provision in the 1996 law, it later became concerned that allowing execution of a judgment against diplomatic property would pose a danger to American diplomatic property abroad and would prevent the United States from using frozen assets as a tool of foreign policy. Consequently, since October 1998 the administration has blocked Mr. Flatow from satisfying his judgment through attachment of Iranian assets frozen in the United States.

AJC welcomed the 1996 law as well as the court decision to impose legal and financial responsibility on Iran for its sponsorship of the deadly attack that killed Alisa Flatow, and, in October 1998, we encouraged the administration to find a workable solution to this important matter. We believe that the Justice for Victims Act strikes a compromise by permitting the president to waive enforcement of a judgment, pursuant to the 1996 Anti-Terrorism Act, against frozen foreign diplomatic assets, on an asset-by-asset basis. The act would deny the president, however, the right to waive enforcement of such a judgment against the real property of a foreign diplomatic mission or its assets, if the property is being used for nondiplomatic purposes (such as rental property) or the assets are sold to a third party. We support S. 1796 in principle and urge the bill's sponsors, the administration, and other interested parties to work toward finding consensus on the bill.

**Secret Evidence Repeal Act (H.R. 2121)**

Late last year, numerous editorials and op-ed columns, echoing claims of civil liberties and pro-immigration advocates, severely criticized the Immigration and Naturalization Service (INS) for its use of classified information, not shared with the accused, in seeking detention or deportation of aliens who are alleged to have been involved in terrorist activity. The criticism has been driven, in large part, by recent judicial determinations regarding the deportation cases of Hany Kiareldeen and Nasser Ahmed, in which classified evidence was involved.

Largely omitted from the public debate surrounding these cases was the fact that the government did not apply the procedures for the use of classified information that Congress had enacted as part of the 1996 Anti-Terrorism Act, known as the Alien Terrorist Removal Act (ATRA). ATRA was intended to reconcile due-process concerns with the need to battle terrorism.

Nonetheless, in the wake of these widely publicized cases, Representatives David Bonior (D-MI) and Tom Campbell (R-CA) introduced the Secret Evidence Repeal Act. The Bonior-Campbell bill would forbid the use of classified information in a deportation proceeding without subjecting that information to examination on the same basis as any other evidence.

AJC has a proud history of support for fair and generous immigration policies, as well as a commitment to due process and civil rights. We view this as entirely consistent with a strong regard for national security concerns, which must be balanced with other national interests in a reasonable manner. We believe that H.R. 2121's categorical ban on the use of classified information in immigration proceedings fails to draw a reasonable balance between due-process concerns and national security interests, a balance that AJC advocated during consideration by the Congress of the 1996 Anti-Terrorism Act.

While ATRA, as enacted in 1996, may be susceptible to improvement, as I stated above, it has never actually been utilized by the INS in the cases that have brought INS practices under scrutiny or, for that matter, in any other case. ATRA, with possible modifications, is a model worth further consideration by Congress. It is untenable, however, to adopt the Bonior-Campbell approach, which makes no accommodation whatsoever for the very real and compelling national security concerns to which the 1996 Anti-Terrorism Act was addressed.

Again, I wish to express my appreciation to you and the other distinguished members of the National Commission on Terrorism for the opportunity to share our concerns with respect to the current U.S. response to international terrorist threats. We greatly appreciate the vital work the commission is tasked to fulfill, and we would welcome any further opportunity to assist your important review of U.S. counterterrorism policies.

## Testimony on Anti-Semitism in Europe and the Middle East to the U.S. Senate Foreign Relations Committee
### April 5, 2000

Mr. Chairman, permit me to express my deepest appreciation to you and to your distinguished colleagues for holding this important and timely hearing, and for affording me the opportunity to testify before the Senate Committee on Foreign Relations about the state of anti-Semitism in Europe and the Middle East. On a personal note, it is a pleasure to see you again.

I have the privilege of representing the American Jewish Committee, the oldest human relations organization in the United States. We were founded in 1906 by a group of prominent American Jewish jurists, diplomats, and businessmen who felt that wherever in the world Jews were threatened, no minority was safe. These esteemed contributors to American civic life—men like Cyrus Adler, Louis Marshall, Jacob Schiff, and Oscar Straus—sought to promote nationally and internationally the concept of legal protection for minorities and the uniquely American idea of pluralism.

They were prompted, I should note, not only by lofty ideals of ending intolerance for all, but also by an immediate concern. The massacres of Jews in czarist Russia in the first years of the twentieth century greatly troubled these noble men, and they organized their response effort by creating the American Jewish Committee.

We at the American Jewish Committee have seen over the decades—and indeed, as we consider the longer timeline of history—a strikingly close correlation between the level of anti-Semitism in a society and the level of general intolerance and violence against other minorities. Indeed, the treatment of Jews within a given society has become a remarkably accurate barometer of the state of democracy and pluralism in a society. Where Jews are safe to practice their religion and express their identity, all citizens are likelier to be secure; and where Jews are endangered, history teaches, it is not long before other groups are targeted and mistreated. Bigotry and xenophobia, whether expressed against Jews or any other vulnerable minority, are threats to the entire social fabric. In effect, it can be said that by dint of our historical experience, Jews have become the miner's canary, often signaling danger before others are touched.

For ninety-four years, the American Jewish Committee has espoused a vision of ethnic and religious understanding worldwide. It has been a compelling and constant vision. Rather than losing relevancy, its message has grown more crucial with the passage of time. This has been especially and painfully apparent since the end of the Cold War, as ethnic and religious tensions seethe and sometimes break out into violence and war.

At the scholarly level, the American Jewish Committee has conducted pioneering research on anti-Semitism. In the post-World War II period, we were proud to sponsor the seminal five-volume series *Studies in Prejudice*, which offered groundbreaking theoretical models, including *The Authoritarian Personality,* still in use today to explain the nature of racism and anti-Semitism. We continue to conduct regular surveys of attitudes toward Jews and other minorities in the countries of Europe and beyond, and to examine tolerance in school curricula and politics through published studies and conferences.

Mr. Chairman, at the outset of my testimony, it seems appropriate to ask an age-old question: What is the essential nature of anti-Semitism? As Professor Daniel Goldhagen of Harvard University has written, in the final analysis the answer is inevitably elusive: "Anti-Semitism ... is only dimly understood. Our apprehension of what it is, how it is to be defined, what produces it, how it is to be analyzed, and how it functions, remains, despite the volumes." The problem lies in the "difficulty of studying its host domain, the mind."[*]

But while the true essence of anti-Semitism may ultimately remain impossible to grasp, its manifestations are easier to identify. Throughout history, anti-Semitism has been inherently intertwined with cynical political aspirations and maneuverings, and with broader and more complex issues of national identity and the social psychology of the fanatic. "The fanatic seeks to oppress all those surrounding him. He uses political oppression, economic domination, social slavery, and the worst of all, oppression of the mind," Nobel laureate Elie Wiesel wrote in a powerful essay in *Das Jüdische Echo*, an Austrian Jewish periodical. "The fanatic defines himself by his victim's pain and fear rather than by his creativity. He feels threatened by a mind or soul that is free."

Although the focus of this testimony is on anti-Semitism in Europe and the Middle East, we fully recognize that the broad problem of intolerance affects every corner of our globe, and indeed may prove one of the most daunting challenges of the new century. Nor is the United

---

[*] Daniel Jonah Goldhagen, *Hitler's Willing Executioners* (New York: Knopf, 1996), p. 34.

States immune. Just last summer, we saw a spate of hate killings in Illinois, Indiana, and California, and arson attacks on three synagogues in Sacramento, among other tragic acts of hate-inspired violence.

Many democratic governments and people in Europe—a continent linked culturally, politically, and economically with our own and embarked on the laudable goal of ever closer regional integration—have embraced new economic and social trends. But we also see a backlash that includes new political and social acceptability for extreme right-wing parties that espouse intolerance and thinly veiled anti-Semitism. Given the brutal history of anti-Semitism in Europe, this requires close scrutiny.

In the Arab world today, the situation is still more disturbing. Here, anti-Semitism is open and unvarnished—contradicting entirely the diplomatic talk of peace in the region and undermining our longing for an end to the Arab-Israeli conflict and full normalization, and a new spirit of cooperation and development in the region.

In both these regions so vital to American interests—Europe and the Arab world—it is crucial for us to understand the sources of anti-Semitism, their scope and magnitude, and the relative danger they portend.

## I. Anti-Semitism in Europe

Allow me, Mr. Chairman, to focus first on Europe. I will not touch on developments in the Former Soviet Union, as my fellow panelist and esteemed colleague, Mark Levin of the NCSJ, will address that topic in his testimony.

There are a number of disturbing incidents and trends that bear watching. It is axiomatic that manifestations of anti-Semitism that are now current in Europe must be taken extremely seriously. Anti-Semitism is the oldest known social pathology, and for centuries Europe has been its primary incubator. Europe has afforded many opportunities to Jews over the centuries, including the freedom to pursue a rich cultural and intellectual life in various countries at various times. But Europe is also the site of blood-soaked chapters of history for the Jews. It was not long ago that one man's sick vision of a new social hierarchy where Aryans were at the top, Eastern Europeans at the bottom, and Jews marked for extinction, caught the brutal fancy of too much of continental Europe's supposedly enlightened population and was greeted with passive indifference by much of the rest.

The American Jewish Committee has identified, and continues to monitor, six sources of anti-Semitism that at one time or another in history have threatened Jews: (1) extreme right-wing extraparliamentary groups; (2) extreme right-wing political parties; (3) ethnically or religiously based models of national identity that distinguish, de jure or de facto, among and between a country's population groups; (4) extreme left-wing extraparliamentary groups; (5) church-based anti-Semitism; and (6) Arab and Islamic extremist groups operating in Europe.

## (1) Extreme right-wing extraparliamentary groups

The most evident sources of anti-Semitic activity in Europe today are fringe groups that are driven by extreme right-wing ideologies and are overtly neo-Nazi. Their targets are Jews, immigrants, guest workers, refugees, Roma and Sinti—in other words, anyone they regard as the "other."

Such groups, which also operate in the United States, are cause for deep concern. They promote hate and are responsible for bone-chilling violent crimes and despicable acts of domestic terrorism. But these issues take on quite another dimension in Europe. While American neo-Nazis may fantasize about an America in which only white Christians have rights, today's extreme-right groups in Europe can actually look back to a not-too-distant history when such an ideology prevailed in Germany, Austria, and beyond, and seek to pick up that historical thread and build upon it.

Anti-Semitism is inextricably intertwined with the worldview of contemporary neo-Nazi groups. Even in societies in which virtually no Jews live, the rhetoric of such groups remains startlingly focused on hatred of Jews. Indeed, at times there almost seems to be an inverse relationship—the fewer the actual number of Jews in a given country, the more shrill the language about the alleged Jewish menace.

There is a certain eerie normality to far-right activity in Europe. Throughout the continent, heavily armed guards stand in front of synagogues and other Jewish institutions around the clock to calm fears inspired by regular bomb threats. It is a shocking sight for visiting Americans, but nothing new for Europeans. Perhaps the wide acceptance of this situation helps to explain why, in a number of European countries, anti-Semitic incidents, including the frequent desecration of cemeteries, fail to elicit much public outcry.

Bizarrely, soccer, the most popular sport in Europe, has also become a visible outlet for anti-Semitic expressions. Fans in Italy have notoriously given voice to pro-Mussolini sentiments and crude anti-Semitism. A banner held up to a competing team at a major national match last year read "Auschwitz is your country and the ovens are your homes," but signs with swastikas are so common that they do not even make the news. Italy, it should be noted, has begun to take steps to address this vulgar—and in Italy, also illegal—behavior, including threats to stop games that are interrupted by offensive signs and penalizing teams. But the problem extends to Holland, Germany, England, and to a culture of soccer fans that exists throughout Europe and beyond.

One of the central components of radical right-wing ideologies is Holocaust denial. It is not simply that deniers want to remove the moral albatross of the Holocaust from the image of fascism—although they *do* clearly want to do this. By maintaining that Jews simply "made up" the Holocaust and have "hoodwinked" the world into believing a lie, the neo-Nazis seek to reverse images and convince the world that they are the victims. Neo-Nazis realize that the shadow of the Holocaust has created a certain sympathetic understanding of the vulnerability of the Jews and the danger of stepping onto the slippery slope of anti-Semitism; therefore denying, distorting, minimizing, trivializing, or in any other way defusing the power of the Holocaust tragedy is seen by neo-Nazis as strengthening their hand and giving further legitimacy and reach to their aims and objectives. Lessons reemphasized in the wake of the Holocaust—such as rejecting anti-Semitism and racism and valuing individual human life—are thus discredited as the product of Jewish "manipulation."

Unfortunately, much of the published material that fuels Holocaust denial in Europe—though its dissemination is illegal in Austria, France, Germany, and Switzerland, among other countries—comes from the United States, where it is produced under the protection of the First Amendment. Moreover, the worldwide Internet has dramatically enhanced the ability of extreme right-wing groups that distort history and espouse anti-Semitism, such as the California-based Institute for Historical Review and the Committee for Open Debate of the Holocaust, to spread their message. Many European officials have told us that their efforts to contain neo-Nazi movements would be strengthened if the United States could find the means to keep a closer eye on the movement of material from American-based neo-Nazi groups. Internet sites are also being founded in Europe to disseminate messages of anti-Semitism and hate. German authorities, who watch anti-Semitic trends with particular vigilance, estimate that the number of propaganda sites in the German language with anti-Semitic content increased 600 percent in 1998.

European and U.S. far-right cooperation also exists in the field of racist and anti-Semitic white-power music, which has become part of the skinhead and younger neo-Nazi culture worldwide. While on the decline in much of Western Europe, due to internal fighting and legal crackdowns, white-power music continues to serve as a medium of cultural communication and to generate millions of dollars for far-right movements.

### (2) Extreme right-wing parties

We see today an increasingly porous border between radical right-wing fringe groups and a growing number of extreme right-wing political parties that have been gaining acceptance in mainstream politics. Most obviously, the newest extreme right-wing party in Germany—which captured nearly 13 percent of the 1998 vote in the state elections of Saxony-Anhalt, although, like other extreme right-wing parties in Germany, its national vote has heretofore been marginal—is run by Gerhard Frey, a Munich publisher of extremist material who propagates the theory of an international Jewish conspiracy against Germany.

Extreme right-wing parties have now entered the mainstream, though it is important to note that these parties have generally gained popularity by appealing to a much broader spectrum of issues in their

**Table 3.1**
**Election Results for Far-Right**
**Parties in Europe**

|                     | Percentage of votes |
|---------------------|---------------------|
| Austria (1999)      | 27.2                |
| Switzerland (1999)  | 23.0                |
| Norway (1997)       | 15.3                |
| France (1997)       | 15.2                |
| Belgium (1999)      | 10.0                |
| Italy (1996)        | 10.0                |
| Hungary (1998)      | 5.5                 |

countries, such as opposition to immigration and to integration in the European Union.

Jean-Marie Le Pen of the National Front Party in France regularly received 14 percent of the French vote, and climbed to 15.2 percent in 1997, though his popularity has gone down since his party split in 1999; Christoph Blocher's Swiss People's Party recently won 23 percent of the national vote, up from 14.9 percent in the election preceding it, making it the second most popular party; Carl Hagen's Progress Party in Norway claimed 15.3 percent of the 1997 vote; Frank Vanhecke's Flemish National Party won 10 percent of the Belgian vote in 1999; Italy's Northern League received just over 10 percent of the vote in 1996; and Istvan Csurka, with his anti-Semitic Hungarian Justice and Life Party, received 5.5 percent of the vote in 1998, becoming the first postwar anti-Semitic party to enter the Hungarian parliament (see table 3.1).

Allow me to spend a moment on Jörg Haider's Freedom Party in Austria, the most successful xenophobic party in postwar Europe (see table 3.2). Originally made up predominantly of aging former Nazis, the Freedom Party generally won between 5 and 6 percent of the vote before Haider took control in 1986—far behind the socialists and conservatives. In 1986, the party jumped to close to 10 percent of the vote.

**Table 3.2**
**Election Results for**
**Austria's Freedom Party**

| Year | % |
| --- | --- |
| Pre-1986 | 5.5 |
| 1986 | 10.0 |
| 1990 | 16.6 |
| 1994 | 22.5 |
| 1999 | 27.2 |

In 1990 its share of the vote went up to 16.6 percent, and in 1994 to 22.5 percent. At that point some observers thought the Freedom Party had peaked, its vote seeming to stabilize at 21.9 percent in 1995 and 22 percent in 1996. But in March 1999 the party won the elections in the province of Carinthia with 42 percent of the vote there, and Haider was elected provincial governor in April. Most recently, in the national elections of October 1999, the Freedom Party won the second-largest number of parliamentary seats by capturing 27.2 percent of the vote.

While we readily acknowledge the resilience of Austrian postwar democracy and its respect for human rights, as well as the fact that 73 percent of Austrian voters *did not* support the Freedom Party, this disturbing development did not entirely surprise us.

The American Jewish Committee has developed close contacts with Jewish and other civic leaders in Austria over the past several decades, and we were keenly aware of the atmosphere in the country prior to the elections. Haider managed to win votes by tapping into several issues in Austrian society. First, he was seen as a bold and telegenic young leader who would introduce change after what was perceived as an interminable and all-too-cozy reign of the conservative-socialist coalition. Second, Haider was seen as someone who would stand up for the "rights" of Austrians against the growing number of refugees who had entered the country in the preceding decade from Eastern Europe and, in particular, the former Yugoslavia. And last but unfortunately not least, Haider appealed to an unsettling Austrian ultranationalism that still exists in the country. He and his associates in the Freedom Party have made statements over the years that cater to the worst sentiments of nostalgia and revisionism in the Austrian populace.* Certainly, we recognize that some of those who cast votes for the Freedom Party do not necessarily harbor racist or anti-Semitic views. Nevertheless, we are troubled by the fact that they are not at all deterred from aligning themselves with those who do.

Furthermore, our own American Jewish Committee surveys of Austrian attitudes (conducted by Gallup in 1991 and 1995) reveal that a significantly higher percentage of Freedom Party supporters than other Austrians are disposed toward Holocaust denial and negative feelings about Jews. These people today remain a core constituency of Haider's party. Though Haider has formally resigned from the party's leadership, no one should be fooled; he remains its guiding light and inspiration. And precisely because he is devilishly clever and chameleon-like, he merits especially close scrutiny—particularly as he certainly seems interested in one day becoming chancellor.

The history of Austrian attitudes bears directly on this hearing. In marked contrast to Germany, the Austrian government, for more than forty years, showed little willingness to face its Nazi past. Indeed, until Chancellor Vranitsky's commendable speeches in 1991 and 1993, which followed on the heels of a self-examination forced on Austria by the Waldheim presidency, the country's leaders waltzed around Austria's central responsibility for the crimes of the Holocaust. The official Austrian line was that the country did not exist between 1938 and 1945 and therefore bore no responsibility whatsoever for what happened on its territory. Moreover, the Allies' declaration in Moscow in 1943 that Austria was the first victim state of the Third Reich provided the needed cover. In Austria, despite some notable efforts, there

---

* Quotations from Jörg Haider and Freedom Party associates (italics added):
Haider: *What I said was that it was the soldiers of the Wehrmacht who brought democracy to Europe, as it is today.* Had they not put up resistance, had they not been posted to the East, had they not led the conflict, then we would have…
*Profil*: What do you mean, "put up resistance?" Wasn't it a campaign of conquest led by the German Wehrmacht?

have still been too few organized attempts to stimulate dialogue on the subject or to face history squarely and unblinkingly. Hence, Haider and his Freedom Party gain entrée into the political mainstream when their rightful place is on the fringes.

The American Jewish Committee applauds the European Union and Israel for their principled decision to reduce diplomatic ties to Austria in the wake of the Freedom Party's inclusion into the ruling coalition.

In neighboring Germany, the fear of a contagion effect from the success of the Freedom Party has so far proved unwarranted. Far-right parties, for instance, captured a negligible portion of the vote in a German state election in Lower Saxony in February of this year. But following on the heels of Haider's victory, we saw in Switzerland the startling success of Christoph Blocher's Swiss People's Party, whose platform strikingly resembles that of Haider. Furthermore, Hungary's far-right party is cause for concern.

Radical right-wing ideologies have gained renewed vigor in recent years—less because their spokesmen have changed tactics or strategies, and more because they are finding increasingly receptive audiences in the larger society for their ideologies of narrowly defined nationalism and xenophobia. In addition, anti-Semitic and hate ideologies are slowly making their way into the larger mainstream press and the political and civic discourse. The recent libel suit of David Irving

---

Haider: If that's what you think, then we must start asking ourselves today what really happened. (Source: Interview with *Profil* magazine, August 21, 1995.)

"[What] you fought for and risked your lives for, [was] to give the younger generations and young people a future within a community in which order, justice, and decency are still considered to be principles.... *There is simply no other reason (to oppose reunions of Waffen-SS veterans), other than it makes some people mad that in this world there are still some people who have character and who stand up for their beliefs, even in the face of strong opposition, and who have remained true to their convictions right up to this day....* Decency will certainly prevail in our world, even if we are currently perhaps not capable of obtaining a majority, but we are mentally superior to the others and that is something very decisive." (Source: Haider's address to former Waffen-SS soldiers at their reunion in Carinthia, 1995.)

"Mass gassings by means of cyclone-B cannot have occurred in such a manner. *The long list of supposed German war crimes is constantly becoming shorter.* Almost none of them can withstand scientific-technical scrutiny. *On the other hand, the actual war crimes of the victorious powers are indisputable.*" (Source: Excerpt from *Zur Zeit* magazine, edited by Haider associate Andreas Mölzer, June 4, 1999.)

against Emory University professor Deborah Lipstadt in England opened a mainstream window on Holocaust denial. Irving has taken Lipstadt to court for defaming his "academic work," and she has had to bring voluminous proof to a London courtroom that, for instance, Jews were in fact gassed at Auschwitz. The verdict in the trial is expected in mid-April, but the case itself has at least temporarily brought talk of Holocaust denial into new circles of quasi respectability.

German political scientist Gideon Botsch caused a stir in Germany in early 2000 when he claimed to observe a shift in anti-Semitic expression to the pages of respected newspapers. His study cited examples of newspapers across the political spectrum that published articles with anti-Semitic undertones. This development might help explain the extremely negative way that some German papers reported on the Jewish Claims Conference, of which the American Jewish Committee is a founding member, during the recent negotiations over compensation for slave and forced labor. Numerous stories depicted the Claims Conference itself and the mostly Jewish lawyers as greedy and self-serving, and a bizarre discussion ensued in mainstream newspapers about whether there are as many Jewish survivors as cited by the Claims Conference.

Indeed, there is reason to believe that recent negotiations about long ignored and only belatedly addressed claims left over from the Holocaust period (Swiss bank accounts, forced and slave labor, stolen art, etc.) have increased anti-Semitism among the general public, a disturbing kind of blame-the-victim response. Surveys of European attitudes conducted by the American Jewish Committee over the last decade point to the same worrisome trends. When asked for their reaction to the statement "Jews are exploiting the memory of the Nazi extermination of the Jews for their own purposes," 16 to 39 percent of citizens of European countries said they agreed, as can be seen in table 3.3.

### (3) National identity models

There has been a revival of the concept of national identity over the last decade. In many European countries, unlike the United States and other modern countries founded by immigrants, citizenship traditionally

**Table 3.3**
**Europeans Who Say They**
**Agree with the Statement:**
**"Jews are exploiting the**
**memory of the Nazi extermination**
**for their own purposes"**
**(in percents of respondents)**

| Country/Date | % |
| --- | --- |
| Switzerland (2000) | 39 |
| Germany (1994) | 39 |
| Austria (1995) | 28 |
| Slovakia (1999) | 25 |
| Czech Republic (1999) | 23 |
| Sweden (1999) | 16 |

Source: AJC country surveys, 1994-2000

has been associated with a national ethnicity or a particular religion. The most brutal periods of anti-Semitism in European history have always coincided with the strengthening of such narrow concepts of national identity, and anti-Semites have capitalized on the notion of the Jew as outsider. Racism in Europe is generally founded on the same concept.

There are several explanations for the recent emphasis on national identity and religion. For one, there is a backlash in some quarters against globalization and the creation of a unified European identity. We saw this in France with the anti-McDonald's campaign and its anti-American undertones. For another, European nations are affected and influenced by the worldwide intensification of identity politics.

National identity is perhaps best exemplified by the language used in various countries. Quite reflexively and unself-consciously, for example, people in Warsaw will speak of "Poles and Jews" when they really are referring to people who hold common citizenship and origins in Poland.

This uncomfortable level of rhetoric about national identity explains the far right's focus on immigration. While concerns about the extent and nature of immigration certainly have a basis in reality and merit serious national discussion, too often the far right has seized upon the immigration issue, exaggerated and thereby fanned existing fears, and claimed the issue as its own. The thirteenth German Shell Youth Study, which has just been released, claims that more than two-thirds of the youth in the former East Germany, and 60 percent of youth in the west, say that there are too many foreigners in Germany today, though the total number of foreigners is less than 10 percent of the German population. The authors' claim that this xenophobia reflects the fear of unemployment and not right-wing extremism hardly seems to justify these numbers. Le Pen, Blocher, Csurka, and others have made anti-immigration central to the platforms of their extremist parties. As mentioned above, Haider's success can in part be attributed to a backlash against Austria's generous policy of accepting refugees during the Bosnian crisis.

But today, more than ever before, pluralism is less an option for societies and more a necessity. Globalization, changing patterns of world migration, and new means of communication make it likely that we will see *more* and not *fewer* international influences penetrating societies that could, in the past, simply close their doors. European governments must regulate immigration and asylum policies so as to maintain stability. But they will also have to reconcile themselves to a degree of movement and change. No country will ever be populated only by "natives"—indeed, few countries ever have been—and attempts to make countries pure in nationality have ended in bloodshed and terror. If the far right gains control of this issue, it will turn a growing pain into a permanent source of unhappiness, fear, and violence.

Mr. Chairman, I wish to call to the committee's attention an immediate problem related to the focus on national identity in Greece. The Greek government is about to issue new identity cards to be used inside Greece and for travel throughout the fifteen-member European Union. According to a new law, these cards will carry a line for the individual's religious identity. The policy is especially traumatic for the small Jewish community. Less than sixty years ago, the bulk of Greek Jewry was exterminated by the Nazis, and the notion of a central government file of all Jews, even in democratic Greece, causes profound anxiety, not to speak of the fear of violence. "Imagine," one Greek Jewish leader told us, "that in this crazy world with its share of anti-Semites, I must show a document everywhere I go that indicates my private religious faith."

Greece is the only European Union country to include religion on a national identity card. Government officials, many of whom have told us they oppose this policy, indicate that it is a concession to the powerful Greek Orthodox Church, which sees a close link between Greek nationality and the church. In this regard, we note with appreciation the mention that this matter was given in the U.S. State Department's 1999 Country Reports on Human Rights Practices and ask this esteemed committee to make its strong disapproval of the new policy clear.

### (4) Extreme left-wing extraparliamentary groups

Two and three decades ago, we saw the strongest expressions of anti-Semitism in Europe coming from another direction—the extreme left. Often cloaked in sympathy for the Palestinian cause and anti-Zionism, extremist left-wing groups such as the Italian Red Brigades and the German Baader-Meinhof Gang collaborated with terrorist groups in acts of violence against Jewish targets. Working in Europe in the late 1970s with the flow of Jewish refugees from the Soviet Union and Eastern Europe, I was personally aware of the very real dangers posed by this nexus. More recently, this threat seems to have been reduced.

Today, however, there is some evidence of a nascent brown-red alliance of fascists and communists. Although more prevalent in the Former Soviet Union than in Europe generally, the blurring of lines between left and right can be seen in manifestations such as the Parti Communautaire National-Européen (PCN) in Switzerland. This group, formerly known as the "Third Way," is active mainly in French-speaking parts of Europe and seeks to unite all "enemies of the system" from the right and left. Similarly, the small Union des Cercles Résistance in France strives to bring together "revolutionaries" from the left and right in opposition to the United States, Israel, and capitalism.

Chants of the 700 neo-Nazis who marched through Berlin's historic Brandenburg Gate on January 30, 2000, to mark the sixty-seventh anniversary of Hitler's taking office in 1933 and to protest the building of a major Berlin Holocaust memorial also sounded tones from the left and right: "Jobs instead of Jewish agitation" was shouted along with "Honor and fame for the Waffen-SS." Finally, with its interest in unknown forces, the New Age movement has recently provided particularly fertile soil for theories of hate that combine traditional elements from the right and left, including Jewish-conspiracy theories. While outlawed in Germany, books about the so-called Illuminati—a concept equivalent to the Jewish "elders"—are often sold at New Age conventions and are best-sellers in many popular European vacation spots.

### A. National action

A great number of people and governments are genuinely concerned about anti-Semitic trends in Europe and actively monitor and combat them. The German government deserves special mention here. It has been steadfast in its efforts to educate the German population about the history of the war—both in the schools and through commemorative and educational public programs. Widespread desire to create a more tolerant society has manifested itself in political, legal, and intellectual discussion and policy. Obviously, as statistics of anti-Semitic and hate-based crime show, German goodwill has not solved the problem completely, but it has managed, to a large degree, to isolate far-right parties and groups.

Nevertheless, the just-released annual survey conducted by the German Federal Agency for the Protection of the Constitution reports that while the number of neo-Nazis and right-wing extremists may be on the decline—from 54,000 to 51,000 between 1998 and 1999—the propensity among neo-Nazis for violence is estimated to have risen by 10 percent in the same period.

Sweden should also be mentioned in this context. After launching a massive national Holocaust education program, Prime Minister Göran Persson proceeded to organize the largest gathering of high-level political officials ever this January—including over a dozen presidents and prime ministers—to discuss the importance of education about the history and lessons of the Holocaust. Our country's delegation to the Stockholm International Forum on the Holocaust was led by Deputy

Secretary of the Treasury Stuart Eizenstat, whose efforts on behalf of Holocaust survivors and the restitution of looted Holocaust-era assets have been indefatigable, inspiring, and decisive. Our only regret is that this historic gathering inexplicably received virtually no media coverage in the United States.

While there are no surefire methods of eliminating anti-Semitism, history has taught us that there are ways to contain and marginalize it, and, conversely, there are responses that only encourage the entry of anti-Semitism into the mainstream. The massive French demonstration led by then-president François Mitterrand in reaction to a particularly vile cemetery desecration in Carpentras in 1990 was an example of leadership turning a terrible event into an important and positive lesson for the future. Likewise, the peaceful candlelight marches that brought together hundreds of thousands of concerned Germans in the wake of attacks on foreigners in Germany have helped marginalize the perpetrators of hate crimes. And, the peaceful—and large—demonstrations against Jörg Haider today in Austria reveal a vocal and determined community of conscience prepared to say no to Haider's narrow vision for Austria.

On the other hand, the deafening silence of Polish president Lech Walesa in 1995, when Father Jankowski, Walesa's parish priest in Gdansk, delivered a vituperative anti-Semitic speech in the presence of the president, is a case study in how not to respond. Similarly, some years ago, following the terrorist bombing of a Jewish restaurant in Paris, the French prime minister, while condemning the attack, remarked that "some Frenchmen" had also died, somehow implying that the French Jews who perished were not Frenchmen as well. While this reaction may have been well-intentioned, its results underscored the notion that Jews are "other" than French.

In 1998, the American Jewish Committee opened an office in Berlin that is monitoring political and social trends there and elsewhere in Europe. We are working closely with the German government, independent foundations, and nonprofit organizations to help strengthen tolerance and civil society, especially in Central and Eastern Europe. The U.S. ambassador to Germany, John Kornblum, has been exceedingly helpful in the work of the Berlin office and has met frequently with delegations of American Jewish Committee leaders, as have ambassadors and their staffs in American embassies throughout Europe. Each time we visit an embassy, we are proud and impressed by the caliber of our nation's representatives abroad. In addition, the friendship and outstanding work of J. D. Bindenagel, the U.S. special envoy for Holocaust assets, deserves special mention.

### B. *Multinational action*

The United Nations and the forty-one-member Council of Europe have helped set the legal norms prohibiting racial discrimination and religious intolerance, but have done very little, by comparison, to report on or take measures to help eradicate anti-Semitism. Strong U.S. engagement is essential to ensure that anti-Semitism is addressed in multilateral arenas in Europe and beyond. Multilateral institutions, as a rule, have not adequately addressed the issue of anti-Semitism, and in the few forums where the subject has come up, they have failed to follow words with action.

The twenty-five-year-old Organization for Security and Cooperation in Europe, of which the United States is one of fifty-three members, has affirmed its concern about anti-Semitism at political meetings, but has never followed up outside them.

The United Nations, founded in the aftermath of the Holocaust, has a rockier record. A 1960 Commission on Human Rights resolution on anti-Semitism was the last mention of this issue for thirty-four years. Worse, the "Zionism is racism" resolution passed by the General Assembly in 1975, rightly described by Secretary-General Kofi Annan as "the low point" in the world body's actions with respect to Jews and Israel, was itself a source of anti-Semitic statements in the world body; in 1991, the resolution was rescinded as a result of a U.S. initiative. Beginning in 1994, other U.S. initiatives brought a series of resolutions calling for the monitoring of anti-Semitic incidents by the special rapporteur on racial discrimination. The United Nations is currently gearing up for a World Conference Against Racism, Racial Discrimination, Xenophobia, and Related Intolerance. We hope anti-Semitism will be a focus of the action plan of the World Conference. Without U.S. backing, it will not be.

Leaders of the United Nations have been more outspoken on the issue of anti-Semitism than state representatives on its political bodies have been. Secretary-General Annan called upon the United Nations to use the fiftieth anniversary of the Universal Declaration of Human Rights to "eradicate anti-Semitism in all of its forms" and High Commissioner for Human Rights Mary Robinson opened the current session of the UN Commission for Human Rights in Geneva this March by including anti-Semitism in a list of "pressing human rights issues which need practical attention."

The Council of Europe, in which the United States has observer status, adopted resolutions in the 1990s recognizing the importance of combating anti-Semitism in Europe. Just last week, under the leadership of its secretary-general, Walter Schwimmer, and with the assistance of the American Jewish Committee, the European Jewish Congress, and the European Union of Jewish Students, a Declaration on Anti-Semitism was adopted at a consultation in Strasbourg, recommending specific action and legislation on the part of European governments. We hope to see these crucial points included in the October 2000 European Conference Against Racism, Racial Discrimination, Xenophobia, and Related Intolerance and, eventually, the World Conference Against Racism. Again, this will only happen if the United States is actively involved.

- The American Jewish Committee urges the government of the United States to ensure that the Council of Europe incorporates the concerns outlined in the Declaration on Anti-Semitism in the conclusions adopted at the European Conference Against Racism, and subsequently at the World Conference Against Racism, and to encourage other governments to implement the declaration continentwide. The European Conference should also propose specific practices to be used by governments to prevent anti-Semitism and racial discrimination and to educate more— and more effectively—about the values that bind our societies one to the other. It should lead to the inclusion of the subject of anti-Semitism in the World Conference Against Racism.
- The American Jewish Committee strongly recommends that the United States not only attend the upcoming preparatory meeting

of the technical working group of the European Conference Against Racism in a few weeks time, but that it actively press for the inclusion of combating anti-Semitism as part of the European plan of action. As indicated above, only the United States has the capacity to catalyze the continent to focus on the remnants of a grim chapter in its own history.

- We recommend that the United States begin to take a more active role in ensuring that the United Nations and other multilateral organizations face the important challenge of reducing anti-Semitism per se.

### (5) Church-based anti-Semitism

Historically, hatred of Jews, pogroms, and physical attacks against Jewish communities often resulted from the stereotypic portrayal of Jews as "Christ killers." On this front there is positive news to share today. The Catholic Church, beginning in 1965 at the Second Vatican Council, and many Protestant churches have taken truly historic steps over the last half century to end the teaching of contempt for Jews and Judaism, and to otherwise distance themselves from the lamentable historical record of church-inspired and church-sanctioned violence aimed at Jews.

Pope John Paul II, who has repeatedly called anti-Semitism "a sin against God and humanity," has made landmark contributions to the relationship between Jews and Catholics throughout his twenty-two-year papacy by recognizing the State of Israel, condemning anti-Semitism, and promoting Catholic-Jewish understanding. His recent visit to Israel significantly enhanced the international attention given his life's work in this area. Several national Catholic bishops' conferences, including those in France, Germany, and Poland, have also gone to great lengths to condemn anti-Semitism strongly. The Lutheran Church, both in this country and in Europe, has taken important steps to apologize for the acts of anti-Semitism, based on the teachings of Martin Luther, committed in its name.

We at the American Jewish Committee and others are deeply engaged in working toward a new and better chapter in Christian-Jewish relations in Europe, the United States, and around the world.

## (6) Arab and Islamic extremist groups operating in Europe

In the 1970s and 1980s, many Palestinian terrorist groups actively sought out Jewish targets in Europe, the most memorable and tragic incident being the murder of Israeli athletes at the 1972 Summer Olympic Games in Munich. In other acts of terrorism, Palestinian extremist groups cooperated with radical left-wing European groups and with communist governments, from which they received logistical and financial support, weapons training, safe havens, and political and diplomatic cover. Below are just a few of the dramatic terrorist incidents during this period aimed at Jewish targets in Europe:

- On June 27, 1976, an Air France jet was hijacked to Entebbe, Uganda, after taking off from Athens airport. Seven members of the Popular Front for the Liberation of Palestine, led by a West German associate, demanded the release of fifty-three terrorists in Israel, Switzerland, West Germany, France, and Kenya in exchange for the 257 hostages.

- On October 3, 1980, in Paris, four people were killed after a twenty-five-pound device exploded under a car outside of the Rue Copernic synagogue in Paris. A moped used in the attack was later traced to a Palestinian who had entered the country under false pretenses.

- On December 27, 1985, in Rome and Vienna, the Abu Nidal organization claimed responsibility for two simultaneous attacks carried out at El Al Airlines counters in airports of the two cities. A total of seventeen people were killed and 116 were wounded in the attacks.

While this cooperation has largely disappeared today with the collapse of the Warsaw Pact, a significant number of Islamic extremist organizations have found safe haven in Western Europe since the late 1980s, where they take advantage of free speech, freedom of movement, and freedom of assembly to produce Islamic extremist materials distributed throughout Europe and the Muslim world. Such material promotes public rallies and fund-raising activities for the cause of jihad, which is interpreted in its military sense as meaning "holy war," including terrorist attacks against Israel and Israeli targets abroad. It is common for such publications to identify Israel and its supporters as forces of evil implanted in the heart of the Muslim world by the United States.

Last month, the London-based Community Security Trust reported that a growing percentage of the anti-Semitic acts carried out in Britain have been initiated by Islamic extremist groups. Anti-Semitic activities throughout Western Europe, ranging from nonviolent to extremely violent, have mirrored this trend. We have also recently received disturbing reports from our colleagues in Western Europe that a number of Jewish institutions, including schools and synagogues, have come under surveillance by individuals using camera and video equipment. There is evidence to indicate that Islamic extremists are carrying out at least some of this surveillance activity.

## II. Anti-Semitism in the Middle East

The phenomenon of Islamic extremist anti-Semitism in Europe is closely linked to anti-Semitism in the Middle East.

While anti-Semitism in Europe must be carefully watched and monitored, the situation in the Middle East is far worse, and politically more dangerous, since it poisons the atmosphere surrounding the Israeli-Arab peace process. Strikingly, while Western nations, especially Germany and also, notably, Sweden, are engaged in dialogue and programs aimed at preserving the memory of the Holocaust, mainstream Arab media are extolling Holocaust denial. While world leaders have repeatedly declared that anti-Semitism is a form of racist action that must be condemned, Arab media, educators, and religious leaders are openly preaching it, and too many political figures are offering it official sanction.

As Israeli and Palestinian negotiators move ahead, however haltingly at times, toward a much-awaited permanent peace settlement, there has been a shocking—and quite frightening—revival of vitriolic anti-Semitism across the Arab world. It is ever-present in countries already formally at peace with Israel, and in others that have opened ties to the Jewish state following the significant peace process breakthroughs over the past decade.

This extraordinary paradox of building peace while actively demonizing the Jewish people is obviously shocking, and requires, we believe, the urgent attention of the Congress. Over the long term, this trend may well undermine efforts to nurture the climate of peace in the region that is essential to assuring the durability of any comprehensive agreement.

Among the latest public statements by Arab leaders denying the facts of the Holocaust were those of the Palestinian Authority-appointed mufti of Jerusalem, Ikrema Sabri, prior to and during the remarkable visit of Pope John Paul II to Israel. "It's true, the number was less than 6 million, and Israel is using this issue to get sympathy worldwide," he said on the Saturday before meeting the pope. The mufti's comments—reminiscent of his wartime predecessor who actually allied himself with Hitler—indicate a deeper and more sinister current espoused by Arab political and spiritual leaders that is reflected in the pages of official newspapers and in school textbooks.

The editor in chief of the official Syrian newspaper *Tishreen* recently asserted in his column and on Syrian radio that "Zionists created the Holocaust myth to blackmail and terrorize the world's intellectuals and politicians." Coming amid efforts to jump-start the stalled Israeli-Syrian peace talks, the editor's views attracted widespread attention and condemnation in U.S. and Israeli quarters, and moved many otherwise supportive Israelis to doubt Syria's reputed strategic decision to reconcile with Israel after an agreement on the disputed Golan. Sadly, though, the *Tishreen* outrage is more the rule than the exception.

From Egypt to Jordan, to the Gulf nations of Qatar and the United Arab Emirates, to the Palestinian Authority, Holocaust denial language has become commonplace in the print and electronic media. The Arab press has repeatedly made the incredible accusation that Israel is spreading poison and disease in Palestinian areas and as far away as the Arab nations of the Gulf. In recent weeks, Arab papers have stepped up their attacks on Israel—and on the Jewish people—by labeling, in vile words and gross caricatures, Israel's prime minister and foreign minister as Nazis. Offensive editorials and columns similar to the *Tishreen* editorial can be found in *Al-Ahram*, *Al-Akhbar*, and *Al-Gumhuriya*, three of the mainstream daily newspapers in Egypt, which signed a peace treaty with Israel twenty-one years ago. One cartoon run on February 29, 2000, portrayed a caricatured David Levy, foreign minister of Israel, painting a swastika onto a building with the caption "Levy's Diplomacy" (see fig. 3.1).

Egypt's leading position in the Arab world gives it enormous influence. Propagating Holocaust denial and slandering Jews can only inhibit relations between the Egyptian people and Israel, and sets a negative example for other Arab countries. Just last week, while President Mubarak was visiting the United States, several Israeli diplomats were invited to a conference at the University of Cairo, but denied entry when they arrived on campus.

In addition to treading on the painfully fresh memory of the Holocaust, that most sensitive of Jewish—and Israeli—issues, the Arab media also engage in other offensive and destructive anti-Semitic rhetoric.

In Qatar, for example, one of two forward-looking Gulf countries to open commercial ties with Israel (the other is Oman), Israel has been accused in the official newspaper of using women to undermine moral values and spread disease in the country—a new accusation suggesting the infamous blood libel against the Jews. "Whether these women are from Israel or from Russia, they have one thing in common: the transmitting of disease and evil in order to cause the collapse of our economy," states *Al-Sharq*. "This is the beginning of Zionist activity in the Gulf region ... for the purpose of totally destroying our leaders."

The Qatari paper goes on to quote, as source material, the notorious anti-Semitic forgery *The Protocols of the Elders of Zion*, a volume widely available in the Arab world and often cited by papers in other Arab countries. A cartoon that appeared in February in *Al-Watan*, a Qatari newspaper owned by the cousin of the emir, depicts Israeli prime minister Barak as a Nazi bombing Lebanon (see fig. 3.2).

In Syria, public school textbooks are filled with vehement hostility toward Israel and the Jewish people. A new study of Syrian textbooks for grades 4 to 11, published by the Washington, D.C.-based Middle East Media Research Institute, reveals state-sponsored curricula replete with anti-Semitism, Holocaust denial, demonization of Israel—and, most appallingly, an open call to exterminate Jews from the earth.

In the Palestinian Authority (PA), which is obligated through signed agreements with Israel to work against incitement, official news organs do not hesitate to join in this bashing of Israel and Jews. *Al-Hayat Al-Jedidah*, the official PA daily with the widest circulation, published a cartoon at the end of last year (see fig. 3.3) depicting a short, grotesque figure labeled with a Star of David as "the disease of the century" situated between an old man, who represents the twentieth century, and a young man, denoting the twenty-first.

According to recent press reports, Hitler's *Mein Kampf*, which is officially permitted for publication and distribution within the Palestinian Authority, is number six on the best-seller list in PA-controlled areas (see fig. 3.4).

Fig. 3.1.

Cartoon in an official Egyptian newspaper
Caption on paint can: "[Israeli Foreign Minister David] Levy's Diplomacy."
Source: *Al-Gumhuriya* (Egypt), February 29, 2000

Fig. 3.2.

Lebanon-Israeli
Nazi Practices

Southern Lebanon

Written on tie: "[Israeli Prime
Minister] Barak."

Cartoon in a Qatari newspaper owned by cousin of the Emir
Source: *Al-Watan* (Qatar), February 21, 2000

Fig. 3.3.

The twentieth century     The disease of the century!!!     The twenty-first century
[depicts a Jew]

Cartoon from an official Palestinian Authority newspaper
Source: *Al-Hayat Al-Jedida* (Palestinian Authority), December 15, 1999

Across the Jordan River, many educated and influential citizens of Jordan, members of the kingdom's professional associations, remain adamantly opposed to any interaction with Israelis, despite the Hashemite Kingdom's historic peace with Israel. In one recent, egregious example, the Jordanian Journalists Association expelled one member, and compelled three others to sign an apology, for committing the "crime" of visiting Israel—fully five years after Israel and Jordan achieved peace.

As the noted Johns Hopkins University scholar Fouad Ajami has observed in his study *The Dream Palace of the Arabs*, "the custodians of political power" in the Arab world determined some time ago that "diplomatic accommodation would be the order of the day, but the intellectual class was given a green light to agitate against the peace."

Fig. 3.4.

1995 Lebanese edition of *Mein Kampf*, today a best-seller in Palestinian Authority-controlled areas

When we raised our ongoing concerns about anti-Semitism in the Arab media during an American Jewish Committee mission last month to Oman, Qatar, the United Arab Emirates, Jordan, and the Palestinian Authority, our interlocutors characterized this poison as "the price of a free press." I must note, however, that one would be hard-pressed to find examples of this sort of condemnation and criticism leveled against the regimes these news organs serve, or any other neighboring regime.

At the same time, when pressed to enhance their relations with Israel, government officials pleaded for patience because, after all, while the government is more than willing to deepen ties with the Jewish state, public opinion is not yet ready.

There is no acknowledgment of any linkage between a people's perception of Israel and the daily venom fed them through the Arab media and school curricula—all sanctioned by the respective Arab governments.

Though the outcome of negotiations may be relations as chilly as those with Egypt, Israel is prepared to take calculated risks to achieve peace because that remains a far better alternative than permanent belligerency. But the antagonistic posture of the Arab media, schools, religious leaders, and intellectuals hardly contributes to creating the necessary climate and culture of peace that is so desperately needed to turn the region from conflict to cooperation.

### Middle East Action

Islamic anti-Semitic activity in the Middle East deserves heightened attention from the United States. It is an inconvenient truth that can no longer be ignored or downplayed or viewed as little more than an Arab negotiating tactic in the complex Arab-Israeli peace talks. There is, in short, an urgent need to reject this behavior unconditionally.

The United States is in an unprecedented position to make a difference in the Middle East—not in all the countries of the region, perhaps, but certainly many. Our government should condemn hateful rhetoric in the clearest of terms. To some degree, at least, the fate of the region depends on it.

## Testimony on the Middle East to Special Session of the UN Commission on Human Rights
## Geneva
## October 17, 2000

Mr. Chairman,

The tragic events of the past few weeks touch us all deeply, irrespective of who we are, where we live, or the manner in which we worship.

For seven years, the Oslo peace process has brought real dividends to the Palestinian people. The American Jewish Committee has actively supported the peace process, and in doing so has reached out to a number of Arab countries represented here today, and has also sought to launch a new chapter in the relationship between the Muslim and Jewish religions.

The very existence of the Palestinian Authority, its various ministries, and its jurisdiction over the daily lives of some 98 percent of the Palestinian people clearly shows that the path to peace lies through negotiations. And it was so recently, for example, that a truly historic, far-reaching peace agreement was put on the negotiating table by Israeli prime minister Ehud Barak, the democratically elected leader of Israel. That opportunity for a breakthrough, however, not for the first time, was lost by the unwillingness of the Palestinian side to engage it. Now, we may have yet another possibility to put the peace train back on the tracks with the welcome news from Sharm el-Sheikh. Let us hope it will indeed yield positive results.

The present special session of the Commission on Human Rights underlines the tragic consequences that result when the road of violence is chosen over the road of dialogue. And like all meetings of the United Nations, today we must strive to see past the rhetoric, to channel our emotions, and to contribute constructively toward the protection of human rights.

Thus, this Commission on Human Rights has the obligation to confront the complex—and I wish to underscore the word "complex"—realities of the present situation. A one-sided discussion that ignores inconvenient facts to the contrary will not help. And a one-sided, politically charged outcome can have grievous, truly counterproductive results on the ground, and therefore must be avoided.

We respectfully submit that this commission ought not fail to address:

**One, the desecration of Jewish religious sites.** The important Jewish holy site of Joseph's Tomb, located in Nablus, was destroyed by a Palestinian mob after the Palestinian police failed to protect it, while the ancient synagogue in Jericho was also damaged. Reference was made this morning to the rebuilding of the Tomb, but mention was not made of the fact that the intended new use is not as a Jewish holy site. These outrages also included the destruction of Jewish holy books and Jewish religious articles. As well, Jewish worshipers at the *Kotel* (also know as the Western Wall) have been denied access to this place of worship, central to the Jewish historical and religious narrative, because of Palestinian rock-throwing. Religious freedom and access to religious sites must be ensured by the commission.

**Two, incitement to hatred by Palestinian Authority officials and by PA-appointed officials.** Why was this documented fact so conveniently ignored by so many of this morning's speakers? We cannot remain silent when the Middle East Media Research Institute translation of a Friday sermon quotes a member of a PA-appointed body exhorting, "Have no mercy on the Jews, no matter where they are, in any country. Fight them, wherever they are. Wherever you meet them, kill them." Or when the Palestinian Broadcasting Authority repeatedly runs films of the intifada, and incites its viewers to take to the streets, where not only stones are used, though some would have us believe this is the case, but live ammunition as well.

Mr. Chairman, over and over hatred is taught—in Palestinian schools, in religious settings, in the Palestinian media. It is verifiable, and it is an incitement to the violation of human rights.

I must also add our profound concern about the dozens of despicable anti-Semitic incidents, including attacks on synagogues, that have occurred in the last two weeks far from the Middle East, but surely encouraged by calls to violence and holy war emanating from there.

**Three, the violations of international law across the Lebanese-Israeli border.** For years, this commission has called upon Israel to respect Security Council Resolution 425. That has now taken place. But the resolution did not end there, and international law certainly does not stop there. Lebanon is obliged to ensure its effective authority in the area. The hostage-taking of Israelis, and the violation of the international border, contradict every norm of civilized behavior, international law, and the UN Charter. The commission must condemn this behavior and its sponsors in clear language.

Mr. Chairman, it is the sacred duty of this commission to protect the human rights of all people. Indeed, historians have documented the vital role played by the American Jewish Committee at the founding of the United Nations in ensuring that the UN Charter included protection of human rights. We are immensely proud of that role and of our subsequent involvement in extending the reach of international human rights both in word and in deed. But human rights protection cannot be inconsistently applied, as some would seek in this case.

Mr. Chairman, the Middle East situation per se is not the only challenge facing this commission. For the concerns that we have laid out in this statement are not political—they are human. And silence or selective outrage in the face of such tragedies would do more than weigh on the individual consciences of the representatives in this room. It would send a message to the whole world that human rights are not universally protected by a single standard for all. How ill-befitting of this commission that would be!

## Testimony on the Middle East to
## 57th Session of the UN Commission on Human Rights
## Geneva
## March 27, 2001

Mr. Chairman,

I speak on behalf of the American Jewish Committee. This organization has a long history of association with the United Nations, dating back to the founding conference in San Francisco. Indeed, historians have credited the American Jewish Committee with an indispensable role in the inclusion of human rights references in the UN Charter, as well as an active part in the adoption of the Universal Declaration of Human Rights and the Genocide Convention. Moreover, as the honorable high commissioner knows well, it was Jacob Blaustein, a president of the American Jewish Committee, who, in 1963, originally proposed the creation of her position in his Dag Hammerskjold Memorial Lecture at Columbia University.

In addition to our steadfast commitment to the extension and protection of international human rights, we have also sought to play a constructive role in advancing mutual understanding among the different nations, races, and religions that define the human family. To this end, on May 2 in Washington, we will be releasing two books under the heading *Children of Abraham*, which aim to familiarize Jews with the beauty and essence of the Islamic heritage and Muslims with the beauty and essence of the Jewish heritage. These books will also shortly be available in Arabic.

Mr. Chairman, it is precisely because of our long-standing dedication to the often-elusive goals of international peace and harmony that I am compelled to express my concern about the direction this commission took at the special session in October and that some would have it take again now.

The abuse of the commission for transparently political purposes frustrates the defense of human rights and complicates still further the quest for peace.

The mission and moral authority of this commission originate in the pursuit of justice. But this justice must never be partial or selective. It must be justice derived from equal treatment. The State of Israel awaits such justice from this body.

Israel has been the only country to be separated from the rest of the world for special examination. In fact, the very construction of the commission's agenda underscores this all too graphically—Item 8 is dedicated to Israel and Israel alone, while Item 9 covers literally the rest of the world.

Further, the mandate for the special rapporteur on the occupied territories is unlike any other. It is open-ended, not subject to review, and it presumes that Israel is guilty of violations at the outset. In addition, the special rapporteur, inexplicably, investigates only Israeli actions, not Palestinian actions.

Palestinian violations of human rights are plentiful and well documented. They must not be ignored, even if politically inconvenient for some of the members of the commission. But then, sadly, some members of the commission also chose to ignore the historic opportunity offered by Israel last year to achieve a watershed peace deal based on unprecedented compromises, only to see it categorically rejected by a Palestinian leadership that once again took a counterproductive all-or-nothing approach.

An inquiry commission was called for by the special session. Had it impartially investigated both sides to this exceptionally complex conflict, the resulting report surely would have included the following proven and pertinent facts:

First, a Palestinian Authority cabinet minister publicly admitted that the violence following Prime Minister Sharon's visit to the Temple Mount in September was a premeditated response after the Palestinian refusal to move forward in the peace talks at Camp David.

Second, Jewish religious sites have been desecrated by Palestinian mobs. This is part of a determined Palestinian campaign, in Jerusalem and elsewhere, to deny the Jewish religious and historical link to the land.

Third, the Palestinian Authority continues its policy of incitement to violence in the media, in schools, and, through some religious leaders, in the mosques. The Palestinian leadership has not yet called for the cessation of the incitement or the violence. We await that call.

Fourth, acts of terror, with devastating consequences, have been perpetrated against Israel, both within the 1967 boundaries and beyond. Again, Palestinian leadership has failed to condemn these acts, much less call for their end.

Instead of an objective study, however, this commission received the report of the inquiry commission (E/CN.4/2001/121), whose lamentable features include a virtual endorsement of Palestinian violence. Nowhere in the report, for example, does one find references to Hamas, Islamic Jihad, or Fatah's Tanzim, though each of these groups has publicly accepted responsibility for attacks on Israeli civilians and soldiers.

The report explicitly advocates Palestinian positions on political topics that are well beyond the commission's mandate and are subject to negotiation between Israel and the Palestinian Authority.

Mr. Chairman, we once again call on this Commission on Human Rights to play a positive role in seeking to protect human rights for all, without prejudice, in the Arab-Israeli conflict. It is not too late. By doing so, this body will be fulfilling its mandate and making a constructive contribution to the region; otherwise, I fear, one-sided actions that fail to take into account all the facts, complexities, and nuances will do this commission a grave disservice and, equally, a grave disservice to the cause of peace.

## Testimony on Iran to
## 57th Session of the UN Commission on Human Rights
### Geneva
### March 29, 2001

Mr. Chairman,

I speak on behalf of the American Jewish Committee, one of the world's oldest human rights organizations, to express a growing concern about the condition of human rights in the Islamic Republic of Iran.

After reading the special rapporteur's report (E/CN.4/2001/39) on human rights in Iran, it is clear that the situation has deteriorated over the course of the past year.

Abuses of human rights can be identified in a number of areas, including: extrajudicial execution of dissidents; killing or imprisonment of journalists; violations of religious freedom; and the persecution and disappearance of members of minority groups.

First, the Iranian government has been responsible for the extrajudicial murders of intellectuals, students, and political dissidents alike, and these killings continue unabated. While the Iranian authorities' lack of cooperation has prevented our obtaining precise numbers, it has been estimated by knowledgeable sources that in the first six months of the year 2000, there were over 130 such executions.

Citizens continue to be prosecuted without a fair or open trial, and are sentenced to death for often ambiguous offenses and in the absence of sufficient procedural safeguards. Iran's judicial and penitentiary systems should, once and for all, be brought in line with international human rights standards.

Second, we are alarmed by reports that numerous journalists and editors have been intimidated or imprisoned, several of whom now face the death penalty. As of January 31 of this year, eleven journalists were imprisoned on charges of "subversive activities against national security" and "defaming the authorities."

If press freedom is an indication of a nation's commitment to basic freedoms of expression, thought, and opinion, it is revealing to discover that since last April more than thirty reformist newspapers and magazines have been banned, in blatant contravention of the relevant protections in the International Covenant on Civil and Political Rights and other documents to which Iran is signatory. Why are the Iranian authorities so fearful of a free press?

Third, religious minorities in Iran are consistently persecuted, and detention and executions are often based solely upon the religion of the victim. Strikingly, apostasy—i.e., "insulting the sanctities of Islam"— is punishable by death.

The Baha'i, a religious group that remains "unrecognized" by the state, faces discrimination on every level. The Iranian government prevents the Baha'is from practicing or teaching their religion, attending university, serving in the army or judiciary, and taking up many other jobs. Baha'i holy sites and cemeteries have been seized, and many individuals have had their personal and business property confiscated. As of June 30, 2000, eleven Baha'is were under arrest for the practice of their faith, and four had been sentenced to death.

Even so-called recognized religions do not escape persecution. In March 1999, Iranian authorities arrested a group of thirteen Jews, which included a number of religious leaders and their students, including a sixteen-year-old boy. After a year's imprisonment without trial, ten were eventually tried behind closed doors on unsubstantiated charges of having illegal contact with "hostile foreign powers" and were sentenced to prison terms of four to thirteen years. Last month, we were pleased to see the release of one of these wrongly accused. We earnestly hope that he will be joined shortly by the nine remaining victims of this miscarriage of justice.

Evangelical Christians are also subjected to repressive measures, and we are concerned by the number of reports that implicate the government of Iran in the murder or disappearance of several Evangelical Christian leaders over the past ten years.

And fourth, the high number of disappearances that occur within Iran is a major cause of concern. For example, between 1994 and 1997, eleven Iranian Jews aged between twenty-two and sixty-four have been reported missing. They disappeared without trace while trying to leave Iran. We ask the Iranian authorities to account for their fate.

Finally, Mr. Chairman, we respectfully urge this commission to take seriously the findings of the special rapporteur and to monitor the implementation of his recommendations to establish and protect human rights within Iran.

We call upon the government of Iran to extend an invitation to the special rapporteur of the Commission on Human Rights to visit the country and to resume full cooperation with him.

We wish to remind the distinguished representatives present here today that the Islamic Republic of Iran is party, inter alia, to the International Covenant on Civil and Political Rights, the Covenant on Economic Social and Cultural Rights, and the Covenant on the Elimination of All Forms of Racial Discrimination. Iran's flagrant disregard for many of the principles of these covenants makes a mockery of international norms and laws.

Mr. Chairman, the Iranian people are the heirs and trustees of one of the world's great civilizations. They deserve better than the intolerance and repression that limit many of their most basic freedoms. And the present regime deserves the reproach and condemnation of the international community for its flagrant disregard of enshrined human rights standards and equal protection for all its citizens.

Mr. Chairman, I thank you.

## Letter on the Middle East to UN Ambassadors
## from the European Union and Associated Countries
## Geneva
## April 6, 2001

Dear Ambassador:

The American Jewish Committee has a long history of involvement in the effort to advance Arab-Israeli peace and reconciliation. We have traveled frequently to the Arab world for meetings with government leaders, as well as to the West Bank and Gaza for the purpose of exchanging views with Chairman Arafat and assessing the situation on the ground.

Moreover, we have sought to strengthen relations between the Muslim and Jewish faiths, fearing that the current tragedy unfolding in the Middle East could otherwise take on an ominous theological dimension that would only further exacerbate an already explosive situation.

Mr. Ambassador, it is against this backdrop that I write to you today regarding the UN Commission on Human Rights. As the European Union and its associated countries consider their position on a resolution submitted under Agenda Item 8, I respectfully urge you to bear in mind several points, which we believe to be of central importance to the discussion.

First, the Commission on Human Rights should act responsibly in the decisions it takes. Any decision ought to enhance the prospects for a resumption of peaceful negotiations, which represent the only realistic path toward an end to the conflict.

Second, the Commission on Human Rights should look at all the facts, not just selected issues. The Palestinian side has committed countless documented violations of human rights since the onset of violence last year, yet at the special session in October these violations were entirely ignored in the resolution adopted (S-5/1), nor are they even remotely reflected in the draft resolution under consideration.

In fact, this current draft is glaringly lacking in balance. It uses inflammatory language, including unsubstantiated and politically motivated references to "war crimes," "the deliberate and systematic killing of Palestinian civilians and children," "flagrant violations of the right to life," and "a major threat to international peace and security in the region and the world."

Third, Israel has the internationally recognized right and responsibility to protect its citizens, who have been the targets of repeated armed attacks. The victims have included women and children.

Fourth, repeated Palestinian calls to launch a "holy war" and to "kill Jews" have been made.

This incitement of the Palestinian populace has been confirmed on Palestinian television and radio, in many mosques, and even in schools, and reawakens serious concerns about whether the ultimate Palestinian goal is the creation of an independent state living side by side and in peace with Israel, or an attempt to destroy Israel itself.

Indeed, listening to several of the governmental and nongovernmental speakers under Agenda Item 8, it was not at all clear whether, in referring to "occupied lands," they were talking about territories seized by Israel in 1967 in a legitimate war of self-defense, or to all of Israel.

And finally, if the Palestinian goal is indeed the creation of an independent state living side by side in peace with Israel, as we earnestly hope it is, it is hard to understand the categorical rejection of Prime Minister Barak's strenuous efforts last summer at Camp David and this January at Taba to negotiate a lasting and comprehensive peace agreement.

Prime Minister Barak extended his hand in peace and put on the table a far-reaching proposal. Instead of engaging it seriously, however, the Palestinian Authority totally rejected it, insisting on the "right of return of Palestinian refugees and their descendants," the practical effect of which would surely mean the end of the State of Israel.

Moreover, it is now abundantly clear that the Palestinian Authority planned the current round of violence to divert world attention from its repudiation of the peace process. Indeed, as the Palestinian communications minister and other leading officials have acknowledged, the violence was premeditated. The calculation was really quite simple: Palestinian violence would trigger an Israeli military response, and the international community would quickly rush to the side of the "weaker" party.

Mr. Ambassador, such premeditated violence and abandonment of the peace table should not be rewarded by the international community. Instead, we submit that the international community should focus on urging a cessation of the violence—an end to the tragic loss of life on both sides—and a resumption of the peace talks, in the spirit of the Madrid Conference and the Oslo Accords and based on UN Security Council Resolutions 242 and 338. Such an approach could make a lasting contribution to the goal we share—a peaceful new era in the Middle East for Palestinians and Israelis alike.

I am grateful for your consideration of these views.

## Testimony on Women and the Taliban to 57th Session of the UN Commission on Human Rights Geneva April 9, 2001

I speak on behalf of the American Jewish Committee. We wish to express our profound concern for the indescribably oppressive conditions endured by women living under Taliban rule in Afghanistan. It is abundantly clear that the Taliban are perpetrating unprecedented, systematic, and widespread gender discrimination against women.

The report of the special rapporteur on violence against women (E/CN.4/2000/68/Add.4) reflects the horrors faced by women in Afghanistan as they fall victim to the Taliban's grotesque interpretation of Islamic law. Moreover, it is with great sadness that we note the absence of any improvement in the situation over the past year.

The UN Charter, the Universal Declaration on Human Rights, and many international conventions enshrine the full and equal rights of both men and women. With these protections established, women should no longer have to endure second-class status anywhere, much less, as in the case in Afghanistan, no status at all.

The Taliban edicts enforced on the lives of Afghan women deny them their most fundamental human rights, indeed suffocate their very existence. Their lives are restricted to such an extent that these women are effectively reduced to silent ghosts.

Forced to wear a *burqua*, a loose veil to ensure that the body is covered from head to toe with only a small cloth screen for vision, the women of Afghanistan face harsh and archaic punishment, such as public flogging, if they are seen to be wavering from the dress code. This physical restriction is symbolic of the attempt to destroy the individual identity of women.

Employment of women has been outlawed, and they are denied access even to the most basic health services. Education for girls over the age of eight has been prohibited. While in their own homes, women must not be seen from the street, and may not step outside their homes unless accompanied by a male relative.

At every turn, even in the smallest details of life, women face emotionally devastating restrictions. For example, they risk being beaten for laughing in public and are forbidden to "walk loudly"—thus shoes that make noise have been outlawed.

The long arm and probing eye of the so-called Ministry for the Propagation of Virtue and the Prevention of Vice, the Taliban's "religious police," enforce these rigid constraints.

This on-going exclusion from any activity deemed to be "un-Islamic" has resulted in virtual house arrest for women. It is therefore unsurprising that a report by Physicians for Human Rights reveals that 97 percent of women in Afghanistan show signs of major depression.

With conflict still raging in parts of the country, women live in constant fear of rape or abduction by Taliban soldiers. There are credible reports, received from women who have fled the country, that a number of Afghan women in danger zones are driven to commit suicide to avoid such a fate.

Mr. Chairman, we regret that the constant threat of intimidation and harassment renders the admirable attempts of international aid workers to promote basic human rights for Afghan women ineffectual.

Without any doubt, the plight of the Afghan women constitutes a matter of the greatest urgency. Unfortunately, Pakistan, Saudi Arabia, and the United Arab Emirates have extended recognition to the Taliban regime. Even more troubling, however, Pakistan has provided indispensable assistance to keep the Taliban in power. In doing so, Pakistan not only legitimizes the Taliban's ruthless actions against women but, as a consequence, shares responsibility for this documented pattern of human rights abuses.

Mr. Chairman, human rights are universal and indivisible. No religious, political, or other banner should be allowed to justify abuses against women, be it the brutal suppression of women under Taliban rule or, for that matter, the horrific practice of female genital mutilation that is inflicted on up to 2 million young women each year, especially in a number of African and Middle Eastern countries.

As a matter of priority, we urge all governments to reaffirm their commitment to implementing the laudable aims of the 1995 Beijing Declaration, which seeks "to advance the goals of equality, development, and peace for all women in the interest of all humanity."

Mr. Chairman, I thank you.

## Letter on the Durban Conference to UN Ambassadors
## Geneva
## July 30, 2001

Dear Ambassador:

As we embark upon the Third Preparatory Committee for the World Conference Against Racism (WCAR) in Durban, South Africa, I would like to share certain deep concerns regarding the tone and direction of the preparations.

When the General Assembly decided to hold the WCAR, we saluted this resolution to advance the global fight against racism—both in its most persistent forms and in its new manifestations.

Now, with just one month before the conference, the process is marred by the introduction of political considerations wholly alien to the themes of the conference and certain language that has been, paradoxically, tinged with racism.

Specifically, I ask your help in ensuring:

First, the conference must not be country-specific. This accepted principle of world conferences helps to prevent their unraveling, and the need to respect it in the case of the WCAR could not be more evident.

Second, the hateful "Zionism is racism" lie, which was on the UN's books from 1975 to 1991, should not be reintroduced, either directly or by implication. Secretary-General Kofi Annan has called that resolution "lamentable," and has said that "deep and painful scars remain." Further, at the opening of today's session of the Preparatory Committee, High Commissioner for Human Rights Mary Robinson stated that it is "inappropriate to reopen this issue in any form here."

Third, references to "the Holocaust" ought to remain in the singular and with a capital "H." The term "the Holocaust" has a historical specificity relating to the Nazi attempt from 1933 to 1945 to eliminate Europe's Jewish population. Efforts to change the term, or to juxtapose it to unrelated events, are historically disingenuous.

Fourth, a serious discussion of anti-Semitism, a pernicious and continuing form of racism, needs to be undertaken at Durban. Both the Strasbourg and Santiago regional conferences recognized the deep roots of anti-Semitism and the need to combat it. I strongly urge your delegation to help assure that it be recognized in the Conference Declaration and Programme of Action.

Finally, the World Conference must address the legacies of slavery, the slave trade, and colonialism that still underpin present-day racism, racial discrimination, xenophobia, and related intolerance. The fight against racism requires an honest understanding of the past and the lessons that it provides. However, we share the view that the conference must, in the final analysis, remain forward-looking if it is to advance the agenda of the fight against racism.

The impact of the Declaration and Programme of Action that are ultimately adopted at the South African meeting should not be underestimated. Born with the imprimatur of a United Nations world conference, the language adopted will provide a powerful basis for future wording of UN resolutions and declarations. It is in this light that we attach such importance to the negotiations now taking place.

I respectfully urge you to help ensure a positive conference outcome in the interests of the integrity of the United Nations and the compelling need to address racism as a concern that affects societies throughout the world.

Please accept the expression of my highest esteem.

# 4. MEDIA ACTIVITY

## Peace and Poison in the Middle East
### *Washington Post*
### May 2, 2000

As Israeli and Palestinian negotiators move toward a much-awaited permanent settlement, there has been a shocking rise in vitriolic anti-Semitism across the Arab world.

This extraordinary paradox of Israeli and Arab political leaders attempting to build peace while official Arab media, schools, religious leaders, and intellectuals actively demonize the Jewish people is startling.

When the Islamic mufti of Jerusalem made deeply painful comments repudiating the facts of the Holocaust, they received wide attention in the Western world because they came during the remarkable visit to Israel of Pope John Paul II.

Likewise, when the official Syrian government newspaper *Tishreen* recently asserted that "Zionists created the Holocaust myth to blackmail and terrorize the world's intellectuals and politicians," the editorial attracted broad attention and condemnation because it appeared amid efforts to jump-start the stalled Israeli-Syrian peace talks.

Less noted was the fact that these two outrages are the rule, not the exception.

Across the Arab world the language of Holocaust denial has become common. Editorials and columns similar to the one in *Tishreen* can be found in *Al-Ahram*, *Al-Akhbar,* and *Al-Gumhuriya*, three of the official daily newspapers in Egypt.

In recent weeks, Arab papers have stepped up their attacks on Israel—and on the Jewish people—by labeling in vile words and in gross caricatures Israel's prime minister and foreign minister as Nazis, and accusing Israel of the most bizarre machinations.

The official newspaper in Qatar, one of two forward-looking Gulf nations to open commercial ties with Israel, has warned that Israel dispatches beautiful women to advance trade—and undermine the sheikdom. "Whether these women are from Israel or from Russia, they have one thing in common: the transmitting of disease and evil in order to cause the collapse of our economy," states *Al-Sharq.*

The official Qatari paper goes on to quote from the notorious anti-Semitic forgery *The Protocols of the Elders of Zion,* which is widely available in the Arab world and is often cited by papers in other Arab countries.

While the Palestinian Authority is obligated through signed agreements with Israel to work against incitement, its official news organs do not hesitate to join in the vituperation of Israel and Jews.

Arab schools are in dutiful step with the editorial writers and columnists.

For example, a new study by the Middle East Media Research Institute reveals that Syrian textbooks for grades 4 to 11 are replete with anti-Semitism, Holocaust denial, demonization of Israel—and, most appalling, an open call to exterminate Jews from the earth!

While the United Nations has declared anti-Semitism a form of racism that must be condemned, Arab intellectuals are preaching it as gospel.

As the noted Johns Hopkins University scholar Fouad Ajami has observed in *The Dream Palace of the Arabs,* "the custodians of political power" in the Arab world determined some time ago that "diplomatic accommodation would be the order of the day, but the intellectual class was given a green light to agitate against the peace."

This has long been the situation in Egypt, where as recently as March 28 several Israeli diplomats invited to a conference at the University of Cairo were denied entry when they arrived. But it also is true in Jordan, where, despite the Hashemite Kingdom's landmark peace with Israel, professional associations remain adamantly opposed to any interaction with Israelis.

When we raised our concerns about anti-Semitism in the Arab media during an American Jewish Committee mission to five Arab countries in March, our interlocutors proclaimed this the price of a "free" press and assured us that comprehensive peace would moderate the media.

At the same time, when pressed on improving their relations with Israel, government officials pleaded for patience because, after all, while the government was more than willing to deepen ties with the Jewish state, "public opinion" was not yet ready.

What a peculiar situation! Is there no acknowledgment of linkage between people's perception of Israel and the daily venom fed them through the Arab media and school curricula—all sanctioned by the respective Arab governments?

Israel is prepared to take calculated risks to achieve peace. But the antagonistic posture of the Arab media, schools, religious leaders, and intellectuals hardly contributes to the climate and culture that are so desperately needed to turn the region from conflict to cooperation.

## Deal Justly, Iran
*Boston Globe*
July 1, 2000

The verdict in the show trial of thirteen Iranian Jews is expected today—the Jewish Sabbath—in Shiraz, Iran. Iranian judiciary officials announced on June 25 that the thirteen, who are accused of spying for Israel, could face the death penalty if convicted. Given the Islamic regime's record—executing seventeen Jews since the revolution in 1979—the prospects for these thirteen, who were imprisoned more than a year ago, appear grim.

From the start, the accusations levied against the Jews, ranging in age from sixteen to forty-eight, have been lacking in credibility. The incarcerated students, rabbis, and lay religious leaders had been providing religious services on a voluntary basis to the Jewish community. For more than five years, the Iranian intelligence service known as the Ministry of Information had these individuals under surveillance, and, on a regular basis, brought them in for questioning about their activities. It is preposterous to believe that these individuals were remotely capable of carrying out acts of espionage while under surveillance in such a tightly controlled society, and, of course, there is no evidence even of a desire or motivation to do so.

The Revolutionary Court trial, closed to outside observers, is an offense to conscience and universal concepts of justice. In a reversal of standard legal norms, the thirteen detainees have been tried without ever being formally charged with a crime. And, during the extended period of imprisonment and trial—ten of the thirteen have been held in pretrial detention for well over a year—accusations against them have been arbitrary and, indeed, increasingly far-fetched.

At first, Iranian authorities accused the thirteen of holding religious classes and printing religious material. Several months later, after their arrest became international news, the Iranian Ministry of Information accused them of spying on behalf of Israel and the United States. Then, stunned by diplomatic protests from dozens of countries, Iranian officials accused them of spying on behalf of Israel, Iraq, and Turkey—and plotting to poison the water supply of Shiraz, an insidious claim eerily reminiscent of medieval anti-Semitic canards.

Since the trial got underway, the only actual evidence presented has been the so-called confessions of the detainees. Defense attorneys, however, responded that the confessions were contradictory and inconsistent with one another, suggesting that, as in all such show trials, the confessions were made under severe duress.

Although Iranian authorities announced at the trial's start that eight Muslims were involved in the alleged espionage plot, only one ever appeared in court, on the last day of the trial, and he denied all charges against him. At the same session, four of the Jewish detainees recanted their confessions, asserting that they had been forcibly extracted.

To state the painfully obvious, the picture looks truly bleak. Yet there is still time for Iran to weigh carefully its judicial decision, and whether it wishes to remain an international pariah or chart a more promising path befitting a country with an ancient and proud civilization in which Islamic, Persian, and Jewish cultures have long enriched one another.

In the final analysis the leaders of this Islamic state would be well served to recall the Koranic verse: "Be steadfast witnesses for Allah in equity, and let not hatred of any people seduce you that you deal not justly. Deal justly, that is nearer to your duty." The world will be watching.

## Palestinians at the Crossroads
### *Die Welt* (Germany)
### October 25, 2000

Meeting earlier this year with the mayor of Kalkilya, a Palestinian town in the West Bank, I was struck by the large painting of the Dome of the Rock, the larger of the two mosques on the Temple Mount, hanging outside his office. Below the mosque was a rat emblazoned with the Magen David, the Jewish star and the symbol of Israel.

A second painting, displayed in the conference room, depicted the land of Israel and the Palestinian territories—from the Jordan River to the Mediterranean Sea—as one country wrapped in a Palestinian flag with al-Quds (Jerusalem) at the center in the shape of a heart.

Anyone visiting this mayor, who is described in the Palestinian world as a moderate, could not help but be haunted by the sinister message of these provocative and sobering paintings.

As I watched with anguish the tragic—and unnecessary—violence that engulfed Jerusalem, the West Bank and Gaza, and Israel, starting on the eve of Rosh Hashanah, these images came back to haunt me.

Durable Israeli-Palestinian peace—indeed, a permanent end to the Arab-Israeli conflict—can only be achieved on the basis of mutual political recognition, mutual respect, and education for peace.

Mutual recognition was achieved in 1993, when Israel and the PLO agreed to embark on an intensive new phase of the peace process, setting the stage for an independent Palestinian state in the West Bank and Gaza and launching a potentially new era of peaceful cooperation.

From the beginning, moreover, both sides agreed that Jerusalem, the most complex issue on the table, as Henry Kissinger foresaw two decades ago, would be left for the final stage of negotiations. That would presumably allow for the development of greater trust between Israelis and Palestinians.

But during the past seven years, the Palestinian Authority has conducted a pernicious campaign to negate any Jewish claims whatsoever to Judaism's holiest city, Jerusalem. Propagation of the false view that the Temple Mount is exclusive to Islam began long before Ariel Sharon's visit.

This campaign has intensified since Palestinian Authority chairman Yasir Arafat spurned Israel's far-reaching offers, including a willingness to explore compromises on Jerusalem, at Camp David this summer. Members of Arafat's cabinet have publicly asserted that the First and Second Jewish Temples never existed, a bizarre claim, all the more so since the Jewish temples are mentioned in the Koran. Nevertheless, the concerted effort to assert an exclusive claim to the Temple Mount is propagated on the Palestinian Authority Web site, through the media, and in the mosques in Palestinian-controlled areas. Myth is being rewritten as history before the world's eyes. So much for mutual respect and education for peace.

To support this campaign, the Palestinian Authority, using the Sharon visit as a pretext for renewed violence, encouraged the attacks on Israelis by spreading through Palestinian media and schools malicious rumors about the Al-Aksa mosque, busing Palestinian children to violent demonstrations, and thereby cynically putting them directly in harm's way. Palestinian police did nothing to quell the brutal violence, and some used their weapons to participate in the assaults.

Abandoning any semblance of critical judgment, too many in the international community bought the simplistic story of Israeli persecution and excessive use of force, without ever asking the tough questions about Palestinian behavior or motives.

And, in the process, too many politicians and journalists, especially here in Europe, also lost sight of the significance of Jerusalem to Judaism, not just to Islam. Somehow, they have forgotten or conveniently ignored Jerusalem's centrality to Jewish history and identity for over 3,000 years, much less the nineteen-year period after Israel's independence in 1948 when Jews were denied any access to their holiest places (under Jordanian control) and the revered Western Wall was nothing more than an alleyway strewn with refuse.

In total contrast, Israel has always recognized the sacred Islamic tie to the Temple Mount, allowing, since 1967, Muslim control of the two mosques, while making every effort to assure free access for all faiths to their holy places throughout Jerusalem.

Now, as Iran and Iraq, and some Islamic religious leaders, among others, call for a holy war to "liberate" Jerusalem and for the wholesale destruction of Israel, Arafat's uncompromising stance on Jerusalem has revealed the Palestinians' deep desire to return to those days of exclusive Islamic control over the cornerstone of Judaism, the Temple Mount and the Western Wall, and once again raised profound concerns about longer-term Arab and Palestinian goals as well.

Jerusalem, as well as the other issues on the table for a permanent agreement, can be resolved, but not through incendiary rhetoric and the calculated use of violence to regain international sympathy and put pressure on Israel for still further compromise.

Palestinian leaders today are at a crossroads. They can abide by previously signed commitments to forswear violence, grasp the outstretched hand of Prime Minister Barak and his government, and begin building true peace—a culture of peace—between neighbors.

Or they can perpetuate conflict. The irrepressible Yogi Berra once said that if you come to a fork in the road, take it. Arafat is at a fork, but, try as he might, he can't have it both ways. For the sake of all the children of Abraham, let him choose the right way, the path of peace and cooperation.

## Stop Tolerating Calls for the Slaughter of Jews
### *International Herald Tribune*
### November 7, 2000

Not since the 1930s have Jews worldwide been exposed to the kinds of threats that were being vocalized on the streets of major cities in recent weeks. From Washington to Ottawa to Paris, pro-Palestinian demonstrators have repeatedly and chillingly crossed the line of civil protest, chanting in Arabic for the "slaughter" of Jews.

This language should never be tolerated in democratic, pluralistic societies. Civic and religious leaders should instinctively condemn it. But, so far, few have recognized the seriousness of these threats, even when the documented record of assaults on Jews worldwide is growing.

The vitriolic hatred is especially volatile in the current context of heightened violence in the Middle East, where some Muslim religious and Arab political leaders have been calling for holy war, jihad, against Israel—and against Jews.

A sermon in the Al-Aksa mosque in Jerusalem, broadcast by the Palestinian Authority, called on Muslims to "eradicate the Jews from Palestine." And a cleric appointed by the Palestinian Authority, addressing worshipers at Friday prayers, declared: "Have no mercy on the Jews, no matter where they are, in any country. Fight them where they are. Wherever you meet them, kill them."

Some among the faithful already believe they are in the midst of such a crusade, and far from the Middle East they have begun to answer calls for war against the Jewish people. Since early October there have been dozens of attacks on synagogues, schools, and other Jewish sites across France, Germany, England, Australia, South Africa, and elsewhere in Western Europe, North America, and Latin America.

In France alone, more than seventy attacks have included destruction of a synagogue, including its five sacred Torah scrolls, near Versailles, desecration of several Paris synagogues, and stone-throwing at children going to or from Jewish schools.

Six years ago, Rashid Baz, in an act of revenge linked to events in the Middle East, opened fire on a van on New York's Brooklyn Bridge, killing Ari Halberstam, one of the yeshiva student passengers. That premeditated murder should be recalled now, especially after shots were fired at a rabbi on a Chicago street, and an Orthodox Jew in London was stabbed repeatedly.

Religious rulings, or fatwas, issued by Muslim clerics calling for jihad against Jews wherever they live encourage this terrorism. One fatwa came from Sheikh Omar Abdel Rahman, who is serving a life sentence in a U.S. prison for his role in the World Trade Center bombing.

Another came from a Muslim group in London associated with Osama bin Laden, the terrorist mastermind sought by the United States. This fatwa has been rapidly and broadly sent through the Internet, the ultimate tool for high-speed dissemination of hate.

Western political leaders, shortsightedly, have generally dismissed the verbal threats as mere rhetoric or characterized the attacks carried out to date as random, isolated incidents. They may not be planned by the same source, but the hateful words espoused by religious leaders and the deafening silence of others in the Arab and Muslim communities surely encourage further assaults.

Whatever one may think about the Arab-Israeli conflict, there can be no justification for this outbreak of raw anti-Jewish violence.

Such incidents in Europe and America are strikingly similar to attacks in areas of the West Bank under the control of the Palestinian Authority, including the destruction of Joseph's Tomb in Nablus, the burning of the ancient synagogue in Jericho, and the cowardly murder of Hillel Lieberman, the rabbi who tried to save the Torah scrolls at Joseph's Tomb.

Given this contempt for Judaism, imagine for a moment what Palestinian demonstrators might do to Jewish worshipers and the sacred Western Wall itself if they managed to break through Israeli security guarding the entrance to the Temple Mount, Judaism's holiest place for 2,500 years.

With the Palestinian Authority stepping up its pernicious campaign to negate Jewish history by falsely claiming that the Jewish temples never existed on the Temple Mount, and with Yasir Arafat vowing to continue the current violence until the Palestinian flag is hoisted atop the ramparts of the walled Old City of Jerusalem, the war against Jews is likely to continue.

Responsible political and religious leaders must speak out clearly and unequivocally against this odious and sinister effort to extend the Arab-Israeli conflict beyond the Middle East, and condemn unconditionally the violence and calls for further attacks against Jews.

Law enforcement, slow to grasp the severity of the situation, must step up its response and recognize the dangers of the blood-curdling injunction to "slaughter the Jews."

One of the costly lessons the world should have learned is that words such as these have enormous power. When Hitler wrote *Mein Kampf* in 1925, calling for the extermination of Jews, few took him seriously. A decade later he began to implement his grotesque plan.

Today's calls for violence threaten not only Jews, but also the very foundation and fabric of Western pluralistic societies.

## How the PLO Intimidates the Media
### *Boston Globe*
### November 25, 2000

Twenty years ago, journalists covering the Palestinian scene in Beirut felt the long shadow of the PLO, a grim reality captured in *From Beirut to Jerusalem*, Thomas Friedman's Pulitzer Prize-winning book.

"The intimidating atmosphere of Beirut never prevented a major breaking news story from being covered in some way," but there were some "important stories which were deliberately ignored out of fear," observed Friedman.

Much has happened over the past two decades as the PLO evolved into the government of a state in the making, but foreign journalists covering the current crisis in the Middle East are finding that intimidation is a principle deeply ingrained in Palestinian society.

Events surrounding the horrific lynching of two Israeli reserve soldiers in Palestinian-controlled Ramallah on October 12 illustrate the point. Palestinian security forces made a vigorous effort to hunt down journalists with cameras and confiscate film and videotape. They were almost successful.

Ramallah, the West Bank seat of the Palestinian Authority and the scene of daily demonstrations, was a natural spot for foreign journalists to cover the unfolding confrontation with Israel. But the lynching was, shall we say, inconvenient for the Palestinian effort to keep the upper hand in the media war.

Until that point, the electronic media had largely presented a simplistic story of stone-throwing Palestinians facing a heavily armed Israeli army and of Palestinian children mercilessly targeted by trigger-happy Israeli soldiers, largely ignoring the widespread Palestinian use of weapons against the Israelis and also failing to ask why children were being placed in harm's way. Such coverage elicited sympathy around the world for the Palestinians, who were seen uncritically as the hapless and victimized underdogs.

A Polish television crew was surrounded by Palestinian security forces who beat them and took their film of the lynching. News crews from other countries had similar experiences.

One Italian TV crew representing a private channel, however, managed to capture the gruesome mob attack on film and sent it to Rome, where it was turned over to other media outlets and replayed around the world. That was the only visual evidence of the lynching available to television stations.

But, in a sign of the fear instilled in foreign journalists, the representative in Jerusalem of RAI, Italian state television, Ricardo Cristiano, sent a letter of apology to Arafat in which he sought to assure the Palestinian Authority that his station never would do such an act that could harm the Palestinians—indeed, he professed his own solidarity with the Palestinians. So much for objective and fearless reporting.

Cristiano's letter, published in the main Palestinian daily newspaper, caused an uproar across Italy. His station subsequently recalled him to Rome, but the damage was done, as other Italian journalists complained that Cristiano had put their lives in danger if they were going to visit Palestinian-controlled areas. (See Appendix, item 6.)

Just as most journalists were reluctant to acknowledge the PLO tactics toward their profession in Beirut, so too, evidently, are some of the foreign journalists traversing the territory of the Palestinian Authority in Gaza and the West Bank.

It took the tragedy in Ramallah to get at least one journalist to come out and report the enormous difficulties—indeed, obstacles—placed in his path.

Mark Seager, a British photographer who was to do a photo essay on Palestinian refugees, considers himself extremely lucky to have left Ramallah alive.

"I was composing the picture when I was punched in the face by a Palestinian," Mr. Seager wrote in the *Sunday Telegraph* of London on

October 22. "Another Palestinian pointed right at me shouting 'no picture, no picture,' while another guy hit me in the face and said, 'Give me your film.' One guy just pulled the camera from me and smashed it to the floor."

The Palestinian crowd displayed "such hatred, such unbelievable hatred," Seager reported. "The worst thing was that I realized the anger that they were directing at me was the same as that which they'd had toward the soldier before dragging him from the police station and killing him. It was murder of the most barbaric kind. I know that I'll have nightmares for the rest of my life." (See Appendix, item 7.)

Those experiences of journalists in Ramallah raise the question of how pervasive is the intimidation of journalists in the Palestinian Authority. It is a question that may not be answered so easily; regrettably, it is not even being discussed openly in the media.

Ironically, those journalists might not even be there were it not for the openness of Israeli society to the news media. More than 300 foreign journalists are accredited to Israel year round, and at this time of crisis that number probably has swelled to well over 1,000.

But they may well be beholden to the will and whim of the Palestinian leadership if they want access and privilege.

And, as Friedman reminds us, recounting his experiences in Beirut as a *New York Times* reporter, in the process some stories do not get told—stories about corruption in the PLO hierarchy, for example, and certainly stories about the ethical dilemma journalists have faced.

Today, among the stories not being adequately addressed, apart from the use of children, are exactly why Arafat has chosen to use confrontation as his preferred means of responding to the far-reaching efforts of Israeli prime minister Ehud Barak to achieve a peace accord, and what Palestinians are hearing in schools and mosques and on Palestinian television and radio regarding hatred of Israel and incitement to violence.

The first casualty in a conflict situation often is the truth, and the Palestinian Authority appears to be making every effort to manipulate with a heavy hand exactly how the media cover it.

## Revisionist History
### *La Tribune de Genève* (Switzerland)
### December 6, 2000

Let me see if I understand M. Berthoud correctly in his one-sided analysis of the Arab-Israeli conflict: For some mysterious reason, he asserts, a war broke out in 1967, which Israel won decisively. Then came a UN peace proposal, which Israel sabotaged, with the connivance of the United States. Since then, Israel's appetite for territory has always outpaced its appetite for peace.

In fact, this is totally revisionist history. Israel was threatened by a war of annihilation in the months leading up to the 1967 Six-Day War. After the war, Israel offered to negotiate peace, using its newly acquired territorial trump cards. The Arab response? The three noes of the 1967 Khartoum Declaration. The PLO response? Renewed support for a charter explicitly calling for Israel's destruction.

Of course, this wasn't the first Arab failure to seize a diplomatic opportunity; Arab maximalism also led to rejection of the 1947 UN Partition Plan. And when the West Bank and Gaza were in Arab hands from 1948 to 1967, there was no move to establish a Palestinian state.

In the late seventies, the U.S.-led Camp David process, which produced the historic Egyptian-Israeli accord, also proposed a Palestinian autonomy plan, but again it was turned down by an all-or-nothing stance.

And now, with a dovish Israeli government in place—which has already completed a unilateral withdrawal from southern Lebanon and tabled the most far-reaching proposals ever made by leaders of the Jewish state, including partition of Jerusalem—what is the Palestinian response? Is it further negotiation or violence? The answer is both obvious and regrettable.

To settle this complex conflict, M. Berthoud, courageous statesmanship on the Palestinian side will also be needed, along the lines of the late Anwar Sadat and King Hussein, and not the mixed signals and erratic course we have instead witnessed. If so, the Palestinians will find a willing partner in Jerusalem today; if not, tragically they will have lost yet another opportunity to turn despair into hope.

## Misrepresenting the Holocaust
*International Herald Tribune*
January 9, 2001

A Palestinian-American, Samir Toubassy, seeks to wrap himself in the mantle of the Holocaust by comparing himself to Jacqueline Waldman, a Romanian Jew who struggled to regain her ancestral home seized by the Nazis.

Hitler's Final Solution—the nearly successful attempt to exterminate all of European Jewry, including 1.5 million children—was a singular event in history. It should not be so glibly invoked to gain sympathy and score political points.

Instead, Mr. Toubassy's plight might well be juxtaposed to that of hundreds of thousands of Jews in Arab countries forced to leave their ancestral homes because of the Arab-Israeli conflict.

While I regret Mr. Toubassy's loss, it came about because of a war declared by Arab nations on the newly created state of Israel, whose right to exist was endorsed by the United Nations six months earlier. Had the Arab world accepted Israel's outstretched hand of peace at the time, Mr. Toubassy might well be living in Jaffa today instead of London.

## Lesson One: Hatred
*Washington Times*
January 12, 2001

Since violent Palestinian-Israeli clashes exploded in late September, few international human rights advocates have asked why there have been so many casualties among children and youths—more than sixty Palestinian children have lost their lives—and how it even came about that scores of children were engaged in this conflict.

The executive director of UNICEF, Carol Bellamy, addressing the UN Commission on Human Rights weeks ago, called on the Palestinian Authority "to take energetic measures to discourage those under age from participating in any violent action because such action places them at risk."

In contrast, the UN high commissioner for human rights, Mary Robinson, after visiting Israel and the Palestinian Authority last month, declared that any suggestion of Palestinians deliberately using their children in the conflict was simply racist.

As recently as last year, a UN Security Council resolution condemned the recruitment and use of children in armed conflict. Similar UN measures include the Convention on the Rights of the Child, which condemns the recruitment of children under fifteen in armed conflicts. The Fourth Geneva Convention strictly forbids the use of civilians, including children, as shields.

But the international community has been content to blame the current tragedy exclusively on Israel's allegedly excessive and wanton use of force, ignoring a pattern of Palestinian leaders encouraging children to participate and religious leaders glorifying the "martyrdom" of the youngest members of that society.

Palestinian use of children in this context stands in sharp contrast to another fierce test of political wills: In the massive Belgrade demonstrations in October calling for Milosevic's ouster, virtually no children could be seen on the streets. Serbian parents and opposition leaders knew there was a high probability of violence and responsibly kept their children out of harm's way.

But when it comes to children in Gaza and the West Bank, the Palestinian Authority seems to adhere—and be held—to a different standard.

How else can one comprehend how the European Union turns a blind eye to the contents of newly introduced textbooks in Palestinian-controlled elementary schools that make no mention of Israel on maps of "Palestine"—a curriculum developed with the financial assistance of the EU?

Instead of being educated from an early age toward becoming open-minded citizens of a future Palestinian state living side by side in peaceful coexistence with Israel—the only realistic outcome of the conflict—Palestinian children are being taught the lessons of hate and the methods of war.

Hatred is reinforced not only in schools, but also during vacation when, for example, tens of thousands of Palestinian children attend camps run by Yasir Arafat's Fatah organization to engage in weapons instruction and lessons in how to kidnap an Israeli soldier.

Moreover, the mufti of Jerusalem, the most influential Islamic cleric appointed by the Palestinian Authority, has stated that "the younger the martyr, the greater and the more I respect him." Of the mothers of these children, the mufti observed, "They willingly sacrifice their offspring for the sake of freedom. It is a great display of the power of belief. The mother is a participant in the great reward of the jihad to liberate Al-Aksa."

With this kind of political and religious leadership, is it any wonder that a twelve-year-old Palestinian boy would tell a reporter from the *Times* of London that he would be happy never to see his adult years?

"I want to die as a martyr. I will go straight to paradise if I do that," said the impressionable youth, whose schooling has taken place entirely during a period in which Israeli and Palestinian leaders engaged in peacemaking.

Or one might consider the Palestinian father, with a hand on the shoulder of his son, telling CNN that he would be satisfied if his child died defending Palestine. Or the Palestinian women in Gaza asserting that they must bear more children to replace others of their offspring who may become "martyrs."

Contrary to widely held perceptions in the West that today's conflict is essentially a reprise of the Palestinian uprising of the late 1980s and early 1990s, the realities in the West Bank and Gaza have changed substantially.

Palestinians control their major population centers—indeed, more than 95 percent of Palestinians live in areas formerly administered by Israelis. Thus, those who wish to attack—and send their children to attack—Israelis must first find them, not down the block, but outside Palestinian towns.

And though the children may be carrying stones, Palestinian adults armed with semiautomatic rifles and other weapons have not hesitated to open fire on Israelis with intent to kill, even while children are sent ahead of them into harm's way.

"What kind of independence is built on the blood of children while the leaders are safe and so are their children and grandchildren?" asked an Arab journalist writing in the London-based Arab newspaper *Al-Sharq Al-Awsat*.

Why are so many Palestinian children dying? It is surely overdue for the international community to pose that question, not just to Israel but to the Palestinian Authority as well.

## Inconvenient Truths
### *Washington Jewish Week*
### January 19, 2001

The last three months of conflict in the Middle East should have shattered preconceived notions among friends of Israel on both the right and left. There are no easy or obvious answers, as the right learns that prolonged occupation is corrosive and inconsistent with Israel's democratic values and the left realizes that its vision of a "New Middle East" is in fact the pursuit of dangerous illusions.

Moreover, demands by Palestinians for a state up to the 1967 boundaries are being intermingled with threats from some Palestinians and their allies in such countries as Iran, Iraq, Lebanon, and Libya to destroy Israel entirely, along with calls to murder Jews wherever they live, even in countries, such as France, far from the Middle East.

Isn't it odd that the current Palestinian-inspired violence erupted against the most dovish government in Israel's history, which was even willing, for the sake of peace, to compromise on Jerusalem, a previously unthinkable position for any Israeli administration? Why has this central fact been so lost in the past three months, as many in the international community once again reflexively place the blame for the outbreak of violence at Israel's doorstep?

The astonishing indifference to historical context is too often the rule of the day for many observers of the Middle East.

How many nations in the world today can claim the same 3,500-year connection between a people, a faith, and a land as the Jewish people with Israel? Or between a people, a faith, and a city as the

Jewish people with Jerusalem? Exhibit A, of course, is the book that forms the earliest cornerstone of Western civilization, the Hebrew Bible. Exhibit B is the prayer book in any synagogue anywhere in the world.

Why does the world so conveniently forget that in 1947, recognizing both an Arab and a Jewish claim to mandatory Palestine, the UN proposed a partition plan that sought to recognize the national aspirations of both peoples, and even accord Jerusalem international status? Recall the response? The Jews agreed; the Arabs, wanting it all, refused and went to war.

What happened between 1948 and 1967, when the West Bank and the eastern half of Jerusalem were under Jordanian control? Were the local Arabs given sovereign rights? Far from it. Jordan annexed the land, and East Jerusalem became a backwater.

Were the Jews given access to their holy sites—the Western Wall and the synagogues in the Jewish Quarter of the Old City—provided for by international agreement? No. Still worse, those sites were systematically desecrated.

Did Gaza, under Egyptian military rule, fare any better than the West Bank? Hardly.

Does the world suffer from amnesia about how Israel came into possession of the Golan Heights, West Bank, eastern Jerusalem, the Sinai, and Gaza? "The existence of Israel has continued too long. The battle has come in which we shall destroy Israel," Cairo Radio declared on May 16, 1967. Not only did Syria go along with Egypt in beating the drums of war, but Jordan also shortsightedly placed its forces under Egyptian control. Israel had no choice but to order a preemptive strike on June 5.

What was the Arab response after the Six-Day War to Israel's readiness to negotiate a settlement that would return virtually all the acquired territory in exchange for peace? As in 1947, the Arabs wanted it all—all of Israel, that is—or nothing, as they declared in Khartoum: "No negotiations, no peace, no recognition."

Yet, when Egypt and Jordan were finally prepared to negotiate, did they not find a responsive Israel and conclude durable peace agreements?

On the creation of refugees, a tragic consequence of every war and not just the Arab-Israeli conflict, why have Palestinian refugees, uniquely throughout the world, been kept in squalid camps for decades rather than resettled, especially in other Arab nations that share a common language and heritage?

Why has only Jordan among the twenty-two members of the Arab League offered Palestinians citizenship? Why was Kuwait permitted summarily to expel 300,000 Palestinians during the Gulf War without a peep from the international community? Why has the international community sustained refugee camps that are incubators of hatred for Israel and the Jewish people for new generations of Palestinians?

Why has the world utterly failed to acknowledge the exodus of 750,000 Jews—no fewer than the number of Palestinian refugees—forced to leave their ancestral homes in Arab countries as a result of seething hatred? Is it perhaps because these refugees were immediately resettled rather than cynically turned into political pawns?

Why has the world failed to understand Israel's profound dilemma in negotiating peace with a nondemocratic and corrupt Palestinian Authority that raises legitimate fears about future commitments to peace? Or the very real strategic vulnerability Israel could face if durable peace does not take root, given especially its narrow width?

And why is the world not asking why Palestinians allow, even encourage, their children to enter into the line of fire, potentially becoming "martyrs" for the cause? This is a price children should never be asked to pay.

In the final analysis, the path of peaceful negotiations and painful compromise is the only alternative for either side if all-out war is to be avoided. Israel has amply demonstrated its commitment to this path; the Palestinians, regrettably but characteristically, continue to send totally contradictory signals. How much longer can the world willfully overlook those inconvenient truths about Palestinian behavior that might otherwise puncture their airtight judgments?

Quotation of the Day
*The New York Times*
March 4, 2001

"American Jews have been always been a step or two behind Israel in understanding Germany's postwar evolution. American Jews have had the luxury of avoiding Germany, even boycotting its products—a luxury Israel could not afford."

Interview
*"Y"*
Magazine of the German Armed Forces
April 2001

**Question**: Mr. Harris, you are the executive director of the American Jewish Committee. What are the aims of your organization?

**Answer**: The American Jewish Committee (AJC) was founded in 1906 by a group of prominent American Jews—of German origin, I might add—who were deeply concerned about a wave of violent attacks against Jews in Eastern Europe. Establishing a permanent organization, they believed, would be the most effective way of helping to ensure the security and well-being of Jews in Eastern Europe, or wherever else Jews were in potential jeopardy.

At the same time, they quickly grasped a fundamental point that has been a guiding principle of AJC ever since—if any minority is threatened, all minorities are endangered; if freedom is abridged for some, everyone is at risk.

Accordingly, AJC has devoted substantial resources to the strengthening of human rights protections and the promotion of understanding among different religious and racial groups. Based on these views, our very first legal action in the U.S. courts—nearly eighty years ago—was to support the right of Catholic parents to send their children to a parochial school if they wished. The effort, I'm pleased to report, was successful.

**Question**: For one year now you have been the chairman of United Nations Watch. What is the main focus of this organization?

**Answer**: UN Watch is a much younger agency than AJC. Established in 1993, it was the brainchild of Morris Abram, president of the AJC in the 1960s and, from 1989 to 1993, the U.S. ambassador to the UN in Geneva.

During his years at the UN, he came to realize that the world body did not always live up to the admirable goals enshrined in the UN Charter. What was needed, he concluded, was a watchdog agency that would measure the UN's performance by the standards it set for itself. He was absolutely right in his vision. With a respected international board and a talented professional staff based in Geneva, that's exactly what UN Watch is doing—offering support to the UN when it is warranted, and providing constructive criticism when it is needed.

**Question**: You have visited the two Bundeswehr universities and the Fuhrungsakademie. What was your message, and what were your impressions?

**Answer**: In January I had the privilege of lecturing at these three distinguished institutions. It was a great honor and a memorable experience.

My principal message was that today Germans and Jews have a common agenda that should draw us closer together and provide a basis for future cooperation. The four key elements of this agenda are: (a) preserving memory both for the sake of the millions of victims of the Third Reich and as a powerful reminder of what can happen if hatred goes unchecked; (b) building a world respectful of democratic values and human rights, and maintaining the closest possible ties among democratic nations, including Germany, the other EU members, the United States, and Israel; (c) serving as an early warning system against extremism and xenophobia; and (d) standing firm against those nations, such as Iraq, that flout the rule of law and threaten peaceful coexistence.

I was impressed by the level of interest and commitment of the administrators, faculty, and students with whom I met. For some it was the first opportunity for such an open discussion between Germans and Jews. Moreover, I must add that, as an American who lectured in

English, I was struck by the widespread fluency in English. Sadly, if the situation had been reversed, I can't imagine too many lecture halls in the United States where hundreds of young people would be able to follow a speech given in German on a complex topic, without the benefit of translation.

**Question**: For several years now there have been regular contacts between the Bundeswehr and the American Jewish Committee. What is your view of these contacts?

**Answer**: Yes, for the past seven years there have been expanding contacts between us. Many Bundeswehr delegations have added AJC to their regular itinerary when visiting the United States, and vice versa.

These meetings have served two important purposes. First, they have exposed a number of American Jews to the Bundeswehr and, as a consequence, broken down psychological barriers and built respect for today's German armed forces. Second, Bundeswehr participants have come away with a far better understanding of the sensitivities, priorities, and challenges of American Jewry, a community numbering nearly 6 million.

I have seen hesitation on both sides—Jews uneasy in the presence of uniformed German officers and German officers unsure of the reception they would receive, especially from elderly Jews—give way to lively conversation and even friendships. It's an invaluable experience for everyone.

**Question**: Holding the office you do at UN Watch has given you an opportunity to gain detailed insight into the problems posed by xenophobia, the propensity to violence against foreigners, and religious fanaticism. What can be done about these problems?

**Answer**: Tragically, the world has long lived with racism, anti-Semitism, and other vicious forms of hatred, and these cancers show too few signs of remission. There have always been those who, to affirm their own self-worth, need to debase or dehumanize others, and in many cases, as we know, this has been translated into violent attacks against individuals, or ethnic cleansing, or genocide.

The twenty-first century poses the ultimate challenge for us. In an increasingly interconnected, multicultural, populous, and, yes, armed world, will we emphasize our common humanity, which overshadows particular cultures, or our ultimately superficial differences? To paraphrase Dr. Martin Luther King, Jr., will we measure people by the content of their character or the color of their skin? And, in a similar vein, will we engage in religious wars driven by triumphalism and rejection of the legitimacy of the views of others, or will we learn to practice mutual respect among the world's many faiths? Frankly, the challenge is as much within each major national or religious group as it is between them—between moderates and extremists, between the tolerant and the intolerant.

What are the antidotes? There is no single surefire formula for combating hatred or xenophobia, but history has taught us what some of the key elements are—enlightened political leadership; respect for democratic values; social stability; inclusive, pluralistic societies; well-trained law enforcement; international cooperation in the face of growing cross-border collaboration among extremist groups; education for tolerance in schools; mutual respect; responsible media; religious leaders who set a positive example; and civil courage, when required, on the part of individuals. In other words, everyone has a role to play, and no one should simply leave it to others to deal with these challenges.

Let's always remember that there is no such thing as moral neutrality in the face of threats to our common good.

**Question**: Through your different contacts, what impressions of Germany have you gained, particularly of the younger generation? Is there something that worries you? Is there reason for optimism? What are your wishes for the way people coming from different nations and cultures should deal with each other?

**Answer**: I have met many young Germans throughout Germany and elsewhere. I have found them to be open and committed to a peaceful and democratic future.

Still, I have concerns, foremost among them the rapid rise in hate crimes, including assaults on Jews and Jewish institutions, in Germany. There was a 40-percent increase in such crimes from 1999 to 2000. This is deeply worrisome. Make no mistake about it: Those who commit such violent acts are targeting both their intended victims and the fabric of German democratic society.

Germany is unquestionably the strongest country in Europe and the leader of the European Union. Slowly emerging from the long shadow of history and with the inexorable passage of time, it is gradually overcoming its past reluctance to assert itself on the global scene. Germany will have to be ever alert to how it manages this important development. I have every reason to believe it will do so with the utmost responsibility, but constant care and sensitivity will be required.

You ask how we should all deal with each other in today's world. The simple yet complete answer was given to us a very long time ago, but too many of us have failed to heed it—"What is hateful unto you, do not do unto your neighbor."

**Question**: Where do you see possible future avenues of cooperation for AJC with German nongovernmental organizations and the Bundeswehr?

**Answer**: We want to develop model collaborative projects. In addition to our long-standing joint activities with the Adenauer and Ebert foundations, several years ago we joined with the Naumann Foundation to promote democracy and civil society in the postcommunist countries of Central and Eastern Europe. We both felt we had a stake in contributing to the successful transition of these nations from tyranny to freedom.

As another example, in 1999, our Berlin office joined with Die Johanniter and the Bundeswehr to conduct an unprecedented humanitarian operation in Macedonia for Kosovar Muslim refugees fleeing Milosevic's oppression.

We look forward to expanded cooperation with the Bundeswehr in the years ahead, especially in the area of tolerance education.

In essence, by our deeds—words alone are cheap—we want to send a message of hope to a world badly in need of it. Sixty years ago, Jews were being exterminated by Nazi Germany in the worst case of genocide in human history. A democratic and peaceful Germany, deeply committed to a responsible international role, has emerged on the ashes of the Third Reich. And Jews, profoundly scarred by the Shoah, nonetheless continue to believe, as our tradition teaches us, that, if we take matters into our own hands, tomorrow can be better than today.

This combination of Germans and Jews working together to advance democracy and assist people in need could well serve as an example of the possibilities of the human spirit. What better gift could we leave to our children and grandchildren?

## An Effort to Erase Jewish History[*]
### *Boston Globe*
### April 7, 2001

Just below the range of the political radar of international communities, eight years after the Oslo Accords were signed, the Palestinian Authority is pursuing a tenacious strategy to delegitimize Israel by recasting the historical Jewish narrative.

The top Islamic cleric in Palestinian society, Sheik Ikrema Sabri, epitomizes this effort to negate the historical Jewish ties to the land where Israel was established. His recent assertion that the Western Wall, the holiest site in Judaism, is a Muslim structure is all too typical of recent statements made by Palestinian and other Arab figures.

This comes a year after Sabri, the mufti of Jerusalem, during the pope's historic pilgrimage to Israel, publicly reiterated his belief that the Holocaust has been grossly exaggerated. The systematic Nazi extermination of 6 million Jews, in the mufti's opinion, is a myth. These statements come not from Hamas or other radical Islamic fundamentalist groups. When the mufti speaks, he does so as the Palestinian Authority's highest religious official, appointed by Yasir Arafat, who has yet to condemn such comments. But then Arafat himself last year claimed that Jesus was born a Palestinian, not a Jew.

Indeed, the effort to undermine the raison d'être for Israel's existence is central to the multifaceted Palestinian strategy that includes armed violence and terrorism, demands for the so-called right of return of Palestinians and their descendants, and continual diplomatic attempts to isolate Israel internationally.

Blithe dismissal of the Western Wall's significance disregards the fact that for over 3,500 years Jerusalem has embodied the religious,

[*] Also published in *Die Welt* (Germany), April 25, 2001

spiritual, and geographic heart and soul of the Jewish people. In a recent interview with the German daily *Die Welt*, the mufti declared: "There is not the smallest indication of the existence of a Jewish temple on this place in the past. In the whole city, there is not even a single stone indicating Jewish history."

Not just the mufti but also members of Arafat's cabinet have publicly asserted that the First and Second Jewish Temples never existed, a truly bizarre claim, all the more so since the temples are mentioned in the Koran.

The zeal to rewrite this Jewish narrative, alleging that there is no historical link between the Jewish people and Jerusalem, emboldens those who view the Jewish people as having no legitimate claims in Israel, of being just another in a long line of foreign invaders.

Abdallah al-Hourani, minister for refugee affairs, told the Palestinian newspaper *Al-Hayat al-Jedidah*, "The Crusaders lived in our land for 242 years, until the liberation of their last outposts, and Israel is like a tree that has flowered on land not belonging to it. No matter how much it is fertilized, it cannot put down roots, and when the fertilizer stops, it will die."

Denying Jewish connections to the land presumably justifies the desecration of Jewish holy sites. Joseph's Tomb in Nablus and an ancient synagogue in Jericho, two West Bank cities transferred peacefully by Israel to Palestinian control in negotiated agreements, are among the sacred Jewish places recently vandalized. Such willful intolerance in the name of Islam is eerily similar to the Taliban's deplorable destruction of ancient Buddhas in Afghanistan.

Portraying the centrality of Jerusalem to Judaism as a myth is no less sinister than Palestinian statements denying the Holocaust that are echoed across the region, from Cairo to Damascus to Tehran, by political officials, religious leaders, and government-controlled media. In doing so, they are hoping to deny Israel the understanding and support it has received as a Jewish homeland in the wake of the Nazi Final Solution.

Illustrative of this is a recent series in the *Tehran Times* saying that Nobel laureate and Holocaust survivor Elie Wiesel is proof that the extermination of Jews did not take place because, well, "He is alive!"

As noted Islamic scholar Khalid Durán points out in his forthcoming book, *Children of Abraham*, the Sacred Scripture condemns the persecution of all believers and the destruction of human life. In the face of this Koranic moral imperative, it is deplorable and shameful that the Holocaust has not evoked a stronger response among Muslims.

The Arab-Israeli conflict over Palestine is no excuse for Muslims to adopt an attitude of indifference with regard to the enormity of the Holocaust.

For the Palestinians and those Arab nations that have yet to accept Israel, repeated wars, terrorism, and economic boycotts have not driven Jews from their ancestral homeland. Thus, the tactic employed with increasing frequency is to question the history of the Jewish people.

Those in the West who ignore or dismiss such statements as merely a rhetorical device miss the point. Over the long run this denial of the historical Jewish narrative not only flies in the face of incontrovertible facts, but makes achieving a peaceful settlement of the conflict still more elusive.

## Middle East Violence
### *International Herald Tribune*
### May 11, 2001

Mr. Brown assails Israel for its policies regarding the Palestinians and faults his Israeli cousin for extending his army duty. In contrast, he proudly states that the bulk of his family avoided fighting in the twentieth century's bloodiest wars, instead resisting tyranny "with the Jewish traditions of dialogue and humanism." Is this for real?

Mr. Brown conveniently ignores certain facts about the Middle East situation. From its founding in 1948, Israel would not have survived a single day without the courage of people like his cousin. The peaceful relationship Israel sought with her neighbors was met with war and the aim of annihilating the fledgling state. Since then, and notwithstanding the welcome peace treaties with Egypt and Jordan, Israel has never been able to let down its guard in its rough neighborhood.

It could have been otherwise. Had the Arab world accepted the UN-proposed partition of the land, there would have been both Arab and Jewish states created in mandatory Palestine. More recently, there was another historic chance to end the conflict. Former prime minister Ehud Barak, with U.S. support, offered a far-reaching deal to the Palestinians, only to see it turned down. What is Israel to do in the face of a negotiating partner that not only can't say yes, but also uses violence and terror to advance its political objectives?

Dialogue and humanism only work if both sides share the commitment; otherwise, Mr. Brown's utopian fantasy translates into catastrophe for Israel. His comments suggest that he would have advocated the same approach during the Holocaust. If only Europe's Jews, perhaps the Allied nations as well, had responded to the Nazi juggernaut with dialogue and humanism, as he implies, then history might have turned out differently. And no doubt you, Mr. Brown, like me, would not have been alive to see it.


## Arab Lobby v. Israel Lobby: Who'll Win?
### *The Jerusalem Report*
### May 21, 2001

Seven years ago, after the White House lawn signing of the Oslo Accords, President Clinton appealed to American Jewish and Arab-American leaders to seek cooperative projects to enhance Mideast peace that also could strengthen Jewish-Arab ties in the United States.

It didn't happen. With very few exceptions, what has emerged is not a new cooperative spirit but increasing competition for the hearts and minds of the American political establishment. The Arab and Muslim lobbies in the United States aim to reduce U.S. foreign aid to Israel, deemphasize Israel's strategic importance for the United States, redefine American notions of terrorism, and end sanctions against Iraq. That effort, which has received too little attention, lends new urgency to efforts to invigorate the tie between Israel and American Jewry and to boost American Jewish political activism for Israel.

Arab- and Muslim-American leaders recognize the critical role Jews play in the special relationship between the United States and Israel, and have concluded that reducing the relative power of the American Jewish community is central to accomplishing their goals. They haven't yet mustered sufficient strength to take on the Jewish community—but the Arab and Muslim populations are growing, mainly through immigration, along with their political savvy and self-confidence. Political candidates come to their organizations' meetings; the media seek their communal views.

The Arab challenge began in the late eighties, during the first intifada. Arab-American organizations orchestrated anti-Israel demonstrations across the United States. They've since vigorously pursued the goal of building the Arab-American community into a political force approaching the influence and standing of the Jewish community.

Meanwhile, Muslim organizations have perpetrated the myth that the Muslim-American population is "over 6 million." Professional demographers dispute that figure. And the researcher who performed a survey for the American Muslim Council later admitted that he was pressured by the group to arrive at the 6 million figure, implying that the actual count is much lower. But 6 million has a special resonance: It would mean that Muslims outnumber Jews in the United States, and it would buttress calls for a redefinition of America's heritage as "Judeo-Christian-Muslim," a stated goal of some Muslim leaders.

Over the past several years a new generation of activists has formed a coalition, American Muslims for Jerusalem, which often parrots the views of Hamas and Islamic Jihad. Its first major campaign was an anti-Israel boycott of the Disney Company's international millennium exhibit, in protest against an Israeli portrayal of Jerusalem as Israel's capital. American Arab and Muslim groups have targeted other companies, including Ben & Jerry's ice cream, which was criticized in October 1998 after an advertisement highlighted Golan Heights water as an ingredient. The ad was dropped. In July 1999, Sprint Communications was attacked for using the Dome of the Rock in an ad for cheap phone rates to Israel—the argument being that its status as part of Israel was still under international discussion.

In response to the Al-Aksa intifada, Arab and Muslim groups have initiated a sophisticated, well-funded public relations campaign in the

United States. Hoping to take maximum advantage of the media-beating Israel has taken, they've sought to portray the Palestinian struggle as akin to the American Revolution. Another series of newspaper ads conjures up Tiananmen Square, with a lone Palestinian youngster facing an Israeli tank.

The American Arab and Muslim communities are increasingly active in the political arena. Though so far their fund-raising abilities and political impact are limited, their vote was courted by the presidential candidates last year. On October 5, George W. Bush held a closed meeting with Arab-American leaders in Michigan, most of whom went on to endorse him. Al Gore met with Arab-American leaders a week later in Michigan, the state with the largest proportion of Arab-American voters.

On some domestic issues, notably in the realm of government intrusion in religion, these communities and American Jews share a common ground. But on the fundamental issues of U.S. support for Israel and the U.S. fight against terrorism, their positions sharply diverge—and that is the heart of the emerging challenge to long-standing U.S. support for Israel.

To meet this challenge, U.S. Jews must keep advocacy for Israel high on the list of communal priorities. Another voice is seeking the ear of lawmakers and officials, and we cannot afford to go silent. But Israel must also wake up. Too often, Jerusalem has underestimated the importance of American Jews in the U.S.-Israel equation, or simply taken American Jewish political advocacy for granted. That is a big mistake.

On this point, the Arab and Muslim lobbies are right—American Jewish support is critical to maintaining the special ties between Washington and Jerusalem. Therefore, anything that might diminish that support—such as alienating Reform and Conservative Jews—could over time negatively affect the U.S.-Israel relationship. Conversely, programs such as Project Birthright that enhance the ties between Israel and American Jewry are likely to bolster that relationship over the long run.

We dare not underestimate the Arab and Muslim lobbies or delude ourselves as to their ultimate objectives. The stakes are too high. The call for action by American Jewry, together with Israel, is clear.

## Middle East Coverage
### *Tribune de Genève* (Switzerland)
### June 5, 2001

Since I arrived in Geneva last year, I have come to rely on *Tribune de Genève* as an important source of information regarding local, national, and international news.

At the same time, I have been disappointed by your coverage of the Middle East since the most recent round of violence began last fall. In the choice of headlines, photographs, articles, and placement, there repeatedly emerges a clear sympathy for the Palestinian side. While every newspaper surely has the right to express a point of view, this is normally reserved for editorials and columns, not news sections.

To illustrate, today's paper carries a large front-page photograph of two healthy-looking Palestinian children in the rubble of a building presumably targeted by the Israeli army. Why was this photo chosen? There is the implication that the children lived in the building, but no evidence. Was the photo staged or spontaneous? The headline above it does not refer to any attack, nor does the caption below, so the photo is not directly linked to the news you are carrying on today's front page. Again, I ask, why was this particular photo chosen at this particular time?

Moreover, in the same newspaper, on page 6, there is a second photo. I confess I do not fully understand this one either. The caption refers to "a Jewish extremist." How do we know that he is a Jewish extremist? Is it because he is described in the caption as "attacking" a Palestinian woman? Attacking verbally? Physically? There is no explanation or indication. Or is he assumed to be an "extremist" simply because he has the appearance of a religious Jew? Or perhaps there is another reason, but, in this case, it is not made known to the readers.

In other words, in presenting an extraordinarily complex conflict, where both sides, not just one, have a case to make, you have opted—at times subtly, at other times more openly—to present one side with far greater sympathy and sensitivity than the other side. In doing so, I fear, you compromise the journalistic integrity that readers of *Tribune de Genève* have come to expect.

## Radio Commentary[*]
## Week of June 11, 2001

On June 1, a Palestinian terrorist outfitted as a human bomb took the lives of twenty young Israelis as they waited to enter a discotheque in Tel Aviv. The terrorist had only one goal—to kill as many Israelis as he could.

This is David Harris of the American Jewish Committee asking everyone to remember these innocent young victims of hate and incitement.

Tragically, Yasir Arafat rejected Israel's far-reaching offer to achieve peace. Instead, the Palestinians launched the renewed campaign of terrorism that has targeted Israeli children, women, and men.

We mourn these latest victims of Palestinian terrorism, and we reaffirm our full solidarity with the government and people of Israel in their age-old quest for peace.

You can read more about support for Israel in the American Jewish Committee's ad in today's *New York Times*, or by logging onto www.ajc.org.

## Travel Letter
### *International Herald Tribune*
## June 22, 2001

You made my day. As a frequent traveler (on behalf of the American Jewish Committee) who has no choice but to use the three New York airports, the news that the Port Authority has finally awakened to the calamitous signage at these gateways brought joy and relief. Of course, one cannot help wondering why it took decades for the responsible officials to tackle an issue that was obvious to anyone passing through these airports even once, but why spoil the moment?

Maybe this bold step will encourage the New York-area authorities to take on another challenge cut from the same cloth—the jumble of

---

[*] The radio commentaries originally aired on WCBS Radio in the New York metropolitan area. They have been expanded to six radio stations in New York, Los Angeles, and Washington.

unhelpful, often confusing, signs that dominate the area's highways. It can be a nightmare for anyone who has not spent a lifetime navigating the region.

For instance, why should one important artery connecting New York and the north be called variously the West Side Highway, Henry Hudson, and Saw Mill parkways? And as if that weren't disorienting enough, unlike Europe, the emphasis in the area seems to be on road names (or numbers) rather than destinations.

Just as air travelers have long known the pleasures of arriving or transiting at Amsterdam's Schipol Airport, New York's new model, so drivers have long known the joy of traveling in countries like Switzerland and finding a remarkably well thought-out system of color-coded and helpful signs—to be found in and around villages, towns, and cities—to lead us from one point to another.

One can only hope that New York officials will be emboldened by their current efforts and press ahead to help travelers beyond the airports as well.

## Middle East Coverage
### *El Pais* (Spain)
### July 16, 2001

The letter on the Palestinian issue was outrageous and cannot be left unanswered.

Ricardo Herren speaks of the "slow holocaust of the Palestinian people perpetrated by Israel," and then compares Israel today with Germany during the Third Reich.

Herren reveals his astonishingly profound ignorance of the Holocaust. The toll included the extermination of 1.5 million Jewish children and the systematic destruction of European Jewish civilization.

During this period, an entire vocabulary of genocide emerged—the yellow star, racial laws, ghettos, deportations, forced marches, slave labor, death camps, gas chambers, and crematoria.

The Israeli-Palestinian conflict is long and complex, and tragedy has befallen *both* sides, but this has nothing to do with Herren's obscene historical analogy. Moreover, his identification with the Palestinians blinds him to political realities.

This conflict could have been solved in 1947-48 had the Arab world accepted the UN Partition Plan, which called for the creation of an Arab and a Jewish state. The Jews accepted, but the Arabs refused and went to war.

The Arab world, which was in control of the West Bank, Gaza, and eastern Jerusalem from 1948 to 1967, could have established a Palestinian state, but chose not to. Instead, Jordan annexed the territories under its jurisdiction, and Egypt imposed military rule on Gaza.

Today the Palestinians could have been on their way to independence if Chairman Arafat had pursued the far-reaching deal offered by Prime Minister Barak last year. But the Palestinians spurned the peace overture and launched a new round of violence, which includes mortar attacks and suicide bombings. Israel, like any nation facing terrorism, must protect its citizens.

Disturbingly, not only do you publish wildly distorted letters, but your headlines, reporting, and cartoons often present a skewed picture. Let me cite three examples from just one week.

On May 19, the day after a Palestinian terrorist killed six Israelis and wounded 100 others in Netanya, you wrote: "Israel responds with combat planes to the suicide attack of a young Palestinian." That headline did not even mention the Israeli victims and left the simplistic impression that this was a conflict between advanced weaponry and youngsters.

On May 22, referring to the report of the Mitchell Commission, the headline read: "The United States demands of Israel a cease-fire and an end to new settlements." How could you not cite the clear call to the Palestinians to end the violence, a central element of the Mitchell report and the American position?

And on May 24, you published an arguably anti-Semitic cartoon. It shows a caricatured religious Jew carrying a Bible in one hand, the Israeli flag in the other, and a gun strapped on his shoulder, while saying: "We are the chosen people of the manufacture of weapons."

Readers deserve better from such a renowned newspaper.

## Farewell, Geneva
*Tribune de Genève* (Switzerland)
July 16, 2001

My family and I were scheduled to spend a sabbatical year in Bologna. Our American friends promised to visit us.

Then life took an unexpected turn. The chairman of the Geneva-based UN Watch, Ambassador Morris Abram, died, and I was asked to succeed him.

When we told our friends—who were already checking the Alitalia timetables for flights to Bologna—that we were going to Geneva instead, they wished us a good year and said they'd see us on our return to New York.

Why such a reaction? I probed and got variations on two themes.

The first was "Geneva is pretty but boring."

And the second was "Why visit a country whose banks demanded death certificates for Nazi victims before releasing funds to heirs?"

Both reactions gave us pause, but UN Watch was located in Geneva and that's where we were headed.

Our year is now at an end, but what a wonderful experience it has been!

If Geneva is boring, we certainly didn't notice. We found it to be a city blessed with charm, culture, and a great location. It's built on a human scale, with thoughtful urban touches—from abundant greenery to intelligent public parking, from well-equipped neighborhood sports complexes to a superb public transport system. In a world increasingly dominated by cacophonous cities, Geneva stands out as an oasis of serenity and gentility.

Okay, so the city of Calvin is not perfect.

It's difficult to understand how the UN can be located here, while Switzerland remains an observer and not a full member. And the amount of smoking, especially among youth, comes as a shock, and secondhand smoke has spoiled more than a few meals in restaurants, which sadly know nothing about nonsmoking sections.

Moreover, the wartime history that troubled our friends, and us, still looms large; in a sense, it's inescapable. Fortunately, though, today's Switzerland is a far more open society.

The noted Argentine writer Jorge Luis Borges was right when he said, *"De toutes les villes du monde ... Genève me semble la plus propice au bonheur"* ("Of all the cities in the world, Geneva seems to me the most suitable for happiness.") Thank you, Geneva, for having given us a wonderful year in a truly unboring place.

## Diplomatic License
## CNN
## August 4, 2001

**Richard Roth, Host**: Race, lies and videotape. Welcome to Diplomatic License. This is Richard Roth in New York.

A world conference on racism without any controversy? You got to be kidding. It's still weeks away, but the third-ever Global Racism Conference sure has garnered a lot of publicity, if nothing else. One item everybody seems to be talking about is language in a draft document that equates Zionism with racism. That's just one issue that the United States and other countries disagree with—so much so, that the United States threatens not to attend. UN officials are scrambling to keep the focus on the big picture.

**David Harris, American Jewish Committee**: The World Conference Against Racism was intended to address the issue of racism and racial discrimination. It's a problem that in one way or another affects every society in this world. To allow a country-specific issue to emerge in Durban is to threaten to destroy the conference. We heard it from Secretary Powell, and we've heard it from the Europeans this week in Geneva. This should not become a country-specific conference. If it does, the conference will unravel.

**Roth**: But won't it be so vague then? Don't you have to name some countries? I mean....

**Harris**: The intent of the UN conference was not to be country-specific at all. If it were, I can give you a list of thirty, forty, fifty, sixty countries where racism is particularly endemic. And, in any case, the Israeli-Palestinian conflict is political in nature and needs to be addressed by the relevant diplomats and politicians, not by such a world gathering.

If we want to begin talking about racism and country-specific situations warranting the world's attention, what about the plight of the Christians in Pakistan? Or Baha'is in Iran, or Christians in Saudi Arabia, or black Christians in Sudan? There's a long list of issues that could easily fall within the scope of the agenda.

Again, I repeat: the Israeli-Palestinian conflict is a political conflict, not a racial conflict. It has no place at the Durban conference.

This conference, to succeed, needs to address best practices in dealing with racism. Racism afflicts every society in the world. And as we become a more interconnected world, more populous and more diverse, the challenge will only grow to advance harmony and combat intolerance.

For this opportunity to be squandered by seeking to politicize a UN conference would be a tragedy. And may I point out, since the subject has come up, that Zionism is nothing more or less than the movement of self-determination of the Jewish people. To seek to equate it with racism is an outrage. And there's still more that concerns us.

I just came from one year in Geneva, where I followed this conference day in and day out. The Arab nations, joined by some Muslim states, are playing fast and loose with the Holocaust, Jewish history, and the legacy of anti-Semitism. They are trying to denigrate the meaning of the Holocaust, and are attempting to diminish the cancerous impact of anti-Semitism over 2,000 years. This is shameful; it turns truth on its head.

I'm afraid that, left unchallenged, we're going to squander a chance to grapple with racism and allow a potentially important world gathering to be hijacked by narrow interests.

Palestinian War Against Jews
*The New York Times*\*
August 14, 2001

In recent days, Palestinian suicide bombers struck again in the heart of Israel. In the worst attack, in Jerusalem, fifteen Jews were killed,

---

\* Published as an AJC "advertorial" in the *New York Times*, as well as in the *International Herald Tribune*, August 23, 2001, and the *New Republic*, September 3, 2001.

including seven children, and 130 others were injured, some critically.

This was the latest in a series of targeted, brutal terrorist attacks on restaurants, discotheques, shopping malls, open-air markets, and public buses throughout Israel.

Victims have included children and the elderly, hawks and doves, the religious and secular, Israelis and foreigners.

To the perpetrators, young Palestinians, it doesn't matter who the victims are—as long as they are Israelis, as long as they are Jews.

Indoctrinated by Palestinian political and religious leaders, they have been taught that suicide attacks are the highest form of martyrdom.

They have been infused with the belief that a glorious "paradise," including the company of virgins galore, awaits those who have killed themselves while killing Jews.

They have been assured that their families will receive generous cash payments for their sacrifice from the Palestinian Authority and from Saddam Hussein's Iraq.

Trained to kill, they have been taught to believe that the world would be a better place without Israel, without Jews.

How many more people in Israel will have to pay with their lives while Chairman Arafat fosters an atmosphere that glorifies suicide attacks?

How many more people in Israel will have to pay with their lives while Arafat fails to imprison the terrorist masterminds under his authority—and pursues a two-faced strategy of talking peace while encouraging violence?

How many more people in Israel will have to pay with their lives while Palestinian media incite hatred, Palestinian schools and camps teach the "virtues" of martyrdom, and religious leaders call for jihad?

And how many more people in Israel will have to pay with their lives while the world overlooks Israel's outstretched hand of peace that could have laid the foundation for an end to the Israeli-Palestinian conflict, only to be rebuffed by Arafat, who, once again, refused to say yes to peace?

## Mideast Misconception
*The New York Times*
August 22, 2001

The attempt by Mary Robinson, the United Nations commissioner for human rights, to equate the "historical wounds of anti-Semitism and of the Holocaust" with the Palestinians' "accumulated wounds of displacement and military occupation" distorts reality.

The attempted symmetry is totally misplaced. The systematic effort to exterminate the Jewish people stands on its own. The Palestinian situation is not comparable. A Palestinian state was offered by the United Nations in 1947, but was rejected in favor of war against the fledgling Jewish state. Last year, Yasir Arafat, the Palestinian leader, rejected a historic offer that could have settled the conflict and instead chose violence.

The Israeli-Palestinian conflict is fundamentally a political conflict, and thus, contrary to what Ms. Robinson said, has no place on the agenda of the United Nations conference on racism.

## The Usual Game Has Ironclad Rules for Ganging Up on Israel[*]
*International Herald Tribune*
August 29, 2001

The concave and convex mirrors in an amusement park create a setting in which for a moment reality is overtaken by the absurd. Imagine, though, that the distortions endure.

Sitting in Geneva for the past year, immersed in the daily business of the United Nations, I often felt encased in a hall of mirrors. The run-up to the UN World Conference Against Racism, which opens on Friday in South Africa, has been a typical case of international diplomacy run amok—a well-intentioned idea hijacked by a group of nations determined to create yet another anti-Israel forum.

---

[*] Subsequently published in *Ha'aretz* (Israel), *Tribune de Genève* (Switzerland), and *Die Welt* (Germany).

How is it possible that after the world's nations agreed months ago that there would be no mention of specific countries in the conference's final document, only one country, Israel, is referred to repeatedly and accused of a long litany of alleged wrongs?

The Arab-Israeli conflict is political and not racial in nature. How is it possible that it has been thrust upon the Durban agenda?

The conference, intended to address the blight on humanity of racism, a worldwide phenomenon, has been diverted from its purpose by the determination of a few, with the acquiescence of many, to launch a frontal attack on Israel and the Jewish people.

Not only have unfounded, indeed unrecognizable, characterizations of Israel and Zionism been thrust front and center, but also the Holocaust and the meaning of anti-Semitism have been distorted in the campaign to undermine the case for Israel's legitimacy. To understand what could well happen in Durban, it is instructive to recall how the UN Commission on Human Rights operates. Just a few months ago the commission convened its annual session in Geneva.

The annual agenda of this gathering of fifty-three nations devotes one part to a discussion of Israel exclusively and another part to discussion of the rest of the world. That is the way the world has been divided up, and too many nations that should know better mindlessly go along with it. Not only does the construction of the agenda create endless opportunities to take the floor and attack Israel, but the political makeup of the United Nations, of which the commission is a reflection, almost inevitably ensures that Israel will find itself with few supporters. Start with the twenty-two-member Arab League. To be sure, the group is far from monolithic; there are radical, centrist, and moderate factions. Even so, as the friendly ambassador of one moderate country said after I asked about his diatribe against Israel: "I had no choice. The pressure on me from other Arab countries was intense and unrelenting. Had I acted differently, there would have been negative consequences."

Another ambassador told me of a European colleague who was chairing a UN meeting a few years ago and in that capacity blocked an Arab parliamentary move. Within days the diplomat was visited by an

Arab delegation with a very clear message: "You will never again be elected to a post within the UN, as we control the majority. Your career here is as good as over."

The fifty-seven-member Organization of the Islamic Conference usually follows the Arab lead, and the 113-member Nonaligned Movement, which includes the Arab League and Islamic Conference nations, does as well—so an automatic majority is created. What chance does Israel have in such an imbalanced setting?

Now the hall of mirrors, where confusion between reality and absurdity reigns, where truth and fairness are turned on their heads, is about to go on show in Durban. A world conference designed to promote tolerance threatens instead to be remembered for giving its imprimatur to the spread of bigotry.

<br>

Commentary
Morning Edition
National Public Radio
August 31, 2001

It seemed like a good idea when it was proposed four years ago: a UN conference against racism.

But like many good ideas, this one went awry.

Despite an understanding that the conference would not focus on any single country, many Arab and Islamic nations couldn't resist turning this international gathering into a forum for bashing Israel, denigrating the Holocaust, and distorting the meaning of anti-Semitism.

I've just returned from a year in Geneva, where I observed the UN up close, particularly the Commission on Human Rights. I witnessed too many countries reflexively going along with such cynical Arab campaigns for shortsighted political or commercial reasons. In doing so, they've allowed truth to be turned on its head.

But there are a few countries, guided by principle, that refuse to go along with this charade. No nation stands taller in this regard than the United States.

Having been asked to serve on the official American delegation, I know just how eager the United States was to participate in the Durban conference. As a nation, we have something to say about our own national experience and much to learn from the experience of others.

And I also realize how much Secretary of State Powell personally wanted to be there.

Yet Washington is unwilling to attend at any cost.

President Bush made this clear in his forceful remarks. Responding to the question of whether "to go or not to go to Durban," the president said that the United States would not participate if Israel, our democratic ally and friend, is singled out for scrutiny.

Some unfairly accuse the administration of turning its back on the world.

The truth is that our government tried valiantly to put this conference back on its original track to deal with contemporary racism worldwide. Months of intense negotiations, however, produced little progress.

This is all sadly reminiscent of two earlier UN conferences on racism, in 1978 and 1983, which were similarly diverted by the anti-Israel crowd. In both cases, under Presidents Carter and Reagan, the United States did not participate, asserting that the American presence could only lend legitimacy to what had become illegitimate exercises.

It's still possible that wise heads will prevail and recognize that this world conference against racism ironically threatens to be remembered as the world conference that promoted bigotry.

But don't bet on it. Representatives of the Egypt-based Arab Lawyers Union have already poisoned the atmosphere by distributing vile anti-Semitic material to arriving delegates in Durban.

Secretary Powell is right to take the high moral ground and sit this one out.

As President George Washington wrote in 1790, "...to bigotry no sanction." Those words, which give expression to our nation's highest ideals, ring as true today as they did over two centuries ago.

## Special Report with Brit Hume
## Fox News Network
## August 31, 2001

**Tony Snow**: The American delegation to the weeklong UN World Conference Against Racism in South Africa will leave early if anti-Israel language remains in the final communiqué. The United States objects to language that condemns Zionism as racism.

David Harris, executive director of the American Jewish Committee, joins us from New York to discuss the conference's controversy.

Mr. Harris, let's begin simply with the "Zionism is racism" charge. That has been leveled for many years by people. How is it, do you think, that the UN has suddenly elevated this to a level at which it may be included in an official communiqué?

**David Harris, American Jewish Committee**: Unfortunately, there's a history here. In 1975, the UN first adopted the so-called "Zionism is racism" resolution because there was, in the UN General Assembly, an automatic majority of nations that was willing to go along with the Arab campaign. It took sixteen years to repeal that "Zionism is racism" canard. It was done in 1991, and we thought we had buried it. But most recently, the Arab nations again, angry at Israel, have revitalized the charge. They have turned to their automatic majority in the UN, and we now see it on the agenda.

**Tony Snow**: The United States, obviously, is going to be opposing this. If it comes to the crunch, is there any redress the United States has, either as a member of the Security Council or whatever, to step in and say that we're simply not going to let this stand?

**Harris**: The United States can make clear that it strongly opposes this, and that it will reassess its views of the United Nations if this persists. And by the way, the United States is not alone. All the Western countries, all the democratic nations, will oppose a revival of the "Zionism is racism" issue. But they may be a minority at the UN, and that's simply a numerical fact.

**Tony Snow**: When you see this sort of thing happening, is it difficult for you to take the UN seriously as a diplomatic body?

**Harris**: I must tell you, it's very painful; it hurts. Zionism is nothing more or less than the quest of the Jewish people for self-determination—the same right that other people have. I might add that the UN has never condemned the right of any other people to self-determination. In the end, though, the fact is it's really a stain on the United Nations itself. And people like Kofi Annan, the secretary-general, have understood this and said so.

**Tony Snow**: But Kofi Annan, in statements opening this particular conference, also pointed to Israel and its treatment of Arabs and, as he said, others living in the, quote, "occupied" territories. He said that it was important to single that out for consideration by the conference.

**Harris**: There are two things I'd say. First, let's be clear. This conference in Durban was intended to address racism throughout the world, and not to focus on any specific country. That was the understanding among all the member nations. In fact, if the conference is to look at individual countries, there is no country that could be immune from charges of racism, and in some cases there could be rather strong charges leveled. The second thing is that Kofi Annan said a number of things in his speech, in addition to what you indicated. He spoke about the importance of remembering the Holocaust, the legacy of anti-Semitism, and Israel's right to exist. These are also important elements that have been overlooked in what the secretary-general said and that do give some context and balance to his remarks in Durban.

**Tony Snow**: Mr. Harris, you just pointed out that every nation has some sense of racial challenge or some problem with it. That being the case, is it really realistic to expect that some broad declaration is going to be anything other than rhetoric?

**Harris**: I suspect not. It will be rhetoric. But again, this could have been a useful conference that might have looked at best-practice models, at how some countries have dealt with racism. Perhaps other countries could learn from those experiences. Instead, what we've seen—and I say this with great regret—is a hijacking of the conference by a determined Arab bloc of twenty-two nations. They have turned to other Muslim nations and some in the nonaligned movement, created a numerical majority, and established special rules for Israel and Israel alone. As a result, I think they have ensured that the conference will be remembered not as a conference against racism but, ultimately, as a conference that promoted racism.

**Tony Snow**: That being the case, you're saying it promotes racism in terms of the "Zionism is racism" equation. Doesn't it also place the United Nations almost in the position of taking sides in the conflict that is now going on in Israel and the West Bank and Gaza?

**Harris**: That's a very good point. The fact is that if the UN wants to be helpful in trying to bring the Israelis and Palestinians closer to peace, this conference will do the exact opposite. It only exacerbates tensions and increases suspicion. So this is not helpful to the pursuit of peace. In fact, what we've seen again is the singling out of Israel in the conference and, moreover, the distribution of anti-Semitic literature by Arab groups. I have here in the studio one document that was prepared by the Arab Lawyers Union, a group that is accredited to this conference, which has the swastika superimposed on the Star of David. This is the kind of material that's being distributed to the delegates at a conference against racism. We've had Jewish delegates in Durban, many Jewish delegates, reporting that they have been harassed. A number of them are afraid for their own physical security. This is not the way the UN should be conducting a conference against racism.

**Tony Snow**: That being the case, Yasir Arafat delivered a pretty angry speech on this topic, and yet we are hearing that, perhaps as early as next week, he'll be meeting with Shimon Peres in Italy to talk about peace. Can you help us put those two stories together and make sense of them?

**Harris**: I wish I could. Yasir Arafat has always been a master of the two-faced strategy, and we're witnessing it yet again. He practices the politics of violence, of terror, and we've seen it in recent weeks in Israel. The discotheque bombing in Tel Aviv, the pizzeria bombing in Jerusalem, it goes on and on. And at the same time, he talks peace. This is the way Yasir Arafat, unfortunately, has conducted his diplomacy for many years. And that's why we're faced with the sad situation we're in. Tony, one year ago, Israel offered an historic proposal to the Palestinians that could have brought this conflict to an end. But rather than engage that proposal, Yasir Arafat walked away, encouraged the violence, and, for the last year, we've seen the results. This is a year that need not have been.

**Tony Snow**: Mr. Harris, we've got about fifteen seconds left. Very quickly, would you have preferred to see Colin Powell go to this conference to make even more palpable U.S. opposition to the resolution?

**Harris**: I know how much he wanted to go, and I know how symbolically important it would have been for the first African-American secretary of state to be there. But to attend under these circumstances would have been to lend legitimacy and stature to a conference that I believe deserves neither.

**Tony Snow**: David Harris, thanks for joining us. We're going to take a break for news. We'll be right back.

## The Lessons After the Chaos[*]
*Forward*
September 14, 2001

Any attempt to grasp the stark reality of what took place in this country on September 11 is bound to fall short. The sheer magnitude and impact of the terror attacks are beyond comprehension.

While no one could have foreseen such a brazen and ambitious assault on the symbols of our nation, the terrorist threat did not begin yesterday nor is it now behind us.

Rather, it's been there crying out for attention for many years.

Think back to the 1983 bombing of the Marine barracks in Beirut; the 1988 downing of Pan Am flight 103; the 1993 bombing of the World Trade Center—whose objective was to topple one of the towers; the 1996 attack on our military personnel in the Khobar Towers in Saudi Arabia; the 1998 destruction of the American embassies in Nairobi and Dar es Salaam; the assault last year on the USS *Cole* in Yemen—not to mention those planned terrorist acts that were foiled by alert U.S. law-enforcement officials.

---

[*] Appeared also in the *Journal News* (Westchester County, New York) and several local Jewish newspapers.

In the name of fanatical political and religious totalitarianism, the United States becomes the preeminent target and terrorism the weapon of choice. And let's be absolutely clear: This is not about Israel, though Israel may also loom large in the demonology of the terrorists. It's about the American, indeed Western, way of life—our values, our modernity, our liberalism, and our courage to stand up to those who challenge a peaceful world order and democratic values.

And those who despise us have not kept it a secret. To the contrary, they have been loud and clear. America is the "Great Satan," they repeat ad nauseam, and, accordingly, it must be destroyed. They've been saying it, but who's been listening?

While no group has claimed responsibility, suspicion points very heavily toward Osama bin Laden and his network. There aren't many other anti-American forces with both the will and the capacity to mount such a complex operation.

Also striking is who's celebrating in the streets—the very same people who welcomed Saddam Hussein's occupation of Kuwait and stood against the U.S.-assembled coalition in the Gulf War. Television images of crowds of Palestinians cheering, blowing car horns, shooting their guns, and passing out sweets in West Bank towns and cities, while America faces arguably the single most calamitous day in our history, will long be etched in our national memory.

As events sink in, which will take a very long time, and as we all reach out to the families of the victims, we need to bear several things in mind.

First, this was beyond an act of terror. It was an act of war. The object was to kill as many Americans as possible and to paralyze our nation's infrastructure.

Second, there is no room for temporizing or psychobabble about seeking to understand the "concerns" or "grievances" of the perpetrators.

Third, terrorists seek to knock a nation off balance, to create ripple effects of fear that lead to self-imposed restraints on behavior. Our national response must be one of unity and resolve. This is a time to come together, to rally around our political leaders, and to refuse to be cowed.

Fourth, we have to be certain that our military, intelligence, and law-enforcement agencies have the sustained capacity—and public support—to respond at every level to the challenges before them. This is not a short-term war, nor is it out in an open battlefield.

Fifth, Afghanistan harbors Osama bin Laden and terrorist training camps. Three nations in the world recognize Taliban rule in the country—Saudi Arabia, United Arab Emirates, and Pakistan—and thus help that regime stay in power.

These three countries cannot have it both ways; they must choose, and if they choose incorrectly, they need to know that they will pay a price, not just from the United States but from civilized nations everywhere. And if other nations are involved in harboring or supporting the terrorists, the same rule must apply.

Sixth, we need to bear in mind that this is not Islam per se in action. To the contrary, it is the perversion of a noble religion by fanatics.

And finally, we must accept the fact that our way of life has, in at least one important sense, changed for a very long time to come. As Israel has learned from painful experience, security is not an option; it's a daily necessity, inconvenient at times, perhaps, but absolutely essential. No security system is foolproof, as we know, but vigilance can go a long way.

September 11 will become embedded in our national consciousness every bit as much as December 7, the "day that will live in infamy." On both days, America was caught by surprise by an enemy seeking to inflict the maximum possible damage on our nation. In 1941, that enemy was confronted and, after four costly years, was vanquished. Let it be said in the years to come that the enemy that challenged America in 2001—and wreaked such havoc—was similarly crushed.

## Radio Commentary
## Week of September 17, 2001

As our nation reels from the deadliest terrorist attacks in our history, we seek comfort in our national unity, our personal faiths, and the examples of those who were taken from us.

We mourn the loss of thousands of lives.

We cannot find enough words to express our appreciation to the city's heroic policemen, firemen, and other emergency workers, too many of whom made the ultimate sacrifice.

We thank city and state officials for their exemplary leadership.

We have confidence that our government will take the measures necessary to punish the individuals, groups, and countries responsible for these horrific terror attacks. Justice demands no less.

And let us all agree:

We shall refuse to give up hope.

We will not let fanatics undo our democratic way of life.

We must never be cowed.

This is David Harris of the American Jewish Committee, wishing us all a year ahead that brings us closer to the realization that we are one human family created in God's image.


## Radio Commentary
## Week of October 1, 2001

The tragic events of September 11 continue to haunt us.

This is David Harris of the American Jewish Committee, struggling, like you, to come to grips with the gravity of the attack on our country.

One thing is painfully clear. This was a well-coordinated attempt to kill as many of us as possible.

It wasn't the first attack on Americans by radical Islamic groups, and, if it's up to them, it won't be the last, either. They have repeatedly said as much.

These groups despise America, indeed, all democratic nations, and moderate Arab regimes as well.

They detest our celebration of freedom, our emancipation of women, and our national goal of building a society composed of citizens of many faiths, races, and ethnicities.

That's why it's so important to grasp what's at stake in the war against terrorism. It's a struggle we must wage, and it's a struggle we must win.

In the Jewish community, we've just celebrated our New Year. May this be a year in which the freedoms we Americans cherish triumph over those who would destroy us.

This is David Harris of the American Jewish Committee.

## Radio Commentary
## Week of October 15, 2001

One of the lessons of history is that evil must be confronted, not avoided. Otherwise, like a malignant cancer, it will only spread.

Osama bin Laden and those terrorist groups and nations that stand with him seek to ignite a war between the Muslim and non-Muslim worlds. In the process, they've proclaimed their desire to destroy America—the Great Satan, as they call us—in the name of their twisted ideology.

After September 11, who doubts their will?

That's why, as with Adolf Hitler and Nazi Germany, there's no room for negotiation, much less compromise, with such diabolical forces.

Our nation, with steady nerves and steely determination, has launched a multipronged war on terrorism.

It won't be a quick or easy war, but it's vitally important for all Americans to remain steadfast and to support our country's efforts.

For more information, please visit our Web site at www.ajc.org.

This is David Harris of the American Jewish Committee.

## Radio Commentary
## Week of October 29, 2001

In the face of the deadly attacks that have struck our country since September 11, we can find inspiration from two of our closest allies.

For a year, Britain stood largely alone against the Nazis.

With unwavering determination and quiet heroism, the British dug in and fought on. They showed an indomitable spirit and helped save the world from evil.

Israel has shown a similar will. Confronted by repeated acts of terror, Israelis know they can't give in. Otherwise, they'd be handing the terrorists a victory.

On June 1, an Arab suicide bomber killed twenty-one Israelis at a Tel Aviv discotheque. In American terms, that would be 1,000 people.

Within days, an Israeli put up a sign near the scene that read: "They won't stop us from dancing."

This is David Harris of the American Jewish Committee, urging us all to proclaim that those who've attacked the United States won't ever stop us from celebrating our freedoms and defending this great nation.

## Radio Commentary
## Week of November 12, 2001

Many of us are asking what more we can do to help our country in the aftermath of September 11.

We began by donating blood, contributing to 9/11 funds, displaying the flag, and reaffirming the values that make this country great.

What else can we do while our nation's men and women in uniform wage war on those who would destroy us?

Here's an idea.

These tragic events have once again revealed our country's dangerous dependence on Middle East oil and the consequences of that vulnerability.

What if each of us resolved today to cut back our use of oil—for example, by driving less, carpooling more, using public transit, thinking smaller when buying a new car, and lowering the thermostats at home a degree or two?

And isn't it time to send a message to our political leaders that we want to see a national energy policy that moves us toward independence and away from dependence?

In times like this, we can all do our share.

This is David Harris of the American Jewish Committee.

## Radio Commentary
## Week of November 29, 2001

No one is born hating, but too many are taught to hate.

One thing we've learned since September 11 is that, in some unexpected places, children are taught to hate us.

Recently, the *New York Times* (October 19, 2001) reported that in Saudi Arabia, tenth graders are warned of "the dangers of having Christian and Jewish friends," and in Pakistan, a million children attending religious schools are taught to "distrust and even hate the United States" (October 14, 2001).

Our planet is increasingly crowded—6 billion people practicing hundreds of faiths and identifying with countless ethnic backgrounds. Either we all learn to respect one another, or else we'll be doomed to more deadly acts inspired by blind hatred.

Our government needs to begin addressing this pressing challenge abroad, starting with those nations ostensibly close to our own. Meanwhile, here at home, let's continue to show the world what mutual respect and understanding are really all about.

This is David Harris of the American Jewish Committee.

## Radio Commentary
## Week of December 10, 2001

This week Jews around the world celebrate Hanukkah.

Hanukkah marks the rededication of the Jewish Temple in Jerusalem, Judaism's holiest site, over 2,000 years ago, after Jews were denied the practice of their religion by the Greek rulers of the time.

More broadly, Hanukkah symbolizes the quest for religious freedom.

For ninety-five years, the American Jewish Committee has been dedicated to protecting religious freedom for all and to building bridges of cooperation among the world's many faiths.

We've made important strides. As the late and admired Cardinal O'Connor said: "No organization in this city, in this country, in this world, has done more to improve Christian-Jewish relations than the American Jewish Committee."

But we still have a long way to go.

To learn more about us and to support our efforts, please visit our Web site at www.ajc.org.

This is David Harris of the American Jewish Committee, wishing you a happy holiday season.

## Arafat Is a Part of the Problem
### Interview in *Jungle World** (Germany)
### December 12, 2001

After the most recent series of attacks, the conflict in the Middle East has intensified further. Following is an interview with David A. Harris, the director of the American Jewish Committee, about the opponents and the boycotters of the peace process.

**JW**: Does Arafat have the situation under control?

**DH**: It's always difficult to judge. We have to work on the assumption that he is capable of exerting control. In the last fourteen or fifteen months, there have been key moments in which Arafat has had an interest in repressing violence and terror. This summer at the Genoa summit of the G-8, for example, Arafat hoped that the G-8 would criticize Israel directly in its final communiqué, so during the summit there was virtually no violence. I believe that, with difficulty, he can exert control. If he cannot exert control, however, it raises an entirely different set of questions—not only who might be in control, but also why should Israel seek to negotiate with a partner who is not even in command of his forces? So I work on the assumption that he is, in fact, in control.

**JW**: Is he therefore also responsible for last week's attacks?

**DH**: Ultimately, yes. The record shows—and intelligence information confirms—that there have been many contacts between Arafat and

---

* *Jungle World* is a German weekly newspaper focused on public policy and geared to a young, left-leaning audience.

Hamas. At times, they play separate cards, but they reach a consensus when it is mutually beneficial. The West sometimes falls too easily for the false argument that we have to protect Arafat because he is weak. According to this logic, the alternatives are worse. These are the arguments that try to justify Arafat's otherwise unjustifiable behavior. The Palestinians are very cleverly trying to exploit this Western fear. Arafat thus maintains Western support in spite of the obvious pattern of playing the diplomatic card on the one hand while using the violence card on the other.

**JW**: The pragmatic reaction of the Israeli government is to hold him responsible.

**DH**: I think the appropriate reaction is to hold Arafat ultimately accountable for what takes place in areas under PA control. Cities like Jenin are under PA control. It is not only the Israelis who hold Arafat responsible, but also the United States. Other countries of good will should do no less. During our visit to Berlin over the past two days, many German leaders with whom we spoke have shown understanding for the essential point that even though they think that Arafat may ultimately be part of the solution, he is without doubt a central part of the problem.

**JW**: What do you think of the Israeli call for seven days without violence before the resumption of negotiations?

**DH**: I don't like to second-guess military and strategic decisions. I don't pretend to be a military expert. The Mitchell Plan envisions four sequential steps. The first is an end to the violence, followed by a cooling-off period. At the end of the day, Israel will be asked to make painful and risky concessions in any peace process. Israelis, therefore, deserve the right to believe that their partner, the Palestinians, can exert control over the violence, whether it is for several days, weeks, or months.

**JW**: This Israeli demand could postpone the negotiating process indefinitely.

**DH**: Yes, but the world cannot realistically expect Israel simply to run into negotiations if its counterpart in the peace process cannot or will not control violence. The continuous violence not only shakes the Israelis' confidence in any possible peace; it also confirms their sense that Arafat is deliberately manipulating violence as a political negotiating tactic. That is why it is terribly important to recall the 1993 Oslo Accords and specifically the letter that Arafat wrote to the U.S. and Israeli governments at the time. In this letter, he pledged to no longer use violence as a means of achieving political aims.

For some strange reason, people around the world choose to ignore this kind of inconvenient truth. It's a form of cognitive dissonance. Given the small size and the vulnerability of Israel's main population centers, why should Israel trust any commitment made by Arafat today in light of his long and well-documented record of broken promises and abandoned commitments?

Most people who have not been to the region simply cannot understand its geography, regardless of how many maps they look at and how many television programs they watch. They simply cannot grasp the strategic risks to Israel involved in any negotiated settlement.

**JW**: How do you assess the threat posed to Israel by foreign extremist groups like Hezbollah?

**DH**: Together with Hamas and Islamic Jihad, Hezbollah continues to constitute a real threat. These three groups seek the destruction of the State of Israel. Unfortunately, this fact receives too little attention in the press. Instead, press reports convey the impression that these groups are merely giving voice to the frustration of the Palestinian people, the difficulties of occupation, or economic deprivation. Groups like Islamic Jihad are not interested solely in removing Israeli settlements from the West Bank. They are interested in removing Israel from the region. This reality is too often lost in the media coverage.

**JW**: Is this true also for Hezbollah?

**DH**: Hezbollah is an Islamist movement very much in the spirit of Al Qaeda, Egyptian Islamic Jihad, and those other groups in the region that advocate Islamic fundamentalism and would like to impose *shari'a*, or Islamic religious law. They would like to create an Islamic state across current political borders, ultimately from Morocco to Indonesia, to unite the *umma*, the worldwide Muslim community. Hezbollah has created a state within a state in Lebanon, but the Hezbollah could not survive without the support of three states: Iran, which provides funding and weapons; Syria, which aids in the transport of these weapons and funds from Iran and has also used Hezbollah as a weapon against Israel; and Lebanon, which has failed until now to exert control over southern Lebanon and therefore over Hezbollah.

It is interesting that when the United States declared Hezbollah a terrorist organization and asked the government of Lebanon to freeze all bank assets related to Hezbollah, the Lebanese government refused.

**JW**: ... with the justification that Hezbollah is a movement of freedom fighters.

**DH**: Yes. Now the challenge is for the United States to persuade Lebanon that it is in its own interest to take action, or to punish Lebanon in some appropriate way if it does not. Hopefully, European states will join the United States in this effort, because some EU countries may have more influence on Lebanon than does the United States.

**JW**: In the military or political sphere?

**DH**: Take France, for example. Traditionally, Syria and Lebanon have had a special relationship with France. When the West seeks to accomplish certain goals in Syria and Lebanon, it therefore often looks to Paris for help. It is important to know whether the French will help in this case. I don't know the answer.

**JW**: Do you see France or Europe more generally to be a true partner of Israel in this context? The Jewish community of France has complained in the last weeks and months that the government in Paris has adopted a one-sided, pro-Palestinian position. Belgium, meanwhile, wants to try the Israeli prime minister for genocide before the War Crimes Tribunal in The Hague.

**DH**: The image of Israel in Europe is a very serious issue for the American Jewish Committee. We have met with European leaders visiting New York in recent weeks, including the French foreign minister. Just before coming to Berlin, we were in Paris for three days, where we met with the French Jewish community and French government officials. The good news is that France is an active member of the U.S.-led coalition against terror and has troops on the ground in Afghanistan as we speak. But beyond Afghanistan, Al Qaeda, and bin Laden, I am not yet sure what degree of consensus there will be between the EU and the United States, and particularly between France and the United States.

Take Iraq, for example. The Bush administration has not yet decided what to do, but if the United States seeks to extend the war on terror to Iraq, the first indications are that the EU reaction would be negative.

If the conflict with Iraq, however, remains on a nonmilitary level, involving political, diplomatic, economic, and financial measures, there might be more of a consensus.

On a related matter, I was quite disturbed by the visit of Syrian president Assad to Europe in July this year. I was in Paris at the time, and the government treated him royally.

**JW**: … as they did in Berlin.

**DH**: Yes, but a little bit less so in Berlin than in Paris. In France, in particular, it sent the wrong message to Assad, because it allowed him once again, as with Arafat, to play the statesman in Paris and talk about shared values, which he did. If you go back and read the official statements, it is quite troubling. France is the home of the Declaration of the Rights of Man and the French Revolution. It is the birthplace of modern democracy. To see Assad trying to reinvent himself as a kindred spirit and soul brother of President Jacques Chirac and the French government is quite upsetting. For its own reasons, the French government seems to play along.

**JW**: What role does anti-Semitism play in this context?

**DH**: To the readers of *Jungle World*, who are very sensitive to this issue, what we see in France is part of a larger trend that I hope the world will soon wake up to. I am not by nature an alarmist, although I am the son of two Holocaust survivors and have always been very sensitive to any threat to human rights, particularly any threat to Jews. The Durban conference—the so-called World Conference against Racism under UN auspices, which took place during the first week of September in Durban, South Africa, and which was very quickly overshadowed by the events of September 11—will be remembered as a vicious outpouring of anti-Semitism. It scared and shocked not only Jews but all people who recognize anti-Semitism as a cancer that infects the heath of democracy in general.

We therefore hope that the French government will take seriously the concerns of the Jewish community today and not seek to minimize them. When French Jews hear shouts of "death to the Jews," or when synagogues are firebombed, it may be the work of individual Muslim teenagers who live in poor suburban areas around Marseilles, Lyons, Strasbourg, or Paris. It may or may not be an organized anti-Semitic campaign, but this fact makes it neither easier for the Jews to accept nor any less dangerous for French society and its values.

After September 11, we once more saw a resurgence of anti-Semitism in the Muslim world in attempts to blame the Jews for the attacks. These allegations evoked age-old anti-Semitic mythology, suggesting that the Jews must have perpetrated the attacks because—these are Arabs speaking, not Jews—only Jews are smart enough to have planned and organized this kind of attack. According to this perverse logic, Jews may have used Arabs to carry out their plans, but the Arabs themselves were incapable of this level of intelligence and organization. The Western world does not take the nature and degree of anti-Semitism in the Arab and Muslim world seriously enough. Instead, such irrational and intense hatred of Jews gets dismissed as a reflection of Arab passion.

For Jews who are themselves survivors of the Holocaust or children of survivors, or for those who not long ago fled Arab countries because of oppression and persecution, it is not so easy to minimize or rationalize these things.

**JW**: What role does the Holocaust play in current European thinking?

**DH**: Some things in Europe change slowly, but they do change. Whether voluntarily or not, most European states have by now confronted their history during the Second World War, and they have all established diplomatic relations with Israel. That was not the case fifteen years ago.

Nevertheless, some European states took advantage of the reparations process essentially to close the books in the historical, emotional, and psychological sense. The event is acknowledged on the anniversary of the liberation of Auschwitz and on other days of remembrance, but without necessarily drawing the lessons for the present. We have failed, I fear, in our efforts to relate the lessons of the past to contemporary Jewish life and the State of Israel.

**JW**: Should Europe withdraw from the Middle East conflict for the time being?

**DH**: It is not useful to speak of Europe as a monolithic entity, and the same consideration applies to the perspectives and behavior of individual states in their relations to Israel. That is why I do not count myself among those who consider Europe to be irredeemably anti-Israel. At the same time, I think that collective European efforts to maintain a self-proclaimed more or less "neutral role" in the Middle East, which at times is rather overtly pro-Palestinian, have negative consequences. If you never choose sides, nonpartisanship becomes nothing more than an excuse. Even though the Europeans, I trust, would never consciously harm Israel, they often overlook important facts that support Israel's case.

**JW**: Are you still relying on the United States as the most important mediator in the Middle East?

**DH**: When representatives of European states come together, however reluctantly, with delegates from those countries intent on condemning Israel—and that is precisely what the signatories of the Fourth Geneva Convention are doing today in Geneva—I ask myself, how can this be? The Fourth Geneva Convention of 1949 was adopted to protect civilians as a response to the horrors of the Second World War. Since then, the convention has been applied only in two cases. In 1999, Israel was cited for its actions in the occupied territories, and today it is happening again, turning history on its head. That is not to say that there are no problems between Israelis and Palestinians, but can we impute good will to the people convening this conference? It reflects very well on the Bush administration that it chose not to participate in the conference.

**JW**: How would you assess further developments in the Middle East?

**DH**: It is difficult to come up with an optimistic prognosis, much as I would like to. There is no country that desires peace as much as Israel, but peace is not foreseeable at the moment. In the long run, though, I see no alternative to peace.

## Trading with Russia
### *The New York Times*
### November 20, 2001

President Bush's decision to seek approval from Congress to lift trade restrictions on Russia (front page, Nov. 14) is momentous, reflecting dramatic changes in the lives of Russian Jews and in world affairs. The 1974 Jackson-Vanik Amendment, by linking trade to the emigration policies of communist countries, sent a message that certain basic freedoms would not be compromised.

It worked. Well over 1.5 million Soviet Jews left oppression to start new lives. Now we are allied with a changed Russia in the war against terrorists. Strengthening this alliance requires new initiatives, and upgraded trade relations are appropriate. But we, and other Jewish agencies, will continue to monitor the condition of Russia's large Jewish community.

## Israel and the Arab-Israeli Conflict:
### A Brief Guide for the Perplexed*
### *The Jewish Week* (New York)
### January 3, 2001

As the magnitude of the horrific events of September 11 sinks in and our nation implements its multifaceted military, diplomatic, and economic response, greater public attention is once again being paid to the Middle East—in the media, on college campuses, and elsewhere. Unfortunately, much of this discussion is misinformed and lacks historical context.

This paper provides some perspectives and talking points, both historical and contemporary. It is not intended as an exhaustive examination of the subject.

---

* This essay, written in October 2001, was also translated into Arabic, French, German, Russian, Spanish, and Turkish.

**The case to be made on behalf of Israel is as strong today as ever.**

When presented with the facts, sensible people should understand:

- Israel's fifty-three-year-long quest for peace and security;
- the real dangers faced by Israel, a tiny country no larger than New Jersey, in a tumultuous, heavily armed neighborhood;
- Israel's unshakable commitment to democracy and democratic values;
- the common enemies of extremism and fanaticism faced by Israel and the United States; and
- Israel's impressive contributions to world civilization in such fields as science, medicine, technology, agriculture, and culture—contributions that are even more remarkable given the country's relative youth and its heavy defense burden.

No country's historical record is perfect, and Israel, like other democratic nations, has made its share of mistakes. But acknowledging fallibility is a national strength, not a weakness. And I'll gladly match Israel's record with that of any other country in the region, indeed well beyond the region, when it comes to the values the West holds dear.

Israel has a proud record and the country's friends shouldn't hesitate to shout it from the rooftops. That record actually begins long before the establishment of the modern state in 1948.

**The Jewish people's link to the land of Israel is incontrovertible and unbroken.**

It spans nearly 4,000 years. Exhibit A for this connection is the Hebrew Bible. The Book of Genesis, the first of the five books of the Bible, recounts the story of Abraham, the covenantal relationship with the one God, and the move from Ur (in present-day Iraq) to Canaan, the region corresponding roughly to Israel. Exhibit B is any Jewish prayer book in use anywhere in the world. The references in the liturgy to Zion, the land of Israel, are endless.

**The same is true of the connection between the Jewish people and Jerusalem.**

It dates back to the period of King David, who lived approximately 3,000 years ago, and who established Jerusalem as the capital of Israel.

Ever since, Jerusalem has represented not only the geographical center of the Jewish people, but also the spiritual and metaphysical heart of our faith and identity. Indeed, the relationship between Jerusalem and the Jewish people is entirely unique in the annals of history.

Jerusalem was the site of the two temples—the first built by King Solomon during the tenth century B.C.E. and destroyed in 586 B.C.E. during the Babylonian conquest, and the second built less than a century later, refurbished by King Herod, and destroyed in 70 C.E. by Roman forces.

As the psalmist wrote, "If I forget thee, O Jerusalem, let my right hand wither; let my tongue stick to my palate if I cease to think of thee, if I do not keep Jerusalem in memory even at my happiest hour."

**Though in forced dispersion for nearly nineteen hundred years, Jews never stopped yearning for Zion and Jerusalem.**

In addition to expressing this through prayer, there were always Jews who lived in the land of Israel, and especially Jerusalem. Indeed, since the nineteenth century, Jews have constituted a majority of the city's population. For example, according to the *Political Dictionary of the State of Israel*, Jews were 61.9 percent of Jerusalem's population in 1892.

The historical and religious link to Jerusalem is especially important because some Arabs seek to rewrite history and assert that Jews are "foreign occupiers" or "colonialists" with no actual tie to the land. Such attempts to deny Israel's legitimacy are demonstrably false and need to be exposed for the lies they are. They also entirely ignore the "inconvenient" fact that when Jerusalem was under Muslim (i.e., Ottoman and, later, Jordanian) rule, it was always a backwater.

**Zionism is the quest for national self-determination of the Jewish people.**

Although the yearning for a Jewish homeland derives from a longing that dates back thousands of years and is given expression in classic Jewish texts, it also stems from a more contemporary reality.

Theodor Herzl, considered the father of modern Zionism, was a secular Jew and Viennese journalist who became appalled at the blatant anti-Semitism fueling the infamous Dreyfus case in France, the first European country to extend full rights to the Jews. He came to the conclusion that Jews could never enjoy full equality as a minority in European societies, since the sad legacy of centuries of anti-Semitism was too deeply embedded. Therefore, he called for the establishment of a Jewish state, which he set out to describe in his landmark book *Altneuland* ("Old-New Land"), published in 1902.

Herzl's vision was endorsed by the British foreign secretary, Lord Balfour, who issued a statement on November 2, 1917:

> His Majesty's Government view with favour the establishment in Palestine of a national home for the Jewish people, and will use their best endeavours to facilitate the achievement of this object, it being clearly understood that nothing shall be done which may prejudice the civil and religious rights of existing non-Jewish communities in Palestine, or the rights and political status enjoyed by Jews in any other country.

In 1922, the League of Nations, entrusting Britain with a mandate for Palestine, recognized "the historical connection of the Jewish people with Palestine."

The rise of Hitler and the Nazi Final Solution, spearheaded by Germany and its allies—and facilitated by widespread complicity as well as indifference to the fate of the Jews—revealed in tragic dimensions the desperate need for a Jewish state. (Apropos, Haj Amin el-Husseini, the mufti of Jerusalem, was among the enthusiastic supporters of the Nazi genocide of the Jewish people.)

Only in such a state, the Zionist movement believed, would Jews not have to rely on the good will of others to determine their destiny. All Jews would be welcome to settle in the Jewish state as a refuge from persecution or as a fulfillment of a "yearning for Zion." Indeed, this latter point fired the imagination of many Jews who settled in what was then a generally desolate Palestine, in the late nineteenth and early twentieth century, out of idealistic convictions, and who laid the foundation for the modern State of Israel.

Israel's adversaries to this day twist the meaning of Zionism and try to present it as a demonic force, with the goal of undermining Israel's raison d'être and isolating the state from the community of nations.

This happened in 1975, when the UN, over the strenuous objections of the democratic countries, adopted a resolution labeling Zionism as "racism." The resolution was repealed by the UN in 1991, but the canard resurfaced earlier this year (of all places) at the World Conference Against Racism in Durban, South Africa. The Arab bloc, however, failed in its latest effort to condemn Zionism in the conference documents. This time many nations understood that the conflict between Israel and the Palestinians is, and has always been, political, not racial.

In this vein, it's well worth remembering the comments of the Reverend Martin Luther King, Jr., on anti-Zionism:

> And what is anti-Zionism? It is the denial to the Jewish people of a fundamental right that we justly claim for the people of Africa and all other nations of the Globe. It is discrimination against Jews, my friends, because they are Jews. In short, it is anti-Semitism.... Let my words echo in the depths of your soul: When people criticize Zionism, they mean Jews—make no mistake about it.

It is also important to stress that non-Jews were not excluded from Israel's nation-building. To the contrary, today one-fifth of Israel's citizens are non-Jews, including over 1 million Arabs, and Arabic is an official national language.

Moreover, Israel's Jewish population has always reflected enormous national, ethnic, cultural, and linguistic diversity, which became even more pronounced in the 1980s, when Israel rescued tens of thousands of black Jews from drought-stricken Ethiopia who were dreaming of resettlement in Israel. The eloquent comments at the time of Julius Chambers, the director-general of the NAACP Legal Defense and Education Fund, bear repeating:

> Were the victims of Ethiopian famine white, countless nations might have offered them refuge. But the people dying every day of starvation

in Ethiopia and the Sudan are black, and in a world where racism is officially deplored by virtually every organized government, only one non-African nation has opened its doors and its arms. The quiet humanitarian action of the State of Israel, action taken entirely without regard to the color of those being rescued, stands as a condemnation of racism far more telling than mere speeches and resolutions.

### The Arab-Israeli conflict was avoidable.

Shortly after its founding in 1945, the United Nations took an interest in the future of mandatory Palestine, then under British rule. A UN commission (UNSCOP, or the United Nations Special Committee on Palestine) recommended to the General Assembly a partition of the land between the Jews and the Arabs. Neither side would get all it sought, but a division would recognize that there were two populations in the land—one Jewish, the other Arab—each meriting a state.

On November 29, 1947, the UN General Assembly, by a vote of 33 in favor, 13 opposed, and 10 abstaining, adopted Resolution 181, known as the Partition Plan.

Acceptance of the Partition Plan would have meant the establishment of two states, but the Arab states and the local Arab population vehemently rejected the proposal. They refused to recognize a Jewish claim to any part of the land and chose war to fulfill their objectives.

On May 14, 1948, the State of Israel was founded. Winston Churchill said at the time: "The coming into being of a Jewish state ... is an event in world history to be viewed in the perspective not of a generation or a century, but in the perspective of a thousand, two thousand or even three thousand years."

Years later, President John F. Kennedy offered his perspective on the meaning of Israel: "Israel was not created in order to disappear—Israel will endure and flourish. It is the child of hope and home of the brave. It can neither be broken by adversity nor demoralized by success. It carries the shield of democracy and it honors the sword of freedom."

Israel's Declaration of the Establishment of the State included these words:

We extend our hand to all neighboring states and their peoples in an offer of peace and good neighborliness, and appeal to them to establish bonds of cooperation and mutual help with the sovereign Jewish people settled in its own land.

Tragically, that offer was ignored.

**On May 15, 1948, the armies of Egypt, Iraq, Jordan, Lebanon, and Syria attacked the fledgling Jewish state, seeking its destruction.**

In the course of this war, launched by the Arabs, civilian populations were affected, just as in all wars. Controversies continue to this day about how many local Arabs fled Israel because Arab leaders called on them to do so or threatened them if they did not, how many left out of fear of the fighting, and how many were compelled to leave by Israeli forces. Importantly, hundreds of thousands of Arabs ended up staying in Israel and became citizens of the state.

But the central point must not be overlooked—Arab countries began this war aiming to wipe out the 650,000 Jews in the new State of Israel, and, by doing so, the Arabs defied the UN plan for the creation of both Arab and Jewish states.

**There have been two refugee populations created by the Arab-Israeli conflict, not one.**

While world attention has been focused on the Palestinian refugees, the plight of Jews from Arab countries, hundreds of thousands of whom became refugees as well, has been largely ignored. Indeed, many experts believe that the sizes of the two groups were roughly comparable. But there was one profound difference—Israel immediately absorbed the Jewish refugees, while the Palestinian refugees were placed in camps and deliberately kept there as a matter of calculated Arab policy and with the complicity of the UN.

**There is no comparable situation in the world today where a refugee population has been cynically exploited in this way.**

Until now, only one Arab country—Jordan—has offered citizenship to the Palestinian refugees.

The other twenty-one Arab countries, with their vast territory and common language, religion, and ethnic roots with the Palestinians, have refused to do so. Why? Sadly, they appear to have little interest in alleviating the plight of refugees living in often squalid camps for two and three generations. Rather, they want to breed hatred of Israel and thus use the refugees as a key weapon in the ongoing struggle against Israel.

Parenthetically—just to give a sense how Palestinians are treated in the Arab world—Kuwait summarily expelled over 300,000 Palestinians working in the country (but never given Kuwaiti passports) when Yasir Arafat voiced support for Iraq in the Gulf War and the Palestinians were seen as a potential fifth column. There was hardly a peep of protest from other Arab countries about what amounted to the expulsion of an entire Palestinian community.

**Unfortunately, the story of the Jewish refugees from Arab countries is not often told.**

When the issue of Jewish refugees from Arab countries is raised, Arab spokesmen often feign ignorance or strenuously assert that Jews lived well under Muslim rule (unlike Jews in Christian Europe). Sometimes they disingenuously argue that Arabs, by definition, cannot be anti-Semitic because, like Jews, they are Semites.

It is certainly true that there was no equivalent of the Holocaust in the Jewish experience in Muslim lands, and it is also true that there were periods of cooperation and harmony, but the story does not end there. Jews never enjoyed full and equal rights with Muslims in Islamic countries; there were clearly delineated rules of behavior for Jews as second-class citizens. Violence against Jews was not unknown in the Muslim world.

To cite but one illustration of the fate of Jews in Arab countries, Jews lived uninterruptedly in Libya since the time of the Phoenicians, that is, many centuries before the Arabs arrived from the Arabian Peninsula, bringing Islam to North Africa and settling—occupying?—lands already inhabited by Berbers, among others.

The vast majority of Libya's 40,000 Jews left between 1948 and 1951, following pogroms in 1945 and 1948. In 1951, Libya became an independent country. Despite constitutional guarantees, the Jews who remained in the country were denied the right to vote, hold public office, obtain Libyan passports, supervise their own communal affairs, or purchase new property. After a third pogrom in 1967, Libya's remaining 4,000 Jews fled, permitted to leave with only one suitcase and the equivalent of $50. In 1970, the Libyan government announced a series of laws to confiscate the assets of Libya's exiled Jews and issued bonds providing for fair compensation payable within fifteen years. But 1985 came and went, with no compensation paid.

At the same time, the government destroyed Jewish cemeteries, using the headstones to pave new roads, as part of a calculated effort to erase any vestige of the Jewish historical presence in the country.

There were an estimated 754,000 Jews in Arab countries in 1948, the year of Israel's establishment; today, there are fewer than 8,000, the bulk of whom live in Morocco and Tunisia.

## Where was the Arab sympathy for the Palestinian population from 1948 to 1967?

With armistice agreements ending Israel's War of Independence, the Gaza Strip was in the hands of Egypt. Rather than consider sovereignty for the local Arab population and the Palestinian refugees who settled there, Egyptian authorities imposed military rule. Meanwhile, the West Bank and the eastern half of Jerusalem were ruled by Jordan. Again, there was no move to create an independent Palestinian state; to the contrary, Jordan annexed the territory, a step recognized by only two countries in the world, Britain and Pakistan.

It was during this period, 1964 to be precise, that the Palestine Liberation Organization (PLO) was founded. Its aim was not the creation of a state in the lands under Egyptian and Jordanian rule, but rather the elimination of Israel and the founding of an Arab Palestinian state in the whole of Palestine.

Article 15 of the PLO Charter clearly revealed this goal: "The liberation of Palestine, from an Arab viewpoint, is a national duty to repulse the Zionist, imperialist invasion from the great Arab homeland and to purge the Zionist presence from Palestine."

In the ensuing years, PLO-sponsored terrorism took its deadly toll, focusing on Israeli, American, European, and Jewish targets.

**How did Israel come into possession of the West Bank, Golan Heights, Gaza Strip, the Sinai Peninsula, and the eastern half of Jerusalem, including the Old City?**

These days, some people reflexively refer to the "occupied territories" without ever asking the question of how they fell into Israel's hands in 1967. Once again, there are those in the Arab world who seek to rewrite history and impute expansionist motives to Israel, but the facts are clear. Here's a quick summary of some of the major events leading up to the Six-Day War:

On May 16, 1967, Cairo Radio announced: "The existence of Israel has continued too long. The battle has come in which we shall destroy Israel." On the same day, Egypt demanded the withdrawal of UN forces that had been stationed in Gaza and Sharm el-Sheikh since 1957. Three days later, the UN announced it would comply with the Egyptian demand.

On May 19, Cairo Radio said: "This is our chance, Arabs, to deal Israel a mortal blow of annihilation…."

On May 23, Egypt's president Gamal Abdel Nasser declared his intention to block the Strait of Tiran to Israeli shipping, thus effectively severing Israel's vital trade links with East Africa and Asia. Israel replied that under international law this was a casus belli, an act of war.

On May 27, Nasser said that "our basic objective will be the destruction of Israel."

On May 30, Jordan's King Hussein placed Jordanian forces under Egyptian control. Egyptian, Iraqi, and Saudi troops were sent to Jordan.

On June 1, Iraq's leader added his thoughts: "We are resolved, determined, and united to achieve our clear aim of wiping Israel off the map."

On June 3, Cairo Radio hailed the impending Muslim holy war.

On June 5, Israel, surrounded by Arab forces likely to attack at any moment, launched a preemptive strike. Within six days, Israel had defeated its adversaries and, in the process, captured land on the Egyptian, Jordanian, and Syrian fronts.

Israel had made strenuous efforts, via UN channels, to persuade King Hussein to stay out of the war. Unlike Egypt and Syria, whose hostility toward Israel was unremitting, Jordan had quietly cooperated with Israel and shared concerns about the Palestinians' aggressive designs. Years later, King Hussein publicly acknowledged that his decision to enter the 1967 war, in which he lost control of the West Bank and eastern Jerusalem, was one of the biggest mistakes he ever made.

**Another lost peace opportunity.**

Shortly after the Six-Day War, Israel indicated its desire to negotiate peace with its Arab neighbors. While Israel was unprepared to relinquish the eastern half of Jerusalem—which contained Judaism's holiest sites and which, despite the terms of the Israeli-Jordanian armistice agreement, had been entirely off-limits to Israel for nearly nineteen years (while Jordan desecrated dozens of synagogues in the Old City)—it was willing to exchange the seized territories for a comprehensive settlement. But Israel's overtures were rebuffed. An unmistakable response came from Khartoum, Sudan's capital, where Arab leaders issued a resolution on September 1 announcing the three noes: "no peace, no recognition, and no negotiation."

**In November 1967, the UN Security Council adopted Resolution 242.**

This resolution, often cited in discussions about the Arab-Israeli conflict as the basis for resolving it, is not always quoted with precision. The resolution stresses "the inadmissibility of the acquisition of territory by war and the need to work for a just and lasting peace in which *every* [emphasis added] State in the area can live in security."

Further, it calls for "withdrawal of Israeli armed forces from territories occupied in the recent conflict," but deliberately omitted use of the word "the" before the word "territories." The U.S. ambassador to the UN at the time, Arthur Goldberg, noted that this was intentional, so that any final settlement could allow for unspecified border adjustments that would take into account Israel's security needs.

The resolution also includes a call for *"termination of all claims or states of belligerency and respect for and acknowledgment of the sovereignty, territorial integrity and political independence of every State in the area and their right to live in peace within secure and recognized boundaries free from threats or acts of force* [emphasis added]."

And, not least, it "affirms further the necessity (a) For guaranteeing freedom of navigation through international waterways in the area; (b) For achieving a just settlement of the refugee problem [Author's comment: Note the absence of reference to which refugee problem, allowing for more than one interpretation of the refugee populations covered.]; and (c) For guaranteeing the territorial inviolability and political independence of every State in the area, through measures including the establishment of demilitarized zones."

On October 22, 1973, during the Yom Kippur War, the UN Security Council adopted Resolution 338, which called for a cease-fire, implementation of Resolution 242 in its entirety, and the onset of talks between the parties concerned. Resolutions 242 and 338 are normally cited together in connection with any Arab-Israeli peace talks.

**The settlements have been a contentious issue.**

No question, but, like just about everything else associated with the Arab-Israeli conflict, there's more here than meets the eye.

After Israel's victory in the 1967 war, and once it became clear that the Arabs were not interested in negotiating peace, Israel, under a Labor-led coalition, began encouraging the construction of settlements, or new communities, in the captured lands. This practice was accelerated under Likud-led governments after 1977.

Whatever one's perspective on the settlements, it's important to understand Israel's motives in moving ahead on this front: (a) Israel contended that the land was disputed—both Arabs and Jews laid claim to it—and since there was no sovereign authority, Israelis had as much right to settle there as the Palestinians; (b) there had been Jewish communities in the West Bank long before 1948, for example, in Hebron and Gush Etzion, both sites of massacres by Arabs in which large numbers of Jews were killed; (c) the West Bank, according to the Bible, represents the cradle of Jewish civilization, and some Jews, moved by faith and history, wanted to reassert that link; (d) the Israeli government believed that certain settlements could serve a useful security purpose; and (e) some Israeli officials felt that building settlements, and thus creating facts on the ground, might hasten the day when the Palestinians, presumably realizing that time was not on their side, would talk peace.

Today, most Israelis agree that any peace agreement with the Palestinians will necessarily entail dismantling many, though not all, of the settlements. Polls repeatedly show that a majority of Israelis accept this prospect, but only in the context of a real peace process. However, Israelis fear that any unilateral decision to withdraw would be viewed by the Palestinians and their Arab supporters as a sign of weakness, not strength, and could only encourage further violence.

In hindsight, this perception of Israeli weakness may have actually been one of the unintended consequences of Israel's unilateral withdrawal from southern Lebanon in 1999. Israeli troops were there for one reason only—not to acquire territory, but to maintain a security zone that would prevent deadly terrorist strikes from Lebanon on the villages and towns of northern Israel.

But periodic attacks by Hezbollah on Israeli soldiers took their toll, and Prime Minister Barak concluded that the benefit to Israel no longer justified the price. He ordered the troops home. Hezbollah declared victory over the seemingly invincible Israel Defense Force (IDF), and this may have emboldened Palestinians in the West Bank and Gaza to believe that they could follow suit and accomplish what no Arab army had succeeded in doing since Israel's founding in 1948, namely, defeat the IDF.

**The possibilities of peace.**

In 1977, Menachem Begin, Israel's first Likud prime minister, took office. That did not stop Egypt's president Anwar Sadat from making his historic trip to Israel the same year and addressing the Knesset, Israel's parliament. An extraordinary peace process ensued, with all the ups and downs that came with a difficult set of negotiations. In September 1978, the Camp David Accords were adopted, containing a framework for comprehensive peace, including a proposal for limited self-government for the Palestinians. (The proposal was rejected by the Palestinians.) Six months later, a peace accord was signed and the thirty-one-year state of war between Israel and Egypt came to an end.

It was a remarkable moment in history. Sadat, virulently anti-Israel and anti-Semitic for much of his life, and the mastermind of Egypt's surprise attack (together with Syria) on Israel that ignited the 1973 Yom Kippur War, teamed up with Begin, the head of Israel's leading right-wing party, to open a new chapter in Arab-Israel relations. It proved that with will, courage, and vision, anything was possible.

But every Arab country, except Sudan and Oman, severed diplomatic ties with Cairo. And in 1981 the Egyptian leader was assassinated by members of Egyptian Islamic Jihad, who would later become brothers-in-arms of Osama bin Laden and his Al Qaeda network.

For its part, Israel yielded the vast expanse of the Sinai (approximately 23,000 square miles), which had provided a critical strategic buffer zone between itself and Egypt. It also gave up valuable oil fields it had discovered in the Sinai, a big sacrifice for a country with no natural resources to speak of. It closed important air bases it had constructed. And, despite Begin's staunch commitment to settlements, it dismantled these enclaves in Sinai.

In doing so, Israel demonstrated very clearly its desire for peace, its willingness to take substantial risks and make sacrifices, and its scrupulous commitment to fulfilling the terms of its agreements.

**Israel and Jordan reached an historic peace agreement in 1994.**

This was a much easier negotiation than with Egypt, since Israel and Jordan already enjoyed good, if quiet, ties based on overlapping national interests vis-à-vis the Palestinians. Israel once again demonstrated its deep yearning for peace and readiness to take the steps necessary to achieve it, including border adjustments and water-sharing arrangements called for by Amman.

**Another opportunity for peace was spurned by the Palestinians in 2000-2001.**

When Ehud Barak took office as prime minister in 1999, he announced an ambitious agenda. The Israeli leader said he would attempt to reach an historic end to the conflict with the Palestinians within thirteen months, picking up where his predecessors had left off, and building on the momentum of the 1991 Madrid Conference and accelerated by the 1993 Oslo Accords. As it turned out, he went beyond what anyone in Israel might have thought possible in his willingness to compromise.

With the active support of the Clinton administration, Barak pushed the process as far and as fast as he could, and, in doing so, he broke new ground on such infinitely sensitive issues as Jerusalem for the sake of an agreement. But alas, he and Clinton failed.

Arafat was not ready to engage the process and make it work.

Rather than press ahead with the talks, which would have led to the establishment of the first-ever Palestinian state, with its capital in eastern Jerusalem, he walked away, after preposterously trying to persuade President Clinton that there was no historical Jewish link to Jerusalem and dropping the bombshell demand of a so-called "right of return" for Palestinian refugees and their generations of descendants. Arafat surely knew that this was an instant deal-breaker, since no Israeli government could ever conceivably allow millions of Palestinians to settle in Israel and thus destroy Israel as a Jewish state.

**Tragically, Arafat revealed himself incapable or unwilling, or both, of pursuing peace at the negotiating table. Instead, he returned to a more familiar pattern—on occasion talking peace while consistently encouraging violence.**

He knew that the media images of heavily armed Israeli troops facing Palestinians in the streets, including children cynically sent to the front lines, would work to his advantage. Israel would be cast in the role of aggressor and oppressor, the Palestinians as downtrodden victims.

It wouldn't be long, he calculated, before the Arab world would angrily denounce Israel, the nonaligned countries would dutifully follow suit, the Europeans would urge still more concessions from Israel to placate the Palestinians, international human rights groups would accuse Israel of excessive force, and the world, plagued by a short memory, would forget that the Palestinian leader had just spurned an unprecedented chance to strike a peace deal.

Moreover, he presumably reckoned, Washington might eventually take a tougher line on Israel, as the result of pressure from Egypt and

Saudi Arabia, two Arab countries that loom large in the worldview of American policy-makers. And finally, there was the long-term possibility that Israel, a first-world country, would begin to tire of the struggle and its daily toll of military and civilian casualties, the negative impact on the nation's mood and psyche—not to speak of its economy—and the potentially growing international isolation.

Some in the media have too uncritically bought the Palestinian spin and, as a consequence, have been less than fully objective and balanced in their coverage of the Israeli-Palestinian conflict. So, too, have a number of international human rights groups, which sometimes seem to have a blind spot for human rights violations in the Arab world, including especially in the Palestinian Authority. And many European Union nations, Germany being the notable exception, haven't always been as understanding of Israel's profound security dilemmas as they should be; it's undoubtedly easier to render judgments on the situation from the safety and comfort of distant capitals.

**What exactly is Israel expected to do to ensure the safety of its citizens? What would other states do in a similar situation?**

We're about to find out, as the United States and its allies respond to Osama bin Laden, Al Qaeda, the Taliban, and possibly some nations that provide shelter and support for terrorist groups. Judging from the military buildup to date and the global diplomatic, political, and financial full-court press, it doesn't look as if "restraint," "dialogue," "compromise," and "understanding" are currently part of Washington's vocabulary vis-à-vis those who attack us, nor should they be.

At the end of the day, Israel tragically finds it has no credible negotiating partner. Instead, its citizens are targeted for murder by suicide bombers who are brainwashed to believe they are destined for martyrdom and sexual ecstasy in paradise.

Despite repeated requests, the Palestinian Authority has proved unwilling to arrest and imprison those responsible for murdering Israelis.

The limits on a Palestinian police force, agreed to in the Oslo Accords, have long since been exceeded, and well-armed and aggressive militia forces are emerging to do battle with Israel. Several of these groups, including the Tanzim and Force 17, are under the direct control of Arafat.

Hamas and Islamic Jihad, two radical groups on the American list of terrorist organizations that are believed to have links with bin Laden's Al Qaeda, operate with relative impunity in the Palestinian-controlled areas.

Cease-fires negotiated with Israel are regularly broken by the Palestinians. Ze'ev Schiff, the highly respected defense correspondent for *Ha'aretz*, noted last year (October 20, 2000) that Arafat agreed to twenty-two cease-fires with Jordan's King Hussein until he was banished from the country thirty years ago and to more than seventy cease-fires during the Lebanese civil war.

The education for peace that is so necessary to laying the groundwork for a new era in the region, regrettably, is absent in the Palestinian Authority. Schools, the media, and the mosques preach hatred of Jews, vilification of Judaism, Holocaust denial, demonization of Israel, and violence.

Perhaps the tragic events of September 11 will help the world grasp the kind of threat Israel has been facing and the rationale for Israel's unflinching response.

Unflinching yes, but also measured. The truth is that Israel could deliver a much more devastating blow to the Palestinians but has chosen not to for a host of diplomatic, political, strategic, and humanitarian reasons.

In the final analysis, even though Israel enjoys military superiority, Jerusalem understands that this is not a conflict that can be won exclusively on the battlefield. Simply put, neither side is going to disappear. This conflict can be resolved only at the peace table, if and when the Palestinians finally realize they have squandered more than fifty years and numerous chances to build a state—alongside Israel, not in its place.

**Israel is a democracy and thinks and behaves like a democracy.**

That's not always easy to do in light of the situation it faces. But, while Israel gets its share of criticism for allegedly heavy-handed methods, the Palestinians, despite all their shrill rhetoric, understand better than anyone that it is precisely Israel's democratic values and rule of law that they regard as the nation's Achilles' heel.

The Palestinians know, even if they don't publicly acknowledge it, that the democratic system puts brakes and limits on Israel's policy options.

They know that Israel has a multiparty political system and that these parties need to differentiate themselves from one another to have any chance of electoral success. In fact, the parties include every viewpoint from extreme left to extreme right, from secular to religious, from Russian Jewish to Arab. In fact, Israeli Arabs currently hold approximately 10 percent of the Knesset seats (and a few of these parliamentarians have identified with Israel's enemies in the current conflict).

They know that public opinion in Israel counts for something and can affect policy; witness the grassroots movement that successfully urged the government to pull out of southern Lebanon.

They know that Israel enjoys a free and inquisitive press.

They know that Israel has an independent judiciary that occupies a respected place in the nation's life.

They know that Israel has a thriving civil society and numerous human rights groups that stress their objectivity and impartiality.

They know that Israel protects freedom of worship for all religious communities, indeed has gone so far as to prevent Jews from praying on the Temple Mount, one of Judaism's holiest sites, specifically to avoid tension with Muslim worshipers at the two mosques built there, and, since the 1967 Six-Day War, has ceded authority for the area to the Waqf, the Muslim religious authority.

They know that Israel cares about world opinion, especially American and European reactions to its policies.

They know that Israel, based on the core values of the Jewish tradition, attaches great importance to ethical and moral standards of behavior, even when, at times, it falls short of them.

And, as a result, they know that there are self-imposed restraints on Israeli behavior precisely because Israel is a democratic state and because, in the final analysis, its government is accountable to the will of the people.

**If only the Middle East resembled the Middle West!**

Wouldn't that augur well for peaceful conflict resolution and regional cooperation? When was the last time that one democratic nation launched a military attack against another democracy? Regrettably, democracy is a very rare commodity in the Middle East.

The Palestinians know how Syria's Assad dealt with Islamic fundamentalists, killing an estimated 10-20,000 in Hama and leveling the city as an unmistakable message to other fundamentalists in the country.

They know how Iraq's Saddam Hussein handled the Kurds, using poison gas to kill thousands and destroying hundreds of Kurdish villages.

They know, as noted above, how Kuwait responded to Palestinian support for Saddam Hussein in the Gulf War by expelling 300,000 Palestinians from the country in one fell swoop.

They know how Saudi Arabia reacted to Yemeni support for Saddam Hussein during the same war. Overnight, the country expelled an estimated 600,000 Yemenis.

And they know how Egypt dealt with its own Islamic radicals in the 1990s—below the radar of the media, without fanfare. Within a few years, thousands of these radicals were either dead or locked up in jails.

The Palestinians count on the fact that Israel will not follow any of these examples. That is Israel's strength as a democracy, but it comes with a price. The Palestinians seek to take advantage of it. But they have made one fundamental error—they have underestimated Israel's will to survive.

**Israelis desperately want peace. At the same time, peace at any price is no peace.**

Israelis want to stop worrying about bombs on buses and in malls. They want to put an end to burying their children, victims of terror or military engagements. In short, they want to lead normal lives, and they have demonstrated their willingness time and again to endorse far-reaching, even potentially risky, compromises in the quest for peace.

Israelis, however, have learned the painful lessons of history. Peace without security can be tantamount to national suicide. And who knows better than the citizens of Israel, who include Holocaust survivors and refugees from communist lands and from Arab extremism, how dangerous it can be to let one's guard down too quickly, too easily?

Are Israelis simply to ignore Iran's and Iraq's calls for Israel's annihilation, their insatiable appetite for acquiring weapons of mass destruction, Syria's hospitality to terrorist groups bent on Israel's destruction, Hezbollah's accumulation of short-range missiles capable of reaching the northern third of Israel, and the blood-curdling calls for suicide attacks against Israel heard in Gaza and the West Bank?

Our world hasn't been terribly kind to the naive, the credulous, or the self-delusional. Despite the doubters at the time, Hitler meant exactly what he said when he wrote *Mein Kampf*, Saddam Hussein meant exactly what he said when he insisted that Kuwait was a province of Iraq, and Osama bin Laden meant exactly what he said when he called for killing as many Americans as possible.

Israel lives in a particularly rough neighborhood. To survive, it has had to be courageous both on the battlefield and at the peace table, passing both tests with flying colors. As Israel faces the unresolved challenges in its region, it deserves both understanding and support.

# 5. AJC INSTITUTIONAL

## Eulogy for Ambassador Morris B. Abram
## April 6, 2000

When Morris died on March 16, I, like many of his legion of admirers, experienced a profound sense of disbelief.

I knew he was eighty-one years old, with an eighty-second birthday coming up on June 19, and I knew that he hadn't been in the best of health.

But I had allowed myself over the years to come to believe that Morris was indestructible, simply because I couldn't imagine a world without him. Sure, he may have lost a half step in his walk and was bent over a bit, but that brilliant and inquisitive mind was still in overdrive, the energy level remained undiminished, and the handwritten notes and phone calls on this or that issue kept coming with regularity. And Morris was still traveling internationally, driving his car, and swimming daily up until just about the very end.

A famous poet once described old age as a time "when the passion is spent and the last race is run." By that definition, Morris never turned old. His passion was never spent; to the contrary, he remained totally engaged on an awesome array of issues—not least regarding Israel, anti-Semitism, and the United Nations. And not only was his last race not run, but, unbelievably, he was still sprinting at the age of eighty-one.

To state the painfully obvious, we have lost a giant: a man who helped shape many of the defining issues of the past sixty years; who refused to be a bystander, instead grasping the essential fact that an individual can make a profound difference in the world around him; who was on a first-name basis with many of the world's principal decision-makers and who could, by dint of his formidable advocacy skills, have a decisive impact on their thinking; whose breadth and depth of knowledge—ranging from medical ethics to education, from the law to

351

international affairs and human rights—whose love of learning and ideas, whose curiosity about everything and everyone around him, was without equal; who, in short, was in love with life and lived each day as if it were both his first and his last.

There is so much that can be said about Morris:

- about the charming juxtaposition of his Fitzgerald, Georgia, twang with his worldliness;

- or about the young man who never had a formal bar mitzvah but who, as an articulate teenager, was actually hired to speak at the bar mitzvahs of others and, years later, rose to become an eloquent spokesman for American Jewry;

- or about his experience at Nuremberg, his agony over the horrors of the Holocaust, and his visceral sense of outrage, throughout his life, not only when anti-Semitism surfaced but, perhaps even more, when it was met with silence, apathy, or rationalization;

- or about his steadfast unwillingness to accept the blatant hypocrisy of undemocratic, corrupt states constantly challenging Israel in the international arena and—still more galling—the cowardice of those nations and individuals who averted their eyes and closed their ears;

- or about his more than forty-year relationship with the American Jewish Committee, beginning in our Atlanta Chapter and including service as our national president from 1964 to 1968, when he involved himself on AJC's behalf in several historic developments—the enactment of the landmark Voting Rights Act of 1965, the adoption of *Nostra Aetate* at Vatican Council II, the mobilization of American support for Israel in the 1967 Six-Day War, and the denunciation before the world of anti-Semitic books published in the Soviet Union;

- or about his deep and abiding love of America, this great and wondrous land, and his belief in the unparalleled moral power of our nation;

- or about his revulsion at the second-class treatment of African-Americans in the South and his lifelong commitment to ensuring equality before the law for all Americans, including equal opportunity for each and every American;

- or about the courtly way he would walk into an office—be it here at AJC, or at the NCSJ, or at the Presidents Conference—and greet each and every employee, fixing his gaze on that person long enough to make that person believe he or she counted, regardless of position;
- or about the legendary dinner parties he hosted at his home, where Morris would begin the dinner discussion by personally introducing everyone at the table in some detail to the entire group and then posing a deceptively simple question for tablewide discussion, such as "What do you think the twenty-first century will look like?"
- or about his long effort to grapple with the question of a Supreme Being and, in this connection, his fascination with the natural order. I can hear him now as he talks with awe about the makeup of the world around us. "David," he would say, "can you imagine that we humans inhale oxygen to survive and exhale carbon dioxide, while the trees and plants need carbon dioxide to survive and therefore exhale oxygen. What a perfect balance! Now how do you think that could have come about?"
- and, of course, about his boundless love for his family—his five children, Ruth, Ann, Morris, Jr., Adam, and Josh, his nine grandchildren, and his beloved wife, Bruna, who flew from Geneva to be with us today.

And even these memories only begin to scratch the surface of the remarkable life of a man who, in the words of the late New York governor Herbert Lehman, could have been the first Jewish president of the United States had the country been ready for a Jew in the White House.

I shall always cherish these and countless other memories of Morris, including our collaboration on the 1987 Soviet Jewry march that brought 250,000 people to Washington and, most recently, our frequent meetings to plan for the absorption by AJC of UN Watch, his chosen institutional legacy, and to prepare for our gala December 1999 dinner in his honor at the Plaza, at which UN secretary-general Kofi Annan, among others, spoke so glowingly about him.

In thinking about today's memorial service, I went back and reread Morris's marvelous autobiography entitled *The Day Is Short*. If you haven't read it, you ought to. Permit me to read just a few paragraphs from the final chapter:

> In the past nine years I have reflected greatly on death. I cannot say that I ever accepted the prognosis [of death from myelocytic leukemia] in June 1973, though all the evidence confirmed it. I did not resist out of fear; it is just that I have always enjoyed life, and in accordance with the primary obligation of my tradition, I choose it, I embrace it. I regard the spirit that burns in every person as holy, never to be extinguished—not even by death—for it shines in the lives of others....
>
> In the days following the diagnosis, I always found relief in the contemplation that if death were the end of existence, it also had a curious and even magnetic fascination for me. A painting on a canvas of infinite size, worked on forever, would be without focus or meaning and probably without beauty. A painting, like life, needs limits. Since I have an almost insatiable craving for knowledge, I found some comfort, too, in the possibility that death may be the greatest as well as the final teacher, the one that provides the key to the ultimate questions life has never answered.
>
> I know that time is limited, and I tend to be in a hurry. I am daily reminded of an ancient Hebrew text that says, "The day is short, the work is great.... It is not thy duty to complete the work, but neither art thou free to desist from it."

Morris, if I'm not interrupting a tablewide discussion that you're currently leading somewhere, I simply want you to know that your spirit *will* live on, for it shines in the lives of the countless people you touched throughout the world, including all of us gathered here in this room today.

# The State of the American Jewish Committee:
## A Ten-Year Perspective
### 94th AJC Annual Meeting
### Washington, D.C.
### May 2, 2000

Ten years ago, the Board of Governors of the American Jewish Committee met in a lovely, strikingly pinkish seaside hotel in St. Petersburg Beach, Florida. The somber, even dark, mood inside the hotel could not have stood in starker contrast to the splendor of the setting. AJC's leaders were meeting to confront an institutional crisis: The organization was in serious financial difficulty, deep cuts in staff and program would be unavoidable, and the wounds of leadership issues in the 1980s were only just beginning to heal.

The *New York Times* reported at the time that "about 40 of the group's 275 employees will be laid off and $1 million will be cut from its $16 million annual budget." In fact, the cuts were even more severe. Rabbi Arthur Hertzberg was quoted in the *Times* article as suggesting that AJC was facing a potentially insurmountable identity crisis and was forced to ask itself, "What is our mission?" In a separate piece in the *Times*, Seymour Lachman, currently a New York state senator, and Barry Kosmin, now head of the Institute for Jewish Policy Research in London, wondered aloud if there was any future for AJC.

But the news was certainly not all bleak. AJC was blessed at the time with a new president, Sholom Comay. If ever there was the right person at the right moment for the job, it was Sholom. In his own understated, yet determined, consensus-building fashion, and working with a single-mindedly devoted team of lay and professional colleagues—and here I must especially note the role played by Shula Bahat—Sholom began to put the building blocks in place for an exciting new era in the life of the American Jewish Committee.

I suppose I, too, was to be one of those building blocks, for Sholom offered me the position of executive director, and the Board of Governors voted its approval in September 1990. This year, then, I will be celebrating my tenth anniversary in the post. My only regret is that

Sholom, a man I deeply admired, is not here to celebrate with me. He met an untimely death in 1991, long before he could see his vision realized.

Sholom believed profoundly in the raison d'être of the American Jewish Committee, an agency he first encountered when he was a student at Brandeis doing research on a paper, and he believed equally profoundly in the agency's future. Indeed, even with the agency down on one knee in 1990, and with some in the Jewish community openly questioning our chances for recovery, he was confidently speaking of the next decade as a time when AJC would reemerge as the preeminent American Jewish institution.

Now predictions, as we know, can be notoriously off-base.

In April 1933, Lewis Douglas, the U.S. budget director, hearing that the United States was going off the gold standard, predicted that this heralded "the end of Western civilization."

In September 1938, British prime minister Neville Chamberlain, speaking from 10 Downing Street, predicted: "For the second time in our history, a British prime minister has returned from Germany bringing peace with honor. I believe it is peace for our time.... Go home and get a nice quiet sleep."

A year later, in May 1939, an editorial in the communist *Daily Worker* predicted: "The whispered lies to the effect that the Soviet Union will enter into a treaty of understanding with Nazi Germany are nothing but poison spread by the enemies of peace and democracy, the appeasement mongers, the Munichmen of fascism." Almost exactly three months to the day later, Germany and the Soviet Union signed a ten-year mutual nonaggression pact.

And in March 1981, President Ronald Reagan predicted that "a drastic reduction in the deficit ... will take place in the fiscal year 1982," only to preside that year over the single largest deficit in American history.

But not all predictions go awry. In fact, some do come true, and it seems fitting, ten years after that fateful meeting in St. Petersburg Beach, to look back and see how close to the mark Sholom really was in forecasting AJC's golden decade.

Now, just as forecasting has its pitfalls, so do retrospectives. In the latter case, the danger is Selective Memory Deficit Disorder.

The automobile industry could justifiably claim, for instance, that the last 100 years have witnessed a veritable revolution in the development of the car. That would be an entirely true statement, but it would fail to reveal some of the bumps along the road.

Last month, the *New York Times* had a wonderful piece on the "ten worst cars of the millennium." They cited, for example, the Renault Le Car. Remember that little gem? One owner commented: "It would put you in mortal danger if you had an accident with anything larger than a croissant." Or the Ford Pinto, which prompted the memorable bumper sticker for the car: "Hit me and we blow up together." Or the legendary Yugo, about which one satisfied owner noted: "At least it had heated rear windows—so your hands would stay warm while you pushed."

And in retrospect, AJC has also had its share of bloopers that won't appear, I assure you, in any copy of the Annual Report or *AJC Journal*.

There was the time we publicly announced the death of an AJC leader, only to be told subsequently that he was still quite alive, thank you.

Or the time the Soviet Émigré Orchestra performed Mozart's *Eine Kleine Nachtmusik* at an annual meeting, and the applause after the first movement was so vigorous and sustained that the orchestra was left with no choice but to rise, take a bow, and angrily leave the stage, even though there were three more movements to be played.

Or the time your executive director, wanting to show off his Hungarian roots at a function hosted by Hungarian diplomats, proposed a toast using the Hungarian equivalent of "cheers" or "*l'chaim*," only to be met with stony silence, as a neighbor quietly pointed out that I had managed to butcher the complex four-syllable word and invoke a raunchy reference to the buttocks instead.

More seriously, though, and far more to the point, with the help of my talented associate, Rebecca Neuwirth, we have prepared a series of tables that highlight some of the principal accomplishments of the agency over the past decade.

Let's begin with the institutional side of the ledger, and I am grateful to Ron Weiner and Cliff Surloff for having organized the financial tables.

The first table (table 5.1) is a schedule showing total revenues. Notice the drop in revenues from 1989 to 1990, and then, of course, the steady progression upward to the 1999 figure of some $35 million.

The second table (table 5.2) indicates our cash and cash equivalents and investments for the ten-year period ending June 30, 1999. The direction speaks for itself.

The third table (table 5.3) reflects total net assets of the agency, and again the trend is evident.

The fourth table (table 5.4) shows the annual change in net assets for the ten-year period ending in 1998. Note that since 1990 we have operated on the basis of a balanced budget or better. This notion is now ingrained as part of our institutional culture. We simply don't spend more than we take in, period.

The next table (table 5.5) documents our schedule of expenses over ten years. Over this period they have risen no more than 30 percent.

And the following table (table 5.6) tracks support services as a percentage of our total expenses. We have kept the number below the high of 23 percent reached in 1989, and, as you will see, for the past four years the percentage has been steadily declining.

These impressive numbers, coupled with our ability to keep the ratio of dollars spent to dollars raised to well under 15 percent, thanks to the magnificent performance of our Development Department, under Jaime Kelstein's leadership, and the Board of Trustees, under Morris Offit's chairmanship, explains why the American Institute of Philanthropy, our industry's watchdog, has ranked us in the top twenty-five major nonprofit groups in the United States from the viewpoint of cost efficiency for three years running. Bear in mind that there are literally tens of thousands of nonprofit agencies in this country. Moreover, we are the only major Jewish group to be listed in this prestigious honor roll.

In terms of our constituency, over the past ten years three significant things have happened:

First, we started counting not only members who might be giving us $100 per year, but also supporters who might be giving us $1,000 per

**Table 5.1**
**AJC Revenues, 1989-1999**
**(in millions of dollars)**

| Year | Total revenue |
|------|---------------|
| 1989 | 19.995 |
| 1990 | 18.600 |
| 1991 | 19.352 |
| 1992 | 21.378 |
| 1993 | 20.881 |
| 1994 | 23.322 |
| 1995 | 22.262 |
| 1996 | 25.092 |
| 1997 | 29.326 |
| 1998 | 34.322 |
| 1999 | 35.000 |

year but for whatever reason weren't formally joining and inexplicably, therefore, were excluded from previous counts.

Second, we launched a direct-mail campaign three years ago that has brought us over 35,000 new contributors. So much for our fear that we might not succeed in direct mail unless we were prepared to frighten Jews with doomsday scenarios. We have succeeded without compromising our integrity or, for that matter, our dignity.

And third, as a successful agency, we have been able to attract new members. The result (table 5.7) is that for the first time in our ninety-four-year history, we have not only crossed the 100,000 threshold but are actually at 105,000 AJC constituents, and Shirley Kohn, our able membership director, is confident that we will continue to experience growth.

Now I don't have to tell you that one of the biggest and most persistent challenges we face is communicating our message to a number of key constituencies, both inside and outside the agency, about who we are, what we do, and how we do it. We've got a "helluva" story to tell, but doing so in a world increasingly driven by sound bites and

**Table 5.2**
**AJC Cash, Cash Equivalents, and Investments,**
**1989-1999 (in millions of dollars)**

| Year | Cash and cash equivalents | Investments |
|------|------|------|
| 1989 | 0.315 | 9.359 |
| 1990 | 0.658 | 10.960 |
| 1991 | 0.916 | 12.404 |
| 1992 | 4.451 | 11.588 |
| 1993 | 4.448 | 12.830 |
| 1994 | 4.778 | 15.359 |
| 1995 | 6.681 | 14.711 |
| 1996 | 5.294 | 20.316 |
| 1997 | 9.432 | 23.011 |
| 1998 | 13.079 | 26.952 |
| 1999 | 17.000 | 28.500 |

fleeting images isn't easy, especially when the story is often complex and multifaceted. We haven't come up with the all-purpose answer yet, assuming one exists, but we have devoted a lot of time and attention to this area. Here are some of the many initiatives we have launched in the last ten years to enhance our communications and outreach abilities. We have:

- created an attractive Web site, www.ajc.org, as a timely forum for internal and external communication;
- initiated a monthly quarter-page ad on the op-ed page of the *New York Times*;
- established a cost-sharing program to encourage chapters to place national ads in local papers;
- founded the Public Relations Committee, currently chaired by Ken Makovsky;
- launched several acclaimed ad series, including "What Being Jewish Means to Me," "What Israel Means to Me," "No One Is Born Hating," and campaigns for Israel's admission to the

**Table 5.3**
**AJC Total Net Assets, 1989-1999 (in millions of dollars)**

| Year | Permanently restricted | Temporarily restricted | Unrestricted | Total |
|------|------------------------|------------------------|--------------|--------|
| 1989 | 10.155 | | -1.471 | 10.604 |
| 1990 | 10.568 | | -2.861 | 9.495 |
| 1991 | 11.036 | | -0.298 | 12.289 |
| 1992 | 14.011 | | 1.052 | 16.512 |
| 1993 | 15.380 | | 1.393 | 18.288 |
| 1994 | 17.335 | | 1.951 | 21.787 |
| 1995 | 17.859 | | 2.933 | 24.082 |
| 1996 | 10.116 | 9.465 | 13.816 | 33.396 |
| 1997 | 10.700 | 12.701 | 16.972 | 40.373 |
| 1998 | 12.688 | 15.420 | 21.773 | 49.882 |
| 1999 | 13.500 | 18.500 | 25.800 | 57.800 |

Western Europe and Others Group (WEOG) and to the Red Cross, etc.;
- distributed the film *AJC Lighting the Torch*, produced by CBS;
- initiated a regular "Letter from AJC's President and Executive Director" sent to a select insiders' list;
- revamped the Annual Report and started distribution to all AJC households;
- and created a new look for the *AJC Journal*, now published on a bimonthly basis.

The last ten years have also seen some vitally important capital improvements, in large part thanks to the generosity of several of you. Only a few of the major undertakings can be mentioned here:
- renovation of the Jacob Blaustein Building, New York, thanks in part to the generosity of the Jacob and Hilda Blaustein Foundation;
- purchase and renovation of Beit Moses to house the Israel/Middle East Office, thanks to the generosity of Alfred and Carol Moses, Amalie Kass, and Claire Lovett, in memory of the Moses parents;

**Table 5.4**
**AJC Annual Increase/Decrease in Net Assets,**
**1990-1999 (in millions of dollars)**

| Year | Operating | Total |
|------|-----------|-------|
| 1990 | -1.197 | -1.109 |
| 1991 | 2.655 | 2.795 |
| 1992 | 2.222 | 3.602 |
| 1993 | 0.744 | 1.776 |
| 1994 | 0.919 | 3.500 |
| 1995 | 1.288 | 2.295 |
| 1996 | 3.798 | 4.318 |
| 1997 | 3.692 | 6.977 |
| 1998 | 4.595 | 9.508 |
| 1999 | 3.694 | 6.528 |

- opening of the Lawrence and Lee Ramer Center for German-Jewish Relations and the Hans Adler Library in Berlin, Germany, thanks to the generosity of Lawrence and Lee Ramer and Dottie Bennett;
- expansion of the Washington, D.C., Office of Government and International Relations;
- and transfer of chapter offices to safe, secure, and well-located facilities.

And last but by no means least, after a slow start, and with welcome prodding from our superb Information Systems and Data Processing Department, we began investing the kinds of sums necessary to keep pace with the dramatic technological advances of recent years. The results are that we have replaced the centralized mainframe systems we once used with a modern, decentralized networked system to improve communications and access to information within the agency, and we have implemented modern client/server-based software programs to enhance computer usage.

Now let me turn to the programmatic side of the past ten years. Again, this will be the "Cliff Notes" version of a much larger and rich-

**Table 5.5**
**AJC Expenses, 1989-1999 (in millions of dollars)**

| Year | Support services | Program services | Total |
|------|------|------|------|
| 1989 | 4.707 | 15.871 | 20.578 |
| 1990 | 4.082 | 15.627 | 19.709 |
| 1991 | 3.642 | 12.916 | 16.557 |
| 1992 | 3.971 | 13.805 | 17.776 |
| 1993 | 3.970 | 15.135 | 19.105 |
| 1994 | 4.162 | 15.661 | 19.823 |
| 1995 | 4.257 | 15.710 | 19.967 |
| 1996 | 4.656 | 16.118 | 20.775 |
| 1997 | 4.752 | 17.598 | 22.350 |
| 1998 | 5.127 | 19.687 | 24.814 |
| 1999 | 5.500 | 21.700 | 27.200 |

er story, and I must apologize in advance for any unintended slight of any aspect of our program.

Before naming some areas of program initiatives, I would like to point out that the overriding goals of our programmatic efforts have been:

- continuation of the proud agency tradition of identifying ascending issues of concern to the Jewish community;
- examination not only of specific issues, but also of the underlying and overarching trends within which these issues play out;
- consideration of both issues and trends in a nonreflexive, nonideological manner that befits an agency of the caliber and sophistication of AJC;
- acknowledgment that we cannot be all things to all people and therefore must pick and choose our issues, with priority accorded to those areas that touch on our core interests;
- recognition that our effectiveness is enhanced if we can leverage the agency's many resources—lay and staff, international, national, and chapter—in an integrated and well-coordinated manner; and

**Table 5.6**
**AJC Ratio of Support Services**
**to Total Expenses, 1989-1999**

| Year | % |
|------|------|
| 1989 | 22.87 |
| 1990 | 20.71 |
| 1991 | 21.99 |
| 1992 | 22.34 |
| 1993 | 20.78 |
| 1994 | 21.00 |
| 1995 | 21.32 |
| 1996 | 22.41 |
| 1997 | 21.26 |
| 1998 | 20.66 |
| 1999 | 20.22 |

- appreciation for the fact that our ultimate goal is to reach the highest levels of decision-making, whether in city councils, state governments, the administration, the Congress, the United Nations, foreign capitals, civil society, the media, or public opinion at large, and to have our views taken seriously and factored into policy-making.

That said, here are some selected—and I emphasize the word "selected"—new program initiatives over the past decade:

- the Arthur and Rochelle Belfer Center for American Pluralism;
- the Sholom Comay Fellows Program;
- the Harriet and Robert Heilbrunn Institute for International Interreligious Understanding;
- the Dorothy and Julius Koppelman Institute on American Jewish-Israeli Relations;
- the Susan and Jack Lapin Fund for Jewish Continuity;
- the Moses Family Institute for Jewish Renewal;
- the Beryl Oppenheimer Memorial Fund for Tolerance Education;

**Table 5.7**
**AJC Members and**
**Supporters, 1996-2000**

| Year | Number |
|------|--------|
| 1996 | 62,776 |
| 1997 | 64,086 |
| 1998* | 84,754 |
| 1999 | 101,978 |
| 2000 | 105,626 |

* Direct mail program begun

- and the Madeline and Bruce Ramer Intergroup Research and Publication Fund.

We have also:

- initiated a charitable choice research program, sponsored by the Pew Charitable Trusts;
- established the Catholic/Jewish Educational Enrichment Program (C/JEEP), with a major boost from the Steven Spielberg Righteous Persons Foundation;
- launched *CommonQuest—The Magazine of Black-Jewish Relations* (a Howard University and AJC project) with a founding grant from the Harry and Jeanette Weinberg Foundation;
- and created the AJC Fellows Program, sponsored by the Joyce and Irving Goldman Family Foundation.

Finally, we have established:

- a new senior management position, assistant executive director for institutional development;
- the Division of European Affairs;
- the Division on Middle East and International Terrorism;
- AJC representation in Warsaw, Poland;
- a merger with Project Interchange;
- an affiliation with UN Watch, full merger slated for January 1, 2001;

- and regular exchange programs with the Israeli Ministry of Education, the Municipality of Jerusalem, the German armed forces, German media, the Naumann Foundation for Central and East European Leaders, and the government of Poland.

One of the programmatic initiatives of which we are most proud and that really bespeaks the agency's success has been the development of ties with world leaders. When we started our diplomatic program in 1993, in connection with the annual UN General Assembly session in the fall, we had exactly—hard to believe, I know—four meetings with foreign ministers. Six years later, we had fifty-two meetings with presidents, prime ministers, and foreign ministers,[1] and, of course, our program extends far beyond these seasonal encounters in New York.

Also on the international scene, we have developed new or expanded offices overseas in Berlin, Warsaw, Jerusalem, and, most recently with our ties to UN Watch, in Geneva.

Moreover, we have created six international partnerships since 1997 with counterpart Jewish organizations in Argentina, Australia, Costa Rica, the Czech Republic, Mexico, and Slovakia, and we look forward to adding to this number.

Here at home, we have worked to further strengthen our chapter network, which, I should point out, was largely protected from the downsizing and restructuring that perforce took place in 1990. New professional staff members have been added for programming, political advocacy, fund-raising, and public relations, and more are on the way.[2] A program fund has been established for the chapters, and local leadership development initiatives have been encouraged and supported. In addition, in 2000 we opened a new office in Connecticut.

---

[1] AJC held bilateral meetings with the leaders of the following fifty-two countries during the opening session of the 1999 UN General Assembly: Argentina, Armenia, Australia, Austria, Azerbaijan, Bahrain, Belarus, Belgium, Bosnia-Herzegovina, Bulgaria, Chile, Croatia, Cyprus, Czech Republic, Denmark, Egypt, El Salvador, Eritrea, Estonia, Finland, Georgia, Germany, Greece, Hungary, India, Israel, Jordan, Kazakhstan, Kenya, Kuwait, Kyrgyzstan, Latvia, Lithuania, Macedonia, Mauritania, Morocco, Oman, Poland, Portugal, Romania, Russia, Slovakia, Sweden, Switzerland, Tunisia, Turkey, Turkmenistan, Ukraine, United States, Uzbekistan, Venezuela, and Yemen.

[2] AJC has added new professional staff in: Atlanta, Boston, Chicago, Cleveland, Dallas, Houston, Long Island, Los Angeles, New Jersey, New York, Palm Beach County, Sarasota, and Washington, D.C., and opened a new office in Connecticut.

Our publications, a hallmark of AJC, continue apace. I can mention here just a tiny fraction of the material we are producing:

- The annual *American Jewish Year Book*, including volume 100 to be published in summer 2000;
- an AJC–Bar-Ilan University bilingual series on Jewish and Israeli topics (eight volumes to date);
- national Holocaust curriculum review studies (four to date),
- national surveys of knowledge and remembrance of the Holocaust (thirteen countries to date);
- *Approaches to Antisemitism: Context and Curriculum,* edited by Michael Brown;
- *A Force Upon the Plain: The American Militia Movement and the Politics of Hate*, by Kenneth S. Stern;
- *Understanding Jewish History*, by Dr. Steven Bayme;
- and *Children of Abraham: An Introduction to Islam for Jews* and *Children of Abraham: An Introduction to Judaism for Muslims*.

One of the innovative features we have introduced is to translate more of our works into other languages, including, depending on the target audience, Arabic and Hebrew, as well as a number of European languages.

One of the most appealing aspects of AJC for me has always been its sense of compassion. It takes to heart the second part of Hillel's trip-tych—"If I am only for myself, what am I?" Thus, AJC has been active over the past decade in responding to any number of humanitarian crises, whether here at home or overseas. A sample of our efforts includes:

- Turkish earthquake relief, 1999;
- reconstruction of three synagogues in Sacramento, California, after firebomb attacks, 1999;
- Kosovo refugee relief, 1999;
- reconstruction of the African-American Gay's Hill Baptist Church in Millen, Georgia, 1996;
- Rwanda relief aid, 1994;
- Argentinian Jewish community after 1994 AMIA bombing;
- and Kurdish aid after the 1991 Gulf War.

Happily, the changes at hand over the past decade, coupled with the agency's traditional commitment to excellence, have not gone unnoticed. The reviews are in, and they're not bad. Here are just a few:

- "The American Jewish Committee is the dean of Jewish organizations in the United States" (*New York Times*);
- "The American Jewish Committee is one of the world's most influential Jewish interest groups" (Reuters);
- "No organization in the world has done more to improve Christian-Jewish relations than the American Jewish Committee" (John Cardinal O'Connor);
- "AJC can play an important role in bringing all of us together as one people" (President Bill Clinton);
- "AJC ... was with us from the beginning in the struggle against the Zionism is racism resolution" (U.S. Senator Daniel Patrick Moynihan);
- "In a remarkable series of advertisements in the *New York Times*, AJC asked a wide array of Jews 'what being Jewish means' to them.... In reading these statements, I was moved" (Professor Alan M. Dershowitz);
- "Only when AJC went public with its tenacious campaign did pensions for East European Holocaust survivors begin to make progress" (*Washington Post*);
- "The American Jewish Committee has pioneered the German-Jewish-American dialogue" (Klaus Kinkel, then German minister of foreign affairs);
- "These [AJC diplomatic] meetings are an integral part of the highly acclaimed involvement of the AJC in assisting Israel's advocacy in the international arena" (Eytan Bentsur, director general of Israel's Ministry of Foreign Affairs);
- "The American Jewish Committee has changed history" (Dore Gold, then permanent representative of Israel to the UN, referring to AJC's leadership role in putting Israel's admission into WEOG on the diplomatic map);
- "For hard-pressed Jewish defense organizations, the AJC offers a positive model of adaptation and change. The Committee's style is a winner in a Jewish community that feels more secure

and less apart from the American mainstream" (Baltimore
*Jewish Times*);
* "The American Jewish Committee is the premier Jewish organi-
  zation in the United States, if not the world" (Leslie Wexner).

But as Shakespeare wrote in *The Tempest*, "What's past is pro-
logue." Everything we have accomplished together sets the stage for
the next decade and beyond, and gives us a wonderful launching pad,
but yesterday's success will not necessarily ensure tomorrow's. We're
going to have to work hard on both the institutional and programmatic
challenges if we are to continue to go from strength to strength.

I have said before, and I would like to say again, that I am truly in
awe of this organization.

I am in awe of its record of accomplishment.

I am in awe of its ambitious mission and mandate.

I am in awe of its thoughtful and deliberative approach to the issues
of the day.

I am in awe of the quality of the lay and staff members it attracts.

I am in awe of the partnership that we have established with one
another.

I am in awe of the carefully crafted balance of the universal and the
particular that reflects the essential nature of who we are.

I am in awe of the reach and clout, the impact and influence of this
organization.

I am in awe of the agency's uncanny instinct to see around corners
and anticipate emerging issues and trends.

I am in awe of the agency's modesty about itself and its oft-demon-
strated willingness to suppress institutional ego in the interests of the
larger issues with which we grapple.

And I am deeply honored to hold the position of executive director.
I mean that from the bottom of my heart. I grow more excited and more
passionate about this agency with each passing day, and I am ever
grateful for the chance I've been given, not least for the indescribably
wonderful opportunity to work with four outstanding presidents—
Sholom Comay, Al Moses, Bob Rifkind, and now Bruce Ramer.

There are many institutional challenges ahead, but let me limit
myself to just three in the interest of time:

First and foremost, we need to ensure the financial well-being of the agency for future generations. Together we have the power to achieve that objective. In anticipation of our centennial anniversary in 2006, AJC is launching a special campaign. Believe me, you'll be hearing much more about it in the coming months.

I'm thrilled by the once-in-a-lifetime opportunity all of us have to mark such a milestone anniversary by providing major gifts and endowment funds that will boost our capacity to respond to the issues ahead, as well as give us the peace of mind to know that there will be a vibrant American Jewish Committee around to safeguard the rights and interests of our children and grandchildren. We Jews should know better than anyone that even in the best of times we need to be alert both to danger and to possibility; AJC fulfills those roles in ways that make us all feel both proud and secure.

Harold Tanner, a veteran of a highly successful Cornell campaign, has been terrific in helping us get ourselves organized. And Leonard Greenberg, as you will see in the latest issue of the *AJC Journal*, started us off with a generous $1 million gift. In fact, as Harold whispered to the Board of Governors assembled in Costa Rica last February, we already have over $6 million in pledges, and we haven't even formally launched the campaign, as we await guidance from the consulting firm we have engaged to assist us in our feasibility study.

Second, AJC has always taken great pride in the quality of the lay members whom we attract to the agency, and with good reason. We need to ensure that in the years ahead we continue to attract the best and the brightest of American Jewry, both young and not so young. In a way this becomes more difficult, and not just for AJC.

Time is everyone's most precious commodity, and to really appreciate AJC requires time. There's no way around it. And fewer people generally seem to be joining organizations. When they do, they may or may not have the patience for the long haul that an organization like ours demands. After all, we live in a world that increasingly focuses on the self and personal fulfillment, and on instant, not deferred, gratification. Agencies like AJC are built on the principle of group consensus and not individual whim; moreover, by the very nature of the issues with which we deal—Jewish security, human relations, human rights, ethnic and religious identity, tolerance and intolerance—we will never be in a position simply to declare victory and close up shop. So we will have to make the case to the best and brightest who are not already with us—why us, why now.

And third, we're somehow going to have to try to keep up with the information and communications technology revolution, itself a daunting task. We're going to have to figure out how we can take advantage of the unprecedented opportunities it provides to get our message out far and wide, to contact people, Jews and non-Jews, whom we've never been able to reach before, and to strengthen our political advocacy through timely and targeted communications.

At the same time, AJC has always cherished the need for careful research and analysis, for nuanced thinking and subtlety, and for face-to-face discussion, debate, and deliberation. In today's world, such values may be viewed as anachronistic, but I don't believe they are, and you wouldn't be here either if you thought they were.

On the programmatic side, what can I say? A few years ago, my son Danny received a toy for his birthday. His younger brother Michael was a bit jealous. He eyed the toy for a few minutes before blurting out, "You know, Danny, I have the exact same toy as you do." He then hesitated when he realized it wasn't quite true, before adding, "Only my toy is completely different."

Perhaps I can use the same logic. The problems ahead are likely to be both eerily familiar and undoubtedly quite different.

Has anti-Semitism disappeared from the face of the earth? Has hate? Can we say with confidence that there will be no more attacks against children in Jewish community centers in southern California? Can we say there will be no more arson attacks against synagogues in Sacramento? Can we say there will be no more crazed killers looking for minority victims in Illinois and Pennsylvania? Can we say that anti-Semitism is a relic of Russia's past and nothing more? Or that the Jews of Iran can now sleep easily because there will be no more kangaroo courts charging Iranian Jews with spurious accusations? Can we say that Holocaust denier David Irving, fresh from his humiliating defeat in a British courtroom, will simply dig a hole and bury himself, along with his like-minded colleagues around the world? Or that Jörg

Haider's seeming resignation from stewardship of the Freedom Party ends concern about anti-Semitism and xenophobia in Austria, or its threat elsewhere in Europe and beyond? Can we assume that the demonization of Jews in a good part of the Arab press has a statute of limitations?

Do we believe that Israel's borders, however they are to be drawn, will be safe and secure from here to eternity? Can we declare the dangers of the Middle East a thing of the past and assume that Iran is building a nuclear weapon only as a deterrent to Iraq, and Iraq is hoping to build a nuclear weapon only as a deterrent to Iran, so they will simply live peacefully with the old Cold War theory of MAD, mutual assured destruction?

Do we assume that pluralism and intergroup harmony are now set in concrete for all time in the United States? Do we believe that we have achieved a universal consensus on the importance of safeguarding the separation of church and state in our country, and therefore can afford to let down our guard? Are we so mesmerized by the reports of a robust economy with the longest period of sustained economic growth in our history that we believe our social ills have disappeared? And is it forever a given that the stranger will be welcome in the American home?

And finally, are we now so certain of the Jewish future that we can leave it to its own natural course? Is Jewish identity now so much a part of the genetic code that we need not concern ourselves with how future generations of American Jews will play out their Jewishness? Have Jews created such a large tent that there is room inside for all the various denominations to live harmoniously and with full appreciation for each other's chosen path? Can we take such comfort from relations between American Jews and Israelis that we need not expend another day's effort in nurturing them? And are we so certain that Israel has conclusively determined what a Jewish and democratic state actually means for its citizens that we can stop wondering about the country's future internal health and cohesion?

Indeed, we have an agenda, a daunting one. And we may never be able to complete it, but history has shown our remarkable ability to make a difference on the big issues—from Catholic-Jewish relations to Holocaust restitution, from human rights protections to repeal of the

"Zionism is racism" resolution, from civil rights to Soviet Jewry. We have been there—not in the bleachers or on the sidelines, but right there in the fray. And we've had more than our share of successes along the way.

We have the recipe—intelligent, caring, dedicated people banded together in a movement we call the American Jewish Committee, who are confident, even brazen, enough to tackle the major pathologies afflicting society, humble enough to recognize there are no easy or quick answers, and committed enough to want to help shape our destiny.

## Tribute to
## Rabbi A. James Rudin
## Washington, D.C.
## May 2, 2000

In one of Jim's weekly columns for the Religious News Service, he wrote of being forced to memorize, as a sixth-grade student, a Joyce Kilmer poem entitled "Trees," including the well-known line: "I think that I shall never see a poem lovely as a tree."

If no poem can ever be as lovely as a tree, then certainly no speech can ever do justice to a thirty-two-year-long career with the American Jewish Committee, especially one as remarkable, prodigious, and successful as Jim's.

But, what the heck, let me try anyway, first by giving you some of the bare-bones facts of his life that may not be entirely familiar to all of you, and then by trying to convey a sense of the magnitude of his achievements.

Of course, what I'm going to share with you are only the facts I know. Who knows what else might be out there? Ben Macintyre, the U.S. editor of the *Times* of London, writing recently of English eccentrics, noted that in his own family "the most celebrated ancestral oddity was a hard-hunting bachelor uncle who smoked a brier pipe and insisted on riding his horse up the stairs, and was revealed only after his death to have been an aunt all along." But let's leave those kinds of stories aside, shall we?

Born in Pittsburgh in 1934, Jim grew up in Alexandria, Virginia, and graduated in 1951 from George Washington High School, having won the "outstanding graduate" award from the school. No doubt, the experience of living in the South, surrounded by Protestants, mostly Southern Baptists, had a significant impact on Jim's future career direction.

After graduating from George Washington University, a distinction Jim shares with Bill Gralnick, he went right to Hebrew Union College and was ordained a rabbi in 1960. Then came two years as an Air Force chaplain, principally stationed in Japan, where (and I am quoting Jim) he "used helicopters, single-engined aircraft, jets, and even horses" to make over ninety-five rabbinical visits in the Far East and to provide pastoral assistance to 2,400 Jewish military personnel. That unusual experience was followed by two years as an assistant rabbi at Temple B'nai Jehudah in Kansas City and four years as the rabbi of Temple Sinai in Champaign, Illinois.

On December 11, 1967, Jim took a fateful step. He wrote to Rabbi Marc Tanenbaum, director of AJC's Interreligious Affairs Department: "I am interested in a position with the American Jewish Committee that can use my skills as a research historian and/or a member of the Interreligious Affairs Department." After an impressive review process, during which AJC contacted no fewer than ten references, Jim received a letter from Eleanor Katz, our personnel director at the time, confirming his appointment as assistant director of the Interreligious Affairs Department.

By the time he joined the AJC staff, and underscoring his lifelong commitment to civic involvement and social justice, Jim had already been involved with Americans for Democratic Action, the NAACP, the Urban League, the Champaign—as in Illinois, that is—Mental Health Society, and voter registration drives in Hattiesburg, Mississippi.

Just to fill out the formal part of Jim's bio, in 1983 he succeeded Marc Tanenbaum as the director of Interreligious Affairs, a post he has held for seventeen years.

Along the way, of course, other things happened to Jim, not least that he married Marcia, a writer with many shared interests, including the dangers posed by religious cults, and they produced two wonderful daughters, Jennifer, whose chosen path is theater and the arts, and Eve, who, together with her husband, Robert, will be ordained as a rabbi later this month.

How wonderfully symbolic that as Jim formally retires, his daughter enters the rabbinate hand in hand with Jim's son-in-law the very same month! Surely this gives new definition to the concept of *nakhes* and continuity. And I'm certain there must be some cosmic meaning in the fact that Robbie's very first position will be as assistant rabbi at our family's synagogue in Bedford, New York.

On April 24, Joyce Purnick, a columnist for the *New York Times* metro section, referred to what she called "that hackneyed phrase, 'the end of an era.'" It may be hackneyed, but I sincerely believe that with Jim's retirement an era has indeed come to an end. Sure, in a sense life goes on, a replacement will be found, and our interreligious work will continue, but for the past thirty-two years Jim has been our address for interreligious work, seventeen of those years at the helm, and, with the notable exception of Murray Friedman, who among us on the staff can recall a time when Jim was not there?

Frankly, I despaired when Jim first came and told me of his plans to retire this spring. But I recalled the comment of a senior on the University of Pittsburgh basketball team, who once boasted: "I'm going to graduate on time, no matter how long it takes." I was hoping, in the same spirit, that Jim, like Jack Benny on his thirty-ninth birthday, might be willing to stay put and stretch out his rite of passage at age sixty-five for at least a couple more years. Obviously, I failed, perhaps underestimating the lure of Sanibel Island, though I'm pleased to report that Jim will be available to us as a part-time consultant. Thank God for whoever coined the concept of consultant!

In his career at AJC, Jim has taken on what he likes to call some of the most "toxic" and "radioactive" issues known to humankind—religion and faith—and he has skillfully—no, magisterially—navigated the potentially fatal shoals of dialogue and discussion, on behalf of AJC and the Jewish people, with much larger and far more potent groups.

Now dialogue and discussion, particularly around such powerful matters as history, identity, beliefs, and core values, can easily lead in one of two directions—paralysis or even regression, on the one hand, or, on the other hand, an all-too-ready willingness to cave, even on basic matters, for fear of otherwise jeopardizing the relationship.

Jim has had this uncanny instinct to forge a third way, to borrow a much-used phrase from Bill Clinton and Tony Blair. He has never compromised on fundamental issues central to Jewish identity and history, nor has he ever closed the door to dialogue or to the search for common ground even when, at first glance, it may seem elusive. In other words, he has learned, and taught us, not only how to agree agreeably—that's easy enough—but, perhaps far more importantly, how to disagree constructively.

That's why he was able to establish such productive relationships at the highest levels with the local, national, and international leadership of the Catholic Church, the Greek Orthodox Church, the various Protestant churches, both mainline and evangelical, and with many Muslim leaders as well.

These leaders knew that in Jim they had an interlocutor of extraordinary integrity and principle, of compassion and concern, of experience and influence, and of sophistication and sensitivity. In other words, they were dealing with a genuine Jewish leader. Abraham Joshua Heschel once said: "The Jewish people is the messenger, but it's forgotten what its message is." Jim never forgot what the message is, or how best to convey it.

In the final analysis, Jim has been a healer of the spirit and the soul—of the cancerous plagues that afflict our societies, from intolerance and bigotry to indifference and oppression—every bit as much as his late and beloved father, Dr. Philip Rudin, was a healer of the body. And therefore, in a way, the oath that our sage Maimonides established over 800 years ago for physicians is the very same oath that Jim has subscribed to as a rabbi.

Maimonides wrote: "The eternal providence has appointed me to watch over the life and health of Thy creatures. May the love for my art actuate me at all times; may neither avarice nor miserliness, nor thirst for glory or for a great reputation engage my mind; for the enemies of truth and philanthropy could easily deceive me and make me forgetful of my lofty aim of doing good to Thy children. May I never see in the patient anything but a fellow creature in pain."

Jim loved his "art," never lost sight of its "lofty aim," and always saw in his fellow human beings, whoever they were, the image of God.

I could go on but, as I said, no comments, no matter how long, could fully address Jim's role at AJC or in the public sphere, whether in the struggle for Soviet Jewry and human rights behind the Iron Curtain or for equal justice and equal opportunity here at home; whether for an end to racial barriers in South Africa or for the victory of religious tolerance over religious triumphalism; whether for Israel's age-old quest for peace and security or for Jerusalem's centrality to Jewish yearning and Israeli sovereignty; whether for greater sensitivity to the daunting ethical aspects of the biomedical revolution or for increased understanding of the innate beauty and not infrequent commonality of all the world's great religions.

Not only was Jim there on every issue, but he unfailingly made a profound difference by dint of his personality, credibility, perseverance, and enviable talent to communicate in a way that was both easy to understand and erudite at the same time.

Mix a decade of higher education at top schools with formative years in Alexandria, Virginia, the U.S. Air Force, Kansas City, and Champaign, Illinois, and, if you're lucky, you get a person like Jim, who can hold his own anywhere and communicate in a way that is easily understood without ever being condescending or simplistic. Hence the success of his weekly column and the steady demand for comment from the media.

Finally, and in the same vein, there's a new book entitled *The Tipping Point* by Malcolm Gladwell. Gladwell talks about the "Law of the Few," which asserts that only certain people can transmit effectively. The author refers to "Connectors, Mavens, and Salesmen." Paul Revere, for instance, was all three rolled into one, Gladwell asserts. Revere knew what the British were up to, making him a Maven; he knew the right people to tell, making him a Connector; and he knew how to tell them effectively, making him a Salesman. To top it off, Paul Revere's message was inherently important, which means it had a high

"Stickiness Factor." And it prompted an effective reaction, which suggests a strong "Power of Context." Under these perfect circumstances, Revere's words spread contagiously and tipped the balance of Colonial behavior. The description of the "Law of the Few" could as easily apply to Jim's entire career at AJC, couldn't it?

It is now my honor, Jim, to present you with our coveted Professional Service Award for 2000, for being our Connector, our Maven, and our Salesman, par excellence, and for being our cherished friend, our admired colleague, and our unrivaled mentor.

And permit me the personal prerogative of offering you a second memento of this evening, namely, the framed original copies of your first letter of inquiry for a job at AJC, dated December 11, 1967, and the letter of confirmation of your appointment from Eleanor Katz, dated April 3, 1968.

### Eulogy for Ruth R. Goddard
### New York
### June 21, 2000

Sure, the day had to come, but still we were caught unprepared. After all, our Ruth was larger than life. She had that special gift to make each of us feel as though she were our Ruth, just as she made us all feel like we were treasured and cared-for members of her extended family. As Ruth approached her ninety-ninth birthday and we at the American Jewish Committee had begun planning for her hundredth birthday extravaganza, she was taken from us.

We wish we could have had just a little more time with Ruth. More time to enjoy her candor and her wit, more time to marvel at her independence and her indomitable spirit, more time to reinvigorate ourselves through her boundless energy, and more time to be blessed by her generosity and her humanity.

But let us not dwell only on our grief today. Let us rather celebrate an extraordinary life fully lived. Ruth herself endured great tragedy, perhaps the greatest tragedy anyone can face—the loss of a child. And yet she chose not to live in bitterness, but to see her son's life as a blessing, remember him with joy, and dedicate herself to helping others.

Each of us gathered here at Temple Emanu-El carries special memories of this unique woman who played so many important roles in our lives—whether as godmother, cherished friend, benefactor, mentor, or colleague. Each of us could share many stories, I'm sure, of how Ruth made us laugh, touched our hearts, or shaped our way of thinking. Yes, she had strong, well-formed views on many an issue. You always knew where Ruth stood on an issue at any given time—all you had to do was ask—and sometimes, not even that—to find out what was on her mind. She was, if I may borrow the title of a best-selling novel, "A Woman of Substance."

Let us learn from this remarkable life lived with both passion and compassion. Let us smile as we remember this incomparably elegant woman who believed that the world could be a better place, and gave of herself so unsparingly to make it so; who demanded excellence in herself and inspired all of us to emulate her example. Let us give thanks for this life lived in truest devotion to the Jewish people and to the highest Jewish values of kindness, justice, and charity.

Ruth always cherished her Jewish identity. Indeed, she would tell the story of how she was scheduled to fly to America on the *Hindenberg* dirigible in 1937, only to be told by her father that she should have nothing whatsoever to do with Germans because of their anti-Jewish policies. She heeded her father's advice and canceled her reservation, coming home by other means. The flight she was to have taken ended in disaster as it approached Lakehurst, New Jersey, killing thirty-six people. Ruth always believed there was a divine message in the story, that her life had been spared for some reason connected to her Jewish identity, that she was here to fulfill a purpose.

For more than half a century at the American Jewish Committee, Ruth was as brilliant a jewel as those she wore so impeccably each time we saw her. Founder of our Women's Campaign Board, most recently honorary chair, Ruth gave generously and unselfishly of her time, experience, and example. Up until just a few weeks ago, she was still working closely with new generations of women—in Ruth's case, there never was a generation gap—helping them to understand AJC's mission, why it meant so much to her, and how they could devote themselves, as she did, to the task of making a difference in the fractured world in which we live.

Whether as the first woman to serve as an AJC national vice president or in any other leadership role, Ruth set the standard of commitment and involvement we all aspire to.

In reflecting on her life's devotion to AJC, I am reminded of the words of the poet Stephen Spender:

*I think continually of those who were truly great ...*
*The names of those who in their lives fought for life, who wore at their*
    *hearts the fire's center ...*
*Born of the sun they traveled a short while toward the sun, and left the vivid*
    *air singed with their honor.*

At our ninety-fifth gala birthday celebration in her honor at the Essex House, I spoke of Ruth's unique combination of *yikhes* and *yiddishkeit*, her acumen and activism, her philanthropy and her flair, her leadership and her largesse, and her courage and her heart. It is these qualities that will sustain and enrich us when we remember the glorious life and the luminous woman who was Ruth Goddard.

As we say on Yom Kippur, "May the beauty of the lives of our dear ones shine forever more, and may our lives always bring honor to their memory."

Ruth, you were truly one of a kind, and we were blessed to have been in your magnetic field.

<br>

Tribute to Bruce Ramer
AJC 95th Annual Meeting
Washington, D.C.
May 3, 2001

Every year we run into the same problem, it seems. No matter how much we try to tinker with the schedule, we just never have enough time for this event. And, with all the VIPs coming this evening, we dare not run late, especially when the president of the United States is known to have two pet peeves—one is cell phones that go off in meetings, so please be warned, and the other is tardiness.

That means my being briefer than I'd like, which isn't easy in this case, because the topic of discussion is Bruce Ramer.

I looked for examples of brevity. The best I could come up with was the following: The students in a creative writing class at a British university were asked to write a concise essay containing the following elements: (1) religion, (2) royalty, (3) sex, and (4) mystery. The prizewinning essay read: "My God," said the queen, "I'm pregnant. I wonder who did it."

It didn't seem to apply to Bruce, so I'll have to extend my remarks a bit.

A true story: A pilot welcomed passengers with the following message: "Our airline is pleased to have some of the best flight attendants in the industry. Unfortunately, none of them are on this flight."

AJC has some of the best Jewish leaders in the country and, fortunately, they are here in this room today to join in paying tribute to Bruce.

Okay, so maybe there are a few, like David Rousso, who are breathing a sigh of relief, thinking that Bruce's departure means no more arm-twisting solicitations. For AJC's sake, I hope David is wrong.

As executive director, I have been blessed to work with four truly outstanding presidents—Sholom Comay, who literally rescued this agency and set it on its present course, and whose untimely death ten years ago this month came as such a shock to all of us; Al Moses, who took the agency to new heights with his extraordinary passion for Jewish and public life, and from whom we had the joy of hearing only a few minutes ago; Bob Rifkind, whose piercing intelligence and soaring eloquence made us all so proud of our association with this organization; and, for the past three years, Bruce Ramer.

I put my thoughts about Bruce on paper because I wanted to try to get it just right. Here's what I wrote:

Dear Bruce,

How could I possibly summarize in just a few sentences the reams of pages I carry inside me about your extraordinary leadership of the American Jewish Committee these past three fleeting years, your unique personal qualities, your indelible impact on the agency, or our brotherly relationship?

Or about your abiding love of family, fierce loyalty and devotion to friends, formidable intellect, courage to speak your mind, clever wit, quick laugh, absence of pretense, and remarkable capacity to juggle a dozen responsibilities—all in need of your immediate attention—without ever missing a beat?

Or about your unswerving dedication to AJC and the Jewish people, passion for public policy issues, and willingness to board a plane for Jerusalem, New Delhi, Skopje, Washington, or New York at a moment's notice, if it might help an Israel in need of friends and support, a Hindu left without a home after an earthquake, a Kosovar Muslim fleeing persecution, or a Jew threatened by anti-Semitism?

Or about the hundreds—thousands?—of meetings you held with kings and queens, presidents and chancellors, prime ministers and foreign ministers, parliamentarians and journalists, and academic and cultural personalities, which advanced the programmatic and institutional interests of AJC in countless ways?

Or about your many and often little known gestures that came from a big heart and a sensitive soul—the personal notes of appreciation you wrote to staff members for a job well done, the phone calls you made day and night prompted by concern and compassion, and the extra minute, even when you didn't have it, for someone who needed your attention?

Hyperbole, I fully realize, is a deeply cherished national pastime, but it is no exaggeration to say that for AJC you have been an exceptional leader and standard-bearer, not to mention a major and unforgettable factor in my own life.

Bruce, you have made a profound difference in the world around you, in the organization to which you have devoted yourself so selflessly, and in the lives of everyone privileged to have collaborated with you. For this and so much more, you have our eternal appreciation.

And let me add a postscript to that letter: Three years ago, the leaders of AJC, people in this room, entrusted this organization to Bruce's leadership. They made an incredibly wise choice.

Bruce has worked around the clock on our behalf, traveled around the globe, used every single ounce of his legendary stamina, approached all of his remarkable contacts near and far on our behalf, and in the process made countless friends for AJC and the Jewish people.

In everything he did, he exemplified the true meaning of leadership. He led by example. He set punishingly high standards for himself. His deeds always outpaced his words. And, like any successful leader, he was not afraid to ask for advice, and he listened carefully when others talked.

In short, this has been an extraordinary three years for all of us.

I trust, Bruce, that you are enjoying this occasion in your honor, in the company of your cherished family. But I also know that it's a poignant moment for you. You've loved this organization in a very profound way, as all of us in this organization have loved you, and it can't be easy for you to step down from the presidency.

Bruce, in the hope of brightening things up just a bit, we have several things to present you.

At the suggestion of Harold Tanner, we've prepared a tribute book, in which you will find many expressions of affection, admiration, and gratitude for your leadership. The comments come from world, national, and local leaders, from friends and associates, and from AJC leaders and leaders of other agencies alike.

And there's more. I took the prerogative of the speaker to prepare three additional gifts for you.

During my sabbatical, I discovered that Albert Camus, the distinguished French writer, and you have at least one thing in common—both of you were soccer goalies. It is in that spirit that I offer you my first present.

The text of this specially prepared calligraphy reads: "I learned that the ball never lands where you expect it. This helped me in life. Albert Camus, author and soccer goalie."

And the dedication below it is as follows: "To Bruce M. Ramer, Princeton varsity soccer goalie, Class of 1955, and President of the American Jewish Committee, 1998-2001. On the field and off, you have always inspired others by your leadership, courage, determination, and teamwork. In admiration and friendship, David A. Harris, Washington, D.C., May 3, 2001."

Now, Bruce is a proud American and in many ways a global citizen, but we can't entirely overlook the California influence, can we? That may help explain one of Bruce's absolute necessities in just about any setting, including the AJC Annual Meeting. The second present—six one-liter bottles of spring water—is given in the spirit of ensuring Bruce's physical survival during the endurance test that Shula organizes each year.

Speaking of water, have you heard this story?

A nomad was walking through the Sahara Desert, desperate for water, when he saw something far off in the distance. Hoping to find water, he walked toward the image, only to discover an elderly Jewish man sitting at a card table with a bunch of neckties laid out on it.

The nomad asked, "Please, I'm dying of thirst. Can I have some water?"

The old man replied, "I don't have any water, but why don't you buy a tie? Here's one that goes nicely with your robes."

The nomad shouted, "I don't want a tie. I need water."

The Jew said, "Okay, don't buy a tie. But to show you what a nice guy I am, I'll tell you that over that hill there, about four miles away, is a restaurant. They'll give you all the water you want."

The nomad thanked the Jew and walked toward the hill and eventually disappeared. Three hours later, the nomad came crawling back to where the old man was sitting.

The elderly man said, "I told you, about four miles over that hill. Couldn't you find it?"

Practically delirious from thirst, heat, and fatigue, the nomad mumbled, "I found it all right. But they wouldn't let me in without a tie."

Bruce, you have the tie and now you have the water. It looks like you're all set, except for one thing.

Anyone who has enjoyed a meal with Bruce, and I've had my share, most memorably in Italian restaurants around the world, knows that, in addition to water—that's still, not sparkling, with no ice, please— there's another essential element to each meal. What is it? Vitamins, of course.

With the help of the legendary Polish-American artist Merck Geritol Pfizer, otherwise known as my invaluable assistant, Alina Viera, we have the ultimate answer for the eternal good health we all wish you, Bruce, and here it is. The inscription reads: "One per year should do the trick." [Present Bruce with a giant-sized, mounted rendering of a vitamin pill.]

Bruce, thank you, a thousand times thank you, for everything. It's been truly great.

## Eulogy for Robert Heilbrunn
## November 20, 2001

As I look over this gathering, I see so many people who, like myself, loved, admired, and respected Bob Heilbrunn. To be sure, we each knew him in a different capacity—as a loving husband, father, grandfather, great-grandfather; as a treasured friend, a cherished mentor—but the qualities that made him unique to this world and special to each of us were no doubt similar.

If I may, I want to tell you about the Bob Heilbrunn I was blessed to know.

Bob was a humble and unassuming man, but I want to make certain that everyone here today knows just how many lives he touched and bettered by his generosity through the American Jewish Committee alone. I'm sure that for every individual in this room, there are comparable stories that can be told.

When Turkey suffered a devastating earthquake that left tens of thousands of families homeless and lives shattered, Bob, along with Harriet—his dear and beloved Harriet—immediately came forward with a generous humanitarian gift through AJC. The Turkish ambassador to the United Nations wrote to us at that time, "It is indeed in trying times such as these that deep-rooted ties of friendship and solidarity among peoples and nations are fortified, as exemplified by the generosity of the Heilbrunns."

Bob, you see, was without doubt one of the finest goodwill ambassadors the Jewish people could ever have hoped for. The result of this gift was to help make possible the building of a school for 400 children in Adapazari, Turkey, and the establishment of an intensive care unit in a neighboring town in the earthquake zone. How many lives were touched by such a humanitarian act? Just imagine, for instance, the long-term impact on the Turkish youngsters of attending a school built specially for them by Bob and Harriet and AJC.

This gift also led to the endowment of AJC's Robert and Harriet Heilbrunn Humanitarian Fund, because he wanted to ensure that we could respond to tragedy quickly and effectively anywhere in the world and without hesitation. And thanks to the vision of Bob and Harriet—and they always operated as a team—we have.

When Hurricane Mitch blew a path of destruction in Central America, AJC could offer lifesaving assistance and help rebuild demolished homes, thanks to Bob and Harriet.

When Muslim refugees from Kosovo fled Serb aggression, AJC helped to provide medical and other critical assistance, thanks to Bob and Harriet.

When thousands of displaced Lebanese refugees who had allied themselves with Israel streamed into the Jewish state after Israel's military withdrawal from southern Lebanon, clothing, blankets, toys, and other necessary items were waiting for them, thanks to Bob and Harriet.

When three synagogues were burned in California on a single day, the targets of hate-inspired arson attacks, AJC was there to help rebuild those sanctuaries, thanks to Bob and Harriet.

In India, where a natural disaster wreaked havoc, AJC could help repair a school serving students of the Hindu, Muslim, and Christian faiths, thanks to Bob and Harriet.

And, as you might well imagine, AJC did not hesitate to step forward when the horrific events of September 11 left thousands dead, including our heroic police and firefighters, thanks to Bob and Harriet.

All of this was possible because Bob Heilbrunn, together with Harriet, his adored wife of sixty-seven years, had a love of humanity that would not, could not, let him sit idly by while others suffered.

The Heilbrunn Institute for International Interreligious Understanding is another example of the legacy he leaves for us all. In particular, the complex relationship between Muslims and Jews was something Bob believed needed to be addressed. Understanding that all too often ignorance leads to fear and intolerance, he wanted to build bridges, human bridges, of respect and mutual understanding.

He was terribly upset about the feelings in the Muslim world directed at Israel and the Jewish people, but in typical fashion he wanted to do something about it, not simply lament the fact from the sidelines. I am so pleased that Bob lived to see the publication of two pathbreaking volumes published by AJC to help each community better understand the other in all its richness, diversity, and complexity. Both volumes, of course, carry the Heilbrunn name.

Bob believed that we should all care for one another and, in the best of what our Jewish heritage has to teach us, welcome the stranger among us.

In that spirit, the rabbis say, when God created the world, only one man, Adam, and only one woman, Eve, were put on the earth—so that everyone who followed, to this day, would derive from the same original mother and father and would thus comprise one human family. No one could claim superior lineage over anyone else.

And we are taught to pursue justice, to do justly, to love mercy, and to walk humbly with our God. We are instructed that it is the quality of our living, and not simply the quality of our life, that really counts.

It is in this moral and ethical tradition that Bob acted.

When compassion was called for, he was impervious to race, religion, or ethnicity. He had a single-minded determination to save and restore lives and, in the process, to make friends for the Jewish community around the world. There are no words sufficient to convey appreciation for such expressions of our common humanity and our shared moral obligation. What a stark contrast to the kind of demented inhumanity that our nation witnessed on September 11!

I know the world is more humane because of the man you, Harriet, and your family cherished, the man I came to know as a precious and generous friend. I am inspired more than ever in my own work, as we all should be, because I have seen that one caring, determined, and gentle individual really can help repair our broken world.

I will miss Bob—seeing him at the beautiful apartment overlooking the park, having lunch at neighborhood restaurants, greeting him at

AJC events, enjoying his gift for humor, and learning from his wisdom and insight.

May Bob's memory forever be a blessing to those countless people, near and far, who were touched by the kindness, generosity, and vision of this extraordinary man.

# APPENDIX

## A Sampling of Images and Words from the European Press
## 2000–2001

During the course of a year-long sabbatical in Europe, I became practically obsessed by coverage of the Middle East conflict and followed especially closely the media in Britain, France, Switzerland, Italy, and Spain—all countries in which language was not a barrier. I was struck both by the degree of attention given to the Middle East and also by the all-too-frequent bias in the coverage. Moreover, it became readily apparent that the sacrosanct line between news and editorial comment was frequently crossed, even in some of the most respected media outlets.

This material is largely drawn from mainstream—and, in many cases, highly influential—media outlets.

### 1. Misleading Headline

Headline reads: "Israel reoccupies part of the Gaza Strip." In this front-page article, there is no mention of the Palestinian attack provoking Israeli action until the inside article on page 4, line 23.

Source: *Le Temps* (Switzerland), April 18, 2001

## 2. Using Images of Children

Pictures of Palestinian children abound in the press, even when they are unrelated to the report, as in this front-page article entitled: "The World Mobilizes to Save the Middle East."

Source: *La Tribune de Genève* (Switzerland), May 22, 2001

## 3. Front-Page Attention Given to Palestinian Suffering

Headline reads: "The War that Kills the Children." A subheadline reads: "Monday, 3 p.m., the farewell of a Palestinian mother to her murdered and martyred daughter near Nablus."

Source: *Paris Match* (France), October 12, 2000

## 4. Appropriating the Holocaust

Cartoon showing two Israeli policemen beating a Palestinian. One officer is saying: "There's no time for me to reflect on the Holocaust."

Source: *La Razón* (Spain), June 9, 2001

## 5. Stereotyped Images of Jews

Front-page cartoon in the wake of the June 1 terrorist bombing of the Tel Aviv discothèque in which 21 Israelis were killed.

Cartoon showing an Orthodox Jew (right) with "settlements" strapped around his waist, depicted as the mirror image of a Palestinian suicide bomber (left), who, incidentally, also looks strikingly like an Orthodox Jew.

Source: *Le Monde* (France), June 4, 2001

## 6. Palestinian Intimidation

Several camera crews, including a Polish team, tried to tape the horrific lynchings in Ramallah in October 2000, but they were either stopped or their tapes were confiscated by Palestinians. An Italian private television station was the only one to succeed; its footage was later broadcast worldwide. Italian state television (RAI) representative Ricardo Cristiano sent a letter to the Palestinian Authority, later printed in a Gaza paper, assuring them that it was not his station that had violated PA press rules.

"We respect the work arrangements between journalists and the Palestinian Authority.... rest assured that this [broadcasting the lynchings of Israelis in Ramallah] is not our way, and we would never do such a thing."

Source: *Jerusalem Post* (Israel), October 19, 2000

## 7. A Journalist's Fear

*Sunday Telegraph* reporter Mark Seager attempted to photograph the Palestinian mob as it was beating the body of one of the Israelis killed in Ramallah.

"One guy just pulled the camera off of me and smashed it to the floor... I was scared for my life.... It was murder of the most barbaric kind. When I think about it, I see the man's head, all smashed. I know that I will have nightmares for the rest of my life."

Sources: *Sunday Telegraph* (United Kingdom), October 15, 2000, and *Daily Telegraph*, October 22, 2000

[Note: The American Jewish Committee sought permission to reprint this eyewitness testimony in ads in the United States, but the newspapers refused to grant it.]

## 8. Misrepresentation

Article announcing the release of the Mitchell Report omits entirely the fact that the very first step demanded by the report was a halt to Palestinian violence.

Headline: "Estados Unidos exige a Israel un alto el fuego y que renuncie a nuevos asentamientos."

Translation: "United States demands of Israel a cease-fire and a halt to new settlements."

Source: *El Pais* (Spain), May 22, 2001

## 9. Out of Their Depths

Terrorists are often treated with kid gloves.

In an interview on page 2, Hamas leader says that Israel has no right to exist. In response, the interviewer asks about his opinions on the Mitchell Report and other aspects of the peace process!

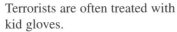

Source: *La Repubblica* (Italy), May 19, 2001

## 10. Of Course, Israel Is to Blame

The blame is on Israel for failing to pursue peace.

Article titled "Sharon rejects the proposal of Arafat to work together for an end to violence." Note the chilling photograph of the father carrying his masked son on his shoulders.

Source: *El Mundo* (Spain), April 21, 2001